The National Wealth of the United States in the Postwar Period

RAYMOND W. GOLDSMITH

ARNO PRESS

A New York Times Company

New York — 1975

Editorial Supervision: Eve Nelson
Reprint Edition 1975 by Arno Press Inc.

Copyright © 1962 by the National Bureau of
  Economic Research, Inc.
Reprinted by permission of the National
  Bureau of Economic Research, Inc.

NATIONAL BUREAU OF ECONOMIC RESEARCH
PUBLICATIONS IN REPRINT
ISBN for complete set: 0-405-07572-3
See last pages of this volume for titles.

Manufactured in the United States of America

———◆———

Library of Congress Cataloging in Publication Data

Goldsmith, Raymond William, 1904-
    The national wealth of the United States in the post-
war period.

    (National Bureau of Economic Research publications in
reprint)
    Reprint of the ed. published by Princeton University
Press, Princeton, N. J., which was issued as no. 10 of
National Bureau of Economic Research's Studies in capital
formation and financing.
    "A continuation of the estimates of national wealth in
volume III of [the author's] A study of savings in the
United States."
    Includes bibliographical references.
    1. Capital--United States. I. Title. II. Series.
III. Series: National Bureau of Economic Research.
Studies in capital formation and financing ; no. 10.
[HC110.C3G6 1975]   339.373   75-19714
ISBN 0-405-07594-4

THE NATIONAL WEALTH OF THE
UNITED STATES
IN THE POSTWAR PERIOD

NATIONAL BUREAU OF ECONOMIC RESEARCH

STUDIES IN CAPITAL FORMATION AND FINANCING

This report is one of a series emerging from an investigation of postwar capital market developments in the United States. The costs of the study were financed by a grant to the National Bureau from the Life Insurance Association of America and from general funds of the National Bureau. The Life Insurance Association is not, however, responsible for any of the statements made or views expressed in the report.

The National Wealth of the United States in the Postwar Period

RAYMOND W. GOLDSMITH

A STUDY BY THE
NATIONAL BUREAU OF ECONOMIC RESEARCH, NEW YORK

PUBLISHED BY
PRINCETON UNIVERSITY PRESS, PRINCETON

1962

Printed in the United States of America

CONTENTS

TABLES

APPENDIX A

Alternative Aggregates and Rates of Change

Main Components of Wealth

Distribution of Wealth Among Sectors

Distribution of Components of Wealth Among Sectors

Wealth Structure of Main Sectors

APPENDIX B

CHARTS

PREFACE

THE estimates of national wealth that are presented and briefly described in this study, like the national balance sheets to be presented in another book, serve a double purpose. Their first objective is to furnish a statistical basis for some parts of the Postwar Capital Market Study. Their second purpose is to serve as a continuation of the estimates of national wealth in Volume III of *A Study of Saving in the United States*,[1] to preserve for use by economic statisticians and analysts the only current series of estimates of tangible wealth in the United States, a series now running back in reasonably comparable form to the turn of the century.

Nobody can be more conscious of the limitations and shortcomings of the estimates presented here than the author, at least nobody who accepts the possibility of, and even the need for, estimates of national wealth and of national balance sheets as part of a system of social accounts. Many of these limitations can be traced to the simple fact that adequate estimates of national wealth are now beyond the power of an individual student; and that the era of shoestring operation in this field is, or should be, past. The time has arrived, I am convinced, for an organized venture on a fairly large scale—within or outside the federal government—a venture that will systematically explore all the basic data available for the construction of national wealth statements; that will experiment with alternative approaches and assumptions; and that will use modern computers in order to put these experiments on a sufficiently broad basis. It is only because nobody seems to be ready to take even the first steps in this direction that I rather reluctantly have made these estimates, and still more reluctantly present the results in their present form. Even in that form the figures shown here may be useful, I hope, for a preliminary exploration of the terrain. Although in need of improvement in many respects, they are not likely to mislead so far as the main conclusions that can be drawn from them are concerned. The estimates should be used only to study the broad outlines of the structure of national wealth in the United States and of changes in it over the postwar period, not for the analysis of fine-structure or of short-term changes.

The study here presented, however, suffers also from shortcomings beyond those that are almost necessarily inherent in a small-scale proj-

[1] *Special Studies*, by Raymond W. Goldsmith, Dorothy S. Brady, and Horst Mendershausen, Princeton University Press, 1956, Part I.

ect in this field. Many of these result from its being written over a period of more than two years in intervals between other more pressing assignments. I am well aware that the text would profit greatly by thorough rewriting, by the expansion of some parts and possibly by the pruning of others. Time and resources—and energy—for such a thorough revision are unfortunately missing. The choice thus is between making available the study as it is, or consigning it to the library of unpublished manuscripts. My impression that the material will be of some use to economists and statisticians even in its present form, and my hope that it will stir some of the users to do better, may be mistaken, but they are the reasons for permitting the study to go to press as it stands.

The original manuscript included two chapters dealing respectively with the conceptual and statistical problems of capital-output ratios and with the interpretation of the actual ratios that can be derived for the United States, primarily for the postwar period, on the basis of the national wealth estimates presented in this study. Similarly, the international comparisons now found in Chapter 7 were supplemented by a comparison of capital-output ratios in the mid-1950's for one to three dozen countries. All this material was finally eliminated—not without regret—from the published version, partly to reduce its bulk; partly because it was somewhat extraneous to the main objective of the study; partly because it proved unfeasible within the limitations of time and resources to break down the nationwide capital-output ratios consistently into sectoral ratios, a breakdown essential for a satisfactory analysis of the whole complex of problems arising in this field; and, finally, because those chapters needed more additional work than could be done without unduly delaying publication of the report.

The text of this book includes only summary tables which, it is hoped, will suffice for the general reader. More detailed tables that should enable users who wish to do so to rearrange the figures to suit their own needs will be found in Appendix A. Appendix B, which probably will be consulted only by specialists, contains the basic data from which the estimates have been built up, and a description of their manipulation in sufficient detail to permit an appraisal of the limitations and validity of the estimates by readers familiar with statistics of this character.

Most of the estimates used in this study were completed in 1959 and the text finished by mid-1960. This will explain why the figures do not extend beyond the year 1958.

In the preparation of the estimates for the postwar period used in this study I have had the patient assistance of Milton Kelenson, while I could not have completed Chapter 3 without the help of Hyman Kaitz. So many statisticians, particularly in the federal government, have been helpful, either with advice or by making available unpublished data, that it would be invidious to mention only a few of them. This, moreover, is the type of debt best discharged not by acknowledging it but by repaying it in kind so far as one is able.

I wish to acknowledge the careful attention given the manuscript by George Soule, Frank W. Fetter, and Theodore W. Schultz of the National Bureau's Board of Directors. The staff reading committee, Frank G. Dickinson, Richard A. Easterlin, and Robert J. Lampman, provided comments and suggestions that were of great value.

Acknowledgment is also made to the members of the Advisory Committee on the Study of the Postwar Capital Market for its assistance in drafting plans for this investigation: W. A. Clarke, George T. Conklin, Jr., W. Braddock Hickman, Norris O. Johnson, Arnold R. LaForce, Aubrey G. Lanston, Robert P. Mayo, Roger F. Murray, James J. O'Leary, Winfield W. Riefler, Robert V. Roosa, R. J. Saulnier, William H. Steiner, Donald B. Woodward, and Eugene C. Zorn, Jr.

The task of editing the manuscript was fulfilled ably by Margaret T. Edgar. The charts were carefully prepared by H. Irving Forman.

RAYMOND W. GOLDSMITH

July 1961

THE NATIONAL WEALTH OF THE
UNITED STATES
IN THE POSTWAR PERIOD

CHAPTER 1

Summary of Findings

1. STOCKS and flows are two basic categories in all economic analysis. The figures on national product, on output in different sectors of the economy, and on the production of different types of commodities, which have come to be used increasingly not only by economists but also by policy makers and in business, must therefore be supplemented by estimates of the stock of tangible assets of different types in the main sectors of the economy. To be comparable among themselves and with flow estimates, these figures must be expressed in the common denominator of market value, for some purposes current value and for others constant value in prices of a given base period.

In the absence of a continuous set of official estimates by the federal government of the value of the stock of tangible assets—excluding only agriculture—the National Bureau has prepared such figures because they were needed as one of the statistical bases of the Bureau's study of the postwar capital market. These estimates are herein made generally available, as they may serve as one of the building bricks of economic analysis of the postwar period.

2. The estimates for reproducible tangible assets follow the "perpetual inventory method," by which the stock of a given category of assets is derived as the cumulation by past expenditures on that category in current or constant prices depreciated in accordance with the average length of life of the asset. The value of nonreproducible assets is estimated independently either on the basis of data of the census type, as for agricultural and public land; or by the application of a typical ratio of land-to-structure value, as in the case of land underlying residential and commercial structures.

Throughout the report estimates are provided on a net (depreciated) and a gross (undepreciated) basis, and on two valuation bases—constant (1947-49) prices and current (replacement) value—and occasionally also on the third basis of original cost. In this summary whichever of these concepts appears to be most relevant in a particular case is used. Neither the gross nor the net stock as here calculated is a direct measure of the productive capacity of the stock of tangible assets. Such a measure will generally lie somewhere between the estimates of the gross and the net stock.

3. The national wealth of the United States (i.e., the aggregate value

3

of all tangible nonmilitary assets located in the United States plus net foreign balance), measured so far as possible by the market value of the assets or the nearest approximation to it, has increased in the postwar period from about $575 billion at the end of 1945 to just over $1,700 billion at the end of 1958, or at an annual rate of fully 8½ per cent. Wealth per inhabitant thus has more than doubled from $4,100 to $9,800, a rise by almost 7 per cent per year.

4. More than one-half of the expansion in the market value of aggregate national wealth and about three-fourths of the increase in wealth per head is a reflection of the rise in the price level during the postwar period. In constant prices of 1947-49, aggregate national wealth has increased from almost $790 billion to nearly $1,250 billion, while wealth per head has risen by one-fourth from about $5,600 to $7,100. The average annual rate of growth thus amounts to about 3⅝ per cent for aggregate wealth and to 1⅜ per cent for wealth per head.

5. As a measure of economic growth, reproducible tangible wealth, which excludes land and subsoil assets, is more appropriate than total wealth. For the entire postwar period the average annual rate of growth of reproducible tangible wealth in constant prices is approximately 4 per cent, and of wealth per capita is 2¼ per cent. These rates are slightly higher than those for total national wealth, because once price fluctuations are eliminated the value of nonreproducible wealth changes but very slowly.

6. The rate of growth of gross reproducible tangible wealth is slightly lower than that for net wealth (which has been used heretofore): 3.5 per cent per year in constant prices for total wealth and 1.7 per cent for wealth per head. As a result, the ratio of the net to the gross value of structures and equipment increased from 0.53 at the end of World War II to 0.57 in 1958, much of the increase occurring during the first part of the period. This increase in the ratio is an indication of a decline in the average age of the stock of reproducible wealth during the postwar period, a decline which in turn reflects a relatively high rate of new investment.

7. Fluctuations in the annual rate of growth of the capital stock— net or gross—clearly reflect the business cycle. Thus, the highest rates of growth were registered in 1948, 1950, and 1955, and the lowest ones in 1949, 1954, and 1958. Average rates of growth over full cycles do not show a definite trend. In each of the three trough-to-trough cycles within the period (on an annual basis 1946-49, 1949-54, and 1954-58), the average aggregate rate of growth of net reproducible wealth in

constant prices was just under 4 per cent per year, and the rate per head slightly in excess of 2 per cent. The rate of growth in the gross stock of reproducible wealth was at a lower level (about 3½ per cent per year for aggregate wealth and 1¾ for wealth per head), but again no considerable difference can be observed among the three full-cycle averages.

8. Although the postwar period is limited to not much more than one decade, considerable changes occurred in the structure of national wealth. These changes reflect differences in the rate of growth of the volume of the different components of national wealth and also changes in the relationship among prices of different types of tangible assets. Most marked and significant among these changes are the decline in the share of nonreproducible wealth and the increase within reproducible wealth of equipment, both producer and consumer durables. These two movements continue trends observable over most of the past century.

9. No sharp change occurred during the postwar period in the share of government in civilian wealth. Business and households each owned, on the basis of current market valuations, slightly more than two-fifths of reproducible tangible wealth, leaving about one-sixth for the government. If military assets are included, the level of the share of government increases, but its relation to total national wealth more broadly defined shows a sharp decline from 30 per cent in 1945 to one-fifth in 1958.

10. Throughout the postwar period, and particularly during the first half of it, the share of owner-operated properties appears to have increased slightly at the expense of rented wealth. Tangible assets rented accounted for only about one-seventh of total national wealth and for about one-sixth of privately owned wealth and were generally limited to three fields: residential real estate, commercial structures, and agricultural land. The share of rented properties shows a marked decline in the case of residential real estate, but no definite trend for agricultural land.

11. The ratio of reproducible tangible assets that are used in the production of commodities for sale to those that are destined for direct nonbusiness use by consumers and public authorities has not changed substantially during the postwar period, if we assume that the second category includes residential structures, structures of nonprofit organizations, consumer durables (except one-half of passenger cars), and one-half of government structures. In that case, about one-half of

reproducible wealth has been used in production while the other half has served consumers and public authorities directly.

12. The outstanding change in the structure of reproducible wealth used in business (production) is the rise in the share of equipment (including livestock) from 27 to 37 per cent, mainly reflecting making up for deficiencies in expenditures on equipment during the period from 1930 to 1945. The share of structures declined only slightly during the postwar period, but that of inventories fell from 23 to 19 per cent. Substantial changes also occurred in the structure of reproducible wealth used directly by consumers. The share of consumer durables rose from 19 per cent in 1945 to 22 per cent in 1958, even though that movement failed to bring the share back to the level of 1929. On the other hand, the share of residential structures in reproducible wealth used directly by consumers declined from 66 to 62 per cent while that of government structures remained at the level of one-eighth.

13. The share of foreigners in assets situated in the United States remained insignificant throughout the postwar period. Additions to national wealth represented by net foreign assets (excluding monetary gold) were likewise very small: 1½ per cent of national wealth in 1958 against ½ per cent in 1946, and foreign assets were responsible for only 2½ per cent of the increase in domestic national wealth during the postwar period.

14. Military assets—excluded from previous figures—have acquired considerable importance since World War II if valued like civilian reproducible wealth on the basis of replacement cost. So valued, they have represented on the average about 8 per cent of civilian reproducible wealth. Since military assets consist largely of equipment, they are much more important if compared only with their civilian counterparts. The average value of military equipment for 1946-58 was equal to one-fifth of total civilian equipment and to as much as two-fifths of civilian producer durables.

15. The structure of the national wealth of the United States and its development during the postwar decade show in general the same characteristics and tendencies that can be observed in the few developed foreign countries for which comparable data are available. Abroad, as in the United States, the share of land in national wealth has tended to decline, and the share of equipment to rise, over the postwar period. The ratio of net to gross national wealth has been similar abroad to the level observed in the United States—around 60 per cent for reproducible tangible assets. A point of difference, not yet satisfactorily ex-

plained, is the higher level of the equipment-structure ratio in foreign countries. Another difference, explainable by the large size and the relative economic self-sufficiency of the United States, is the lower ratio of foreign assets and liabilities to national wealth.

16. The rate of growth of national wealth among developed foreign countries during the postwar years, and even after the period of reconstruction, appears to have been at least as rapid as in this country.

CHAPTER 2

Scope and Character of Estimates

No SYSTEM of national accounts can be regarded as complete without balance sheets for the nation and for the main sectors distinguished in the accounts.[1] No theory of economic fluctuations or growth— whether based primarily on broad statistical aggregates or derived from cross-section studies of behaviorally significant magnitudes—is likely to succeed unless it incorporates stock variables in addition to the flow variables that have constituted the sole tools for constructing earlier theoretical or econometric models. Awareness of this fact is reflected in the stress in the recent literature on the Pigou effect, introduction of stock variables into the consumption function, controversies about the capital-output ratio following its introduction into the discussion by Harrod and Domar, and attempts to dynamize input-output tables by the addition of stock-flow coefficients.

If these assertions are correct—and they would probably find acceptance among the majority of economists—there is urgent need for a set of estimates of economic stocks (real and financial assets, liabilities, and net worth) in about the same detail and of the same quality as the flow data that are now available. Yet very little has been done in developing such estimates. There are no official estimates of stocks of tangible assets with the exception of a few types (e.g., inventories) and of one sector (agriculture). The resources devoted inside and outside the government to work on national wealth statements and balance sheets are trifling compared with those used in the methodological, statistical, and analytical study of flows.

This disparity between the need for comprehensive and detailed information on stocks and the scanty data available in official or other statistics may justify the publication of the annual estimates of national wealth in the postwar decade that are presented here, notwithstanding their methodological and statistical limitations which are pointed out throughout this report. Companion estimates of intangible assets, of liabilities, and of net worth of the main sectors of the economy have also been completed. In conjunction with the estimates of national wealth, they permit the preparation of national and sectoral balance sheets and will be presented and discussed in a forthcoming National Bureau book.

[1] See, for instance, National Accounts Review Committee, *The National Economic Accounts of the United States: Review, Appraisal, and Recommendations*, New York, National Bureau of Economic Research, 1958, p. 112.

It is to be hoped that comprehensive estimates of national wealth will not again depend upon individual effort, albeit aided in this study by clerical assistance and by the cooperation of some government agencies producing the relevant basic data. The time has come for lifting the derivation of national balance sheets and of national wealth statements to the same level of intensity that for years has been accepted in national income estimation, in flow-of-funds work, and in input-output analysis. This means the organization of a large-scale project, within the government or outside of it, having at its disposal specialists in the different fields of economic statistics who are essential for building up the estimates, and equipped with the facilities and the authority to collect primary data on the many aspects of measurements of stocks where they are now lacking.

It will be years, even under the best circumstances, before an adequate and up-to-date set of stock estimates can be prepared and be carried back far enough to permit the study of long-term trends. Until then theorists, econometricians, and students of national accounts must work with the rough estimates which can now be put together. The set presented here was developed as part of the National Bureau's Postwar Capital Market Study and is intended to continue similar, often still rougher, estimates for the period 1896 to 1945, published in Volume III of *A Study of Saving in the United States*, and to supersede the preliminary figures for 1945-49 in the same publication.[2] The figures should, however, serve many other purposes, as the earlier estimates of national wealth and national balance sheets apparently have done.[3]

Respect for the presumed needs of one's fellow workers in the field and of the users of the estimates prompts the desire to give full explanation of sources and estimating procedures. The following pages briefly summarize the main methods and sources and—more important—point to a number of conceptual or statistical weaknesses in the figures. A set of annotated tables which permit those interested to follow in reasonable detail every step in the construction of the estimates will be found in Appendix B of this volume. Some material bearing on the reliability of the estimates will be found in Chapter 5.

The exact scope of tangible assets included in an estimate of national

[2] *Special Studies*, by Raymond W. Goldsmith, Dorothy S. Brady, and Horst Mendershausen, Princeton University Press, 1956.

[3] Preliminary figures for some dates after 1949 have been published in *Statistical Abstract of the United States* (e.g., 1959, pp. 324-325), in *Historical Statistics of the United States* (1960 ed.), and in the Thirty-Seventh Annual Report of the National Bureau of Economic Research (1957, p. 34). These figures should be regarded as superseded by the present estimates, wherever there are differences.

wealth is not of great importance so long as the figures are shown in sufficient detail to enable each user to isolate or to combine those types of assets that seem best fitted for his analytical purposes. The estimates presented here are based upon a rather broad definition of national wealth and therefore include separate figures—often unavoidably rough—for categories not always covered by estimates of national wealth, such as consumer durables, government civilian structures, military equipment, forests, and subsoil minerals. No figures, however, are shown for a few other categories of tangible assets, because there is no basis for even rough estimates, particularly on an annual basis: for instance, consumers' holdings of semidurable and nondurable commodities, works of art and collectors' items. There is, however, enough evidence about the order of magnitude involved to conclude that they are very small in proportion to total tangible assets of the nation or of major sectors.[4] The omission of any estimates for the value of three important natural resources (air, sunlight, water) and of human resources, on the other hand, is based both on the unavailability of a basis for calculation, and on the conviction—not shared by all students of this problem—that these items have no place in an estimate of national wealth of an economy where these resources cannot be appropriated and hence have no market price in an economy in which slavery does not exist.

The present estimates constitute essentially a continuation of the series for the period 1896 to 1949 previously published in slightly varying versions.[5] For reproducible tangible wealth the estimates are derived by the "perpetual inventory" method; the estimates of the stock of each type of reproducible tangible assets are obtained by cumulating the capital expenditures for that type of assets for a number of years equal to the assumed length of the asset's useful life. New capital expenditures, equal to gross expenditures less retirements

[4] See Goldsmith, "A Perpetual Inventory of National Wealth," *Studies in Income and Wealth*, Vol. 14, New York, National Bureau of Economic Research, 1951, pp. 36–38.

[5] (1) *Ibid.*; (2) *idem*, "The Growth of Reproducible Wealth of the United States of America from 1805 to 1950," *Income and Wealth of the United States; Trends and Structure*, Income and Wealth Series II, International Association for Research in Income and Wealth, London, Bowes and Bowes, 1951; (3) *A Study of Saving in the United States*, Vol. III, Tables W-1 to W-8.

For discussion of the general approach and of methodological questions, the reader is referred to the first two publications above, and to Goldsmith, "Measuring National Wealth in a System of Social Accounting," *Studies in Income and Wealth*, Vol. 12, New York, NBER, 1950. A description of the figures for the years before 1946 will be found in the tables of (2) and (3) above. Detailed estimates for 1945-58 are given in the annotated tables of Appendix B of this book.

during the same period, are used in the estimation of the gross stock and net expenditures, equal to gross expenditures less depreciation in the calculation of the net stock. Three sets of estimates have been prepared for each type of asset, based respectively on (1) original cost, (2) constant (1947-49) cost, and (3) replacement cost; but only the constant and current (replacement) value estimates are shown, since original cost figures are of very limited value for economic analysis. The constant cost estimates are obtained from the original expenditure figures by means of a price index (1947-49 = 100) appropriate to the type of expenditure. The replacement cost estimates are derived from the constant cost figures by reflation (multiplication of the constant value figures) with the same indexes.

The elements in the calculation of capital stock are shown in the tabulation below. For every type of reproducible asset being distinguished estimates of the nine separate flows are listed in columns 1 and 2, the cumulation and combination of which yield estimates of the six desired concepts of capital stock of column 4. Here k designates gross capital expenditures; r, retirements; d, capital consumption allowances; m, new capital expenditures; n, net capital expenditures; G, gross capital stock; and N, net capital stock; the one and two bars above the symbols, indicate, respectively, values expressed in constant (1947-49) prices and current (replacement) costs rather than original cost (unbarred); and the subscripts v and t stand for the length of life of an asset and for the date to which the estimate refers.

Concept and Valuation Base	Capital Expenditures (1)	Capital Consumption (2)	Capital Formation (3)	Capital Stock (4)
Gross				
Original cost	k	—	k	—
Constant (1947–49) cost	$\bar{k}$	—	$\bar{k}$	—
Replacement cost	$\bar{\bar{k}}$	—	k	—
New				
Original cost	k	$\bar{r}$	$k - r$	G
Constant (1947–49) cost	$\bar{k}$	$\bar{r}$	$\bar{k} - \bar{r}$	$\bar{G}$
Replacement cost	$\bar{\bar{k}}$	$\bar{\bar{r}}$	$\bar{\bar{k}} - \bar{\bar{r}}$	$\bar{\bar{G}}$
Net				
Original cost	k	d	$k - d$	N
Constant (1947–49) cost	$\bar{k}$	$\bar{d}$	$\bar{k} - \bar{d}$	$\bar{N}$
Replacement cost	$\bar{\bar{k}}$	$\bar{\bar{d}}$	$\bar{\bar{k}} - \bar{\bar{d}}$	$\bar{\bar{N}}$

The derivation of the different stock estimates is summarized in the following simple formulas:

(1) $$G_t = \sum_a^t (k_j - r_j) = \sum_a^t k_j - \sum_a^t r_j = \sum_a^t k_j - \sum_{a-v}^a k_j \quad (a = t - v)$$

(2) $$\bar{G}_t = \sum_a^t \bar{g}_j = \sum_a^t (g_j \pi^{-1}{}_{jb}) \qquad\qquad (g_j = k_j - k_{j-v})$$

(3) $$\bar{\bar{G}}_t = \sum_a^t g_j \pi_{tb} = \bar{g}_t \pi_{tb} \qquad\qquad (\bar{g}_j = k_j \pi_{jb} - k_{j-v}\pi_{(j-v)b})$$

(4) $$N_t = \sum_a^t (k_j - d_j) = \sum_a^t n_j \qquad\qquad (n_j = k_j - d_j)$$

where $\quad d_j = \dfrac{1}{t} \sum_{j-v}^{j} k \quad$ or $\quad (1 - \gamma) N_{j-1}$

          (straight line)   (declining balance)

(5) $$\bar{N}_t = \sum_a^t (\bar{k}_j - \bar{d}_j) = \sum_a^t \tilde{n}_j$$

(6) $$\bar{\bar{N}}_t = \left[\sum_a^t (\bar{k}_j - \bar{d}_j) \right] \pi_{tb} = \bar{N}_t \pi_{tb}$$

The subscripts indicate, respectively, the date to which the estimate refers t; the beginning of time o; the period during which the expenditures were made j; the length of life of the asset v; and the base period of the price indexes b. The symbol π_{jb} stands for the price index for period j on the basis of prices in period b.

The relationship between the periods for which expenditures are cumulated in deriving gross and net stocks is indicated in the following equations, which are valid for calculation in original cost or constant prices:

$$G_t = \sum_0^t g$$

$$= \sum_0^t (k - r)$$

$$= \sum_0^t k - \sum_0^{t-v} k \qquad (\text{since } r_t = k_{t-v})$$

$$= \sum_{t-v}^{t} k$$

$$N_t = \sum_{0}^{t} n$$

$$= \sum_{0}^{t} k - \sum_{0}^{t} d$$

$$= \sum_{0}^{t} k - \left(\sum_{0}^{t-v} k + a \sum_{t-v}^{t} k \right)$$

$$= (1 - a) \sum_{t-v}^{t} k$$

(where a is the average ratio of accumulated depreciation to original cost of assets still in the stock, and $\sum_{0}^{t-v} k$ are assets fully written off)

Thus, both gross and net stock estimates require expenditure estimates only for the period t-v, which of course varies in length from asset to asset, though the estimates can also be obtained—theoretically—by summing new or net capital expenditures since the beginning of time. (There is no practical point to this alternative since all new or net capital expenditures for periods more than v years ago are zero.)

For nonreproducible and foreign assets no similar standardized method of calculation is available. (None is needed for inventories as these can be estimated directly.) For these assets we must try to find other methods approximating market value in current or constant (1947-49) prices. In the case of nonagricultural privately owned land, the largest component of nonreproducible assets, the estimates are usually based on land-structure value ratios for which some quantitative evidence is available, although its comprehensiveness and accuracy leave much to be desired outside the field of single family homes. For agricultural land, census figures and estimates based on them, both representing close approaches to market value, can be used. For public land, vacant lots, forests, and for all subsoil assets, very rough estimates of presumed market value are all that can now be contrived.[6]

[6] Because of the method of estimation—tying land to the values of structures— which we are forced to use owing to the paucity of direct data, it is possible that the increases in the values of undeveloped land during the postwar decade have been understated. There are many reports about large relative increases in the value of land of this type, particularly on the outskirts of cities and along highways. Unfortunately no sufficiently systematic and comprehensive investigation appears to have been made to permit a direct estimate of the value of nonfarm land not underlying

The fact that the estimates for most components of reproducible tangible wealth—specifically for structures and equipment—are built up from gross capital expenditure series makes it very difficult to take account of changes of ownership of reproducible tangible wealth that occur among sectors after an asset has come into existence. To do so it would be necessary to have, for each type of asset, figures on the balance of transactions between each pair of sectors, or at least a figure for the net balance of trade for each sector and each type of asset. Such figures generally are not available for either reproducible tangible wealth or for nonreproducible assets. As a result, the estimates presented here for the wealth of individual sectors reflect in most cases a picture of reproducible tangible wealth originally acquired by the different sectors—subject to errors as these figures may be—rather than a record of assets held at a given point of time.

This specific source of error becomes more important as one sector's net acquisition or sale of a given type of tangible assets from or to other sectors becomes larger compared with its original capital expenditures. For sectors as broad as designated here, net balances are probably small compared with original acquisitions, particularly for long periods of time. There have, however, been types of transactions in tangible assets among sectors—apparently dealing mostly with nonreproducible assets—that were relatively substantial and that tended continuously in the same direction. Probably the most important example is the sale of agricultural land by the farm sector to the nonfarm, household, and business sectors. One of the few cases involving reproducible assets and transfers of substantial size, though occurring over a relatively short period, is the sale of government owned plants, equipment, and residences to private business, local governments, and households after World War II. The acquisition of large stockpiles of agricultural and mineral products by the federal government may be regarded as another example, although such transactions are treated here as original acquisitions by the government. Some of these transfers have been taken into account in the estimates, while most of them had to be ignored because no figures were available or because estimation was too time consuming in view of the magnitudes involved.

It thus should be recognized that the estimations of wealth by sector are subject to errors that do not affect estimations of aggregate national

structures. This is a field in which a systematic nationwide investigation is urgently needed.

wealth or of wealth by type of assets, both of which of course are invariant to changes of ownership among domestic sectors.

There is one problem bearing upon the scope and character of the estimates used in this study which apparently has been disturbing many users of national wealth estimates—the possibility of double counting, which is presumed to be present in particular when the value of government assets, primarily nonreproducible assets such as land, is included in national wealth.

The argument is that to include government assets, such as roads and streets in addition to the value of adjoining private properties already included at market value, constitutes double counting, since part of the market value of those private properties reflects the proximity of roads and streets and other government structures. Hence, it is argued, the value of roads and streets is already implicitly included in the value of the adjoining private properties and must not be added separately to the estimates of aggregate national wealth. It is difficult to accept this argument for reproducible tangible assets if national wealth is regarded as the sum of the market values of all separate tangible assets, or an approximation of market values such as replacement cost. Obviously, the replacement cost of roads and streets, i.e., their original cost of construction adjusted for capital consumption and changes in construction cost, does not differ in any essential way from the replacement cost of other reproducible tangible assets.

The argument, therefore, must be limited to the value of government nonreproducible assets, particularly land. Since the market value of all land, whether privately or government owned, is affected by many factors and in turn affects other components of national wealth, the value of land underlying roads and streets, or more generally of government owned land, cannot be excluded simply because its existence affects the value of adjoining private land. Private structures also affect the value of adjoining private land, but this does not lead to the exclusion of the value of land underlying these structures from national wealth. The value of the land underlying railroad tracks or structures like universities or Rockefeller Center is not excluded from national wealth, although the existence of the structures is likely to affect the value of adjoining properties, and specifically the land element in their values. The fact that many types of government land, including land underlying roads and streets, have no easily ascertainable market value has practical importance, and is a reason for caution in interpreting the estimates. It is not a sufficient reason, however, for excluding the value of these types of government land, the more so since such values are often actually ascertained when private land is condemned for government use.[7]

The practical solution of these controversies is the same as that proposed in the case of several other points in dispute. It is to present separate estimates for the disputed items, and then let the users adjust the totals in accordance with their taste, since it is impossible to show in one table figures for all possible concepts of national wealth, let alone to indicate in each case when analysing the figures how the interpretation would be affected if a different concept had been used. In accordance with this principle the values attributed to government owned properties, and to the land underlying them specifically, are shown separately in the aggregate in the text and Appendix A tables and in more detail in the Appendix B tables.

---

[7] So far as actual quantitative relations go, the question whether or not the land under roads and streets should be included separately in an estimate of national wealth and, if so, how its value should be estimated is of secondary importance. The site value of roads and streets does not constitute a separate element in our estimation of the value of all land owned by state and local governments. However, since our estimates are tied to the bench-mark estimate for 1946 (*A Study of Saving in the United States*, Vol. III), they implicitly include an allowance for the site value of roads and streets. This value can be put roughly at about 2 per cent of total net national wealth (excluding military assets) in 1946, and at about 1 per cent in 1958. The importance of the site value of roads and streets is still smaller for gross national wealth. On the other hand, the implicit allowance for the site value of roads and streets is not negligible in comparison with the estimated value of all public land (about one-half in 1946 and two-fifths in 1958) or with the total net wealth of state and local governments. Therefore, it may make a difference whether or not separate allowance is made for the site value of roads and streets. Even in this narrow field it is not likely, however, that any major trends during the postwar period would be affected by the choice between including and excluding the site value of roads and streets.

CHAPTER 3

The Elementary Algebra of National
Wealth Estimation

IN A static economy in which gross capital expenditures are the same every year and net capital formation (as well as new capital formation) is zero,[1] the value of the gross stock of reproducible tangible wealth is equal to the product of a year's gross capital expenditures and the weighted average life of reproducible tangible assets, disregarding changes in distribution of expenditures within the stable total and ignoring the existence of a retirement distribution and possible changes in it. In the same situation the net stock is equal to one-half the gross stock. So long as changes in the distribution of gross capital expenditures among items of differing life span occur, but no account is taken of the retirement distribution and changes in it, the ratio of net to gross stock will deviate from 0.50, but it will return to this value ultimately after the distribution has become stabilized, more specifically after a period equal to the life span of the longest lived type of assets.

The common situation is one in which both total capital expenditures and their distribution among types of durable assets change continuously; in which actual retirements are distributed around their actuarial dates; and in which total capital expenditures have an upward trend. In such a situation the gross stock will be smaller than the product of current capital expenditures and their weighted average life, while the ratio of net to gross stock will exceed 0.50. Formulas are helpful for an analysis of estimates of reproducible tangible wealth, particularly of structures and equipment, and are sometimes useful as a preliminary check on the calculations.[2] Formulas were developed for the relations between gross capital expenditures, k, gross stock, G, net stock, N, and for the ratio of net to gross stock at t under simplified assumptions—initially on the assumptions, later to be relaxed, of a stream of capital expenditures continuously increasing (or decreasing) at a rate of $100 \times g$ per cent per year;[3] for straight-line depreciation;

---

[1] We recall that net capital formation equals gross capital expenditures minus capital consumption allowances, and new capital formation equals gross capital expenditures minus retirements.

[2] I am greatly indebted to Hyman Kaitz for assistance in developing the formulas, particularly the more complicated ones.

[3] The correct expression for a continuously increasing (or decreasing) rate of

for zero scrap value ratio, s; for a constant length of life, v; and for no retirement distribution (i.e., retirement of all assets at exactly the time their assumed life expires). In these formulas, the rate of capital expenditures, the growth rate, and the value of the gross and net stock may be regarded as representing either aggregate or per head values, and as expressed in original cost, current prices or constant (deflated) prices.

We then have for every type of capital expenditure and the reproducible tangible assets[4] resulting from them:

$$(1) \qquad G_t = k_t \left(\frac{1 - e^{-gv}}{1 - e^{-g}} \right)$$

$$(2) \qquad N_t^{(1)} = k_t \left[\frac{1 - \dfrac{1}{gv}(1 - e^{-gv})}{1 - e^{-g}} \right]$$

$$(3) \qquad \frac{N_t^{(1)}}{G_t} = \frac{1}{1 - e^{-gv}} - \frac{1}{gv}$$

Under these simplified conditions gross and net stock depend upon only three factors: (1) the current level of capital expenditures k_t, which may also be understood as a cycle average of k or as the trend value of k at t—; (2) the rate of growth of expenditures, g; and (3) the product of the rate of growth and the length of life, gv. The ratio of net to gross stock is determined solely by the third factor, the product of rate of growth and length of life. Table 1 shows for selected values of rate of growth and length of life, that should encompass most of the situations actually encountered, first, gross and net stock at a given date as multiples of the rate of capital expenditures at that date, and second, the ratio of net to gross stock.

The ratio of gross and net stock to the current rate of expenditures will vary widely among different types of structures and equipment. It is larger for a given rate of growth of expenditures, the longer the life of the asset; and smaller for a given length of life, the higher the rate of growth of expenditures. Differences in the ratio of net to gross stock among various types of assets, on the other hand, are likely to

---

expenditures is $(e^g - 1) \times 100$ rather than $100 \times g$ per cent per year, but the difference is minor for the rates of growth usually encountered.

[4] The formulas are also applicable with appropriate conceptual modifications to intangible assets. Gross capital expenditures, for example, become new issues or loans made, and net capital expenditures become changes in amounts outstanding or net flows.

TABLE 1

RELATIONS BETWEEN CAPITAL EXPENDITURES, GROSS STOCK, AND NET STOCK, ON
ASSUMPTION OF CONTINUOUS GROWTH OF EXPENDITURES, STRAIGHT-LINE
DEPRECIATION, NO RETIREMENT DISTRIBUTION, AND ZERO SCRAP VALUE

Growth of Capital Expenditures (per cent per year)	Length of Life (years)	*Gross Stock*	*Net Stock*	Net Stock to Gross Stock (per cent)
		as Multiples of Current Rate of Capital Expenditures[a]		
(1)		(2)	(3)	(4)
0	5	5.00	2.50	50.0
	10	10.00	5.00	50.0
	20	20.00	10.00	50.0
	50	50.00	25.00	50.0
	100	100.00	50.00	50.0
1	5	4.90	2.50	50.4
	10	9.50	4.85	50.8
	20	18.15	9.35	51.6
	50	39.35	21.30	54.1
	100	63.20	36.80	58.2
2	5	4.80	2.45	50.8
	10	9.15	4.70	51.6
	20	16.65	8.85	53.3
	50	31.90	18.50	58.2
	100	43.70	28.70	65.7
3	5	4.70	2.40	51.2
	10	8.75	4.60	52.5
	20	15.30	8.40	55.0
	50	26.15	16.25	62.1
	100	32.15	23.10	71.9
5	5	4.50	2.35	52.0
	10	8.05	4.35	54.1
	20	12.95	7.55	58.2
	50	18.80	12.95	68.9
	100	20.35	16.40	80.7
10	5	4.15	2.25	54.1
	10	6.65	3.85	58.2
	20	9.10	6.00	65.7
	50	10.45	8.45	80.7
	100	10.50	9.45	90.0

[a] Rounded to nearest 0.05.

be much less pronounced. Most actual values for this ratio will lie between 0.50 or slightly less, and approximately 0.70.

In actual life capital expenditures, of course, do not follow the strict exponential path which is assumed in the formulas. Even if the fluctuations are regular in proportion to the trend value—say sinusoidal—

there remains a discrepancy between gross or net stock calculated by the perpetual inventory method on the basis of annual figures and that calculated approximately by the formulas, particularly if length of life is not an integral multiple of the length of the cycle in expenditures.

Deviations of gross and net stock and of the net-gross ratio approximated by the formulas and calculated on the basis of annual capital expenditures are likely to be small, so long as fluctuations of capital expenditures around the trend are fairly regular. They are likely to be modest, with a maximum deviation of not more than, say, one-fifth from their trend value, and to have relatively short wave lengths, say, three to five years. During and immediately after large irregular or protracted deviations from trend, gross and net stock and the net-gross ratio calculated by formula may differ significantly from the comparable values derived by more detailed calculations. It is therefore inadvisable, for instance, to use the formulas for the war and first postwar years. Insofar as expenditures in constant prices show less marked deviations from their growth trend than expenditures in current values, as is usually the case, calculation by formula will be more reliable for the former than for the latter.

One mathematical model of a sinusoidal movement about a basic straight-line logarithmic trend is

$$(4) \qquad y = Ae^{gt}\left(1 + \frac{c}{100}\sin\frac{2\pi t}{d}\right)$$

where y is the sum of the continuous growth value and the sinusoidal component; g is the rate of growth per year; t is a point of time specified (in years); c is the maximum percentage deviation of expenditures from their straight-line trend; and d is the period of the cycle (in years).[5] This leads to

$$(5) \qquad y_t = \frac{\bar{k}tge^{gt}\left(1 + \frac{c}{100}\sin\frac{2\pi t}{d}\right)}{1 - e^{-g}}$$

[5] A is a constant whose numerical value is determined within the framework of a particular set of values for the other terms in the equation. It disappears from any ratio, such as the ratio of net to gross stock, or the ratio of net stock calculated under one set of specifications to that derived under another set.

Alternatively, $A = \dfrac{\bar{k}_i g}{1 - e^{-g}}$ where $\bar{k}_i$ is the capital expenditure in the reference year calculated from the logarithmic straight-line trend.

The formula shows (to mathematicians, at least) that the deviations from the straight-line logarithmic trend are smallest for an asset life which is an exact multiple of the cycle length, and are greatest for asset life which deviates from an integral multiple of the cycle length by one-half the cycle length. The formula also indicates that the gross stock calculated on the basis of a sinusoidal movement is most pronouncedly below that calculated for a straight-line logarithmic trend when the calculation is made for a date midway between a trough and a peak; and is most pronouncedly above the straight-line logarithmic trend at a date midway between the peak and the trough. It can furthermore be seen from the formula that the percentage deviations between alternative gross stock calculations are independent of asset life length, so long as the latter is an integral multiple of the cycle life. When the asset life is not an integral multiple of the cycle length, the percentage deviation of the sinusoidal gross stock from the logarithmic straight-line trend is also a function of the length of the asset life and decreases with increasing asset life.

The relationships inferred in general terms from the formula are illustrated in Table 2 for a particular case in which it is assumed that gross capital expenditures increase at an annual rate of 4 per cent; that the cycle lasts for four years; and that the maximum deviation of annual capital expenditures from their trend is 10 per cent, 50 per cent, and 100 per cent, respectively. It is then seen that the maximum deviation of the gross stock from its straight-line logarithmic trend rapidly decreases with the length of life of the asset. In the case of an asset of ten years' life, for instance, the maximum deviation is not much over 6 per cent if the cyclically fluctuating amounts of gross capital expenditures range from one-half to one and one-half times their trend value. For long-lived assets the deviations become practically negligible. If asset life is as long as fifty years, which is not unusual for many types of structures, the maximum deviation of the stock is less than 2 per cent if gross capital expenditures swing from 50 per cent to 150 per cent of trend, and are not much in excess of 3 per cent if the assumption is made that expenditures fluctuate between zero and twice their trend value. These figures illustrate the fact that the danger in approximating capital stock estimates on the basis of the trend in gross capital expenditures lies not so much in the cyclical movements of capital expenditures around their trend as in sharp, discontinuous, or long deviations from the trend.

TABLE 2

MAXIMUM DEVIATION OF SINUSOIDAL GROSS STOCK FROM GEOMETRIC
TREND GROSS STOCK

(four year cycle length; 4 per cent annual growth)

Asset Life (years)	Limits of Swing (per cent of trend values)		
	90 to 110	50 to 150	0 to 200
2	6.4	31.9	63.8
3	2.3	11.5	23.0
4	0.2	1.2	2.5
5	1.4	6.8	13.7
6	2.1	10.7	21.3
7	1.1	5.3	10.6
8	0.2	1.2	2.5
9	0.8	4.1	8.2
10	1.3	6.4	12.9
19	0.5	2.4	4.8
20	0.2	1.2	2.5
21	0.4	2.2	4.4
47	0.3	1.5	3.0
48	0.2	1.2	2.5
50	0.3	1.7	3.3

In Table 3 estimates of the capital stock are given for two important items—industrial machinery and residential structures—using both the formulas and the cumulation of annual expenditure figures. For both items comparative data are provided for two years (the end of 1945 and of 1956), for two price bases (original cost and 1947-49 prices), and on the basis of the indicated year's actual value as well as its trend value. These two items have been selected as representatives of very long-lived items (residential structures, 80 years) and rather short-lived ones (industrial machinery, 20 years). The choice of the two bench-mark years was guided by the desire to test the effects of the simplified method of calculation in periods when actual expenditures were con-siderably below (1945) or above (1956) their trend value.

It will be seen that, as would be expected, the estimates of gross and net stock based on the formulas are much closer to the figures derived by the accumulation of annual actual expenditure data when the trend values of the last year's expenditures are used rather than that year's actual expenditures. For trend values, all of the sixteen ratios lie

TABLE 3

RESULTS OF ESTIMATION OF STOCK BY ACTUAL CUMULATION
AND BY FORMULA, END OF 1945 AND OF 1956
(cumulated stock = 1.00)

| | Gross Stock Based on Year's | | Net Stock Based on Year's | |
| | Actual Value | Trend Value[a] | Actual Value | Trend Value[a] |
	(1)	(2)	(3)	(4)
Industrial Machinery[b]				
End of 1945				
Original cost	1.62	0.92	1.61	0.91
Base period cost	1.59	0.94	1.60	0.95
End of 1956				
Original cost	0.80	0.96	0.83	0.99
Base period cost	0.82	0.97	0.83	0.99
Residential Structures[c]				
End of 1945				
Original cost	0.30	0.83	0.30	0.83
Base period cost	0.23	0.86	0.23	0.86
End of 1956				
Original cost	2.02	0.69	1.87	0.65
Base period cost	1.72	0.85	1.65	0.82

NOTE: Cumulated stock is estimated on the assumption of no retirement distribution, no scrap value; and by straight-line depreciation. Formula stock is estimated on the assumption of exponential growth, and no scrap value; and by straight-line depreciation.
a Straight-line logarithmic trend over lifetime of asset.
b 20-year life.
c 80-year life.

between 0.65 and 0.99, and eight of them do not deviate by more than 10 per cent from the value obtained by full cumulation of actual annual data. The difference between the two estimates using expenditure trend values is considerably smaller for the shorter-lived industrial machinery than for the long-lived residential structures. It will also be noted that the ratio is highest in all cases for base period than for current prices, the differences being particularly pronounced for residential structures in 1956 when actual expenditures were much farther above their trend values in current than in constant prices as a result of the sharp rise in construction costs.

The deviation of the estimates obtained by formula on the basis of the indicated single year's actual expenditures vary widely from those obtained by annual cumulation. The large size of most of the deviations makes it clear that formula estimates can be used only if the indicated year's expenditures that enter the formulas represent a trend rather than an actual value.

The ratios for the estimates of gross to net stock are almost identical for both items, both years, both price bases, and actual as well as trend values.

It is now necessary to look at the effect of abandoning some of the simplifying assumptions made in the basic formulas. Allowance for scrap value affects only the net stock and is relatively simple to incorporate into the formulas. Designating the ratio of scrap value to original cost by s, we have

$$(6) \qquad N_t^{(2)} = (1 - s)N_t^{(1)} + sG_t; \quad \text{or}$$
$$N_t^{(2)} - N_t^{(1)} = s(G_t - N_t^{(1)})$$

The ratio of the net to the gross stock is affected proportionately and becomes

$$(7) \qquad \frac{N_t^{(2)}}{G_t} = \frac{N_t^{(1)}}{G_t}(1 - s) + s$$
$$= \frac{N_t^{(1)}}{G_t} + s\left(1 - \frac{N_t^{(1)}}{G_t}\right)$$

The difference between the net-gross ratio with and without allowance for scrap value is not likely to be very substantial. For an asset with a life of twenty years and a scrap value of 10 per cent, on which expenditures increase at an average annual rate of 3 per cent, for example, the ratio of net stock to current expenditures will be 9.10 instead of 8.40 without allowance for scrap value. If the net-gross ratio without scrap value allowance is 0.50 and the ratio of scrap value to original cost is 0.10, the net-gross ratio with allowance for scrap value will be 0.55. Similarly, the ratio rises from 0.60 to 0.64 and from 0.80 to 0.82 if allowance for a scrap ratio of one-tenth is made. The difference thus is less important the higher the net-gross ratio without scrap value allowance and, of course, the smaller the scrap value in proportion to original cost.

A considerable modification, on the other hand, is introduced into the formulas for net stock and for the net-gross ratio, if use is made of declining balance instead of straight-line depreciation, in which case allowance must be made for scrap value. Here we have, if d—more precisely $(1 - e^{-d})$—is the ratio of declining balance depreciation allowance to the value of the stock at the beginning of the period, and if s', the scrap value appropriate to declining balance depreciation, is e^{-dv}

(8)
$$N_t^{(3)} = k_t \left[\left(\frac{g}{g+d} \right) \left(\frac{1 - e^{-v(g+d)}}{1 - e^{-g}} \right) \right]$$
and

(9)
$$\frac{N_t^{(3)}}{G_t} = \left[\left(\frac{g}{g+d} \right) \left(\frac{1 - e^{-v(g+d)}}{1 - e^{-gv}} \right) \right]$$

The ratio of the net stock under declining balance straight-line method (s' and s being the respective scrap value ratios)[6] is

(10)
$$\frac{N_t^{(3)}}{N_t^{(2)}} = \frac{\left(\frac{g}{g+d} \right)(1 - s'e^{-gv})}{1 - s\left[1 - \frac{1}{gv}(1 - e^{-gv}) \right] + s(1 - e^{-gv})}$$

The value under declining balance will thus be considerably lower. In the case of an annual growth rate of 5 per cent, a useful life of ten years, scrap values of 10 per cent, and depreciation rates of 10 per cent (straight line) and 20 per cent (declining balance), the declining balance net worth at three times the current rate of capital expenditures is equal to about 70 per cent of the straight-line stock.[7]

[6] In the straight line case, s and v (and hence the depreciation rate) may be specified independently, but under declining balance depreciation the value of s' and d are jointly determined.

[7] In one of the few cases in which the net stock of reproducible wealth has been calculated by both methods on the basis of the same set of capital expenditure figures—Australia for 1947 to 1956—the following ratios were obtained:

| | Scrap Value Ratio | Annual Depreciation Rate (per cent) | | a | $\frac{N_t(3)}{N(1)}$ | |
		Straight Line	Declining Balance		1947	1956
Dwellings	0.05	1¾	4	2.80	0.62	0.68
Other private structures	.06	2	5½	2.75	.63	.65
Agricultural equipment	.09	5	11½	2.30	.74	.76
Nonfarm equipment	.09	5	11½	2.30	.69	.75
Public works	.05	2½	7¼	2.90	.58	.68
Five categories	—	—	—		.62	.69

See J. M. Garland and R. W. Goldsmith, "The National Wealth of Australia," *The Measurement of National Wealth*, Income and Wealth Series VIII, 1959, p. 354.

Another simplification implicit in the formulas is likewise of small quantitative importance. This is the assumption that all reproducible tangible assets of a given type have identical lives, i.e., that those acquired during a given period are actually retired or scrapped simultaneously after the number of years corresponding to their assumed length of life. Actually, of course, the members of a given "cohort" of structures or machines of a given type—to apply the term familiar from population statistics to assets originating in the same year—are retired after having lasted for a varying length of time which may be assumed to center around the assumed length of life for the entire cohort. As a result, gross and net stock and net-gross stock ratios will deviate from the values indicated by the formulas, but the differences are likely to be small for the usual combinations of length of life and rate of growth of expenditures.

If account is taken of the distribution of actual retirement dates—assumed to be normal, i.e., symmetrical and bell-shaped—the gross stock will be above the value found by the formulas which disregard retirement distribution, but the difference will not be much above 5 per cent and will be below 3 per cent if gv is below 0.5 or above 4.5.[8] The net-gross ratio will be slightly below the value of 0.50 expected according to the formula (with stable capital expenditures and binomially symmetrical retirement distribution) because of the increase in gross stock value resulting from the allowance for retirement distribution, and will differ less from 0.50, less the longer the life of the asset.[9] For example, for assets with a ten-year life, the net-gross ratio, allowing for retirement distribution, will be 0.43, while it will rise to 0.46 for assets with twenty-year life and to 0.485 for those with a life of fifty years.[10]

If there is good reason to assume that the length of life of a type of reproducible durable asset has changed in regular fashion, this change can be allowed for in the formulas, even though at the cost of con-

[8] Eric Schiff, "Gross Stocks Estimated from Past Installations," *Review of Economics and Statistics*, May 1958, p. 176.

[9] Schiff, "Reinvestment Cycles and Depreciation Reserves under Straight-Line Depreciation," *Metroeconomica*, April 1957. The author does not investigate the effect of an increasing trend in expenditures, but it does not appear likely that this would substantially affect the results derived on the assumption of constant expenditures.

[10] Neither the basic formulas nor the more detailed calculation based on annual expenditure data, which are used in this paper, make allowance for retirement distribution. Such an allowance is, however, made in the capital stock estimate of the Machinery and Allied Products Institute.

siderable complication. We will then have, introducing the symbol b to indicate the annual rate of change in v,

$$(11) \quad N_t^{(5)} = k_t \left[\frac{1 - e^{-gv}}{1 - e^{-g}} + \frac{g}{v(g-b)^2} \left(\frac{e^{-gv}[v(g-b) + 1] - e^{-bv}}{1 - e^{-g}} \right) \right]$$

and, since gross stock is unaffected (provided length of life either increases or decreases by less than $\frac{100}{v}$ per cent per year),

$$(12) \quad \frac{N_t^{(5)}}{G_t} = 1 + \frac{g}{v(g-b)^2} \left(\frac{e^{-gv}[v(g-b) + 1] - e^{-bv}}{1 - e^{-gv}} \right)$$

The net stock obviously will be larger or smaller than under the constant life calculation depending upon whether length of life is assumed to have increased or decreased during the period covered by the calculation.

Thus, fortunately, two deviations from more carefully calculated figures that are introduced by the use of simplifying formulas—the disregard of scrap value and of retirement distribution—tend in opposite directions. They will partly cancel each other, though usually the offset will not be complete. There are no similar offsets to two other deviations—the variations of actual capital expenditures around their exponential trend, and changes in length of life—but there is no reason to assume that these two factors will lead to a systematic difference between estimates of gross and net stock and of the net-gross ratio approximated by simplified formula and calculated in a more detailed fashion.

The estimates of national gross and net stock of reproducible tangible assets are nothing but sums of the estimates for stocks of different types of such assets—the estimates discussed so far in this section—while the national net-gross ratio is a weighted average of the ratios for the constituent types of structures and equipment.[11] If we are willing to make the same simplifying assumptions for aggregate national capital expenditures that were made for expenditures on individual assets— exponential growth of expenditures, unchanged length of life, and

---

[11] In principle, the same method can be applied to inventories. However, there is no information on capital expenditures for inventories, i.e., inventory purchases, and the margin of error in estimating the average life of inventories is relatively great. Since we have a reasonable basis for estimating inventories on original cost and for adjustment to other valuation bases, applying the perpetual inventory method to inventories is unwarranted. Indeed, figures for expenditures on inventories would probably have to be derived by multiplying the estimated inventory holdings at a given date by the reciprocal of the assumed length of the inventory period.

simultaneous retirement of all assets installed during one period—the same formulas can be applied to obtain national gross and net stock estimates and the national net-gross ratio from aggregate national capital expenditures.

Deviations of actual capital expenditures, life spans, and retirement distribution from the underlying simplifying assumptions are likely to lead to smaller differences between the calculations based on annual figures and those obtained by applying the summary formulas to national aggregates or averages than is the case for many individual assets. The reason is that national capital expenditures show milder and more regular swings around their trend than the expenditures on many individual assets show, because there is more scope on a national scale for the offsetting effects of variety in the movements of components. Similarly, the retirement distribution may be more symmetrical—although it will have a wider time range—than for many individual types of assets.

If these were the only factors, the formulas could be applied to aggregate national capital expenditures with more confidence than to individual assets. There is, however, one characteristic of national capital expenditures which makes the formula for gross and net stock more hazardous to use on a national scale. This is the much greater physical and economic variety in the assets that result from capital expenditures. True, even the narrowest category of capital expenditures with which we must operate in actual statistical work covers structures or equipment differing considerably with respect to the trend and variability of expenditures and the length of life and the retirement distribution. This variety, however, is magnified in the national aggregates. The length of life, for instance, will stretch all the way from as little as three years to as much as one hundred years. Average length of life may therefore vary more for the national aggregate, as the composition of total expenditures changes, than is the case for capital expenditures on specific types of assets.[12]

[12] This statement does not apply to all types of capital expenditures. For example, the length of life of automobiles changed more during the last thirty years—and in a different direction—than is probably the case for aggregate national capital expenditures.

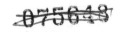

CHAPTER 4

Growth of Total National Wealth

The Postwar Period

ACCORDING to the estimates presented in this report—from now on qualifications will be omitted unless there is a specific reason for them—the net civilian national wealth[1] of the United States in current prices increased from a total of about $575 billion at the end of 1945 to $1,700 billion thirteen years later (Chart 1). The annual average rate of growth for the decade thus is slightly above 8.5 per cent. As the prices of tangible assets rose considerably during that period—slightly more than the general price level represented by the gross national product deflator—the average rate of growth in constant (1947-49) prices was substantially lower, averaging 3.5 per cent a year for the period as a whole. The rate of increase is further reduced to 1.8 per cent per year if account is taken of population growth.

As a result of the somewhat more rapid growth of reproducible than of nonreproducible tangible wealth, all rates of growth are slightly higher if attention is limited to reproducible wealth. For this, the major part of national wealth, which comprises structures, equipment, and inventories, the rate of growth after adjustment for price changes averaged 3.9 for the period. Real reproducible wealth per head of the population increased at the rate of 2.1 per cent for the thirteen-year period as a whole.

The year-to-year movements in the rate of growth of real wealth, shown in Chart 2, reflect, as would be expected, the cyclical fluctuations during the period. Growth was particularly rapid in 1948, the peak year, with a rate of 4.9 per cent compared with the average of 3.5 per cent for the entire period; for 1950 and 1951, 4.3 per cent; and for 1955, 4.5 per cent. The smallest increases were registered in the three recession years since the end of World War II, in 1958, 2.3 per cent, in 1949, 2.6 per cent, and in 1954, 2.9 per cent.[2]

For the three trough-to-trough cycles occurring within the period the rate of growth in total civilian deflated national wealth averaged[3]

---

[1] The difference between net national wealth and gross national wealth, which will be discussed later, is that reproducible tangible assets are included at their depreciated value in net national wealth but are carried at their undepreciated value in the estimates of gross national wealth until their assumed useful life expires.

[2] These figures are taken from Table A-4.

[3] First and last year of cycle assigned weight of one-half.

CHART 1
Gross and Net Total Wealth, 1945-58

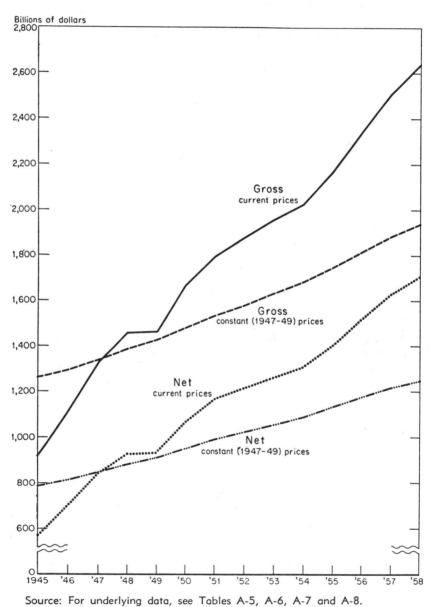

Source: For underlying data, see Tables A-5, A-6, A-7 and A-8.

CHART 2
Annual Rate of Change of Net and Gross Reproducible Wealth, 1946-58

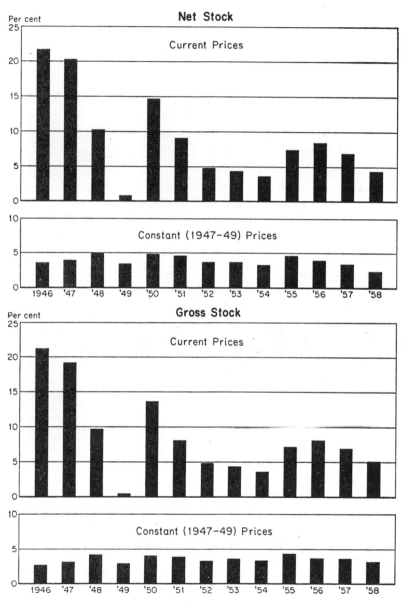

Source: Underlying data from Tables A-3 and A-4.

3.9 per cent, 1946-49; 3.7 per cent, 1949-54; and 3.5 per cent, 1954-58. A similar slight decline is shown for the two peak-to-peak cycles of 1948-53, 3.8 per cent, and 1953-57, 3.6 per cent.

The rates of growth for the postwar period are only slightly different if a somewhat broader or narrower concept of national wealth is adopted. This is evident from Table 4. Using the broadest concept, for which estimates have been made—total civilian wealth including consumer durables plus military assets—the average rate of growth of deflated wealth for the period 1945-58 is 3.0 per cent, noticeably lower than that for civilian wealth (3.5 per cent) because of the relatively small increase in military assets over the period as a whole. Inclusion of military assets, moreover, reverses the position of the two halves of the period. If military assets are included, the rate of growth in the first half—practically entirely before the Korean War—is considerably lower with 2.6 per cent than it is in the second half, when it reaches 3.4 per cent, just the opposite of the relationship for civilian wealth for which the rates are 3.9 per cent (1946-51) and 3.3 per cent (1952-58).

Under the narrowest concept of national wealth—a concept rarely explicitly used—which may be regarded as equivalent to business wealth, and which excludes not only consumer durables but also all durable assets of government and nonprofit institutions and all housing, the rate of growth of deflated wealth averages 3.4 per cent for the entire postwar period, compared with 3.5 per cent for the standard concept (total civilian wealth).

Taking trough-to-trough cycles, the growth rate for business wealth shows a continuous decline—from 3.9 per cent for the 1946-49 cycle to 3.4 per cent and 3.2 per cent in the two following cycles. This is similar to, but more pronounced than, the reduction in the rate for total civilian wealth from 3.9 per cent to 3.5 per cent. Using peak-to-peak cycles, the rate of growth of business wealth falls from 3.6 per cent in 1948-53 to 3.1 per cent in 1953-57, while that for all civilian wealth declines only slightly from 3.8 per cent to 3.6 per cent and that for nonbusiness wealth (mainly housing, consumer durables, and government structures) increases from 3.8 per cent to 3.9 per cent.

The trend of growth of national wealth thus depends on the scope of assets included. There is some indication of a decline in the rate of growth over the postwar period for business wealth, but none for household and public wealth. A longer time span is needed before one can be sure that the movements over the years since the end of World War II reflect long-time trends.

TABLE 4

AVERAGE RATE OF GROWTH OF REAL (DEFLATED) NATIONAL WEALTH, VARIANT DEFINITIONS, SELECTED PERIODS, 1946-58

(per cent per year)

PERIOD	Total Including Military (1)	CIVILIAN Consumer Durables Included (2)	CIVILIAN Consumer Durables Excluded (3)	Business (4)	HOUSEHOLD AND PUBLIC Consumer Durables Included (5)	HOUSEHOLD AND PUBLIC Consumer Durables Excluded (6)	Population (7)	Employment (8)
			A. NET WEALTH					
1946-58	3.03	3.50	3.09	3.46	3.70	2.84	1.73	1.81
1946-51	2.61	3.89	3.16	4.12	3.73	2.38	1.74	3.04
1952-58	3.38	3.32	3.02	2.80	3.67	3.23	1.72	0.76
1946-49a	2.16	3.86	3.10	3.91	3.82	2.46	1.78	3.26
1949-54a	3.49	3.71	3.10	3.39	3.78	2.87	1.69	0.58
1954-58a	3.45	3.54	3.23	3.16	3.81	3.32	1.75	1.54
1948-53a	3.32	3.76	3.18	3.63	3.84	2.80	1.69	0.82
1953-57a	3.57	3.58	3.19	3.05	3.94	3.32	1.75	1.44
			B. GROSS WEALTH					
1946-58	2.74	3.50	2.81	3.12	3.71	2.57	1.73	1.81
1946-51	2.33	3.40	2.76	3.59	3.31	2.15	1.74	3.04
1952-58	3.09	3.58	2.85	2.71	4.06	2.95	1.72	0.76
1946-49	2.04	3.28	2.54	3.27	3.32	2.06	1.78	3.26
1949-54	2.72	3.56	2.95	3.36	3.68	2.70	1.69	0.58
1954-58	3.38	3.73	2.95	2.80	4.26	2.97	1.75	1.54
1948-53	2.52	3.57	3.00	3.50	3.60	2.60	1.69	0.82
1953-57	3.29	3.74	2.98	2.89	4.24	3.04	1.75	1.44

SOURCE: For basic figures, see Tables A-6 and A-8.
a First and last year weighted one-half (in cols. 1-6).

During the postwar period, the rates of growth of gross national wealth, adjusted for price changes, are considerably lower than those for net national wealth (except in the case of civilian wealth including consumer durables), reflecting the relatively rapid rise of capital expenditures and the consequent reduction of the average age of the stock of reproducible assets. For aggregate gross reproducible tangible wealth excluding inventories—and it is only for this segment that gross and net stock differ—the average rate of growth is 3.5 per cent a year against 4 per cent for the net stock of structures and equipment.[4] The difference is relatively small for consumer and government durables, but very pronounced for the reproducible assets of business. This difference reflects the sharp rise in expenditures on business structures and equipment, within the postwar period and also in comparison with the prewar decades, an acceleration which results in a large excess of depreciation allowances over retirement.[5] As a result the rate of growth averages 3.6 per cent for the gross stock of business structures and equipment compared with a rate of 4.1 per cent for the net stock.

The relative difference between the rates of growth of net and gross stock are, of course, more pronounced when allowance is made for growth in population or labor force. The per-head rates of growth for deflated gross stock are then about one-fifth lower than those for net stock, if all reproducible assets are taken together (1.8 per cent against 2.2 per cent a year); but they are almost halved in the case of business structures and equipment (1.4 per cent against 2.4 per cent).

When national wealth estimates, adjusted for price changes, are used in economic analysis, neither gross nor net stock can be regarded as a measure of productive capacity or changes in it. While much depends on the technique used to deflate current capital expenditures and on other peculiarities of the data and their manipulation, it is likely that, in general, productive capacity in the sense of output at practically full utilization of resources will grow at a rate somewhere between the rates indicated by net and gross wealth.

An important characteristic of national wealth is thus provided by the ratio of its net value (net of depreciation) and its gross value (net of retirements) which is shown in Chart 3. This ratio, which applies only to structures and equipment, is an indicator of the proportion of

---

[4] For basic figures see Tables A-6 and A-8.

[5] Both series, as used in this report, are based on conventional length-of-life assumptions. There is little doubt, however, that the excess would persist if information were available on actual retirements.

CHART 3

Net-Gross Stock Ratio of Selected Assets, 1945-58
(current prices)

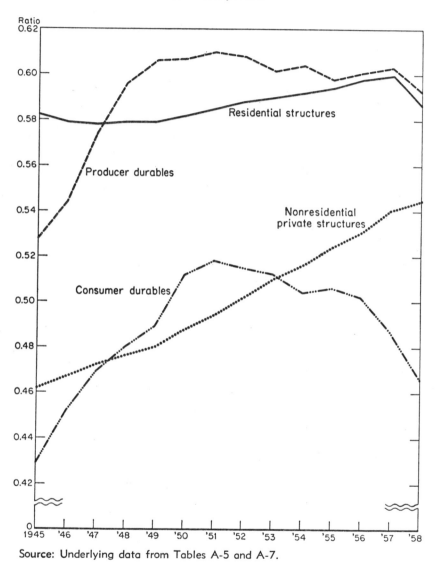

Source: Underlying data from Tables A-5 and A-7.

the original investment in structures and equipment which is still unrecovered on the basis of the length-of-life assumption and the depreciation schedule that are applied. To the extent that both, as well as the adjustment for price changes, are realistic, the ratio measures the proportion of useful life expired and provides an indication of the proportion of original investment still available for use in production.

The ratio (which would be 0.50 in a static economy in which the amount of gross capital expenditures is the same, year after year[6]) stood—on the basis of current prices of the net and gross stock—at 0.53 at the end of 1945, advanced gradually to 0.57 in 1956 and 1957, and then dropped slightly to 0.56 in 1958. Producer durables and structures both show ratios of about 0.59 for 1958 in contrast to only 0.47 for consumer durables. The levels of and changes in the net-gross ratios for individual types of assets can be followed, on an annual basis, in Table A-65. The level for the two main constituents, business plant and equipment, and household and public structures and consumer durables, started at about the same level—50 and 56 per cent, respectively, in 1945—but the ratio advanced to about two-thirds in 1958 for business plant and equipment while remaining practically stationary for the second category.

A Longer Perspective

In a question such as the rate of growth of a nation's capital stock, long-range perspective is essential. How does the rate of growth of national wealth in current prices observed during the postwar decade compare with American experience in the past? And how does its distribution among changes in the price level, in population, and in real capital per head compare? Table 5 tries to answer this question insofar as a few summary figures can do so.[7]

In comparison with three semicentennial periods before World War II—1805 to 1850; 1850 to 1900; and 1900 to 1945—the growth of wealth during the postwar period is characterized by the following features:[8]

1. The decline in the share of nonreproducible assets, particularly farm land, continued (Chart 4). This will be discussed in the first section of Chapter 5. What follows is limited to reproducible wealth.

---

[6] Cf. Chapter 3.

[7] It is hardly necessary to stress that the wealth estimates for the nineteenth century are considerably weaker than those for the last sixty years, imperfect as the latter are. The very broad comparisons made here may not, however, be seriously affected.

[8] The margin of error in the figures, of course, increases as we go back in time.

TABLE 5

DISTRIBUTION OF GROWTH OF REPRODUCIBLE TANGIBLE WEALTH, EXCLUDING MILITARY, AMONG INCREASE IN POPULATION, CHANGE IN PRICE LEVEL, AND GROWTH OF REAL WEALTH, SELECTED PERIODS, 1805-1958

(per head)

	Successive Periods					*Periods Ending 1958*			
	1945 to 1958	1929 to 1945	1900 to 1929	1850 to 1900	1805 to 1850	1929 to 1958	1900 to 1958	1850 to 1958	1805 to 1958
	(1)	(2)	(3)	(4)	(5)	(6)	(7)	(8)	(9)
A. ANNUAL PERCENTAGE RATE OF GROWTH[a]									
1. Nonmilitary wealth, current value	8.80	2.17	5.91	5.20	4.40	5.21	5.56	5.31	5.21
2. Population	1.73	0.86	1.62	2.40	3.00	1.25	1.43	1.89	2.20
3. Wealth per head[b]	7.07	1.31	4.29	2.80	1.40	3.96	4.13	3.62	3.01
4. Price level[c]	4.93	1.98	2.62	0.30	−0.80	3.19	2.91	1.74	1.02
5. Real wealth per head[d]	2.14	−0.67	1.67	2.50	2.20	0.77	1.22	1.88	1.99
6. Real wealth	3.87	0.19	3.29	4.90	5.20	2.02	2.65	3.77	4.19
B. PER CENT OF TOTAL GROWTH RATE									
1. Nonmilitary wealth, current value	100.0	100.0	100.0	100.0	100.0	100.0	100.0	100.0	100.0
2. Population	19.7	39.7	27.4	46.2	68.2	24.0	25.7	34.3	42.2
3. Wealth per head[b]	80.3	60.3	72.6	53.8	31.8	76.0	74.3	65.7	57.8
4. Price level[c]	56.0	91.2	44.3	5.8	−18.2	61.2	52.3	31.6	19.6
5. Real wealth per head[d]	24.3	−30.9	28.3	48.1	50.0	14.8	21.9	34.1	38.2
6. Real wealth	44.0	8.8	55.7	94.2	118.2	38.8	47.7	68.4	81.4

SOURCE: Data from Income and Wealth Series II, p. 306; and Tables A-1 and A-2, below.

[a] Calculated from ratio between value at beginning and at end of period.

[b] Line 1 less line 2.

[c] Implicit; calculated as difference between lines 3 and 5.

[d] Line 6 less line 2.

2. The current value of reproducible tangible wealth grew very rapidly (Chart 5). The rate of almost 9 per cent a year is well in excess of that for any of the three semicentennial periods. It is at least as high as that observed for any ten-year period for which we have separate estimates, including the decades 1860-70 and 1912-22 which cover the two preceding war and postwar inflations.[9]

[9] The rate of growth for the period 1860-70 was only 4 per cent for the aggregate and 1.7 per cent for the current value of reproducible wealth per head if Willford I. King's estimates are used (*The Wealth and Income of the People of the United States*, New York, Macmillan, 1919, pp. 256-259). The rate of growth for the period 1912-22 is estimated at 8 per cent for aggregate reproducible wealth in current prices and 6.5 per cent for wealth per head. If we select for this comparison the

CHART 4

Share of Nonreproducible Constituents in Total Wealth, Selected Years, 1900-58
(current prices)

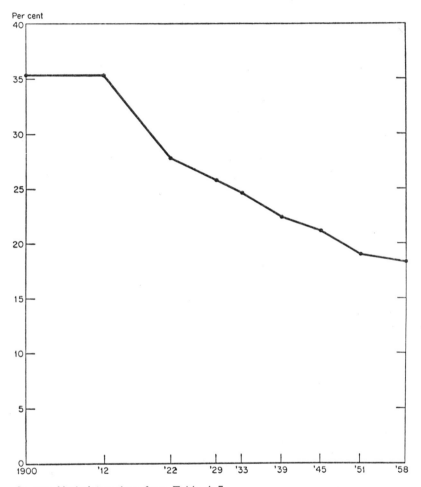

Source: Underlying data from Table A-5.

3. Rising prices accounted for a high proportion of the growth of the current value of reproducible wealth (Chart 6). For the postwar

---

period 1939-48 which is more appropriate in its location relative to the years of actual warfare, the rate of growth (9 per cent in the aggregate and 7.5 per cent per head) during the World War II decade equals the partly overlapping postwar period.

CHART 5

Total Net Wealth, Excluding Military, Selected Years, 1900-58

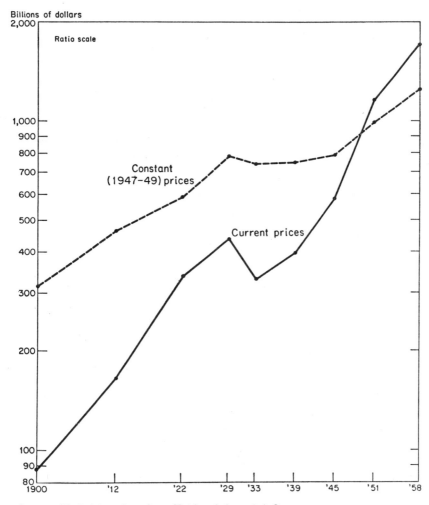

Source: Underlying data from Tables A-1 and A-2.

period as a whole almost three-fifths of the total increase in the current value of tangible wealth is attributable to the price factor. It is, however, worth notice that the share of the rise of prices in the growth of the current value of wealth during the decade 1946-55 is not much above that for the average of the entire period 1900-45 in which the absolute

CHART 6

Annual Rate of Change of Net Reproducible Wealth, Selected Periods and Years, 1900-58

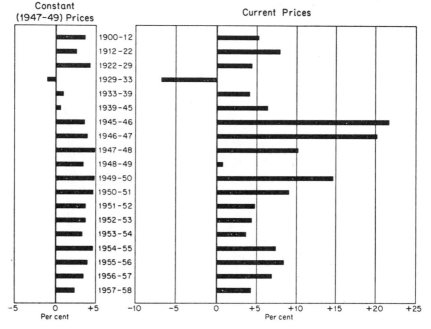

Source: Underlying data from Tables A-3 and A-4.

rate of growth of the current value of wealth was considerably smaller. During the nineteenth century as a whole, on the other hand, only a negligible part of the growth of the current value of reproducible wealth was attributable to a rise in the price level of durable goods.

4. The growth of population showed a relatively low share in the increase of real reproducible wealth. During the postwar period, more than two-fifths of the increase in total real wealth was absorbed by the increase in the number of people, compared with a share of almost three-fifths in the preceding half-century, a share of one-half for the second half of the nineteenth century, and a share of three-fifths for the period 1805 to 1850.

5. The rate of growth of reproducible wealth per head of 2.2 per cent per year—for the economist, probably the most relevant of all these measures—is slightly above the average for the entire period from 1805

to 1945; only slightly below the average for the entire nineteenth century; and far above the average for the period 1900-45 as a whole. What is more significant, the rate is slightly above the average for the first three decades of the twentieth century (1.7 per cent), although somewhat below the average for the new era of the twenties (1922-29, 2.5 per cent).

6. The relation between the rates of growth of national wealth in the postwar period, comparing concepts of different scope, is partly similar and partly different from what it had been in the 1900-45 period and—possibly more relevantly—in the 1900-29 period (Table 6 and Chart 7). The postwar period resembled the first three decades of the century, in that the rate of growth of household and public wealth (including consumer durables) was higher than that of business wealth (3.7 per cent against 3.5 per cent, both adjusted for price changes but before adjustment for population growth). On the other hand, the first three decades do not exhibit the marked excess within household wealth of the rate of growth of consumer durables over that of housing and government structures that characterized the postwar period. Finally, the difference between the rates of growth of total and civilian wealth was, of course, absent in the 1900-29 period (though it was even more pronounced in the 1929-45 period), since military assets were of negligible size until World War II.

7. Because of the existence of long swings in many basic economic series, one must be very careful to interpret the level of the rate of growth of national wealth or components of it, during the postwar period, as indicating a change in trend. The existence of such swings in the case of reproducible tangible wealth is indicated in Table 7, which shows the average annual rate of change of reproducible tangible wealth in constant (1929) prices for the fifteen reference cycles since 1896 distinguished by the National Bureau. Taken alone, the average rate of growth for the three postwar cycles of about 4 per cent per year is high, since the same average for the preceding twelve cycles is slightly below 3.5 per cent. However, the high rate for the three postwar cycles, particularly the second and third, may well reflect the top of a long swing rather than a change in trend, similar for example to cycles 8 to 10 (1921-32), which showed an average rate of growth of 3.5 per cent a year; or to cycles 2 to 4 (1900-11), with an average of 3.75 per cent.

8. On the whole, when attention is limited to broad aggregates, the similarities between the growth of national wealth in the postwar

TABLE 6

National Wealth Per Head, Selected Years, 1900-58

END OF YEAR	ALL NONBUSINESS WEALTH				REPRODUCIBLE TANGIBLE NONBUSINESS WEALTH			
	Total	Consumer Durables		Business Wealth	Total	Consumer Durables		Business Wealth
		Included	Excluded			Included	Excluded	
	(1)	(2)	(3)	(4)	(5)	(6)	(7)	(8)
A. NET DOLLARS PER HEAD, CURRENT PRICES								
1900	1,144	488	410	656	772	367	288	405
1912	1,718	718	577	1,001	1,135	545	404	590
1922	3,061	1,484	1,200	1,577	2,136	1,083	800	1,053
1929	3,587	1,937	1,593	1,650	2,559	1,407	1,062	1,152
1933	2,621	1,482	1,278	1,139	1,914	1,079	875	835
1939	3,015	1,779	1,532	1,237	2,329	1,416	1,161	920
1945	4,062	2,382	2,020	1,680	3,144	1,567	1,567	1,215
1945	4,097	2,444	2,115	1,653	3,249	1,736	1,736	1,183
1951	7,480	4,291	3,504	3,189	5,964	3,594	2,808	2,370
1958	9,781	5,671	4,566	4,111	7,873	3,678	3,678	3,090
B. NET DOLLARS PER HEAD, CONSTANT (1947-49) PRICES								
1900	4,094	1,935	1,654	2,159	2,888	1,482	1,201	1,405
1912	4,826	2,354	2,014	2,473	3,486	1,817	1,477	1,669
1922	5,382	2,746	2,400	2,636	3,921	2,013	1,668	1,908
1929	6,352	3,553	3,085	2,799	4,673	2,620	2,153	2,052
1933	5,886	3,427	3,032	2,459	4,334	2,518	2,123	1,816
1939	5,699	3,390	2,952	2,309	4,358	2,655	2,217	1,703
1945	5,429	3,174	2,738	2,255	4,202	2,525	2,090	1,677
1945	5,608	3,324	2,915	2,283	4,429	2,793	2,384	1,636
1951	6,364	3,738	3,030	2,626	5,126	3,133	2,425	1,993
1958	7,097	4,246	3,336	2,851	5,830	3,628	2,719	2,202

(continued)

TABLE 6
(concluded)

| END OF YEAR | ALL NONBUSINESS WEALTH | | | | REPRODUCIBLE TANGIBLE NONBUSINESS WEALTH | | | |
| | Consumer Durables | | | Business Wealth | | Consumer Durables | | Business Wealth |
	Total (1)	Included (2)	Excluded (3)	(4)	Total (5)	Included (6)	Excluded (7)	(8)
C. AVERAGE PERCENTAGE RATE OF CHANGE PER HEAD, NET WEALTH IN CURRENT PRICES								
1900-12	1.38	1.65	1.65	1.14	1.58	1.71	1.73	1.44
1912-22	1.10	1.55	1.77	0.64	1.18	1.02	1.22	1.35
1922-29	2.40	3.75	3.65	0.86	2.54	3.83	3.61	1.04
1929-33	-1.92	-0.91	-0.43	-3.29	-1.90	-1.00	-0.35	-3.10
1933-39	-0.54	-0.18	-0.45	-1.05	0.09	0.78	0.72	-1.07
1939-45	-0.81	-1.10	-1.26	-0.40	-0.61	-0.84	1.00	-0.30
1945-51	2.13	1.98	0.65	2.36	2.47	1.93	0.28	3.34
1951-58	1.57	1.84	1.38	1.18	1.86	2.12	1.65	1.42
1945-58	1.83	1.90	1.04	1.72	2.14	2.03	1.02	2.30
1900-29	1.53	2.12	2.17	0.90	1.67	1.98	2.03	1.31
1929-58	0.38	0.62	0.27	0.06	0.77	1.13	0.81	0.23
1900-58	0.95	1.36	1.22	0.48	1.22	1.55	1.42	0.78

Source: Based on data in Tables A-1 and A-2.

43

CHART 7

Growth of National Wealth, Alternative Definitions, Selected Years, 1900-58

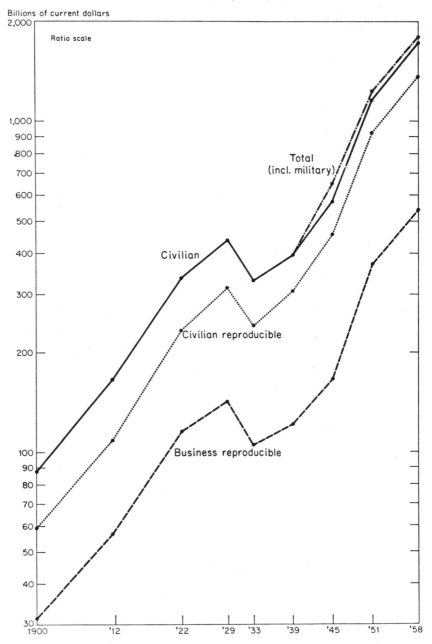

Billions of current dollars

Ratio scale

Total
(incl. military)

Civilian

Civilian reproducible

Business reproducible

Source: Underlying data from Tables A-1 and A-5.

44

TABLE 7

RATE OF GROWTH OF TOTAL REPRODUCIBLE TANGIBLE ASSETS OVER NBER REFERENCE CYCLE PHASES, 1896-1958

Line	Dates of Reference Cycles			Average Yearly Standing ($ billion of 1947/49)			Per Cent Change from Preceding Phase		Per Cent Change from Preceding Cycle[a]		Per Cent Change Per Year from Preceding Phase	
	Trough	Peak	Trough	Expansion	Contraction	Full cycle	Expansion	Contraction	Total	Per Year	Expansion	Contraction
	(1)			(2)	(3)	(4)	(5)	(6)	(7)	(8)	(9)	(10)
1.	1896	1899	1900	112.8	120.4	114.7		+6.7	+14.6	+3.6		+3.4
2.	1900	1903	1904	129.0	138.6	131.4	+7.1	+7.4	+16.3	+3.9	+3.6	+3.7
3.	1904	1907	1908	149.8	161.8	152.8	+8.1	+8.0	+12.6	+3.6	+4.0	+4.0
4.	1908	1910	1911	169.2	177.8	172.1	+4.6	+5.1	+10.1	+3.4	+3.1	+3.4
5.	1911	1913	1914	186.4	195.6	189.5	+4.8	+4.9	+11.4	+2.8	+3.2	+3.3
6.	1914	1918	1919	208.6	221.2	211.1	+6.6	+6.0	+8.4	+2.4	+2.6	+2.4
7.	1919	1920	1921	227.0	230.8	228.9	+2.6	+1.7	+6.9	+2.8	+2.6	+1.7
8.	1921	1923	1924	239.5	255.3	244.8	+3.8	+6.6	+14.3	+4.8	+2.5	+4.4
9.	1924	1926	1927	273.5	292.8	279.9	+7.1	+7.1	+12.5	+3.1	+4.7	+4.7
10.	1927	1929	1932	308.2	319.5	315.0	+5.3	+3.7	-3.8	-0.2	+3.5	+1.5
11.	1932	1937	1938	201.5	311.1	303.1	-5.6	+3.2	+10.4	+1.5	-1.4	-1.1
12.	1938	1944	1946	333.6	337.0	334.5	+7.2	+1.0	+13.2	+2.3	+2.1	+0.2
13.	1946	1948	1949	368.9	398.0	378.6	+9.5	+7.9	+25.1	+5.8	+4.6	+5.2
14.	1949	1953	1954	464.7	510.1	473.8	+16.8	+9.8	+18.6	+3.9	+6.4	+3.8
15.	1954	1957	1958	552.4	590.5	561.9	+8.3	+6.9			+4.1	+3.4

SOURCE: 1896-1945, *A Study of Saving* . . . , Vol. III, Table W-3. 1946-58, Table A-26 below (converted to 1929 prices).

[a] Base average of preceding cycle.

period and that observed in the preceding century are much more pronounced than the differences. The growth of national wealth in the years 1946-58 has followed the pattern of the preceding two or three generations. Differences in detail naturally exist, and there will be occasion to point out some of them in greater detail in Chapter 5.

CHAPTER 5

Changes in the Structure of National Wealth

THE revival of interest in national wealth estimates during the past decade has been accompanied by a realization that the value of these figures for economic analysis resides much less in broad national aggregates than in breakdowns which permit comparisons among types of wealth or among groups of wealth holders, and breakdowns which also enable the analyst to relate the wealth estimates to the income derived from the same type of assets or by the same groups of holders. Of the two breakdowns, changes in the structure of national wealth among its components have been given more attention by economists, probably because analysis of the distribution of national wealth among groups requires the simultaneous consideration of tangible assets, financial assets, liabilities, and net worth. This chapter deals primarily with the breakdown of tangible assets by type and secondarily with the distribution of the ownership of tangible assets among the various sectors of the economy.

Changes in the relations between components of national wealth differ, depending on whether the analysis is conducted on the basis of original cost, current (market or replacement), or constant (base period) values. What is more disturbing, changes in the structure of national wealth also depend to some extent on the choice of the price basis. This may be true even if the base periods are only twenty years apart, as seen from a comparison of the distribution of national wealth by type during the first part of the postwar decade in 1947-49 prices, given in this report, with a similar distribution based on 1929 prices, derived from previously published estimates.[1]

In order not to complicate the discussion unduly, we shall concentrate in this chapter on changes in the structure of national wealth as reflected in current values (replacement cost for reproducible tangible wealth), drawing attention only occasionally to instances of changes in the structure of national wealth that differ significantly in pattern when

NOTE: The discussion in this section is based for the period beginning with 1900 on the estimates shown in the relevant Appendix tables, which in turn are taken for the period 1900 to 1935 from *A Study of Saving in the United States*, Vol. III, *Special Studies*, 1956. For the nineteenth century the rough estimates in "The Growth of Reproducible Wealth of the United States of America from 1805 to 1950," Income and Wealth Series II, London, 1952 (pp. 247ff.), were used.

[1] *A Study of Saving . . .* , Vol. III, Table W-3.

deflated figures are used. The interested reader, however, can follow the movements on both bases in summary form in Tables 6 to 12, and in detail with the help of Tables A-9 to A-14 and A-19 to A-24.

Reproducible and Nonreproducible Tangible Wealth

The primary distinction usually made in the analysis of the structure of national wealth is that between nonreproducible assets, represented chiefly by land, and reproducible assets, which consist chiefly of structures, equipment, and inventories.

During the postwar decade the ratio of the current value of nonreproducible tangible assets declined only very slightly from almost 21 per cent to 19½ per cent, as shown in Table 8. The drop was fairly regular, amounting on the average to nearly one-tenth of a percentage point or about ⅜ per cent of its own level per year. It reflected primarily the relatively slow increase in the aggregate current value of farm land—the quantity of which, of course, hardly changed in the face of a considerable expansion of the physical volume of reproducible tangible wealth, however measured. As a result the share of agricultural land in national wealth declined from about 8 to 6 per cent.[2]

This decline thus was not due to either of two factors which may be thought responsible. It was not due, first, to the lag in an increase in the price of agricultural land. In fact, the price of agricultural land advanced slightly more between 1945 and 1958 than the price level of all reproducible tangible wealth increased, measured by the ratios of current to its deflated values, that is, by about 115 per cent against

---

[2] An explanation of the substantial increase in the value of land at constant prices, which is shown in Table 8, is appropriate, since it might be presumed that the value of land at constant prices should by definition remain unchanged. This increase is the result of the method of estimating the value of nonagricultural land, particularly land underlying residential and nonresidential buildings. The value of these categories of land in constant (1947-49) prices at any one date is obtained by applying, to the constant price values of structures, land-structure ratios derived from the relationship between land and structure values in current prices at the same date. Hence, if the constant price value of structure increases relatively more than the land-structure ratio declines, and of course if the land-structure ratio remains unchanged, the value of land in constant prices will rise. This is not unreasonable economically. In an expanding economy land is often upgraded, that is, its value is increased in constant prices even in the absence of improvements. Thus, the transformation of farm acreage into urban land increased the value of total land between, say, 1900 and 1960, whether we use the 1900 prices or the 1960 prices or any intermediate years' prices of land of a given type. The increase in the aggregate value of land in constant prices shown in Table 8 is thus the effect of what may be called the change in the "mix" of different types of land that occurred during the period of observation.

TABLE 8

REPRODUCIBLE AND NONREPRODUCIBLE NET WEALTH,
SELECTED YEARS AND PERIODS, 1945-58

Year	Total Wealth		Reproducible Wealth		Nonreproducible Wealth	
	Military Assets		Military Assets		Military Assets	
	Included	Excluded	Included	Excluded	Included	Excluded
	(1)	(2)	(3)	(4)	(5)	(6)
A. ABSOLUTE VALUES, CURRENT PRICES ($ billion)						
1945	649	576	530	457	119	119
1951	1,220	1,165	984	929	236	236
1958	1,791	1,702	1,456	1,367	335	335
B. ABSOLUTE VALUES, CONSTANT (1947-49) PRICES ($ billion)						
1945	889	788	723	622	166	166
1951	1,037	991	844	798	193	193
1958	1,308	1,244	1,086	1,022	222	222
C. PERCENTAGE SHARES, CURRENT PRICES						
1945	100.0	100.0	81.7	79.3	18.3	20.7
1951	100.0	100.0	80.7	79.7	19.3	20.3
1958	100.0	100.0	81.3	80.3	18.7	19.7
D. PERCENTAGE SHARES, CONSTANT (1947-49) PRICES						
1945	100.0	100.0	81.3	78.9	18.7	21.1
1951	100.0	100.0	81.4	80.5	18.6	19.5
1958	100.0	100.0	83.0	82.2	17.0	17.8
E. PERCENTAGE RATE OF GROWTH PER YEAR, CURRENT PRICES						
1949-51	11.09	12.46	10.86	12.55	12.09	12.09
1951-58	5.64	5.56	5.76	5.67	5.13	5.13
1945-58	8.12	8.69	8.08	8.79	8.29	8.29
F. PERCENTAGE RATE OF GROWTH PER YEAR, CONSTANT (1947-49) PRICES						
1945-51	2.60	3.89	2.62	4.24	2.54	2.54
1951-58	3.37	3.30	3.66	3.60	2.02	2.02
1945-58	3.02	3.59	3.18	3.89	2.26	2.26

SOURCE: Data from Tables A-5, A-6, A-25, and A-26.

85 per cent. Second, it was not due, or due only to an insignificant degree, to the declining share of the value of agricultural land in total tangible assets of agriculture. This share was approximately the same in 1958 as twelve years earlier—about one-half. Among nonfarm sectors, the share of land (including forests and subsoil assets) held up until 1951 and declined very slightly, from 16 to 15 per cent over the entire decade.

The decline in the share of land in total national wealth during the postwar decade continued a trend that can be observed as far back as national wealth estimates reach. From 1900 to 1945, for instance, the share of land was almost cut in half from 35 per cent to about 20 per cent. This meant a decline by about one-third of one percentage point per year, or by approximately 1.25 per cent of its average level. Thus, the decline in the share of land during the postwar decade was considerably smaller in absolute terms than the diminution that had been experienced over the preceding half century.

During the nineteenth century the decline in the share of land in national wealth had proceeded quite regularly at the rate of about one-fifth of one percentage point per year so far as the very rough estimates utilized in Table 9 can be trusted. As during the postwar decade this continuous decline in the share of land reflected primarily the diminishing importance of agriculture within the American economy and was not due, or only to a minor extent, to a decline in the share of land in total tangible assets of agriculture[3] or in total tangible assets of the other sectors of the economy.

Wealth for Production Versus Wealth for Consumption

Another significant division of tangible wealth is by assets used for production and those devoted directly to individuals' welfare (consumption). The separation—which of course is not identical with the distinction between profit-making and nonprofit-making assets—is not entirely unambiguous conceptually or statistically. However, the result cannot be very far off quantitatively from what more precisely allocated figures would yield, if we regard as tangible wealth used for consumption residential and institutional structures and the land underlying them; consumer durables, except one-half of the stock of passenger cars;[4] one-half of government civilian structures;[5] and—

[3] The share of land in the tangible assets of agriculture may be put very roughly at close to three-fifths in 1805, 1850, and 1900, although the share probably was somewhat above that level in 1805, and somewhat below it in 1880. The figures permit only the tentative conclusion that the ratio of land to total tangible assets in agriculture failed to show an obvious or marked trend during the nineteenth century.

[4] The exclusion of one-half of the stock of passenger cars is intended as a rough recognition of the fact that a substantial proportion of intracity and interurban transportation between home and place of work depends on consumer owned and operated passenger cars. To that extent at least passenger cars are direct substitutes for trolley cars, buses, and railroad coaches; and indirect substitutes for part of railroad track, coaches and locomotives.

[5] Only one-half of government structures is allocated to wealth used for consump-

TABLE 9

SHARE OF LAND IN NATIONAL WEALTH, SELECTED YEARS, 1805-1958

(current values in billions of dollars)

Year	Total			Agriculture			Other Sectors		
	Tangible[a] Wealth (1)	Land[b] (2)	Share of Land (3)	Tangible Wealth (4)	Land (5)	Share of Land (6)	Tangible Wealth (7)	Land (8)	Share of Land (9)
1805	1.23	0.65	0.53	0.95	0.60	0.63	0.28	0.05	0.18
1850	7.2	3.0	0.42	4.1	2.5	0.61	3.1	0.4	0.13
1880	37.7	13.0	0.36	13.5	7.6	0.56	24.2	5.4	0.22
1900	87.7	30.9	0.35	24.5	14.5	0.60	63.2	16.4	0.26
1929	439.1	113.5	0.26	64.4	34.9	0.54	374.7	78.6	0.21
1945	576.2	121.2	0.21	86.7	43.5	0.50	489.5	77.7	0.16
1958	1702.3	310.8	0.18	182.6	87.6	0.48	1519.7	223.2	0.15

Source: 1805-80: Goldsmith, "The Growth of Reproducible Wealth of the United States of America from 1850 to 1950," Income and Wealth Series II, Tables I, II, IV and V.

1900 and 1929: *A Study of Saving . . .*, Vol. III, Table W-1.

1945 and 1958: Tables A-5 and A-52.

[a] Including consumer durables and net foreign assets, but excluding military assets.

[b] Including forests and subsoil assets.

rather arbitrarily—one-half of government land. Thus, all nonresidential structures and the land underlying them, all producer durables, all private inventories, farm land, and one-half the stock of passenger cars and of government structures and land are regarded as assets for production.

Such an allocation, in which tangible assets of a given type are assigned either to wealth for consumption or to wealth for production throughout the entire period, cannot take account of the shift of certain activities between household and business that occurred during the period. For instance, a larger proportion of passenger traffic facilities of railroads may have served immediate consumption—for pleasure travel—in 1900 than in 1960. If so, a larger share of the reproducible tangible assets of railroads should have been allocated to wealth for consumption in 1900. (Actually no such allocation was made in either year, all tangible assets of railroads having been allocated to wealth for production throughout the period.) It is unlikely that these shifts, not all of which tended in the same direction, were large enough to change the general outlines of the distribution of national wealth between production and consumption use.

The distribution of tangible wealth between assets for welfare and for production has hardly changed over the postwar decade, keeping close to a 45-55 per cent division, as Table 10 shows. This stability, however, is the result of an increase in the share of consumer durables large enough to offset a moderate decline—in proportion to its starting level—in the share of residential structures. The absence of a trend in the distribution of tangible wealth between assets for welfare and for production is in contrast to the trend in the preceding half-century,

---

tion because a considerable part of the reproducible tangible wealth owned by the government, particularly state and local governments, serves what are under any reasonable definition productive functions and has a close counterpart in the private sphere. This applies particularly to water and sewerage facilities, gas and electric plants, reclamation and flood control work, and river and harbor improvements. These categories accounted in 1946 for more than one-fifth of the total value of reproducible government assets (J. E. Reeve, *et al.*, "Government Component in the National Wealth," *Studies in Income and Wealth*, Vol. 12, New York, NBER, 1950, pp. 514ff.). If only one-half of roads and streets are added, as primarily serving business transportation or substituting for facilities of the business type like railroad tracks, the share of tangible government assets used for productive purposes rises to above two-fifths. Allocation of parts of nonresidential buildings and miscellaneous structures, which together represent about three-tenths of reproducible government assets, would bring the share of productive assets to at least one-half. It would be considerably in excess of one-half if city streets were also regarded as productive assets.

TABLE 10

CIVILIAN WEALTH FOR PRODUCTION AND WELFARE, SELECTED YEARS AND PERIODS, 1945-58

(values in billions of dollars)

| | NET WEALTH | | | | GROSS WEALTH | | | |
| | Total | | Reproducible | | Total | | Reproducible | |
	Production (1)	Welfare (2)	Production (3)	Welfare (4)	Production (5)	Welfare (6)	Production (7)	Welfare (8)
A. ABSOLUTE VALUES, CURRENT PRICES								
1945	311	265	227	230	468	450	384	414
1951	642	523	471	458	927	870	757	804
1958	961	741	700	667	1,377	1,259	1,131	1,170
B. ABSOLUTE VALUES, CONSTANT (1947-49) PRICES								
1945	422	367	304	318	642	621	525	572
1951	537	454	400	398	769	765	632	709
1958	661	583	505	517	957	980	802	913
C. PERCENTAGE SHARES, CURRENT PRICES								
1945	54.0	46.0	49.7	50.3	51.0	49.0	48.1	51.9
1951	55.1	44.9	50.7	49.3	51.6	48.4	48.5	51.5
1958	56.5	43.5	51.2	48.8	52.2	47.8	49.2	50.8
D. PERCENTAGE SHARES, CONSTANT (1947-49) PRICES								
1945	53.5	46.5	48.9	51.1	50.8	49.2	47.9	52.1
1951	54.2	45.8	50.1	49.9	50.1	49.9	47.1	52.9
1958	53.1	46.9	49.4	50.6	49.4	50.6	46.8	43.2
E. PERCENTAGE GROWTH PER YEAR, CURRENT PRICES								
1945-51	12.84	12.00	12.94	12.16	12.06	11.61	12.23	11.70
1951-58	5.93	5.10	5.82	5.52	5.82	5.37	5.90	5.51
1945-58	9.07	8.23	9.05	8.53	8.70	8.18	8.92	8.32
F. PERCENTAGE GROWTH PER YEAR, CONSTANT (1947-49) PRICES								
1945-51	4.10	3.61	4.60	3.81	3.29	3.77	3.14	3.54
1951-58	3.01	3.64	3.45	3.81	3.16	3.60	3.46	3.68
1945-58	3.50	3.62	3.98	3.81	3.12	3.79	3.31	3.66

SOURCE: Data from Tables A-5 and A-6.

when the share of tangible wealth serving consumption increased noticeably from only about 30 per cent in 1880 and more than 35 per cent in 1900 to close to 45 per cent in the 1930's.[6]

[6] So far as the rough estimates permit a conclusion, the share of tangible assets used for consumption was fairly stable between 1805 and 1880. In fact, if attention is limited to reproducible tangible wealth, the share of assets for consumption seems to have declined between 1805 and 1850. This trend indicated by the rough estimates is not unreasonable, as one would expect that during most of the nineteenth

Structures, Equipment, and Inventories

This division shown in Table 11 and Chart 8 is of significance primarily for productive reproducible tangible wealth. It is to some extent arbitrary, particularly with respect to the distinction of some types of equipment from the structures in which they are installed, and to the classification of livestock which may be regarded as a form of either inventory or equipment.[7]

The outstanding change during the postwar decade is the increase in the share of producers' durable equipment in productive reproducible wealth shown in Table 11. It rose between 1945 and 1958 from 22 per cent to 29 per cent if livestock is excluded, although the advance was only from 26 to 31 per cent if it is included, because the share of livestock alone in productive reproducible assets declined from 4 to 3 per cent.[8] This increase in the share of equipment (producer durables) was offset partly by the fall in the proportion of inventories from 23 to 19 per cent including livestock, and from 19 to 16 per cent excluding livestock. The share of nonresidential private structures increased slightly from 34 to 36 per cent. These movements, however, can be regarded as reflecting to only a relatively small extent significant long-term trends. They are largely the result of postwar readjustments and of the very low level of expenditures on equipment from 1930 through 1945. It was only around 1950 that equipment (excluding livestock) regained its share of 1929 in productive reproducible wealth.

The increasing share of equipment observed during the postwar decade, however, continues a trend visible at least since 1880.[9] At that time about one-sixth of productive reproducible wealth consisted of equipment (excluding livestock), a figure apparently little changed over the preceding three-quarters of a century. The share then rose to

---

century the share of tangible assets used for production increased with industrialization, but that this increase ceased when consumer durables began to gain in importance, beginning with the introduction of the automobile early in the twentieth century. On the basis of these considerations one might have expected the share of tangible assets used for production to increase until about the turn of the century, but the figures, such as they are, place the turning point near the end of the third quarter of the nineteenth century.

[7] The test probably should be the length of useful life of the individual livestock unit. From that point of view, the classification probably should be changed from inventories to equipment, as the relatively long-lived dairy cattle came to account for an increasing proportion of the total value of livestock.

[8] Detailed data from Table A-5.

[9] Goldsmith, Income and Wealth Series II, p. 306.

TABLE 11

MAIN CATEGORIES OF CIVILIAN WEALTH, SELECTED YEARS AND PERIODS, 1945-58
(values in billions of dollars)

	Net Wealth[a]				Gross Wealth[a]			
	Structures (1)	Equipment (2)	Inventories (3)	Non-reproducible (4)	Structures (5)	Equipment (6)	Inventories (7)	Non-reproducible (8)
A. ABSOLUTE VALUES, CURRENT PRICES								
1945	286	95	53	121	522	200	53	121
1951	545	246	110	222	983	439	110	222
1958	833	379	130	311	1,424	721	130	311
B. ABSOLUTE VALUES, CONSTANT (1947-49) PRICES								
1945	408	119	74	168	746	255	74	168
1951	466	214	94	181	841	381	94	181
1958	593	297	110	203	1,011	572	110	203
C. PERCENTAGE SHARES, CURRENT PRICES								
1945	49.7	16.5	9.2	21.0	56.9	21.8	5.8	13.2
1951	46.8	21.1	9.4	19.1	54.7	24.4	6.1	12.4
1958	48.9	22.3	7.6	18.3	54.0	27.4	4.9	11.8
D. PERCENTAGE SHARES, CONSTANT (1947-49) PRICES								
1945	51.7	15.1	9.4	21.3	59.1	20.2	5.9	13.3
1951	47.0	21.6	9.5	18.3	54.8	24.8	6.1	11.8
1958	47.7	23.9	8.8	16.3	52.2	29.5	5.7	10.5
E. PERCENTAGE GROWTH PER YEAR, CURRENT PRICES								
1945-51	11.38	17.18	12.94	10.64	11.13	14.00	12.94	10.64
1951-58	6.25	6.37	2.42	4.93	5.44	7.34	2.42	4.93
1945-58	8.57	11.23	7.15	7.53	8.03	10.37	7.15	7.53
F. PERCENTAGE GROWTH PER YEAR, CONSTANT (1947-49) PRICES								
1945-51	2.24	10.27	4.07	1.25	2.02	6.92	4.07	1.25
1951-58	3.50	4.79	2.27	1.65	2.67	5.98	2.27	1.65
1945-58	2.92	7.29	3.10	1.47	2.37	6.41	3.10	1.47

SOURCE: Data from Tables A-5, A-6, A-7, and A-8.
[a] Not including monetary metals and net foreign assets.

over one-quarter in 1929, gaining about two percentage points every decade, or advancing every year on the average by 1 per cent of its own level. If this trend had continued at the same absolute intensity after 1929 it would have led in 1958 to a share of equipment in reproducible productive wealth of about 30 per cent. Continuation of the trend at the same relative intensity would have led to a ratio between 33 and 34 per cent in 1958. The actual level of 34 per cent is thus right

CHART 8

Distribution of Net Reproducible Wealth Among Main Assets,
Selected Years, 1900-58
(current prices)

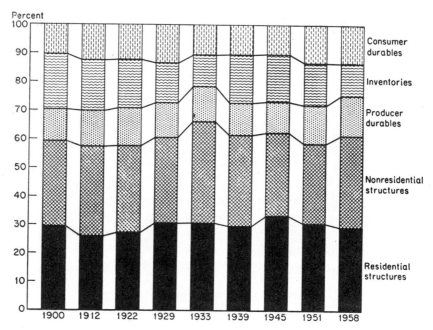

Source: Underlying data from Table A-5.

in line with the extrapolated trend.[10] This is what the general observations of the tendency toward the use of more and more complicated machinery would lead one to expect.

A similar shift occurred among components of reproducible wealth used for consumption, taking the form of an increased share of consumer durables compared with residential structures. In 1958 the value of consumer durables amounted to 44 per cent of that of residential structures, a substantial advance from the 30 per cent of 1945. As in the case of producer durables, this advance was partly a reflection of the low level of purchases between the Great Depression and the end of World War II, and partly a continuation of long-term trends. In

10 The figures are virtually the same if constant prices are used. The actual level of 32 per cent in 1958 then compares with extrapolated values of 30 per cent and 34 per cent, respectively.

1929, for instance, consumer durables accounted for 44 per cent of the value of residential structures, the same proportion that prevailed in 1958. At the turn of the century, however, the ratio had been around 35 per cent.[11]

For many purposes of analysis it is desirable, and sometimes even essential, to break down the aggregate stock of producer durables by type of equipment. The available figures, unfortunately, are far from satisfactory for this purpose. Expenditures on producer durables are given for only about one dozen broad classes of equipment, and even this limited breakdown is available only through 1954.[12] Many of the price indexes used to deflate the expenditures series leave much to be desired. Finally, the estimates of the useful length of life of the different types of equipment are rough, and can be applied only to the total of all different items that are combined in each of these classes. Therefore, the estimates of net and gross stock of the different types of producer durables must be interpreted with great caution. The fact that the tendencies they show for the postwar decade agree well with what is known from other sources may, however, increase confidence in the figures.

The main changes in the distribution of the stock of producer durables in the postwar decade are increases in the share of electrical machinery, instruments, office equipment, and motor vehicles, and sharp declines in the share of railroad equipment and ships. The largest category, industrial machinery and equipment, which accounts for almost one-half of the total stock of all producer durables, showed only a small decline.[13] Electrical machinery, office machinery, and instruments, together, represented at the end of 1954 almost one-fourth of the total value, in 1947-49 prices, of producer durables, against a share of not much over one-sixth at the beginning of the period. This increase, most of which is attributable to electrical machinery, though the rise is proportionately sharpest for instruments, is in line with the technological changes during the period. Unfortunately, separate figures cannot yet be provided for types of machinery particularly closely

11 In constant prices the shares are 50 per cent in 1900, 47 per cent in 1929, 27 per cent in 1945, and 53 per cent in 1958.

12 In order to continue estimates of stock figures for the entire postwar decade, a necessary assumption was that total expenditures on producer durables were distributed in the same proportions among types for the years 1955-58 as for the preceding seven years.

13 These statements are based on estimates in constant prices. They are valid also if current price estimates are used, except that on that basis the share of industrial machinery shows a small increase, as can be seen from Tables B-128 and B-129.

connected with the process of automation, or even a distinction between old and new types of machinery, both of which would be particularly valuable for economic analysis. The sharp increase in the share of trucks, buses, and passenger cars owned by business—from 4 per cent in 1945 to 9 per cent of all producer durables in 1954—reflects primarily the replenishment of a stock depleted by low replacements during the war period but is also indicative of the expansion of the intercity truck fleet. Hence, only part of the increase may be regarded as reflecting a long-term trend. The sharp decline of the share of railroad equipment and ships from more than 17 per cent to only slightly over 10 per cent mirrors the declining relative importance of the two industries that use such equipment.

A similar breakdown is equally important in the case of consumer durables, the aggregate for which grew during the postwar period by as much as 180 per cent (1947-49 prices), or by more than 8 per cent per year. This aggregate is a compound of one group of consumer durables—automobiles and household appliances, mostly electrical, including radio and television sets—the stock of which grew at the astonishing average rate of 14 per cent per year after adjustment for price changes; and of another group—consisting of furniture, house furnishings, jewelry, watches, and books—which showed an average rate of growth of the net stock of only 4.5 per cent per year. The reasons for these differences are fairly obvious. The extraordinary increase in the value of the net stock of passenger cars—at a rate of 15 per cent per year in 1947-49 prices—reflected primarily the replacement of a stock that had been run down far beyond customary standards as a result of unavailability of new cars during the war years, but was also influenced by a spread of car ownership, due to the general high level of income, and by an upgrading among types of cars, made possible by the same favorable income experience. The almost equally sharp rise in the stock of what may be called household machinery, averaging about 12.5 per cent a year, on the other hand, may be attributed primarily to the introduction of entirely new types of commodities (for example, television sets and air conditioning equipment) or the sharp decline in the relative price of others (such as radios, washing machines, and heaters). These are typically "new products," and their rapid growth is in sharp contrast to the much slower increase of furniture (5 per cent per year) and particularly house furnishings (only about 1.5 per cent per year). Although furniture basically must be classified, like the other items showing relatively lower rate of growth, as an "old product," changes in style preferences together with the high level of new household formation may have lifted furniture into a somewhat intermediate position between the slowly and the very rapidly expanding types of consumer durables.

Domestic and International Wealth

In many countries the growth and structure of reproducible tangible wealth cannot be understood without considering the country's international financial relations, primarily the ebb and flow of its capital imports and exports. In the United States during the postwar decade these relations have been statistically of small importance, if attention is concentrated, as it must be here, on the share of domestic tangible wealth owned by foreigners or of the foreign assets held by U.S. residents.

The share of foreign ownership of tangible assets situated in the United States is negligible, even if we assume that the total foreign direct investment in nonfinancial businesses is represented by tangible assets, and if we regard foreign holdings of shares in American nonfinancial publicly owned corporations as equivalent to a pro rata ownership of their tangible assets. In that case foreign ownership, although rising in current value from about $5 billion in 1946 to $12 billion in 1958, accounted in both years for only a little over 0.5 per cent of total national wealth. This figure, because of its derivation, is almost certainly an overstatement of the actual ownership by foreigners of tangible assets situated in the U.S. What is more relevant, there does not seem to be any major type of tangible assets for which foreign ownership is more than marginal.

If foreign investments by American owners are treated similarly, we have to account at the end of 1946 for about $6 billion of direct investments in nonfinancial businesses operating abroad, and for holdings of stocks in publicly owned foreign corporations of about $1 billion. This total of $7 billion was equivalent to about 1 per cent of the national wealth of the United States. Notwithstanding a sharp increase in the value of these types of foreign investments, which rose in 1958 to nearly $30 billion, about nine-tenths of which consisted of direct investments in nonfinancial enterprises, they were equivalent to less than 2 per cent of total national wealth.[14]

14 While these figures, which are based on estimates made by the Department of Commerce in connection with its studies of the balance of payments, understate the current value of direct foreign investments, reflecting as they do book values rather

In considering the international aspects of national wealth we may, however, also want to take account of the net balance of intangible claims and liabilities, including the claims of the United States Treasury against foreign governments, insofar as they are definite enough to permit valuation. In 1946 the net balance of claims was very small, liabilities offsetting most of the claims. Twelve years later the net credit balance had risen to about $6 billion, but yet amounted to less than 0.5 per cent of national wealth. Even the most liberal interpretation of net foreign assets, including both tangible and intangible assets, would thus add only about 1.5 per cent to total domestic national wealth in 1958 and would leave it virtually unchanged for 1946.

This reduction in foreign assets and liabilities to almost insignificance in the over-all picture of the national balance sheet of the United States is a rather recent phenomenon, although foreign investments have never been statistically very important since the turn of the century. In 1929, when the relative importance of foreign investments for the U.S. probably reached its statistical peak, they accounted for about 3 per cent of domestic national wealth. Throughout the nineteenth century the U.S. had been a debtor country on balance. However, net foreign investments in the U.S. apparently were never in excess of 5 per cent of total national wealth, and showed a declining trend throughout the century, falling to about 3 per cent in 1850 and fluctuating around that level during the second half of the century.

The share of foreign investment is, of course, higher when net foreign investments are compared, not with total national wealth but—what is economically more appropriate—only with reproducible tangible assets, since most of the foreign investments found their way into assets other than land. In that case, net foreign investment may have accounted for almost 10 per cent of domestic reproducible tangible wealth at the beginning of the nineteenth century and for as much as 5 per cent even in 1850, further slowly declining to about 4 per cent in 1900 and, of course, becoming negative rather than positive from World War I on.

Military and Civilian Wealth

Military durable assets have become too important and the change in their absolute and relative value too pronounced during the postwar

---

than market values, a tentative adjustment would still leave the share for 1958 not much above 2 per cent and would not substantially affect it for 1946.

decade to be ignored altogether in an analysis of national wealth. The discussion whether durable military assets are an intrinsic part of national wealth or only an intermediary item in a complete accounting for all stocks of physical assets will, of course, continue. Furthermore, however military assets are treated from the conceptual point of view, the user must be aware that the estimates which can be contrived at the present time, in the absence of a comprehensive or statistically satisfactory inventory in current or constant prices compiled by the federal government, are affected by a very substantial margin of uncertainty. This results mainly from the uncertainty about the length of life that should be assigned to some of the most important types of military equipment in a period of rapidly changing military technology, and the consequent high incidence of obsolescence. There are, however, two developments which are sufficiently well established not to be unduly affected by these uncertainties, and at the same time are relevant for an analysis of national wealth during the postwar decade.

The first is the fact that, however estimated, military assets have ceased to be of negligible size compared with civilian wealth, and indeed have become larger than several types of civilian assets that would be regarded as important in any analysis. For the average of the period 1946-58 military assets were equal, on the basis of current or replacement values, to at least 6 per cent of total civilian wealth. Their share was somewhat higher (8 per cent) if attention is limited to reproducible tangible assets and, of course, was considerably more important if the comparison is made between military and civilian equipment (excluding in both cases structures and inventories). In that comparison it appears that the value of military equipment was equal, for the average of the postwar decade, to about one-fifth of total civilian equipment, but to almost two-fifths of producer durables alone.

The second fact is that, unlike the upward trend in civilian tangible assets, the net value of the stock of military durables diminished markedly between the end of World War II and 1950. As a result, the share of military in total tangible assets declined from 13 per cent to 5 per cent. The substantial increase in the stock during the 1950's—at least in current prices—was just sufficient to prevent a further decline in the share of military assets.

Because of its large size and still more because of the sharp fluctuations in its value, the inclusion of the stock of military assets in national wealth produces a change in the level and particularly in the movements of the rate of growth of wealth during the postwar decade. Thus the average annual rate of growth of reproducible tangible wealth in constant (1947-49) prices is reduced by the inclusion of military assets from 3.9 per cent to 3.2 per cent. The effect, of course, is relatively more pronounced on the rate of growth per head, which is lowered by the inclusion of military assets from 2.2 to 1.5 per cent per year. This effect, however, is entirely limited to the first half of the decade for which the rate of growth of civilian wealth of 4.2 per cent is reduced to 2.6 per cent by the inclusion of military assets. For the second half of the period the rate is hardly affected, actually being increased from 3.6 per cent to 3.7 per cent. Thus, the most spectacular effect of the inclusion of military durables is in the comparison between the two halves of the postwar decade. For civilian wealth alone the rate of growth is substantially higher for the first than for the second half—4.2 per cent against 3.6 per cent. If military assets are included, the relationship is reversed, and the rate of growth appears to have risen from 2.6 per cent in the first half to 3.7 per cent in the second half of the decade. Any interpretation of the over-all rate of growth of national wealth in the postwar decade depends decisively on whether or not military assets are included, that is, on the decision whether or not military structures and equipment should be regarded as a part of a nation's stock of assets. That decision, in turn, will depend on whether, in the world of today, military assets are regarded as a necessary complement to civilian wealth.

Ownership of National Wealth

Since ownership is a financial concept and national wealth a real concept, the analysis of the ownership of tangible assets alone is of limited significance, but there is considerable interest in the extent to which tangible assets used for production or consumption are owned by their operators or must be rented by their users.[15]

The distribution of ownership of total national wealth or of reproducible tangible assets did not change significantly during the postwar decade, if attention is limited to the three very broad groups of business enterprises, households, and government, as can be seen from Table 12 and Chart 9.[16] Throughout the period, business enterprises

---

[15] The distribution of ownership of tangible assets, of course, is not identical with the distribution of net worth because the debt-asset ratio differs among sectors. The difference is particularly pronounced in the case of the federal government.

[16] For details, see Tables A-29 to A-32.

CHART 9

Distribution of Total Nonmilitary Wealth Among Sectors,
Selected Years, 1900-58
(current prices)

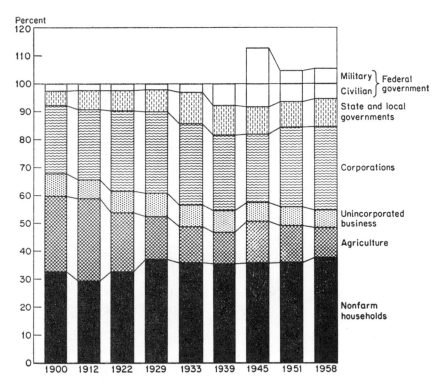

Source: Underlying data from Table A-19.

owned, on the basis of current valuations, almost one-half of total civilian tangible wealth, while households owned slightly more than one-third, leaving about one-sixth for the government.[17] If military assets are included, the level of the share of government increases, but its relation to total national wealth in the broader definition shows a sharp decline from 30 per cent in 1945 to about 20 per cent in the

[17] Nonprofit institutions are included with households. The business sector includes all of agriculture and hence also farm residences and farmers' consumer durables. If these are shifted to the household sector—a shift which produces more homogeneous figures—the share of business is decreased by between 2 and 3 percentage points and that of households increased accordingly. Trends are not affected by this shift.

TABLE 12

DISTRIBUTION OF OWNERSHIP OF NATIONAL WEALTH AMONG MAIN SECTORS, SELECTED YEARS AND PERIODS, 1945-58

(values in billions of dollars)

	Net Wealth					*Gross Wealth*				
	Nonfarm Households[a]	Agriculture	Business	Government, Military Assets Excluded	Government, Military Assets Included	Nonfarm Households[a]	Agriculture	Business	Government, Military Assets Excluded	Government, Military Assets Included
	(1)	(2)	(3)	(4)	(5)	(6)	(7)	(8)	(9)	(10)
A. ABSOLUTE VALUES, CURRENT PRICES										
1945	204	87	182	106	177	354	116	305	143	294
1951	418	153	410	184	239	699	206	629	262	449
1958	638	183	620	262	351	1,064	257	939	375	601
B. ABSOLUTE VALUES, CONSTANT (1947-49) PRICES										
1945	277	113	257	142	242	483	151	429	200	408
1951	362	124	342	163	209	606	170	526	233	388
1958	486	132	559	200	263	927	188	638	285	437
C. PERCENTAGE SHARES, CURRENT PRICES										
1945	35.4	15.0	31.6	18.1	30.7	38.6	12.6	33.2	15.6	32.0
1951	35.9	13.2	35.2	15.8	20.5	38.9	11.5	35.0	14.6	25.0
1958	38.1	10.6	36.1	15.3	20.4	40.4	9.8	35.6	14.2	22.8

(continued)

TABLE 12 (concluded)

	Net Wealth					Gross Wealth				
	Nonfarm House-holds[a]	Agri-culture	Business	Government, Military Assets		Nonfarm House-holds[a]	Agri-culture	Business	Government, Military Assets	
				Excluded	Included				Excluded	Included
	(1)	(2)	(3)	(4)	(5)	(6)	(7)	(8)	(9)	(10)
D. PERCENTAGE SHARES, CONSTANT (1947-49) PRICES										
1945	35.2	14.3	32.6	18.0	30.7	38.2	12.0	34.0	15.8	32.3
1951	36.5	12.6	34.5	16.4	21.1	39.5	11.1	34.3	15.2	25.3
1958	39.0	10.6	34.5	16.0	21.1	42.7	9.7	32.9	14.7	22.6
E. PERCENTAGE GROWTH PER YEAR, CURRENT PRICES										
1945-51	12.70	9.87	14.50	9.98	5.13	12.01	10.04	12.82	10.62	7.31
1951-58	6.60	2.59	6.09	5.18	5.64	6.19	3.21	5.89	5.26	4.25
1945-58	9.38	5.89	9.89	7.37	5.41	8.83	6.31	9.04	7.70	5.65
F. PERCENTAGE GROWTH PER YEAR, CONSTANT (1947-49) PRICES										
1945-51	4.56	1.56	4.88	2.32	-2.47	3.85	1.99	3.45	2.58	-0.84
1951-58	4.30	.90	7.27	2.97	3.34	6.26	1.45	2.80	2.92	1.71
1945-58	4.42	1.20	6.16	2.67	0.64	5.14	1.70	3.10	2.76	0.53

SOURCE: Data from Tables A-15 to A-22, inclusive.
[a] Including nonprofit organizations.

fifties. As government ownership of land is substantial, even on the basis of its present market value or an approximation to it, the share of the government in reproducible wealth is slightly lower than its share in total tangible wealth, but still it has remained fairly stable at approximately one-sixth throughout the period.

Three main changes in the distribution of ownership of tangible assets may be observed during the postwar period. The first is the increase in the share of corporations from 25 to 30 per cent. This has been accompanied by a slight decline in the share of nonfarm unincorporated business from 7 to 6 per cent. The second main change is the decline in the share of agriculture from 15 to 10 per cent. The third is the reduction of the share of the civilian assets of the federal government from 8 to 5 per cent of total national wealth. The movement is even more pronounced if military assets are included, in which case the federal government's share is cut in half from 20 to 10 per cent.

The decline of the share of government in national wealth is a rather new development, although there is a precedent for it in the period 1912-29. Throughout the nineteenth century and until World War I the share of government showed an increasing trend, though at a moderate rate. During the thirties the share moved sharply upwards, the combined result of a considerable increase in the value of tangible assets owned by the government—including monetary metal—and a stagnation in the value of private wealth. As a result of the decline of the postwar period, the federal government's share in civilian national wealth in 1958 was back to the level of the mid-1930's.

The increasing share of corporations in national wealth is in line with the trend observed between 1900 and 1929 but interrupted during the thirties. The 1929 peak was reached again in 1951 and the 1958 share was 1.5 percentage points above that of 1929. It will be interesting to see whether the trend will continue during the sixties. The decline in the share of agriculture also resumes a trend in evidence from 1900, and even earlier, to 1939, but briefly interrupted during World War II. This decline which now has reduced the share of agriculture in national wealth to less than its 1939 low was, however, less pronounced than the decline of farmers' share in population.

Information is not sufficient for a comprehensive separation of tangible assets into those used by owners and those rented by operators. It is, however, known that renting is practiced on a large scale for only three types of tangible assets, agricultural land, residential structures, and commercial real estate. On the basis of shares of rental properties of approximately two-fifths in the value of urban residential real estate and of one-fourth of agricultural land, and an allowance for other rental use of tangible assets, particularly in the field of commercial real estate, the share of national wealth rented may be put at approximately one-seventh for the postwar decade, leaving about six-sevenths to be operated or used by owners, including corporate owners. The share of rented properties is considerably higher for land, where it approaches one-fourth, than the share for reproducible tangible assets, which remains around one-tenth. The proportion of tangible assets rented is much smaller for business—less than one-tenth—than among households, where it is as high as one-fifth as a result of the still relatively large proportion of rented residential structures. It is negligible in the case of tangible assets used by the government.

Combining the rough indications about the main types of rented property suggests that the share of rented properties in total national wealth remained between one-fourth and one-fifth from 1900 to World War II. The ratios of the two out of three main components about which statistical information is available—tenanted farm property and rented residential property—failed to show definite long-term trends. At the end of World War II, the proportion of rented properties probably had declined to approximately one-sixth, and it seems to have averaged one-seventh since 1950.

While no comprehensive close estimates can be made, it is likely that the rented share of national wealth has declined during the postwar period, possibly from one-sixth at the beginning to not much over one-eighth at the end. The sharp decline in the share of rental housing from about 35 per cent of the value of all dwelling units in 1945 to only 28 per cent thirteen years later has been the main factor in this development.[18] It continues a trend in evidence, although not without interruption, since at least the turn of the century. In the case of farm land, the trend toward a declining share of land not owned by operators—observable only since the Great Depression—seems to have come to a halt during the postwar decade.[19] Virtually nothing is known statistically about the movement of the share of rental properties in the third field in which they are important, urban commercial buildings.

[18] Robert E. Lipsey, "Housing in the National Balance Sheet," in Goldsmith and Lipsey, *Studies in the National Balance Sheet*, in press, NBER, 1962.

[19] *Statistical Abstract of the U.S.*, 1958, p. 762. The value ratios must be estimated since 1950 on the basis of the proportion of the number of tenant farms.

Current Versus Constant (1947-49) Prices

Only if the prices of all categories of durable assets showed the same price movements could the student of changes in the structure of national wealth ignore differences between distributions based on current (replacement) values and constant (deflated) values and be absolved from deciding which of the two bases is relevant for the purpose of the investigation. The wider the changes in the relative prices of different types of tangible assets are, the larger are the differences between the results of the two sets of estimates, and the more important is a careful consideration of the effects of price movement on the interpretation of the statistics.

For an analysis of the statistics of national wealth the crucial developments of the postwar decade are, as they were in previous periods, the relative price movements of structures, equipment, inventories, and land and, in particular, the apparent upward trend in the relative price of structures compared with commodities. This tendency has the result that an increase in the share of structures in national wealth or reproducible tangible assets appears larger (or the decline smaller) when current values (replacement cost) are used as the basis of comparison than it appears when the analysis is based on deflated prices. This is true whether the years 1947-49 are selected as the base period, as here, or the year 1929 is chosen, as in *A Study of Saving in the United States* or in Simon Kuznets' studies.[20]

In Table 13 changes during the period 1945-58 in the share of the main tangible assets in national wealth are compared on the basis of current values and 1947-49 prices. The difference between the two sets of figures is easiest to follow in columns 7 and 8, which show the proportional change in the share of the various assets on the two bases of valuation, and in column 9, which expresses the change in the current value share as a ratio of the change in the constant price share. The share of reproducible tangible wealth in total national wealth, for example, increased by 1.2 per cent in current values but by 4.0 per cent in 1947-49 prices, or by three and one-third times as much. On the other hand, the share of nonreproducible assets declined by 4.7 per cent in current prices, but fell by 15.1 per cent in 1947-49 prices.[21]

[20] See, for example, his "Long-Term Changes in the National Income of the United States of America since 1870," Income and Wealth Series II.

[21] The absolute changes in the shares of reproducible and nonreproducible assets, in terms of percentage points of total national wealth, are, of course, equal but of opposite sign on both valuation bases.

TABLE 13

PERCENTAGE CHANGE IN SHARE OF MAIN TYPES OF TANGIBLE ASSETS IN NET NATIONAL WEALTH, 1945-58

TANGIBLE ASSETS	SHARE IN NET NATIONAL WEALTH Current Prices			1947-49 Prices			Percentage Change in Share, 1947-58		Change in Current Value Share as Ratio of 1947-49 Price Change[a]
	1945	1958	Change 1945-58	1945	1958	Change 1945-58	Current Prices	1947-49 Prices	
	(1)	(2)	(3)	(4)	(5)	(6)	(7)	(8)	(9)
Reproducible Wealth	79.31	80.29	+0.98	78.99	82.17	+3.18	+1.24	+4.03	0.31
Structures	49.56	48.93	−0.63	51.73	47.65	−4.08	−1.27	−7.89	0.16
Nonfarm residential	24.85	22.99	−1.86	25.17	23.18	−1.99	−7.48	−7.91	0.95
Nonfarm nonresidential	9.72	10.53	+0.81	10.35	9.19	−1.16	+8.33	−11.21	−0.74
Mining	1.35	1.87	+0.52	1.43	1.78	+0.35	+38.52	+24.48	1.57
Farm	2.83	2.12	−0.71	2.82	2.27	−0.55	−25.09	−19.50	1.29
Institutional	1.21	1.54	+0.33	1.47	1.43	−0.04	+27.27	−2.72	−10.03
Government	9.60	9.88	+0.28	10.49	9.80	−0.69	+2.92	−6.58	−0.44
Equipment	16.47	22.25	+5.78	15.09	23.86	+8.77	+35.09	+58.12	0.60
Producer durables	8.44	11.75	+3.31	7.80	11.03	+3.23	+39.22	+41.41	0.95
Consumer durables	8.03	10.50	+2.47	7.29	12.83	+5.54	+30.76	+75.99	0.40
Inventories	9.13	7.62	−1.51	9.41	8.84	−0.57	−16.54	−6.06	2.73
Livestock	1.69	1.06	−0.63	1.89	1.20	−0.69	−37.28	−36.51	1.02
Crops	1.03	0.47	−0.56	1.00	0.86	−0.14	−54.37	−14.00	3.88
Nonfarm	5.95	5.61	−0.34	6.06	6.06	—	−5.71	—	b
Public	0.46	0.48	+0.02	0.46	0.72	+0.26	+4.35	+56.52	0.08
Monetary gold and silver	4.15	1.49	−2.66	2.76	1.82	−0.94	−64.10	−34.06	1.88
Nonreproducible Wealth	20.69	19.71	−0.98	21.01	17.83	−3.18	−4.74	−15.13	0.31
Agricultural	8.08	5.95	−2.13	7.63	4.81	−2.82	−26.36	−36.96	0.71
Nonagricultural	12.61	13.76	+1.15	13.38	13.02	−0.36	−9.12	−2.69	−3.39

SOURCE: Data from Tables A-9 and A-10.
a Col. 7 divided by col. 8.
b Indeterminate.

The most pronounced discrepancies among major categories of wealth are shown in the movements of the share of structures, consumer durables, inventories, and gold. The changes in the shares were in the same direction on both valuation bases but were more pronounced in constant (1947-49) prices than in current prices for structures and consumer durables, while the opposite relationship prevailed for inventories and gold. The explanation in all cases can be found in the course of relative asset prices, that is, the relation between the movement of the price of the asset in question and the average of tangible asset prices. This is more evident in the sharper decline in the share of gold stock in current prices than in 1947-49 prices: the price of gold remained unchanged on both bases, but the average current price of tangible assets increased considerably. On the other hand, the much larger decline in the share of structures in constant than in current prices reflects the sharper increase in the cost of construction compared with the rise in prices of equipment or of inventory goods. This discrepancy in turn may be traced primarily to the slower increase of productivity in the construction trades compared with the manufacturing industries. The much sharper increase in the share of consumer durables on the basis of 1947-49 prices is due to their relatively small absolute price rise during the postwar decade. Similarly, the decline in the share of inventories results largely from a decline in the relative price of crop products in the face of a substantial advance in the general price level.

In view of the significant differences in the movement of the shares of components of national wealth on the two bases—observable not only during the postwar decade but also in earlier periods—the selection of the valuation basis is of more than academic importance for an analysis of changes in the structure of national wealth. The decision should not depend upon the admittedly unsatisfactory nature of many of the deflators that must now be used, but rather on the assumption that the indexes used as deflators could correctly measure changes in the prices—whether visualized as market values or as replacement cost—of physically identical or closely comparable commodities. Even if this condition were met, the use of current values is indicated for some purposes of analysis and the reduction to a constant price basis for others. Wherever tangible assets are combined with intangible assets or compared with debt and net-worth figures, current values are appropriate, though occasionally the original cost of the different assets to the owner may also be relevant. Constant (deflated) values rarely have any use when tangible assets are regarded as part of national or sectoral balance sheets, or when the problems these estimates are supposed to illuminate are primarily financial. On the other hand, when the purpose of the analysis is the measurement of the rate of growth of the stock of tangible assets, the use of deflated figures is almost always essential. Then the only or predominant question will be whether the figures actually do measure changes in the physical volume of durable assets, provided an unambiguous definition of physical changes in stock can be framed. Doubt about the valuation basis to be used may thus remain chiefly in analyses comparing wealth estimates with income estimates. Probably the most important instance which requires a choice is that of capital-output ratios.

Gross and Net Stock of Wealth

If the purpose of estimates of national wealth, and particularly of reproducible tangible assets, is not so much the determination of the accounting value of the stock, i.e., its unabsorbed original cost adjusted or unadjusted for price changes, or the economic theorist's favorite—capitalized expected future earnings—but a measure of the stock's capacity for current production, it can be argued that the value of the gross (undepreciated) stock is a better approximation than the value of net (depreciated) stock. The argument would be entirely convincing if all durables were like Holmes's deacon's masterpiece, the "wonderful one-hoss shay." The less durable assets behave like this famous vehicle, the more will the productive capacity[22] of an asset decline stepwise, either with straight-line depreciation, declining balance depreciation, or some other accounting device for writing off its original cost (less scrap value) during its useful life, rather than, like the one-hoss shay, "all at once and nothing first." In practice, a figure somewhere between net and gross stock, in terms of either replacement cost or base-period cost, may provide the best workable approximation to an accounting measure of capacity.

It is known from the formulas discussed in Chapter 3 that, as the rate of capital expenditure accelerates, the value of the net stock will

---

[22] The definition of "current productive capacity" is by no means without difficulty. Obviously, prime cost, including cost of repair and maintenance, cannot be entirely neglected, but how is it to be taken into account? One possibility is to include the potential output of a durable asset in productive capacity, so long as the prime cost of its operation is not above the average full cost of the item that could replace it most economically. This definition may be satisfactory for some purposes, but of course cannot as yet be translated into statistical terms.

rise more rapidly than that of the gross stock, and the net-gross ratio will increase. What is relevant, however, in this comparison is the average rate of growth of capital expenditures over a period extending from the date for which the stock estimate is made back to the presumed date of installation, a period equal to the assumed length of life. Thus, in comparing the rate of growth of gross and net stock of the various types of durable assets at the end of 1945 and 1958, the relevant rate is the rate of growth—say, for an item of twenty years' life—from 1926 through 1945 as against the rate of growth for the period 1938 to 1958. The periods to be compared are thus much longer, and the part of the period for which they overlap relatively more extended in the case of long-lived structures than in that of relatively short-lived producer and consumer durables. One would therefore expect differences in the rate of growth of the net and the gross stock between 1945 and 1958 to be relatively smaller for structures than for equipment. Since capital expenditures increased for most types of assets at a more rapid rate over the period ending in 1958 than during an equally long period terminating in 1945—whether in current or constant prices—one would also expect the rate of growth between 1945 and 1958 to be generally lower for the gross than for the net stock.

These expectations are borne out in Table 14, which compares the net and gross rates of growth of the main components of reproducible tangible wealth (other than inventories, gold, and net foreign assets for which, of course, gross and net stock are identical) for the entire postwar period. During the 1945-58 period, the net stock of reproducible tangible wealth in constant (1947-49) prices rose by 69 per cent, while the increase amounted to only 58 per cent for the gross stock. The annual rates of growth thus were 4.1 per cent for the net stock against 3.6 per cent for the gross stock. Since the increase in population was the same in both cases (1.8 per cent per year) the difference between the rate of growth of the net and the gross stock was much larger on a per head basis—2.3 per cent for the net stock, but only 1.8 per cent for the gross stock.

The differences in the rate of growth of the net and the gross stock are considerably larger in absolute terms for equipment than for structures—0.9 per cent against 0.6 per cent—but they are almost identical at about one-eighth in relative terms. Among structures, however, two groups can be distinguished. For residential structures, the largest and longer lived component, the difference is quite small—2.9 per cent for net against 2.7 per cent for the gross stock. The differences are much

TABLE 14

COMPARISON OF RATIOS OF GROWTH OF GROSS AND NET CAPITAL STOCK,
1945-58

(per cent per year, except ratios)

Item	Current Prices			Constant (1947-49) Prices		
	Gross	Net	Ratio	Gross	Net	Ratio
	(1)	(2)	(3)	(4)	(5)	(6)
Total reproducible tangible wealth	8.63	8.96	0.96	3.59	4.12	0.87
Structures	8.03	8.57	.94	2.37	2.92	.81
Residential	7.81	8.05	.97	2.69	2.91	.92
Nonresidential nonfarm	8.00	9.36	.85	1.47	2.57	.57
Mining	9.38	11.42	.82	3.44	5.33	.65
Farm	5.59	6.28	.89	1.19	1.86	.64
Institutional	9.05	10.72	.84	1.78	3.35	.53
Government	8.78	8.93	.98	2.91	3.03	.96
Equipment	10.36	11.25	.92	6.40	7.29	.88
Producer durables	10.50	11.53	.91	5.34	5.84	.91
Consumer durables	10.23	10.95	.93	7.24	8.17	.89

SOURCE: Tables A-5, A-6, A-7, and A-8.

larger, absolutely and relatively, for nonfarm, nonresidential structures, and for several of the smaller components—farm, mining, and institutional structures—reflecting the substantial acceleration of capital expenditures during the period ending in 1958 compared with that ending in 1945.

The ratio of the rate of growth of gross to net stock is closer to unity, i.e., the difference between the two rates is smaller, for current than for constant price estimates (except for producer durables, where the ratios are equal), and the difference is substantial for most types of structures. The direction of the difference is to be expected: expenditures in current prices have been increasing at a more rapid rate than at constant prices, because the trend of prices has been upward for most of the half-century before 1945.

One would, of course, like to check the rates of growth of both the net and the gross stock of total reproducible tangible wealth and of its main components against independent estimates of capacity. Such estimates, unfortunately, do not exist for the entire economy—unless the increase in real national product in years equally close to full employment were accepted as a measure of capacity—and they are also missing for virtually all large sectors of the economy for which estimates of capital stock are available, except for manufacturing and mining.

Capital Stock of the Main Industries

Since private business enterprises, even excluding agriculture and residential real estate, account for over one-third of total national wealth, a further breakdown by industry will be most desirable for an understanding of the changes in the structure of national wealth. Unfortunately, it is not as yet possible to present such a breakdown in a way that, while consistent over long periods of time, ties in exactly with the national estimates of the different types of wealth.[23] Figures are available, however, for the two largest sectors of private nonfarm business enterprises, manufacturing and mining, on the one hand, and railroads and public utilities, on the other. Since these two groups appear to have accounted for about three-fourths of the total fixed capital of all nonfarm business enterprises since the turn of the century, a study of them goes quite far to substitute for a complete breakdown of the wealth of the nonfarm business sector.

The outstanding feature in the distribution of the total fixed assets of manufacturing and public utilities during the postwar period, as it appears in Table 15, is the sharp decline of the share of railroads at the expense of manufacturing and mining and still more of all other public utilities. In this respect the postwar period is but a continuation of the half century before World War II. During that period the share of railroads in the fixed assets of manufacturing, mining, and public utilities declined from about one-half to not much over one-quarter, and that of manufacturing and mining increased from almost one-third to nearly one-half. Since the share of the three groups together appears to have remained fairly stable at approximately three-fourths of the total for nonfarm business enterprises, these changes can also be interpreted as reflecting similar movements in the share of the three groups in the total fixed assets of nonagricultural business.

[23] The difficulty does not lie in the scarcity of estimates for the capital stock in individual industries. Rather it lies in the existence of several bodies of material, independently derived from different sources, and of different scope, detail, valuation basis, and reliability. This material cannot be combined in a way to fit exactly the over-all estimates of the value of plant and equipment of nonagricultural business enterprises derived by the perpetual inventory method, the set which in turn constitutes an integral part of the estimates of reproducible tangible wealth underlying this study. In particular, the separate estimates for structure and for equipment of nonagricultural business derived by the perpetual inventory method cannot be completely reconciled with the sum of the estimates of structures and equipment in the main sectors—manufacturing and mining, public utilities, and other nonfinancial business—that can be pieced together from other information available for these sectors. As these difficulties affect primarily the period before World War II—there are no similar figures for all main sectors in the postwar period—they need not be discussed here.

TABLE 15

FIXED ASSETS OF MANUFACTURING, MINING, AND PUBLIC UTILITIES, SELECTED YEARS,
1899-1956

(amounts in billions of 1929 dollars)

	Absolute Figures				Percentage Shares		
End of Year	Manufacturing and Mining	Railroads	Other Public Utilities	Total	Manufacturing and Mining	Railroads	Other Public Utilities
	(1)	(2)	(3)	(4)	(5)	(6)	(7)
'99	9.7	15.2	5.6	30.5	32	50	18
'29	30.9	23.8	20.1	74.8	41	32	27
'37	25.9	21.0	21.3	68.2	38	31	31
'48	36.5	22.3	23.0	81.8	45	27	28
'56	54.1	24.8	37.2	116.1	47	21	32

SOURCE: Col. 1, Table 16, line 14; Cols. 2 and 3, Table 17, lines B-1 and B-7.

The changes in the distribution of the fixed capital stock of manufacturing among about a dozen main industries can be followed in Table 16. Addition of inventories and land probably would change the picture only to a minor extent.

Between 1948 and 1956 the value (in 1929 prices) of the fixed assets of all manufacturing industries increased by 48 per cent or 5.0 per cent a year, a rate somewhat in excess of that for plants and equipment of all business or for national fixed assets. Differences in the rates of growth among major manufacturing industries are reflected in their changing share in the fixed assets of total manufacturing shown in Table 16. Shifts in this eight-year period were quite substantial even in the stock of fixed assets and, of course, were considerably more pronounced for gross or net investment in fixed assets. The chemical industries sharply increased their share from 9 to about 14 per cent of the total, the result of an increase of 125 per cent or about 10.5 per cent a year. The smaller "other transportation equipment" industry (primarily aircraft) more than tripled its share. The very large metal industries showed a smaller but still noticeable increase from less than 32 to over 34 per cent. On the other hand, the share of the food, textile, leather, forest products, and printing industries declined considerably, and that of petroleum refining to a lesser degree. Using a broader and economically more relevant grouping, it appears that during the postwar period the durable goods industries expanded plant and equipment much more rapidly than the nondurable goods

TABLE 16

PERCENTAGE DISTRIBUTION OF NET FIXED CAPITAL OF MANUFACTURING, SELECTED
YEARS, 1900-56, 1929 PRICES

	1956 (1)	1948 (2)	1937 (3)	1929 (4)	1900 (5)
1. Food products	9.6	12.0	14.6	14.7	21.5
2. Textiles and products	4.5	6.5	8.2	10.8	15.9
3. Leather and its manufactures	0.3	0.5	0.7	1.0	2.5
4. Rubber products	1.1	1.3	1.0	1.6	0.6
5. Forest products	3.1	4.5	5.7	7.3	12.7
6. Paper, pulp, and products	4.5	4.2	4.7	4.4	3.4
7. Printing and publishing	2.6	3.1	3.3	3.4	4.7
8. Chemicals	13.8	9.1	6.7	5.6	5.0
9. Petroleum refining	17.2	19.8	16.1	13.0	1.3
10. Stone, clay, and glass products	3.2	3.2	4.8	5.5	5.3
11. Metal and its products	38.1	33.5	32.4	30.4	25.9
Iron and steel products		14.1	15.1	13.7	11.3
Nonferrous metals and products	34.4	3.3	4.0	3.7	4.4
Machinery		9.6	6.9	7.0	8.7
Motor vehicles		4.7	4.5	4.6	0.4
Other transportation equipment	3.6	1.1	1.8	1.4	1.2
12. Miscellaneous	2.2	2.4	1.7	2.4	1.4
13. Total, shares	100.0	100.0	100.0	100.0	100.0
14. Total (billions of 1929 dollars)	54.1	36.5	25.9	30.9	9.7

SOURCE: 1899-1948, Daniel Creamer, Sergei Dobrovolsky, and Israel Borenstein,
*Capital in Manufacturing and Mining: Its Formation and
Financing*, Princeton for NBER, 1960, Table A-9.

    1956, Creamer, "Postwar Trends in the Relation of Capital to
Output in Manufactures," *American Economic Review*, May
1958, p. 253 (with some minor alterations to preserve com-
parability).

industries did—at the rate of 6.9 per cent a year compared to only 2.8
per cent for the nondurable goods industries. In consequence, they increased their share in the fixed assets of all manufacturing industries
from 50 to 58 per cent.[24,25]

These postwar developments are in the same direction as, though
more pronounced than, the prewar trends in the growth and distribution of manufacturing plant and equipment. Between 1899 and 1948
the durable goods industries increased their share in the fixed assets of
total manufacturing from 49 to 51 per cent, expanding plant and

[24] For purposes of this calculation, the industries on lines 5, 8, 10, and 11 of Table
16 have been regarded as durable goods industries, and all others as nondurable
goods industries.

[25] If petroleum refining is excluded from nondurable goods industries, the rate of
growth of their fixed assets is reduced to 2.5 per cent, and their share in plant and
equipment of all manufacturing declines from 30 per cent to less than 25 per cent.

equipment at the rate of 2.8 against 1.7 per cent for the nondurable goods industries excluding petroleum refining.[26] The postwar decline in the share of the textile and food industries from 18.5 to 14 per cent, in particular, is in line with the decline from 37.5 to 25.5 per cent between 1899 and 1929 and from 25.5 to 18.5 per cent in the following twenty years.

In the public utility sector, the basic structural change evident in Table 17 has been the continuous—and since World War I rapid—

TABLE 17

PERCENTAGE DISTRIBUTION OF NET PLANT AND EQUIPMENT OF PUBLIC UTILITIES, SELECTED YEARS, 1899-1956

	1956 (1)	1950 (2)	1945 (3)	1937 (4)	1929 (5)	1912 (6)	1899 (7)
A. CURRENT PRICES							
1. Railroads	38.0	44.9	54.3	51.3	54.2	61.2	71.2
2. Street and electric railways	1.0	1.5	2.5	4.1	6.0	11.5	9.7
3. Electric light and power	26.0	22.0	17.3	19.3	15.8	7.7	2.5
4. Telephone	12.0	9.6	6.0	5.7	5.1	5.7	4.1
5. Other	23.0	22.0	20.0	19.6	18.8	13.8	12.5
6. Total, shares	100.0	100.0	100.0	100.0	100.0	100.0	100.0
7. Total (billions of dollars)	135.0	87.3	50.9	40.9	43.9	19.5	9.0
B. CONSTANT (1929) PRICES							
1. Railroads	40.0	46.7	53.8	53.8	54.2	62.8	74.0
2. Street and electric railways	1.0	1.6	2.5	4.4	6.0	11.8	9.7
3. Electric light and power	23.0	19.3	17.1	16.7	15.8	9.0	2.7
4. Telephone	13.0	10.5	6.5	5.5	5.1	2.2	.9
5. Other	23.0	22.0	20.2	19.6	18.8	14.3	12.7
6. Total, shares	100.0	100.0	100.0	100.0	100.0	100.0	100.0
7. Total (billions of dollars)	62.0	48.4	41.2	42.3	43.9	33.0	20.8

SOURCE: 1899-1950, Derived from Melville J. Ulmer, *Capital in Transportation, Communications, and Public Utilities: Its Formation and Financing*, Princeton for NBER, 1960, Tables B-1, C-1, D-1, E-1, F-1, G-1 and H-1.

1956, Rough estimates based on gross and net capital expenditures in 1951-56 derived from *Statistics of Income, 1950* and *1956*.

decline in the share of the railroads and street railways, and the corresponding increase in the share of the electric power and telephone industries.[27] The railroads (including street railways) at the turn of

[26] If petroleum refining is included the rate for nondurable industries is 2.7 per cent a year.

[27] Among public utilities, it makes little difference whether or not inventory and land are included in the calculations.

the century still accounted for over four-fifths of the capital stock of all public utilities. Their share had declined to three-fifths by 1929 and lost only a few percentage points until the end of World War II. In the postwar decade it resumed its rapid decline, falling to less than 40 per cent by 1956. The electric power and the telephone industries continued during the postwar period to increase their share in the capital stock of all utilities, but at a rate considerably more rapid than between 1929 and 1945 (the telephone industry at a more rapid rate than at any time since 1899).

CHAPTER 6

Reliability of the Estimates

THE assessment of the reliability of economic statistics, specifically statistics derived from a system of national accounts, and the estimation of the margins of error to which they are subject are notoriously difficult, both conceptually and practically. As a result it is extremely rare to find estimates of the probable or possible error accompanying calculations of national product, investment, saving, national wealth, and similar magnitudes notwithstanding the obvious advantages that such specifications would have to the user of the figures.

In the absence of a theoretical framework or of practicable methods that would permit a systematic assessment of the margins of error in such estimates, the minimum that readers may ask for is the comparison of the results of a specific estimation or measurement with the results of other measurements of the same magnitude. Such a comparison, of course, will not give information on the direction or size of the error, because the margin of error in the measurements used for comparison is also unknown. In addition, it cannot be assumed that the true value of a sought-for magnitude can be obtained by applying to the various estimates of the same object the natural science techniques which presuppose repeated measurement of the same, or a generically equal, object by the same method or instrument. In a field such as national wealth, where many of the basic data and the estimates derived for them are unavoidably weak, comparison of the results obtained by different methods or by using different basic data is particularly important.

Since we have defined our measure of national wealth as the market value, or the nearest approximation to it, of tangible assets, and since we have derived our estimates of national wealth for most types of reproducible assets by the perpetual inventory method (i.e., by cumulating gross capital expenditures, depreciating them, and adjusting them for price changes), we must look for purposes of checking and comparison to bodies of data which reflect the market value of various types of tangible assets that are not derived by the perpetual inventory method. Similar checks can also be used to compare our estimates of the value of land insofar as they are linked to the perpetual inventory estimates of the value of structures.

Unfortunately, a comparison of this type is possible only for two, though very important, types of reproducible assets, residential real estate and commercial and industrial real estate combined. For several other important types of tangible assets, particularly plant and equipment of business corporations and of the federal government, a less satisfactory though still valuable comparison is possible. For these assets we may compare the original cost, depreciated or undepreciated, as calculated by the perpetual inventory method with the figures shown in the books of the owners. This comparison will give us a clue as to whether the figures for gross capital expenditures used and the assumptions made regarding the length of life of the different types of tangible assets are reasonably close to actual capital expenditures as entered on the owners' books and the depreciation rates applied by them. We are thus left without the possibility of effective comparison for consumer durables, the tangible assets of state and local governments, and a few types of assets of quantitatively less importance, such as standing timber and subsoil assets. We also have no check on the figures used for farm land, inventories, and monetary metals, but this is not a serious defect, since the figures used in our estimates are based on comprehensive data of an official character, which may be regarded as being very close to the market values of the assets in question.

Residential Real Estate

In this field there are two sets of figures against which the perpetual inventory estimates can be checked. The first are the data on value of residential real estate in the *Census of Housing, 1950*; the second, the estimates of the value of residential real estate in 1956 derived on the basis of assessed valuations in the *Census of Government, 1957*.

CENSUS OF HOUSING, 1950

Table 18 permits a comparison of the estimates of the value of residential real estate in 1950 used in this report with three other estimates, one of which is based, like our figures, on the perpetual inventory estimate, while the two others are derived from data in the *Census of Housing*. It is, of course, the latter bench mark which provides an effective test of the figures used here.

For April 1950, the date of the housing census, the structure value of residential real estate as used in this study may be estimated at approximately $250 billion, a figure derived by interpolation between

TABLE 18

COMPARISON OF ESTIMATES OF VALUE OF NONFARM RESIDENTIAL REAL ESTATE,
BASED ON CENSUS AND PERPETUAL INVENTORY FIGURES, 1950 AND 1956

(billions of dollars)

	Total	Structures	Land
Based on Census of Housing, 1950[a]			
Grebler and associates[b]	260.0		
Reid[c]	274.1		
Based on perpetual inventory, 1950[d]			
Grebler and associates[b]	212.5	173.6	38.9
NBER[e]	249.2	215.0	34.2
Based on assessed valuations, 1956			
Census[f]	355.9		
NBER[e, g]	380.0	328.2	51.8

[a] As of April 1950.
[b] Grebler, Blank, and Winnick (see footnote 1, p. 82), p. 370.
[c] Reid, *loc.cit.*
[d] As of end of 1949.
[e] Excludes public housing.
[f] Communication from Bureau of the Census, Government Division (Oct. 19, 1959).
[g] As of end of 1955.

the calculated values for the ends of 1949 and 1950. This compares with two independent estimates of $260 and $274 billion, respectively, which were derived from the information on the number of dwellings and the average value of owner occupied dwellings provided by the census. The average value of tenant occupied dwellings must be estimated, primarily from information on rent payments, since it is not reported in the census. Differences in this item are partly responsible for the variations between the two aggregate bench-mark estimates.

The estimate used in this report is thus 4 per cent, or 10 per cent below the bench mark derived from the housing census, depending whether the aggregate bench-mark estimate of Grebler and associates or of Reid is accepted. The difference in either case is not unduly high, given the many estimates that must be used in developing the figures, among them, the step-up of reported construction expenditures, particularly in the earlier years; the assumption of an eighty-year life of residential structures adopted in the calculation; and the estimates of the relation of land to structure values. While the level of the estimates of residential real estate used in this report thus appear to be compatible with census figures for the one date for which comparison is possible, judgment about the acceptability of the perpetual inventory method in this field, particularly in the measurement of trends rather than levels, must wait until similar comparisons can be made for the year 1960 for which census data will again be available.[1]

CENSUS OF GOVERNMENT, 1956

As a part of the 1956 census of government, the Census Bureau determined the assessed value of all locally assessed residential real estate (including vacant lots) and used these figures as the basis of an estimate of the market value of residential real estate. The bridge between assessed and market values was the ratio between these two values determined from a random sample of nearly 700,000 properties made during the first six months of 1956.

On the basis of this approach the market value of residential structures, including the land underlying them (but excluding vacant lots), may be estimated at $356 billion.[2] This estimate may be regarded as referring to early 1956 and may therefore be compared with an average of the perpetual inventory estimates for the ends of 1955 and 1956, which comes to $380 billion. While an entirely satisfactory comparison would call for small adjustments of the perpetual inventory estimate in order to make it fully comparable with the census figure, the comparison of the unadjusted figures is sufficient here. On that basis, the difference between the two estimates is fairly small—$24 billion or 6 per cent—so that the census estimate may be taken as a corroboration of the order of magnitude of the perpetual inventory estimate used here.

Commercial and Industrial Real Estate

Comparison of the census estimates for "commercial and industrial real estate" derived from assessed valuations with relevant figures in our national wealth estimates is very difficult. In principle, the census figures include all locally assessed privately owned commercial and

---

[1] For a comparison of estimates based on perpetual inventory and census figures of the value of residential real estate for earlier bench-mark years, see R. W. Goldsmith, *A Study of Saving in the United States*, Vol. II, Princeton University Press, 1955, pp. 391ff.; Leo Grebler, David M. Blank, and Louis Winnick, *Capital Formation in Residential Real Estate: Trends and Prospects*, Princeton for NBER, 1956, pp. 368ff.; Margaret G. Reid, "Capital Formation in Residential Real Estate," *Journal of Political Economy*, April 1958, p. 147. The relevant figures will also be found in *Historical Statistics of the United States*, 2nd ed., 1960, p. 388, with comments, p. 383.

[2] The original source (*Census of Government, 1956*, Vol. V, p. 81) shows only a combined estimate for all locally assessed real estate ($690 billion). The breakdown, including the separate estimate for nonfarm nonresidential real estate, was kindly provided by the Government Division of the Bureau of the Census.

industrial property. This concept undoubtedly includes land and structures, but it is unfortunately not known whether or to what extent it also covers equipment. It is probable that most types of equipment are excluded, but there is a definite possibility that, at least in some states, fixed equipment is included.

It is thus impossible to match the census figure with an exactly corresponding estimate from our national wealth calculation. The best that can be done is to compare the census estimate of $142 billion with our estimates of commercial, industrial, and private social and recreational structures and the land underlying them, excluding public utilities since most of their property is state assessed and hence not included in the census totals. We then obtain a figure of $129 billion which can be compared with the census estimate of $142 billion. Thus the census estimate is considerably but not radically above ours ($13 billion or 10 per cent). Whether the difference can be accounted for by machinery that is included in the census estimates is uncertain, but it is certainly not impossible. Another part of the difference may well be due to the minor part of public utility property that is locally assessed. (Local assessment of about one-tenth of public utility property would suffice to account for the entire difference.)

Corporate Depreciable Assets

For corporate depreciable assets (structures and equipment), comparisons between the estimates presented in this study and independent measures can be made only on the basis of original cost rather than of current market values. This comparison is possible because *Statistics of Income* tabulates annually the gross and net book value of the depreciable assets of all corporations submitting balance sheets as part of their tax returns—figures accounting by size of assets for very close to 100 per cent of all corporations. While the book value of depreciable assets as shown in corporate balance sheets submitted to the Treasury is not identical with original cost, because of occasional write-ups and write-downs of properties particularly in connection with mergers and similar operations, the two values are sufficiently close conceptually to justify the comparison.

Table 19 compares for each year of the postwar period the gross and net book value of the depreciable assets of all nonagricultural corporations, as reported in tax returns, with the gross and net original cost of structures and equipment derived by cumulation and, for net assets, depreciation of expenditures on structures and equipment.

TABLE 19

COMPARISON OF ORIGINAL COST OF CORPORATE DEPRECIABLE ASSETS,
NBER ESTIMATES AND TAX RETURNS, 1945-57

(billions of dollars)

	GROSS VALUE				NET VALUE[a]			
			Difference				Difference	
	NBER[b]	IRS[c]	Level	Annual Change	NBER[d]	IRS[c]	Level	Annual Change
	(1)	(2)	(3)	(4)	(5)	(6)	(7)	(8)
1945	140.4	132.5	7.9		74.2	80.2	—6.0	
1946	147.7	142.5	5.2	—2.7	81.6	87.6	—6.0	0
1947	160.0	156.6	3.4	—1.8	93.4	98.6	—5.2	0.8
1948	175.6	172.7	2.9	—0.5	106.9	111.3	—4.4	0.8
1949	189.2	186.6	2.6	—0.3	117.3	120.6	—3.3	1.1
1950	205.6	199.8	5.8	3.2	129.3	128.9	0.4	3.7
1951	224.9	218.0	6.9	1.1	142.8	142.7	1.1	0.7
1952	244.6	233.3	11.3	4.4	157.8	152.7	5.1	4.0
1953	264.2	249.2	15.0	3.7	172.3	162.7	9.6	4.5
1954	283.2	265.6	17.6	2.6	184.6	172.9	11.7	2.1
1955	302.0	287.2	14.8	—2.8	197.5	185.1	12.4	0.7
1956	325.4	314.2	11.2	—3.6	215.2	202.5	12.7	0.3
1957		342.5				219.8		

NOTE: Corporations in agriculture, forestry, and fishery are excluded.

a Gross value less depreciation.

b Original cost values from Tables B-14, B-42, B-121, B-126, and B-127, minus original cost values from Tables B-16, B-43, B-54, B-55B, B-56, and B-58.

c *Statistics of Income*, various issues. Since the figures include up to 1953 depletable and intangible assets, the figures reported for 1945 through 1953 have been reduced by 3.8 per cent, the ratio of depletable and intangible total capital assets shown by the statistics for 1954.

d Cumulated original cost expenditures from Tables B-5, B-7, B-8, B-46, B-99, B-101, B-102, B-103, B-104, B-107, B-108, B-109, and B-119, minus those from Tables B-15, B-40, B-45, B-49, B-50, B-52, B-53.

For gross value of the stock of depreciable assets, the two estimates are quite close. While the figures derived by the perpetual inventory method are in every year slightly above those reported in corporate tax returns, the difference does not exceed 7 per cent in any year. Moreover, the increase in the gross value of depreciable assets for the post-war decade as a whole or for its two halves is virtually identical in the two series, notwithstanding some substantial differences in a few individual years. This close similarity between the gross value of corporate plant and equipment derived by the perpetual inventory method and reported in corporate tax balance sheets must mean one of two things. First, it may mean that the capital expenditures on plant and equipment underlying the perpetual inventory estimates are very close to the capital expenditures entered by corporations in their own books (or, more correctly, the set of books they keep for tax purposes); and that the estimates of the length of life of the different types of reproducible assets used in the perpetual inventory method are close to those employed by corporations in their own accounts. Or, second, it may mean that, insofar as there are deviations between the figures underlying the perpetual inventory method and those used in the corporation's own accounts—and undoubtedly there are—those deviations happen to cancel out, not only for the entire decade but for most individual years, when all nonagricultural corporations and all types of depreciable assets are combined. It is unfortunately not possible to determine whether the satisfactory correspondence in the aggregate series is the effect of only moderate discrepancies for individual industries and individual types of assets, or whether it is the result of very wide but fortuitously offsetting deviations.

The correspondence between the perpetual inventory and the Internal Revenue Service series is not as satisfactory for net (depreciated) values. Here the level of the perpetual inventory estimates is slightly (7.5 per cent) below the IRS figures at the end of World War II, but slightly (6.3 per cent) above it in 1956. As a result, the increase in the net value of corporate plant and equipment during the postwar decade is considerably smaller in the IRS series ($123 billion) than in the perpetual inventory estimates ($141 billion). Since the rise in gross value was almost identical in both series, the difference in the movement of the net values must reflect higher depreciation accumulation in the IRS series: the increase in depreciation reserves (the difference between gross and net values) is $61 billion for the IRS series compared with $44 billion for the perpetual inventory estimate.

The difference is in the expected direction. The perpetual inventory figures are derived on the assumption of constant straight-line rates of depreciation for a given type of asset. In contrast, the rates underlying the IRS figures have varied, and it is reasonable to assume that, as a result of both relaxations in tax legislation and changes in corporate accounting practices, there has been a general tendency toward increasing rates of depreciation on comparable assets, particularly by taking advantage of provisions for accelerated depreciation offered at several times throughout the postwar decade, and, near the end of the period, by a partial shift to declining balance depreciation. There is, however, no evidence that the length of useful life of comparable types of structures and equipment has generally shortened—and sharply so after

1954, if the tax returns are accepted. It may be claimed, therefore, that the perpetual inventory estimates reflect economically relevant changes in the stock of plant and equipment of corporations more accurately than do the corporate balance sheets submitted to the Treasury, and that the difference between the increase in the depreciation reserves is a measure—at least a rough one—of the excessive depreciation taken in tax returns.[3]

Farm Machinery

An additional check is possible for farm machinery against an independent, as yet unpublished, estimate developed by Zvi Griliches on the basis of the number of farm implements of different types and their current prices around the end of 1956. These estimates indicate a gross value of total farm machinery and equipment of $33.2 billion (of which $12.4 billion is accounted for by tractors) against a figure of $29.1 billion in our estimates. Griliches' figures thus are about 10 per cent higher for total machinery and equipment, most of the difference occurring in tractors. On a net basis, his estimates at $14.9 billion (of which $5.8 billion is accounted for by tractors) are only slightly below ours ($15.2 billion, of which $5.4 billion is for tractors).

Private Land

After completion of our calculations, a bench-mark estimate of the value of private noninstitutional land in 1956 became available, which had been derived by splitting estimates of the value of total real estate into structure and land values on the basis of assessed valuations for

[3] The discrepancy between depreciation accruals calculated according to the perpetual inventory method and those reported in corporate tax returns is particularly pronounced in the years 1955-56 after the liberalization in the Revenue Act of 1954. In these two years, tax depreciation was on the average about $3.7 billion above the perpetual inventory figures. An estimate by the Machinery and Allied Products Institute (*Statistical Notes to Capital Goods Review*, No. 38, May 1959, p. 3) puts the 1955-56 additional depreciation allowances claimed—in comparison with straight-line depreciation, the method used also in the perpetual inventory estimates—at an annual average of $3.3 billion, thus providing an explanation for most of the difference between allowances in that period. For the years 1950 through 1954 the MAPI adjustments, then primarily on account of accelerated amortization, averaged $0.7 billion per year. For this period, however, there is no difference between depreciation accruals under the perpetual inventory method and those reported in tax returns.

The discussion here, it should be emphasized, is in terms of original cost. No allowance is made, therefore, for the underdepreciation that may be involved in basing depreciation allowances on original rather than replacement cost.

the two types.[4] This estimate puts the value of land in 1956 at $243 billion with a range, reflecting sampling error, of $227 to $272 billion.[5] The most nearly comparable figure from our estimates is $207 billion,[6] or about one-seventh less than the mid-point of the range, though less than one-tenth below its lower boundary. Since the alternative estimate is available only as an aggregate for all private land, it is not possible to be certain where the differences lie or to venture a guess as to which estimate is likely to be closer to the true value—if such a term may be used at all in so complicated a conceptual and statistical situation.

State and Local Highways, Roads, and Streets

A comparison of the estimates for the gross and net value of state and local highways, roads, and streets utilized in this report with two independent estimates may be worthwhile, although the other estimates are also derived by the perpetual inventory method.[7]

The estimates of Farrell and Paterick (which were unavailable when the original estimates were made for *A Study of Saving in the United States,* and which were discovered only after the estimates had been revised and brought up to date) and ours differ in the following respects: (1) Farrell and Paterick make no allowance for expenditures before 1914. Since our estimates assume a life of thirty years, this fact cannot account for any difference in the estimates after 1939. (2) Farrell and Paterick use an annual expenditure series developed by the Bureau of Public Roads (which includes actual payments for right of way excluded in our figures), while we utilize figures derived from the Census Bureau's *Financial Statistics of State and Local Governments.* The difference between the two expenditure series, both of which, in turn, are not entirely identical with the figures for cost of construction of state and local highways in *Construction Statistics,* are relatively small for longer periods. (3) The deflators applied to the original expenditure series differ slightly. (4) While our estimates are based

[4] J. S. Keiper, E. Kurnow, C. D. Clark, and H. H. Segal, *Theory and Measurement of Rent,* Philadelphia, Chilton, 1961.

[5] *Ibid.,* pp. 244-245.

[6] This is the sum of the estimates for residential land ($55 billion), vacant lots ($21 billion), private nonresidential land ($42 billion), farm land ($74 billion), and forest land ($15 billion).

[7] F. B. Farrell and H. P. Paterick, "The Capital Investment in Highways," *Proceedings of the Thirty-Second Annual Meeting of the Highways Research Board,* January 1953; and J. E. Reeve, *et al.,* "Government Component in the National Wealth," *Studies in Income and Wealth,* Vol. 12, New York, NBER, 1950, p. 520.

throughout on a length of life of thirty years, Farrell and Paterick use separate estimates for the main components of expenditures which, when averaged, increase over the period from somewhat over twenty-five years in 1914-19 to about thirty-five years in 1947-52. For this reason Farrell and Paterick's estimates for 1952 should be above those developed here, disregarding other differences, and the discrepancy should increase with time.

Reeve's estimate, the derivation of which is not known in the same detail, also uses basic series and assumptions which differ slightly from those utilized in our estimate. For example, depreciation is set at 3 per cent for the first twenty-two years and 0.67 per cent for the next fifty-one years, but he follows the same basic approach.

The comparison of the actual estimates presented in Table 20 shows that the Farrell-Paterick estimates are virtually identical with those used here for gross stock and are moderately above those for net stock and slightly more so in 1952 than in 1945, both these differences being in the expected direction. The Reeve estimate, which is available only on a net basis, is practically the same as the Farrell-Paterick figure for 1939, but is somewhat above the other two estimates in 1945.

Reproducible Tangible Wealth of the Federal Government

Comparison is possible here also only on the basis of original cost; moreover it can be made only for gross rather than net values. The basis for comparison is provided by the Federal Property Inventory, which has been compiled for the last few years and which, in the case of reproducible tangible assets, is in principle based on original cost of acquisition to the federal government. This should make the figures conceptually comparable with the original cost estimates derived by the perpetual inventory method, at least for structures and equipment.

Table 21 shows that, for total reproducible assets of the federal government as well as for structures and equipment, the perpetual inventory estimates used in this study are slightly above the figures of the Federal Property Inventory. For structures and equipment together, the difference at the end of 1956 amounts to about $13 billion, or 8 per cent. The relatively small difference between the two figures, considering the numerous possible sources of discrepancy, may be taken to indicate that the perpetual inventory method has in the past allocated approximately the correct amounts to capital expenditures by the federal government. It indicates, too, that the assumptions about

TABLE 20

COMPARISON OF ESTIMATES OF GROSS AND NET STRUCTURE VALUE OF STATE AND
LOCAL HIGHWAYS, ROADS, AND STREETS, SELECTED YEARS, 1929-52

(billions of dollars; replacement cost)

	Gross Value			Net Value				
Year	NBER (1)	Farrell-Paterick (2)	(1): (2) (3)	NBER (4)	Farrell-Paterick (5)	Reeve (6)	(4): (5) (7)	(4): (6) (8)
1929		8.0			6.5			
1939		19.0			14.0	14.3		
1945	34.0	35.0	0.97	18.9	22.0	25.7a	0.86	0.74
1949	46.9	45.0	1.04	23.6	28.5		0.83	
1952	59.7	60.7	0.98	30.5	36.9		0.83	

SOURCE, BY COLUMN

(1 and 4) 1929-39: From worksheets for *A Study of Saving* . . . .
1945-52: Gross values from cumulation of constant (1947-49) expenditures for highway construction, Table B-138; original expenditures, Tables B-136 and B-140, converted to constant (1947-49) values by applying annual average highway index from Table B-143. Replacement cost then derived by multiplying cumulative gross values in constant prices by year-end deflation from Table B-143.
Net values from Table B-138 and from state and local portion of Table B-150, less value of "other construction" from statistical worksheets.

(2 and 5) 1929-45: Values in 1953 prices read off from Figure 4 of Farrell and Paterick, *op.cit.*, and adjusted to current prices by construction cost index in its Table 1.
1952: *Ibid.*, pp. 7 and 10.
These figures exclude expenditures made before 1914 which are included in cols. 1 and 4.

(6) J. E. Reeve, *et al.*, *op.cit.*, p. 487.

a 1946.

length of life of the different types of assets made in applying the perpetual inventory method correspond roughly to the actual lives, since the federal inventory includes—at full undepreciated original cost—all items of structure and equipment not actually discarded.

The reasonably good correspondence in the aggregate figure may, of course, hide offsetting differences of considerable size for different types of assets. Table 21 indicates that this is so, even when only a few broad categories of assets are distinguished. The correspondence remains satisfactory for military equipment, the item for which a substantial discrepancy would have been the least surprising. For both civilian and military structures, however, the perpetual inventory estimates are considerably higher—by about one-half and one-fourth respectively—than the Federal Property Inventory figures. The dis-

TABLE 21

COMPARISON OF NBER AND FEDERAL PROPERTY INVENTORY ESTIMATES OF FEDERAL REPRODUCIBLE ASSETS, 1956

(billions of dollars; original undepreciated cost)

	Federal Property Inventory (1)	Hubbell (2)	NBER (3)
Civiliana			
Structures	16.5	} 29.0	25.1
Equipment	10.6		5.8
Inventories	14.5	6.1	12.6
Total	41.6	35.1	43.5
Military			
Structures	21.8	22.9	26.7
Equipment	} 109.5	97.2	107.6
Inventories		6.3	5.9
Total	131.3	126.4	140.2
Total	173.1	161.5	183.7

SOURCE, BY COLUMN

(1) Averages of figures for June 30, 1957 and 1956 from *Federal Real and Personal Property Inventory Report . . . as of June 30, 1958* (Committee on Government Operations, U.S. Congress, 1959), pp. 11 and 139. Structures outside the U.S. are excluded.

(2) Robert Hubbell, unpublished estimates.

(3) Civilian: Cumulation of original cost gross expenditures from Tables B-158 to B-162, and B-165, plus AEC gross stock from Table B-172A, plus inventories from Tables B-156 and B-173.
Military: Table B-172A.

a Including government corporations and the Atomic Energy Commission.

crepancy may be due to an overestimation in our calculations of either capital expenditures made by the federal government or the length of life of structures or of both. On the other hand, the perpetual inventory estimate of civilian equipment is considerably lower—by about two-fifths—than the Federal Property Inventory figure. This may reflect an underallocation of the proportion of total produced equipment that is bought by the federal government, or an underestimation of its actual life. The fact that the combined totals for civilian structures and equipment are considerably closer in the two estimates than the totals are for either of the two components suggests that the definitions of structures and equipment in the two series may differ considerably.

The comparison of the perpetual inventory estimates of federal reproducible assets with the bench mark provided by the federal inventory thus suggests that, while the estimates for structures and equipment together seem to be of the correct order of magnitude, great care must be taken in using the perpetual inventory estimates for any one of the components of federal reproducible assets. The Federal Property Inventory figures are not yet complete, refined, and reliable enough for us to be sure that they are in all respects superior to the estimates derived by the perpetual inventory method, but the substantial differences between the two series undoubtedly suggest caution in the use of the latter.[8]

Since the fiscal year 1952, an alternate estimate of the capital expenditures of the federal government (excluding stockpiles but including acquisition of land and structures) has been available from the Census Bureau.[9] These figures are in the aggregate slightly above the estimates used in this report. For the entire period from 1952 to 1957 the excess amounts to about 6 per cent. However, the census figures are considerably above ours for construction—which accounts for only about one-fifth of the total capital expenditures of the federal government—and exceed them for 1952-57 by almost one-fifth. On the other hand, the census figures for other capital expenditures, mostly military equipment, are about one-tenth below our estimates, probably because of some differences in classification. Differences for individual years, of course, are sometimes substantially larger. Since the census figures are not given in sufficient detail to permit the application of the perpetual inventory method, since they are provided only for fiscal years and are not available before 1952, they have not been used in the derivation of our estimates. The effect, if used, on our estimates of the stock of structures and equipment of the federal government between 1952 and 1958 would be small, particularly in the case of the net stock.

Conclusion

For all assets examined, the available bench-mark figures corroborate the order of magnitude of the perpetual inventory estimates used in this study, at least for broad asset categories. This gives some assur-

---

[8] A third estimate (Table 21, col. 2), which came to our attention only after the calculations were completed, is in the aggregate slightly (7 per cent) below the Federal Property Inventory figures and somewhat more (15 per cent) below our own estimates. This is a result chiefly of higher estimates on our part for civilian inventories and military structures. Hubbell's and our figures are almost identical for civilian structures and equipment, and are only 12 per cent apart for the largest item, military equipment.

[9] See *Census of Government, 1957*, Vol. IV, 3, p. 14; and *Annual Summary of Government Finances* (Bureau of the Census), various issues.

ance that the perpetual inventory method can be used to derive such estimates, and that no large-scale mistakes have been made in its application to the national wealth of the United States in the postwar period—provided we accept the census data used here for comparison as sufficiently accurate. We do not yet have satisfactory bench-mark figures for either narrower asset categories, or for holdings of tangible assets cross-classified by sectors. Even here, however, the comparisons that can be made do not clearly point to a distortion, at least, in the perpetual inventory estimates.

CHAPTER 7

Some International Comparisons

UNDERSTANDING of the structure of the national wealth of the United States, of its growth, and of its relation to income would be considerably deepened if we could compare our situation with that of other countries, particularly countries similar to the United States in their economic and institutional structure. Comparison of the present situation of foreign countries in different stages of their economic development with that of the United States in earlier stages of its history might be particularly interesting and suggestive. Unfortunately, adequate comparisons of this type are not yet possible and cannot be presented here. Limitations of time and resources have ruled out the thorough exploration, examination, and adjustment of the data available for foreign countries, necessary for an adequate international comparison. Moreover, the relative scarcity of reliable and sufficiently detailed estimates of national wealth for foreign countries and the disparity in the methods of estimation used would make such comparisons both difficult and precarious. We must therefore be satisfied with a much less ambitious approach.

All that is attempted in this chapter is the comparison of a few basic structural characteristics of national wealth for varying groups of countries—sometimes less than ten, sometimes as many as forty—during the 1950's. Even this limited comparison has been made possible only by the recent publication in Income and Wealth Series VIII of national wealth estimates for a number of countries for which they were not previously available, and by the inclusion in the introduction to that volume of a set of comparative tables based on these country papers.[1] Any attempt to go beyond the countries and dates covered in Income and Wealth Series VIII does not in the present situation promise an increase in information commensurate with the effort required, except in the analysis of marginal capital-output ratios, omitted from this report.

The comparisons center on three basic aspects of national wealth:

[1] *The Measurement of National Wealth*, "Introduction," by Raymond W. Goldsmith and Christopher Saunders; "Statistics of National Wealth for Eighteen Countries," by Th. van der Weide (Income and Wealth Series VIII, London, Bowes and Bowes, 1959).

1. The structure of net national wealth in current prices, i.e., the distribution of total national wealth among the main types of tangible assets
2. The distribution of net national wealth among the three main economic groups—business enterprises, households, and government
3. The ratio of net to gross reproducible tangible wealth

Structure of National Wealth

THE SHARE OF LAND

For broad international and historical comparisons one of the two or three crucial ratios characterizing the structure of national wealth, and possibly the one most revealing of a country's economic status, is the proportion of land (particularly agricultural land) to total national wealth.

This share now stands at about 17 per cent in the United States, after having declined fairly steadily from 25 per cent in 1929, 35 per cent in 1900, and 45 per cent in the middle of the nineteenth century.[2] The shares are remarkably similar for most European countries for which the figures are available, as shown in Table 22. They are slightly below the United States level for Belgium and the Netherlands, and slightly above it for West Germany and Luxemburg, lying for all countries between one-seventh and one-fifth of the value of total tangible wealth. For Sweden, the ratio is substantially below that of the United States, about one-eighth. It probably would still be somewhat lower for the United Kingdom, for which no current estimate is available. Unfortunately, only one underdeveloped and primarily agricultural country, India, is included in the comparative tabulations of Income and Wealth, Series VIII. Here the land–tangible assets ratio is, of course, much higher and amounts to close to 50 per cent, indicating an approximate equality between the value of land and of reproducible tangible assets. Ratios of this magnitude will probably be found in many of the predominantly agricultural countries in Southeast Asia, the Middle East, Central America, and Africa.[3] Such ratios are not at all surprising

[2] The estimates for the United States are taken (unless otherwise indicated) for the period since 1900, from the appendix tables to this report, and for the nineteenth century, from R. W. Goldsmith "The Growth of Reproducible Wealth of the United States of America from 1805 to 1950," Income and Wealth Series II, London, 1951.

[3] For Honduras, an estimate not utilized in Table 22 (E. Tosco, *La Riqueza de Honduras*, mimeographed, September 1957) puts the share at 44 per cent.

TABLE 22

SHARE OF LAND IN NATIONAL WEALTH, SELECTED COUNTRIES AND YEARS, 1950-56

Country	Date	Land as Per Cent of All Tangible Assets		Land as Per Cent of Tangible Assets Excluding Consumer Durables	
		Total	Agricultural	Total	Agricultural
		(1)	(2)	(3)	(4)
1. United States	1955	17	5	18	6
2. Sweden	1952	11	2	12	2
3. Belgium	1950	14		16	
4. Netherlands	1952	15	12	18	15
5. Australia	1956	17	9	18	10
6. West Germany	1955	20		22	
7. France	1954		14		15
8. Yugoslavia	1953	26	23	29	25
9. Norway	1953				2
10. Luxemburg	1950			20	10
11. South Africa	1955			28	
12. India	1950			51	45

SOURCE: Van der Weide, *op.cit.*, Table I.

if it is recalled that we need look back only about a century to find in the United States equally high shares of land in total tangible wealth. Yugoslavia and South Africa, two countries ranking in their economic development between the industrial countries of Europe and North America and the agrarian countries of the tropics and subtropics, show land-wealth ratios of about 30 per cent.

The ratio of agricultural land to total wealth in the United States of 6 per cent, a ratio which is more characteristic of economic development than the all-land ratio since the latter includes urban land of high locational value, is among the lowest in the world. It is, however, above that for some Scandinavian countries and probably for Great Britain, and compares with ratios of approximately 15 per cent in France and the Netherlands, 25 per cent in Yugoslavia, and 45 per cent in India.

The ratio of all land to total national wealth thus combines two main components. The first is the ratio of agricultural land to national wealth shown in columns 2 and 4 of Table 22. This ratio is likely to decline in the course of economic development, as agriculture gradually accounts for a declining share of labor force and output. The second component is the ratio of nonagricultural (mainly urban) land to national wealth. It is not evident that this ratio will have a definite long-term trend. In some phases of economic development, particularly during rapid urbanization, the ratio may rise. During others it may fall, particularly when improvements in transportation reduce the scarcity value of land in urban centers. It is, however, to be expected that the second component of the land–national wealth ratio, reflecting locational advantages, will increase in importance in comparison with the first component, which is largely the result of differences in physical characteristics such as soil fertility, though locational factors also play an important role in it.

THE EQUIPMENT-STRUCTURES RATIO

A second important ratio is the relation of the value of equipment (producer and consumer durables) to structures shown in Table 23.

TABLE 23

RATIO OF EQUIPMENT TO STRUCTURES, SELECTED COUNTRIES AND YEARS, 1950-55
(per cent)

Country	Date	Ratio of Total Equipment to Structures, Consumer Durables		Ratio of Enterprise Equipment to Structures, Dwellings	
		Included (1)	Excluded (2)	Included (3)	Excluded (4)
1. United States	1955	50	29	35	85
2. Belgium	1950	75	47	54	265
3. Luxemburg	1952		69	81	165
4. Netherlands	1952	88	42	58	124
5. West Germany	1955	70	42	47	105
6. Norway	1953		38	46	88
7. Yugoslavia	1953	58	37	38	71
8. Canada	1955	71	39	49	95
9. Union of South Africa	1955		34	36a	53a
10. Colombia	1953		29	33	47
11. Japan	1955	81	38	43	72
12. India	1950		25	27	57

SOURCE: Van der Weide, loc.cit.
a Excluding government corporations and public enterprises.

While this ratio now stands at about 50 per cent in the United States, it is substantially higher for each of the few countries for which the information is available: about 70 per cent for Canada and West Germany; 75 per cent for Belgium; fully 80 per cent for Japan; and almost 90 per cent for the Netherlands. If consumer durables are excluded, in all but two of the eleven countries the ratio of producer durables to all structures is higher than in the U.S. The median ratio for these eleven countries of slightly less than 40 per cent compares with an American ratio of slightly less than 30 per cent.

For purposes of analysis, it is probably preferable to limit the comparison to business and government enterprises, excluding dwellings as well as consumer durables. The picture then is somewhat different. The United States with a ratio of producer durables to enterprise structures of 85 per cent is close to the median for the eleven foreign countries for which the information is available. The ratio is considerably higher than in the U.S. in all Western European countries for which it can be calculated—Belgium, Luxemburg, the Netherlands, and West Germany—and slightly higher in Canada and Norway. It is lower only in definitely underdeveloped countries—in descending order, Japan, Yugoslavia, India, Union of South Africa, and Colombia.

It is not easy to explain these relationships, particularly in view of the well-known status of the U.S. as a highly mechanized country with an ample stock of consumer durables. In only a few countries, particularly in Japan and to a lesser extent in West Germany, does the relatively small value of the stock of dwellings explain the high ratio of equipment to structures. Relative costs—particularly the relatively high cost of building construction in the U.S.—may provide part of the answer. Incompatibilities in coverage and completion as well as differences in length of life probably are all responsible for some of the difference. Much more data and analysis, as well as a detailed examination of the derivation of the estimates underlying Table 23, however, are needed before a satisfactory explanation can be attempted.

THE SHARE OF FOREIGN ASSETS

There is at least one point at which the structure of the national wealth of the United States differs from that of many, if not most, foreign countries—the share of both foreign assets and foreign liabilities in total national wealth. This statement unfortunately cannot be documented in detail, since only a few foreign countries have sufficiently accurate or continuous estimates of their foreign assets and liabilities for comparison with those of their domestic wealth.

In the United States, foreign assets represented only 5 per cent of domestic tangible wealth including monetary metals, and not more than 3.5 per cent excluding them, even at the end of the first postwar decade (1956). Foreign liabilities (including all foreign investments in the U.S.) amounted to over 2 per cent of domestic tangible wealth, leaving a net balance of 3 per cent including monetary metals and of not much over 1 per cent excluding them. These ratios are apparently considerably below those that can be inferred for many foreign countries, both developed European and underdeveloped non-European countries. In Belgium and the Netherlands, for instance, the net foreign balance constitutes 10 and 7 per cent, respectively, of national wealth.

In the countries which in the past have been heavy importers of foreign capital, the net foreign balance is usually negative, since foreign liabilities, in the form of both borrowing abroad and foreign ownership of domestic assets, are larger than those countries' foreign assets, including their holdings of monetary metals. In Canada, for instance, the net foreign balance is equal to about 12 per cent of national wealth; in Latin America (as a whole) somewhat less than 10 per cent; in Australia 5 per cent (the result of foreign assets of 2 per cent and foreign liabilities of 7 per cent of national wealth); and in Norway to 1.5 per cent.[4] There is little doubt that net foreign liabilities are in similar or even larger proportions of national wealth for a number of underdeveloped countries in Southeast Asia, Africa, and Latin America, although exact statistical calculations are not feasible, chiefly because of the lack of estimates of national wealth.

OWNERSHIP OF TANGIBLE ASSETS

The distribution of reproducible tangible assets among business enterprises, households, and governments—which, of course, is not identical with the share of these three groups in national equity—shows considerable international differences. In the United States in 1955 nearly one-half of tangible assets were operated by business enterprises (if farms are included); two-fifths represented dwellings and consumer durables operated by households; and a little over one-eighth were operated by the government. These ratios would not be substantially changed by the inclusion of nonreproducible assets, particularly land.

Of the countries for which the necessary data are available (Table 24) two—Belgium and Canada—show a share of the government in reproducible tangible wealth only slightly higher than the ratio found in the United States. A few other countries show a markedly higher ratio, averaging one-fifth of total reproducible tangible wealth—the Netherlands, West Germany (partly estimated), and Japan. Of the

---

[4] Most of these ratios are derived from information in the country papers in **Income and Wealth Series VIII.**

TABLE 24

DISTRIBUTION OF OWNERSHIP OF REPRODUCIBLE TANGIBLE WEALTH,
SELECTED COUNTRIES AND YEARS, 1950-56

(per cent of reproducible tangible wealth)

COUNTRY	Date	REPRODUCIBLE WEALTH OF ENTERPRISES				REPRODUCIBLE WEALTH OF HOUSEHOLDS		REPRODUCIBLE WEALTH OF GOVERNMENTS	
						*Dwellings*a		*Government Owned Enterprises*	
		Total	Dwellingsa	Government	Private Nonresidential	Includeda	Excluded	Included	Excluded
		(1)	(2)	(3)	(4)	(5)	(6)	(7)	(8)
1. United States	1955	76	30	2	44	43	13	13	11
2. Belgium	1950	77	36	5	36	51	15	14	8
3. Netherlands	1952	66	20	5	41	42	22	18	12
4. West Germany	1955	75	25			40	15		10
5. France	1954	65	17b	20	28	30+	13	42	22
6. Yugoslaviac	1953	76	22	47	7	34	12	59	12
7. Canada	1955	71	19	2	50	35	16	15	13
8. Australia	1956		31		29	41	10	30	
9. Japan	1955	64	14	6	44	34	20	22	16

SOURCE: Van der Weide, *op.cit.*, Table III.

a Includes all dwellings; hence cols. 1, 2, and 5 overlap.
b Excluding farm dwellings.

c Collective peoples' ownership included in cols. 3, 7, and 8.

countries for which the ratio can be calculated—all basically free-enterprise countries—the share of the government is highest in France, where the available estimates put it at approximately two-fifths. Almost as high a ratio would probably be obtained for Australia.

The share of households in the ownership of tangible wealth in the Netherlands and West Germany is similar to the American level of two-fifths. It is somewhat lower—in the order of one-third—in Australia and Japan, chiefly because of the relatively low share of dwellings in national wealth. On the other hand, the ratio is substantially above the American level in Belgium because of the high proportion of dwellings in the estimates of national wealth.

The share of private business enterprises (including farms but excluding government owned enterprises) is not very different from the American ratio of somewhat below one-half in most of the other countries for which estimates are available.

Ratio of Net to Gross Wealth

The ratio of the net to the gross value of reproducible tangible assets—the significant ratio, since there is no difference between the two components for inventories and for land—is astonishingly similar for the few countries for which estimates are available, as Table 25 shows.

The four foreign countries for which the ratio can be calculated—West Germany, Netherlands, Yugoslavia, and Australia—all show a ratio of net to gross reproducible tangible wealth of very close to 60 per cent which is the figure obtained for the United States.[5] The ratios are also very similar for most of the main components of reproducible tangible assets such as dwellings and producer durables. Substantial differences appear only in the ratios of nonresidential private structures, government structures, and consumer durables, but they are not systematic. For private nonresidential structures as well as consumer durables, the net-gross ratio for the United States is low

[5] Such a ratio can be the result of numerous combinations of rates of growth of expenditures and their average length of life. It may, for instance, represent the combination of a 2 per cent growth and a life of slightly more than 60 years, an unlikely high value for the average of all capital expenditures; of a growth of 3 per cent and a life of slightly more than 40 years; of a growth of 4 per cent and a life of a little over 30 years; or, again a less likely combination, of 5 per cent growth and 25 years' life. Hence, several countries may show the same net-gross ratio although capital expenditures have increased at considerably different rates in the past, provided only that there are offsetting differences either in the distribution of capital expenditures among items of differing durability or because similar items are retained in the stock for longer or shorter periods.

TABLE 25

RATIO OF NET TO GROSS REPRODUCIBLE TANGIBLE WEALTH,
SELECTED COUNTRIES AND YEARS, 1952-56

(per cent)

	United States (1956) (1)	West Germany (1955) (2)	Netherlands (1952) (3)	Yugoslavia (1953) (4)	Australia (1956) (5)
Reproducible tangible wealth, including item 9	60	60	61		59
Reproducible tangible wealth, excluding item 9	62	59	61	62	61
Structures, private	58	57	61	58	56
Structures, dwelling	56	60	61	51	57
Structures, other private	53	55	61	66	53
Structures, government	59	50	50a	57a	57a
Equipment, private, including item 9	55	61	59		53
Equipment, private, excluding item 9	60	58	57	56	56
Consumer durables	50	67	61		49

SOURCE: Col. 1, Tables A-5 and A-7.
    Cols. 2 to 5, Van der Weide, op.cit., Table II.
a Includes government equipment.

compared with most of the other countries for which data are available, while it is high for government structures.

In view of our limited information about the foreign data's reliability and scope, and of the many factors that could be responsible for differences in the net-gross ratio for individual types of assets, no attempt to explain each of these differences will be made. It is more remarkable that, notwithstanding the differences of five countries' structure of reproducible tangible assets, length of life of the different types of assets, and time shape of the capital expenditure streams which underlie the ratio, the over-all ratio of net to gross reproducible tangible wealth is practically identical. This near identity, of course, may be, and probably is, at least in part, the result of offsetting differences in the various factors that determine the national over-all ratio.

Rate of Growth of National Wealth in the Postwar Period

The number of countries for which the rates of growth of real national wealth during the postwar period can be calculated is so small that not much can be concluded from a comparison of the figures shown in

Table 26 and Chart 10, with the rate of growth of national wealth in the United States.[6] It is fairly evident, however, that unless the foreign countries for which the data are available are entirely untypical of the world outside, the rate of growth of real reproducible wealth per head, during the postwar decade and after, was at least as rapid abroad as in the United States. In Europe and the (former) British Dominions, the stock of tangible wealth apparently has grown faster than in the U.S., a relation partly explained by the rapid reconstruction in a number of European countries. The rate of growth in the underdeveloped countries, about which unfortunately little is known outside of Latin America, seems to have been, at best, as rapid and generally somewhat slower than in the U.S.

TABLE 26

RATES OF GROWTH OF REAL NATIONAL WEALTH IN POSTWAR PERIOD, SELECTED COUNTRIES AND PERIODS, 1945-58

(per cent per year)

COUNTRY	Period	AGGREGATE REPRODUCIBLE WEALTH Consumer Durables		Population (3)	REPRODUCIBLE WEALTH PER HEAD Consumer Durables	
		Included (1)	Excluded (2)		Included (4)	Excluded (5)
1. United States	1945-58	3.9	3.4	1.7	2.2	1.7
2. Argentina	1945-55		2.9	2.2		0.7
3. Colombia	1945-53		3.6	2.2		1.4
4. Australia	1947-56	4.6	4.6	2.4		2.2
5. United Kingdom	1947-57		3.4	0.4		3.0
6. South Africa	1945-55		5.2	2.0		3.2
7. Canada	1947-55	6.8	6.2	2.9	3.9	3.3
8. West Germany[a]	1948-55		5.4	1.9		3.5
9. Norway	1945-55		5.6	1.0		4.6

SOURCE: Country papers in Income and Wealth Series VIII, except for United States (Table A and for United Kingdom (*National Income and Expenditures*, U.S. Department of Commerce various issues).

a Only fixed reproducible assets.

The calculation of rates of growth of reproducible national wealth by means of the comparison of estimates of (deflated) wealth at two points of time, or of the comparison of a period's cumulated net capital expenditures with the stock of capital at the beginning of the period, is limited by scarcity of data for the nine countries listed in Table 26. It is, however, possible to derive rough approximations of

6 Cf. Chapter 4.

CHART 10

Average Annual Rate of Growth of Real National Wealth Per Head
in Postwar Period, Selected Countries and Periods, 1945-58

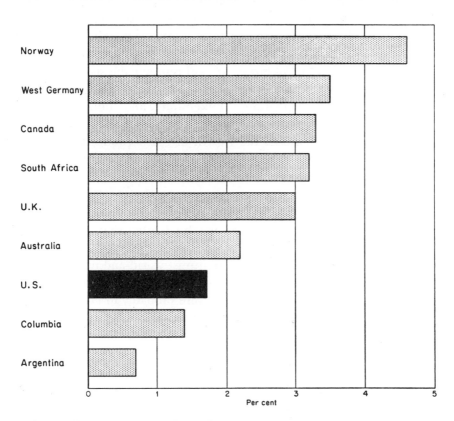

Source: Underlying data in Table 26.

the rates of growth of reproducible tangible wealth in the postwar
period for another half-dozen countries for which bench-mark estimates
of national wealth in the postwar period are available. One of two
approaches must be accepted for reducing the available estimates of
gross capital expenditures (in prices that underlie the bench-mark
estimates of national wealth) for the postwar period to a net basis.
One is using the ratio of depreciation allowances to gross capital
expenditures derived from the countries' official national accounting
statements; the other is by applying a standard ratio, based on the
theoretical relationship between gross and net capital expenditures,

that corresponds to a given rate of growth of capital expenditures in the past and an assumed length of life of reproducible tangible assets.[7]

Most of the countries for which additional rough estimates thus become available show a rate of growth per head of reproducible tangible wealth (excluding consumer durables) during the postwar period—usually between 1950 and 1957—which is definitely above the rate of 1.75 per cent observed for the United States. This is undoubtedly so for Japan, with a rate of growth of real reproducible assets per head of at least 4 per cent, and for Belgium, with the rate of about 3 per cent. For France, the Netherlands, Luxemburg, and India, the rate of growth seems to have been at about the same level as for the United States. Only in Sweden does the growth of real reproducible tangible assets per head seem to have been definitely below the U.S. level.

The inclusion of these additional countries, notwithstanding the lesser reliability of the estimates that can be derived for them, thus seems to reinforce the conclusion drawn from Table 26, that the rate of growth of reproducible wealth in the United States during the entire postwar period, and still more during the 1950's, was at best as rapid as in the rest of the non-Communist world and may well have proceeded at a slightly slower rate than in those countries. The comparable rates in Communist countries were probably in most cases well above the U.S. level, although the absence of published bench-mark estimates of the stock of reproducible tangible assets makes documentation difficult.[8]

This relationship—the absence of a lead in the American rate of growth—probably is in contrast to the experience in the prewar period, but it is in line with the fact that real income per head also increased more rapidly in many foreign countries during the postwar period (again excluding Southeast Asia) than in the United States. However, the position of foreign countries compared with the U.S. appears to have been more favorable with respect to the rate of growth of reproducible tangible wealth than with respect to income, with the result that, insofar as a judgment is possible, the capital-output ratio rose more (or fell less) in the rest of the world than in the U.S.

[7] Cf. Chapter 3.

[8] With the gross investment rates of between 20 and 30 per cent encountered in most Communist countries, the high net-gross capital expenditure ratios, and the rapid rate of growth, in real per head terms, of the volume of national product and capital expenditures, the stock of capital is bound to increase by much more than 2 per cent a year, even if the average reproducible capital-output ratio at the beginning of the postwar period had been very high in international comparison—which is unlikely.

Changes in the Structure of Wealth During the Postwar Period

There is not enough statistical material available for foreign countries to permit a statistically founded comparison between the changes in the structure of national wealth that have taken place in the United States during the postwar period with those that have occurred abroad.

The figures at hand for a few countries (Germany, Canada, Australia) and fragmentary material for a few others make it likely, however, that the changes were in the same direction abroad as those observed in the United States after World War II. Thus, the share of **reproducible tangible** assets appears to have continued its increase at the expense of the share of land. Within reproducible tangible assets, the share of equipment has increased substantially. While it advanced in the postwar decade from 13 to 19 per cent in the U.S., it rose during approximately the same period from 24 to 30 per cent in Germany, from 23 to 29 per cent in Canada, and from 17 to 18 per cent in Australia. Similar changes appear to have taken place also in a number of underdeveloped countries, where they accompanied the increase in the share of manufacturing in national output, but figures are missing to document statistically the shift in the structure of national wealth.

APPENDIXES

Appendix A

APPENDIX A contains the detailed tables on the components of national wealth of the United States during the postwar period on which much of the text of Chapters 1 and 4-6 is based. All tables show annual figures for the period 1945 through 1948. In many, figures for a few bench-mark years back to the turn of the century (1939, 1929, 1922, 1912, and 1900) are also given for comparative purposes, but that was not possible in all tables because some estimates, particularly those for gross national wealth, were not available for years before 1945. In the tables, two values for 1945—usually differing but little—are shown. The first of these in each table, taken from *A Study of Saving* . . . ,[1] is comparable with the bench-mark date estimates back to 1900; the second belongs to the set of annual estimates for the postwar period.

Figures are shown in hundred—or ten—million-dollar units (billions of dollars, with one or two digits) for the convenience of users who want to perform further calculations with them. There is not, of course, any implication that the estimates are accurate to the nearest ten or hundred million dollars. Indeed, in most cases the last digit or the last two digits shown are not significant.

The sources and methods of estimates are described briefly in Chapter 2 of the text. Detailed notes on the derivation of the figures, together with the underlying data from which the estimates were derived, will be found in the Appendix B tables.

Appendix A consists of five sets of tables. The first tables in each set present absolute figures, and are followed in some sets by tables showing percentage distributions and annual and period rates of change to facilitate the use of the material by analysts.

The first set (Tables A-1–A-4) presents estimates of the alternative main aggregates of national wealth in current and constant (1947-49) prices, on a net and a gross basis and in absolute figures, as well as in the form of year-to-year percentage changes. One of the purposes of these tables, besides providing a summary of the estimates, is to permit users to see the effects on the estimates of alternative concepts of national wealth.

The second set (Tables A-5–A-14) may be regarded as the core of Appendix A. It consists of ten tables showing the estimates for the

[1] Raymond W. Goldsmith, *A Study of Saving in the United States*, 3 vols., Princeton University Press, 1955-56.

fourteen main components of wealth from which the aggregate figures have been built up. Estimates are again given in current and constant prices; on a net and a gross basis, in absolute figures as well as in percentages; and in the form of year-to-year rates of changes. Some additional breakdowns, particularly for more than a dozen categories of producer durables and of consumer durables, for military assets, and for foreign assets and liabilities are given in the Appendix B tables.

The third set (Tables A-15–A-34) is devoted to estimates of the total wealth of the seven main sectors and certain combinations of them. Separate tables are provided for total and for reproducible wealth alone. They permit comparison of the distribution of national wealth, on different valuation bases and in accordance with different definitions, among the main sectors, and are intended to facilitate the study of cyclical and trend movements in the wealth of different sectors.

In the fourth set (Tables A-35–A-49) the distribution of wealth among sectors is shown for each component of national wealth. Usually, of course, only a few sectors show holdings of a given form of wealth, in particular because relatively minor holdings often of necessity were ignored in the preparation of the estimates.

The fifth set (Tables A-50–A-64) presents information on the wealth structure of the seven main sectors by showing, for bench-mark years from 1900 to 1945 and then successively for each year end from 1945 through 1958, all the types of tangible assets held by each sector. These tables constitute the basis for the study of the tangible wealth structure of each sector and the changes therein.

Appendix A
Tables

TABLE A-1

National Wealth of the United States, Excluding Military Assets, Alternative Main Aggregates, Current Prices

(billions of dollars)

End of Year	NET STOCK								GROSS STOCK			
	All Wealth				Reproducible Tangible Wealth				Reproducible Tangible Wealth			
	Total[a] (1)	Nonbusiness Consumer Durables Included (2)	Excluded (3)	Business (4)	Total (5)	Nonbusiness Consumer Durables Included (6)	Excluded (7)	Business (8)	Total (9)	Nonbusiness Consumer Durables Included (10)	Excluded (11)	Business (12)
1900	87.9	37.5	31.5	50.4	59.3	28.2	22.1	31.1				
1912	165.4	69.1	55.5	96.4	109.3	52.5	38.9	56.8				
1922	334.5	162.2	31.2	172.4	233.4	118.3	87.3	115.1				
1929	439.4	237.3	195.1	202.1	313.5	172.3	130.1	141.1				
1933	330.5	186.9	161.2	143.6	241.3	136.0	110.3	105.3				
1939	396.8	234.0	201.5	162.7	307.4	186.3	152.8	121.1				
1945	571.4	335.1	284.2	236.3	442.3	271.5	220.5	170.9				
1945	576.2	343.7	297.5	232.5	457.0	290.5	244.3	166.5	798.8	509.4	401.2	289.4
1946	700.9	411.2	351.6	289.7	556.2	344.1	284.4	212.1	967.9	608.9	477.2	359.1
1947	843.5	498.8	425.4	344.7	668.4	413.4	340.0	255.0	1,153.2	731.8	575.3	421.3
1948	928.4	544.4	459.1	383.9	736.5	452.4	367.1	284.2	1,265.2	800.6	623.1	464.6
1949	932.0	547.2	456.0	384.7	742.2	456.0	364.8	286.2	1,270.9	800.1	613.7	470.8
1950	1,067.1	623.5	512.1	443.6	851.8	520.9	409.5	331.0	1,444.5	908.2	690.9	536.3
1951	1,164.6	668.1	545.6	496.5	928.6	559.5	437.1	369.0	1,560.5	971.3	734.7	589.2
1952	1,214.1	703.1	575.4	511.0	972.9	591.4	463.8	381.2	1,636.6	1,025.4	777.7	611.2
1953	1,259.3	733.5	598.7	525.7	1,015.3	618.4	483.7	396.8	1,708.3	1,069.6	806.4	638.7
1954	1,306.3	762.4	623.7	543.9	1,052.6	642.6	503.9	409.9	1,771.1	1,111.5	836.4	659.6
1955	1,401.9	822.5	671.7	579.4	1,130.4	694.3	543.5	436.1	1,897.5	1,197.0	898.8	700.4
1956	1,518.1	884.0	720.7	634.1	1,226.2	746.5	583.1	479.7	2,049.7	1,285.8	960.2	763.8
1957	1,629.8	934.6	761.0	695.1	1,311.3	787.1	613.5	524.1	2,190.7	1,360.4	1,003.8	830.3
1958	1,702.8	981.1	802.3	721.7	1,367.6	825.1	646.4	542.4	2,300.7	1,436.0	1,052.2	864.8

(continued)

112

(1) Sum of cols. 2 and 4.
(2) Col. 3 plus Table A-38, col. 1.
(3) Col. 7 plus Table A-50, cols. 3, 4, 7; Table A-51, col. 3; Table A-52, col. 4; Table A-54, col. 4; Table A-55, col. 4; Table A-56, cols. 4 and 8.
(4) Col. 8 plus Table A-52, cols. 5, 9, 10; Table A-53, col. 4; Table A-54, cols. 5, 9 to 11.
(5) Sum of cols. 6 and 8.
(6) Col. 7 plus Table A-38, col. 1.
(7) Table A-35, col. 1; Table A-50, col. 6; Table A-51, cols. 2 and 4; Table A-55, cols. 3, 5 to 7; Table A-56, cols. 3, 5 to 7.

(8) Table A-52, cols. 3, 6 to 8; Table A-53, cols. 3, 5, 7 to 9; Table A-54, cols. 3, 6, 7, 8.
(9) Sum of cols. 10 and 12.
(10) Col. 11 plus Table A-49, col. 1.
(11) Table A-46, col. 1; Table A-57, col. 6; Table A-58, cols. 2 and 4; Table A-62, cols. 3, 5 and 6; Table A-63, cols. 3, 5 to 7.
(12) Table A-59, cols. 3, 6 to 8; Table A-60, cols. 3, 5, 7 to 9; Table A-61, cols. 3, 6 to 8.

a Totals for bench-mark years from 1900 to 1945 differ slightly from those shown in Table A-5, col. 2, and in Raymond W. Goldsmith, *A Study of Saving in the United States* (3 Vols., Princeton University Press, 1955–1956), Vol. III, Table W-1, because of rounding.

TABLE A-2

NATIONAL WEALTH OF THE UNITED STATES, EXCLUDING MILITARY ASSETS, ALTERNATIVE MAIN AGGREGATES, CONSTANT (1947–49) PRICES

(billions of dollars)

	NET STOCK								GROSS STOCK			
	All Wealth				Reproducible Tangible Wealth				Reproducible Tangible Wealth			
		Nonbusiness Consumer Durables				Nonbusiness Consumer Durables				Nonbusiness Consumer Durables		
End of Year	Total (1)	Included (2)	Excluded (3)	Business (4)	Total (5)	Included (6)	Excluded (7)	Business (8)	Total (9)	Included (10)	Excluded (11)	Business (12)
1900	314.6	148.7	127.1	165.9	221.9	113.9	92.3	108.0				
1912	464.7	226.6	193.9	238.1	335.6	174.9	142.2	160.7				
1922	588.2	300.1	262.4	288.1	428.5	220.0	182.3	208.5				
1929	778.0	435.1	377.8	342.9	572.3	320.9	263.7	251.4				
1933	742.2	432.1	382.3	310.1	546.5	317.5	267.7	229.0				
1939	748.4	444.5	386.9	303.9	572.0	347.9	290.2	224.1				
1945	763.7	446.5	385.2	317.2	591.1	355.2	293.9	235.8				
1945	788.1	467.2	409.7	320.9	622.3	392.5	334.9	229.8	1,096.7	695.7	558.5	401.0
1946	812.7	476.3	411.6	336.4	644.1	398.5	333.8	245.6	1,124.6	709.1	563.8	415.5
1947	845.9	497.5	423.7	348.4	669.2	412.4	338.6	256.8	1,159.2	732.8	574.7	426.3
1948	882.6	517.4	435.3	365.2	702.3	429.8	339.7	272.5	1,207.1	762.2	589.3	444.9
1949	910.4	538.5	448.1	372.0	726.4	448.4	358.0	278.0	1,241.2	787.1	603.7	454.1
1950	949.2	561.3	458.4	387.9	761.9	469.9	367.0	292.1	1,291.0	818.2	618.2	472.8
1951	990.8	582.0	471.8	408.8	798.2	487.7	377.5	310.5	1,340.8	845.6	634.2	495.2
1952	1,022.5	601.3	485.5	421.3	828.0	505.9	390.1	322.1	1,384.6	874.2	651.8	510.5
1953	1,055.3	623.6	500.3	431.7	858.9	526.9	403.6	332.0	1,434.7	909.9	671.6	524.7
1954	1,086.3	646.6	516.7	439.7	887.0	547.8	418.0	339.2	1,482.7	946.2	692.0	536.6
1955	1,131.6	677.8	536.5	453.8	928.2	576.4	435.1	351.8	1,546.0	991.4	715.6	554.6
1956	1,174.6	702.6	553.1	472.0	965.2	599.3	449.8	365.9	1,603.8	1,031.5	736.5	572.3
1957	1,216.3	726.3	570.0	490.0	998.9	620.4	464.1	378.5	1,663.0	1,075.6	756.3	587.4
1958	1,244.4	748.4	588.8	496.0	1,022.3	640.0	480.3	382.3	1,715.0	1,117.4	777.8	597.6

SOURCE: Same as for Table A-1, using figures in constant (1947–49) prices.

114

National Wealth of the United States, Annual Percentage Rates of Change, Current Prices

	NET STOCK								GROSS STOCK			
	All Wealth				Reproducible Tangible Wealth				Reproducible Tangible Wealth			
Year or Period	Total	Nonbusiness Consumer Durables Included	Excluded	Business	Total	Nonbusiness Consumer Durables Included	Excluded	Business	Total	Nonbusiness Consumer Durables Included	Excluded	Business
	(1)	(2)	(3)	(4)	(5)	(6)	(7)	(8)	(9)	(10)	(11)	(12)
1912[a]	5.41	5.22	4.84	5.55	5.23	5.34	4.82	5.15				
1922	7.29	8.91	8.98	6.00	7.88	8.45	8.42	7.31				
1929	3.97	5.59	5.83	2.30	4.30	5.55	5.86	2.94				
1933	−7.38	−6.15	−4.89	−8.99	−6.76	−6.09	−4.22	−7.59				
1939	3.09	3.83	3.80	2.15	4.06	5.34	5.58	2.32				
1945	6.27	6.16	5.89	6.41	6.30	6.51	6.30	6.19				
1946	21.64	19.53	18.18	24.60	21.70	18.45	16.41	27.38	21.19	19.53	18.94	24.08
1947	20.35	21.30	20.98	18.99	20.17	20.13	19.54	20.22	19.14	20.18	20.55	17.32
1948	10.07	9.14	7.92	11.37	10.18	9.43	7.97	11.45	9.71	9.40	8.30	10.27
1949	00.39	0.51	−0.68	0.20	0.77	0.79	−0.63	0.70	0.45	−0.06	−1.51	1.33
1950	14.50	13.94	12.30	15.31	14.71	14.23	12.25	15.65	13.65	13.51	12.57	13.91
1951	9.14	7.15	6.54	11.92	9.01	7.41	6.73	11.48	8.03	6.95	6.33	9.86
1952	4.25	5.23	5.46	2.94	4.77	5.70	6.10	3.30	4.87	5.57	5.85	3.73
1953	3.72	4.32	4.04	2.87	4.35	4.56	4.29	4.09	4.38	4.31	3.69	4.49
1954	3.73	3.94	4.17	3.46	3.67	3.91	4.17	3.30	3.67	3.92	3.72	3.27
1955	7.32	7.88	7.69	6.52	7.39	8.04	7.85	6.39	7.13	7.69	7.46	6.18
1956	8.29	7.47	7.29	9.44	8.47	7.51	7.28	9.99	8.02	7.42	6.83	9.05
1957	7.36	5.72	5.59	9.61	6.91	5.41	5.17	9.25	6.87	5.80	4.54	8.70
1958	4.48	4.98	5.43	3.82	4.27	4.79	5.29	3.49	5.02	5.55	4.82	4.15
1900–29	5.71	6.57	6.49	4.91	5.91	6.45	6.30	5.35				
1929–58	4.78	5.01	4.99	4.49	5.21	5.55	5.68	4.75				
1900–58	5.24	5.79	5.74	4.70	5.56	6.00	5.99	5.05				
1945–58	8.69	8.40	7.91	9.11	8.80	8.38	7.76	9.51	8.48	8.30	7.70	8.79
1945–58[b]	8.86	8.55	8.06	9.31	8.96	8.49	7.88	9.75	8.63	8.44	7.85	8.95

Source: Computed from figures in Table A-1.

[a] Calculated from value at beginning and end of period except for last line, which is the average of annual rates of change. First line refers to period 1901–12.

[b] Average annual rates of change.

TABLE A-4
NATIONAL WEALTH OF UNITED STATES, ANNUAL PERCENTAGE RATES OF CHANGE, CONSTANT (1947–49) PRICES

| | NET STOCK | | | | | | | | GROSS STOCK | | | |
| | All Wealth | | | | Reproducible Tangible Wealth | | | | Reproducible Tangible Wealth | | | |
Year or Period	Total (1)	Nonbusiness, Consumer Durables Included (2)	Excluded (3)	Business (4)	Total (5)	Nonbusiness, Consumer Durables Included (6)	Excluded (7)	Business (8)	Total (9)	Nonbusiness, Consumer Durables Included (10)	Excluded (11)	Business (12)
1912[a]	3.30	3.57	3.58	3.06	3.53	3.64	3.67	3.37				
1922	2.39	2.85	3.07	1.92	2.47	1.35	2.51	2.64				
1929	4.08	5.45	5.35	2.52	4.22	6.98	5.38	2.70				
1933	−1.18	−0.11	0.29	−2.55	−1.16	−0.27	0.45	−2.36				
1939	0.14	0.47	0.20	−0.34	0.80	1.60	1.44	−0.36				
1945	0.34	0.07	−0.07	0.72	0.50	0.28	0.13	0.86				
1946	3.12	1.95	0.46	4.83	3.50	1.53	−0.33	6.88	2.54	1.92	0.96	3.62
1947	4.09	4.45	2.94	3.57	3.90	3.49	1.44	4.56	3.08	3.36	1.94	2.60
1948	4.34	4.00	2.74	4.82	4.95	4.22	0.32	6.11	4.14	4.00	2.54	4.37
1949	3.15	4.08	2.94	1.86	3.43	4.33	5.39	2.02	2.82	3.26	2.44	2.07
1950	4.26	4.23	2.30	4.27	4.89	4.79	2.51	5.07	4.01	3.96	2.40	4.10
1951	4.38	3.69	2.92	5.39	4.64	3.79	2.86	6.23	3.86	3.34	2.59	4.75
1952	3.20	3.32	2.90	3.06	3.73	3.73	3.34	3.80	3.27	3.38	2.78	3.00
1953	3.21	3.78	3.13	2.47	3.73	4.15	3.46	3.07	3.61	4.09	3.03	2.79
1954	2.94	3.69	3.28	1.85	3.27	3.97	3.57	2.17	3.35	3.99	3.03	2.25
1955	4.17	4.83	3.83	3.21	4.64	5.22	4.09	3.71	4.27	4.77	3.41	3.38
1956	3.80	3.66	3.09	4.01	3.99	3.97	3.38	4.01	3.74	4.04	2.93	3.19
1957	3.55	3.37	3.06	3.81	3.49	3.52	3.18	3.44	3.69	4.27	2.68	2.64
1958	2.31	3.04	3.30	1.22	2.34	3.16	3.49	1.60	3.13	3.88	2.85	1.74
1900–29	3.17	3.77	3.83	2.54	3.33	3.64	3.68	2.96				
1929–58	1.64	1.87	1.52	1.31	2.03	2.39	2.08	1.50				
1900–58	2.40	2.82	2.67	1.92	2.68	2.01	2.87	2.22				
1945–58	3.58	3.65	2.78	3.47	3.89	3.79	2.75	4.07	3.50	3.71	2.58	3.12
1945–58[b]	3.58	3.70	2.84	3.41	3.88	3.84	2.82	4.01	3.50	3.71	2.58	3.12

SOURCE: Computed from figures in Table A-2.
[a] Calculated from value at beginning and end of period except for last line, which is the average of annual rates of change.
[b] Average annual rates of change.

NET STOCK OF MAIN TYPES OF TANGIBLE ASSETS, CURRENT PRICES
(billions of dollars)

End of Year	Total		Structures			Producer Durables		Livestock	Inventories
	Military Included (1)	Military Excluded (2)	Residential (3)	Private Nonresidential (4)	Public Civilian (5)	Private (6)	Public (7)	(8)	(9)
1900		87.7	17.4	15.5	2.0	6.4	0.1	3.1	6.8
1912		165.2	28.4	28.3	5.9	13.6	0.2	5.7	11.0
1922		334.3	63.2	55.8	15.5	30.7	0.2	5.4	27.2
1929		439.1	95.9	70.6	23.4	37.8	0.6	6.5	31.5
1933		330.2	74.3	59.0	26.2	28.6	0.6	3.2	18.7
1939		395.6	91.2	63.5	33.8	33.4	0.8	5.1	25.3
1945		570.4	133.6	80.8	50.7	46.7	3.4	9.7	42.5
1945	648.9	576.2	152.4	77.9	55.3	45.3	3.3	9.7	42.9
1946	775.4	700.9	178.5	99.0	67.9	55.4	3.1	11.9	56.3
1947	911.7	843.5	216.7	116.9	81.1	70.7	3.0	13.3	66.7
1948	991.7	928.4	234.2	127.9	87.3	84.6	2.9	14.4	71.6
1949	986.3	932.0	231.6	128.4	86.1	94.0	2.9	12.9	66.7
1950	1,121.5	1,067.1	267.4	144.4	95.5	107.0	3.0	17.1	79.4
1951	1,219.5	1,164.6	286.0	156.2	103.2	120.3	3.3	19.5	90.9
1952	1,276.9	1,214.1	301.7	165.6	111.4	128.4	3.6	14.8	92.1
1953	1,330.6	1,259.3	313.5	176.0	116.2	136.9	3.9	11.8	96.0
1954	1,380.9	1,306.3	324.8	184.0	122.5	145.3	4.2	11.2	95.9
1955	1,481.2	1,401.9	351.4	199.2	133.1	152.1	4.7	10.7	102.6
1956	1,602.5	1,518.2	375.5	215.4	145.7	172.4	5.0	11.1	111.2
1957	1,716.2	1,629.7	392.1	241.2	156.9	187.6	5.5	14.1	112.7
1958	1,791.7	1,702.8	411.3	254.2	168.2	194.0	5.9	18.1	111.8

(continued)

TABLE A-5 (concluded)

End of Year	Consumer Durables (10)	Private Land Agricultural (11)	Private Land Residential (12)	Private Land Nonresidential (13)	Public Land (14)	Monetary Metals (15)	Net Foreign Assets (16)	Military Assets (17)
1900	6.1	16.1	4.4	6.5	4.0	1.6	−2.3	72.7
1912	13.6	33.6	7.0	10.2	7.5	2.5	−2.1	74.5
1922	30.9	45.0	15.4	19.8	12.6	4.4	8.2	68.2
1929	42.2	38.0	24.1	36.1	15.3	4.8	12.4	63.3
1933	25.7	25.0	18.7	22.1	15.4	4.7	8.1	54.3
1939	32.5	26.1	22.9	22.2	17.4	19.6	1.7	54.4
1945	51.0	48.1	31.1	24.9	24.0	22.9	1.7	54.8
1945	46.3	46.6	22.6	31.9	20.5	23.9	−2.3	62.8
1946	59.6	50.3	26.3	39.4	25.9	24.4	2.8	71.3
1974	73.4	55.9	31.9	46.7	29.7	26.7	10.9	74.6
1948	85.3	59.5	34.6	54.4	30.4	28.2	12.9	79.3
1949	91.2	59.2	34.2	53.0	29.6	28.5	13.8	84.3
1950	111.3	70.3	39.6	56.4	35.5	26.8	13.4	86.6
1951	122.5	80.6	42.2	61.2	37.6	26.8	14.4	88.9
1952	127.6	80.2	44.4	65.5	36.6	27.4	14.7	
1953	134.8	76.2	46.2	69.7	36.0	26.3	15.9	
1954	138.7	79.0	47.8	75.0	36.5	26.0	15.4	
1955	150.8	84.0	51.8	82.0	38.4	26.1	15.4	
1956	163.4	88.7	55.4	90.3	39.7	26.5	17.9	
1957	173.6	95.0	57.9	101.8	41.0	27.5	22.8	
1958	178.8	101.3	60.7	108.0	40.8	25.4	24.3	

SOURCE, BY COLUMN

(1) Cols. 2 plus 17.
(2) Sum of cols. 3 to 16.
(3) Table A-35, col. 1.
(4) Table A-36, col. 1 minus cols. 6 and 7.
(5) Table A-36, cols. 6 and 7.
(6) Table A-37, col. 1 minus cols. 6 and 7.
(7) Table A-37, cols. 6 and 7.

(8) Table A-53, col. 8.
(9) Table A-39, col. 1 minus Table A-5, col. 8.
(10) Table A-38, col. 1.
(11) Table A-41, col. 5 plus Table A-42, col. 1.
(12) Table A-40, col. 1.
(13) Table A-41, cols. 2, 3, 4, 6 plus Table A-43, col. 1.

(14) Table A-41, cols. 7 and 8.
(15) 1900–45, *Study of Saving*, Table W-1, col. 18; 1945–58, Table A-44, col. 1.
(16) Table A-45, col. 1.
(17) Table A-15, col. 10.

NOTE: Agricultural land includes forests.

TABLE A-6

NET STOCK OF MAIN TYPES OF TANGIBLE ASSETS, CONSTANT (1947–49) PRICES

(billions of dollars)

End of Year	Total		Structures			Producer Durables		Livestock (8)	Inventories (9)
	Military Included (1)	Excluded (2)	Residential (3)	Private Nonresidential (4)	Public Civilian (5)	Private (6)	Public (7)		
1900		313.9	75.6	59.6	9.5	20.9	.2	13.6	18.6
1912		463.5	109.6	93.1	21.0	38.1	.5	13.7	23.5
1922		587.0	138.2	111.1	28.2	49.6	.3	15.2	40.7
1929		778.8	200.0	138.5	44.5	60.4	.9	13.7	49.8
1933		743.0	192.4	134.6	56.3	51.9	1.0	15.0	38.2
1939		747.5	189.5	122.3	66.5	53.1	1.2	14.0	47.1
1945		760.6	184.5	111.7	69.6	62.1	4.5	15.1	58.3
1945	888.8	788.5	211.1	114.0	82.7	57.1	4.2	14.9	59.3
1946	897.0	812.7	213.2	116.3	81.6	63.0	3.6	14.3	65.2
1947	915.7	845.9	216.8	118.5	81.5	72.4	3.1	13.6	65.0
1948	941.5	882.7	222.7	121.4	82.3	82.0	2.8	13.4	69.6
1949	961.8	910.4	228.2	124.0	84.8	87.8	2.7	13.6	68.5
1950	995.1	949.8	236.5	127.2	87.9	94.0	2.7	14.0	72.4
1951	1,036.7	991.0	243.9	131.2	90.5	100.7	2.8	14.6	79.9
1952	1,073.8	1,022.4	251.2	135.2	93.5	106.4	3.0	14.8	82.8
1953	1,113.2	1,055.4	259.1	139.7	96.7	112.2	3.2	14.6	86.3
1954	1,146.6	1,086.4	267.2	144.4	100.7	116.3	3.4	14.8	86.7
1955	1,192.7	1,132.1	277.9	150.2	105.3	120.3	3.5	15.0	91.3
1956	1,236.2	1,175.0	287.3	155.8	110.0	126.1	3.7	14.7	94.3
1957	1,278.6	1,216.4	295.6	161.9	115.3	131.8	3.9	14.3	95.0
1958	1,308.0	1,244.4	303.9	166.9	121.9	133.3	4.0	14.9	95.0

(continued)

TABLE A-6 (concluded)

End of Year	Consumer Durables (10)	Private Land Agricultural (11)	Residential (12)	Nonresidential (13)	Public Land (14)	Monetary Metals (15)	Net Foreign Assets (16)	Military Assets (17)
1900	21.7	45.9	19.0	22.4	11.5	2.3	−6.9	
1912	32.7	58.6	27.2	29.8	16.9	3.7	−4.8	
1922	37.8	58.2	34.0	33.6	21.1	7.1	12.0	
1929	57.3	57.2	50.0	54.7	26.2	7.5	18.2	
1933	49.8	56.3	48.1	42.0	34.1	7.3	15.8	
1939	57.6	53.1	47.1	39.0	35.0	19.0	3.1	
1945	61.3	58.1	43.1	33.3	35.5	22.3	1.2	
1945	57.5	60.2	31.3	47.7	29.5	21.7	−2.7	100.3
1946	64.7	57.4	31.5	48.6	28.2	22.2	3.0	84.2
1947	73.8	56.8	32.0	48.6	28.7	24.5	10.6	69.8
1948	82.2	55.8	32.8	50.1	29.4	26.0	12.2	58.9
1949	90.4	56.1	33.6	51.2	30.3	26.2	12.9	51.4
1950	102.9	57.5	34.8	51.7	31.3	24.5	12.0	46.0
1951	110.2	57.9	35.9	53.5	33.2	24.5	12.3	45.6
1952	115.8	57.4	36.9	54.5	33.3	25.0	12.5	51.4
1953	123.3	56.9	38.0	55.6	32.6	23.9	13.4	57.9
1954	129.8	57.1	39.1	57.1	33.2	23.6	12.8	60.2
1955	141.3	56.9	40.7	58.9	34.4	23.6	12.5	60.6
1956	149.5	57.7	42.1	61.0	34.0	23.9	14.5	61.2
1957	156.3	58.4	43.4	63.0	34.5	24.8	18.0	62.2
1958	159.7	59.8	44.6	64.6	34.2	22.7	18.9	63.6

SOURCE: Same as for Table A-5, using figures in constant (1947–49) prices, except for col. 17, for which the source is Table A-16 col. 10.
NOTE: Agricultural land includes forests.

TABLE A-7

Gross Stock of Main Types of Tangible Assets, Current Prices

(billions of dollars)

End of Year	Total		Structures			Producer Durables		Livestock (8)	Inventories (9)
	Military Included (1)	Excluded (2)	Residential (3)	Private Nonresidential (4)	Public Civilian (5)	Private (6)	Public (7)		
1945	1,068.1	917.8	261.8	168.5	91.7	85.9	6.2	9.7	42.9
1946	1,298.0	1,112.7	308.4	212.1	115.6	100.4	7.2	11.9	56.3
1947	1,524.8	1,328.2	374.6	247.5	139.5	120.3	8.0	13.3	66.7
1948	1,653.5	1,457.0	404.6	268.5	153.6	139.4	7.4	14.4	71.6
1949	1,633.3	1,460.8	400.2	267.5	149.0	154.1	5.7	12.9	66.7
1950	1,837.1	1,659.7	459.2	296.8	166.7	175.6	5.7	17.1	79.4
1951	1,982.8	1,796.5	488.8	316.0	179.2	196.9	5.8	19.5	90.9
1952	2,069.0	1,878.1	513.3	330.2	194.1	210.9	6.2	14.8	92.1
1953	2,141.8	1,952.3	531.5	345.2	200.5	227.1	6.7	11.8	96.0
1954	2,208.7	2,025.0	548.7	356.8	209.9	240.4	7.2	11.2	95.9
1955	2,361.8	2,169.1	591.5	380.4	225.7	254.3	8.0	10.7	102.6
1956	2,558.9	2,341.6	627.9	405.8	246.0	286.2	9.2	11.1	111.2
1957	2,741.1	2,508.9	653.1	446.2	260.3	309.9	10.4	14.1	112.7
1958	2,862.1	2,635.8	684.1	466.3	274.0	326.2	11.0	18.1	111.8

(continued)

TABLE A-7 (concluded)

| End of Year | Consumer Durables (10) | Private Land | | | | Monetary Metals (15) | Net Foreign Assets (16) | Military Assets (17) |
		Agricultural (11)	Residential (12)	Nonresidential (13)	Public Land (14)			
1945	108.0	46.6	22.6	31.9	20.5	23.9	−2.3	150.2
1946	131.7	50.3	26.3	39.4	25.9	24.4	2.8	185.3
1947	156.5	55.9	31.9	46.7	29.7	26.7	10.9	196.6
1948	177.5	59.5	34.6	54.4	30.4	28.2	12.9	196.5
1949	186.4	59.2	34.2	53.0	29.6	28.5	13.8	172.5
1950	217.2	70.3	39.6	56.4	35.5	26.8	13.4	177.4
1951	236.6	80.6	42.2	61.2	37.6	26.8	14.4	186.3
1952	247.7	80.2	44.4	65.5	36.6	27.4	14.7	190.9
1953	263.2	76.2	46.2	69.7	36.0	26.3	15.9	189.5
1954	275.1	79.0	47.8	75.0	36.5	26.0	15.5	183.7
1955	298.2	84.0	51.8	82.0	38.4	26.1	15.4	192.7
1956	325.7	88.7	55.4	90.3	39.7	26.5	17.9	217.3
1957	356.6	95.0	57.8	101.8	41.0	27.5	22.8	231.9
1958	383.8	101.3	60.7	108.0	40.8	25.4	24.3	226.3

SOURCE, BY COLUMN

(1) Col. 2 plus Table A-17, col. 10.
(2) Sum of cols. 2 to 16.
(3) Table A-46, col. 1.
(4) Table A-47, col. 1 minus cols. 6 and 7.
(5) Table A-47, cols. 6 and 7.
(6) Table A-48, col. 1, minus cols. 6 and 7.

(7) Table A-48, cols. 6 and 7.
(8) Table A-5, col. 8.
(9) Table A-5, col. 9.
(10) Table A-49, col. 1.
(11) Table A-5, col. 11.
(12) Table A-5, col. 12.

(13) Table A-5, col. 13.
(14) Table A-5, col. 14.
(15) Table A-5, col. 15.
(16) Table A-5, col. 16.
(17) Table A-17, col. 10.

NOTE: Agricultural land includes forests.

TABLE A-8

Gross Stock of Main Types of Tangible Assets, Constant (1947–49) Prices
(billions of dollars)

| End of Year | Total | | Structures | | | Producer Durables | | Livestock | Inventories |
	Military Included (1)	Excluded (2)	Residential (3)	Private Nonresidential (4)	Public Civilian (5)	Private (6)	Public (7)	(8)	(9)
1945	1,470.6	1,262.5	362.6	246.3	137.4	109.6	7.9	14.9	59.3
1946	1,503.4	1,293.2	368.2	249.3	138.6	113.9	8.2	14.3	65.2
1947	1,538.2	1,335.8	375.1	251.1	140.3	123.3	8.2	13.6	65.0
1948	1,571.2	1,387.4	384.7	254.7	143.5	135.1	7.2	13.4	69.6
1949	1,588.8	1,425.3	393.8	258.2	148.1	144.1	5.4	13.6	68.5
1950	1,630.3	1,478.3	405.8	261.3	153.2	154.7	5.1	14.0	72.4
1951	1,688.6	1,533.5	417.2	265.7	157.6	164.9	5.0	14.6	79.9
1952	1,736.2	1,579.1	427.9	269.2	162.6	174.8	5.3	14.8	82.8
1953	1,784.3	1,631.0	439.5	273.9	167.8	184.8	5.6	14.6	86.3
1954	1,829.4	1,682.0	451.5	279.7	173.5	192.7	5.9	14.8	86.7
1955	1,896.2	1,749.4	466.3	286.7	180.1	201.1	6.2	15.0	91.3
1956	1,968.6	1,813.1	479.9	293.3	186.4	209.7	6.7	14.7	94.3
1957	2,037.8	1,880.4	492.7	299.6	192.2	217.8	7.3	14.3	95.0
1958	2,089.2	1,937.0	505.8	306.3	199.0	224.1	7.6	15.0	95.0

(continued)

123

TABLE A-8 (concluded)

| End of Year | Consumer Durables (10) | Private Land | | | Public Land (14) | Monetary Metals (15) | Net Foreign Assets (16) | Military Assets (17) |
		Agricultural (11)	Residential (12)	Nonresidential (13)				
1945	137.2	60.2	31.3	47.7	29.5	21.7	−2.7	208.1
1946	145.3	57.4	31.5	48.6	28.2	22.2	3.0	210.2
1947	158.1	56.8	32.0	48.6	28.7	24.5	10.6	202.4
1948	172.9	55.8	32.8	50.1	29.4	26.0	12.2	183.8
1949	183.4	56.1	33.6	51.2	30.3	26.2	12.9	163.6
1950	200.1	57.5	34.8	51.7	31.3	24.5	12.0	152.1
1951	211.4	57.9	35.9	53.5	33.2	24.5	12.3	155.1
1952	222.3	57.4	36.9	54.5	33.3	25.0	12.5	157.0
1953	238.3	56.9	38.0	55.6	32.6	23.9	13.4	153.3
1954	254.3	57.1	39.1	57.1	33.2	23.6	12.8	147.4
1955	275.8	56.9	40.7	58.9	34.4	23.6	12.5	146.9
1956	295.0	57.7	42.1	61.0	34.0	23.9	14.5	155.5
1957	319.3	58.4	43.4	63.0	34.5	24.8	18.0	157.4
1958	339.6	59.8	44.6	64.6	34.2	22.7	18.9	152.1

SOURCE: Same as for Table A-7, using figures in constant (1947–49) prices, except that Table A-6 is used rather than Table A-5, and Table A-18 instead of Table A-17.

NOTE: Agricultural land includes forests.

TABLE A-9

Percentage Distribution of Net Stock of Tangible Assets, Current Prices

	Total		Structures			Producer Durables			
	Military								
End of Year	Included (1)	Excluded (2)	Residential (3)	Private Nonresidential (4)	Public Civilian (5)	Private (6)	Public (7)	Livestock (8)	Inventories (9)
1900		100.00	19.88	17.70	2.30	7.34	0.08	3.56	7.80
1912		100.00	17.16	17.14	3.56	8.20	0.10	3.42	6.68
1922		100.00	18.90	16.70	4.64	9.18	0.05	1.61	8.13
1929		100.00	21.84	16.07	5.32	8.60	0.13	1.48	7.16
1933		100.00	22.49	17.86	7.93	8.66	0.18	0.96	5.67
1939		100.00	23.05	16.06	8.53	8.45	0.20	1.30	6.40
1945		100.00	23.42	14.16	8.89	8.18	0.60	1.71	7.45
1945	112.62	100.00	26.46	13.52	9.60	7.87	0.57	1.69	7.45
1946	110.63	100.00	25.47	14.12	9.68	7.90	0.45	1.70	8.03
1947	108.08	100.00	25.69	13.85	9.61	8.38	0.36	1.57	7.91
1948	106.81	100.00	25.23	13.78	9.41	9.12	0.31	1.55	7.71
1949	105.83	100.00	24.84	13.78	9.24	10.09	0.31	1.38	7.16
1950	105.10	100.00	25.06	13.53	8.95	10.03	0.28	1.60	7.44
1951	104.71	100.00	24.55	13.41	8.86	10.34	0.28	1.68	7.80
1952	105.17	100.00	24.85	13.64	9.18	10.58	0.29	1.22	7.59
1953	105.66	100.00	24.90	13.98	9.22	10.88	0.31	0.93	7.62
1954	105.71	100.00	24.86	14.08	9.38	11.12	0.32	0.86	7.34
1955	105.66	100.00	25.07	14.21	9.49	10.85	0.33	0.76	7.32
1956	105.55	100.00	24.73	14.19	9.60	11.36	0.33	0.73	7.32
1957	105.31	100.00	24.05	14.80	9.63	11.51	0.34	0.86	6.92
1958	105.22	100.00	24.13	14.93	9.88	11.41	0.34	1.06	6.57

(continued)

TABLE A-9 (concluded)

End of Year	Consumer Durables (10)	Private Land Agricultural (11)	Private Land Residential (12)	Private Land Nonresidential (13)	Public Land (14)	Monetary Metals (15)	Net Foreign Assets (16)	Military Assets (17)
1900	6.90	18.29	5.00	7.39	4.56	1.87	−2.67	
1912	8.23	20.32	4.24	6.16	4.54	1.53	1.27	
1922	9.26	13.47	4.61	5.91	3.77	1.31	2.45	
1929	9.62	8.66	5.48	8.23	3.48	1.10	2.82	
1933	7.79	7.57	5.65	6.68	4.66	1.44	2.45	
1939	8.22	6.61	5.78	5.60	4.40	4.96	0.44	
1945	8.93	8.43	5.45	4.36	4.20	4.01	0.18	
1945	8.03	8.08	3.92	5.53	3.56	4.15	−0.40	12.62
1946	8.51	7.18	3.75	5.62	3.70	3.48	0.40	10.63
1947	8.70	6.63	3.78	5.53	3.52	3.16	1.30	8.08
1948	9.19	6.41	3.73	5.86	3.27	3.04	1.39	6.81
1949	9.79	6.35	3.67	5.69	3.18	3.05	1.48	5.83
1950	10.43	6.59	3.71	5.29	3.33	2.51	1.25	5.10
1951	10.51	6.92	3.62	5.26	3.23	2.30	1.24	4.71
1952	10.51	6.61	3.66	5.39	3.01	2.26	1.21	5.17
1953	10.70	6.05	3.67	5.53	2.86	2.09	1.27	5.66
1954	10.62	6.02	3.66	5.77	2.79	1.99	1.18	5.71
1955	10.75	5.99	3.69	5.85	2.74	1.86	1.10	5.66
1956	10.76	5.84	3.65	5.95	2.61	1.74	1.18	5.55
1957	10.65	5.83	3.55	6.25	2.52	1.69	1.40	5.31
1958	10.50	5.95	3.57	6.35	2.40	1.49	1.43	5.22

SOURCE: Based on figures shown in Table A-5; col. 2 equals 100 per cent.   NOTE: Agricultural land includes forests.

126

TABLE A-10

PERCENTAGE DISTRIBUTION OF NET STOCK OF TANGIBLE ASSETS, CONSTANT (1947–49) PRICES

End of Year	Total		Structures			Producer Durables		Livestock	Inventories
	Military Included (1)	Military Excluded (2)	Residential (3)	Private Nonresidential (4)	Public Civilian (5)	Private (6)	Public (7)	(8)	(9)
1900		100.00	23.85	19.05	3.04	6.68	0.07	4.34	5.96
1912		100.00	23.64	20.09	4.52	8.21	0.11	2.95	5.07
1922		100.00	23.55	18.92	8.44	8.44	0.04	2.59	6.93
1929		100.00	25.68	17.78	5.72	7.75	0.12	1.76	6.40
1933		100.00	25.90	18.12	18.12	6.99	0.15	2.02	5.14
1939		100.00	25.35	16.36	8.90	7.10	0.17	1.87	6.30
1945		100.00	23.42	14.18	8.84	7.88	0.58	1.92	7.41
1945	112.72	100.00	26.77	14.46	10.49	7.24	0.56	1.89	7.52
1946	110.36	100.00	26.23	14.31	10.04	7.75	0.44	1.70	8.02
1947	108.25	100.00	25.60	13.99	9.61	8.56	0.51	1.60	7.67
1948	106.67	100.00	26.23	13.75	9.33	9.20	0.32	1.52	7.88
1949	105.65	100.00	25.07	13.62	9.31	9.64	0.30	1.49	7.52
1950	104.85	100.00	24.92	13.43	9.25	9.90	0.28	1.48	7.63
1951	104.60	100.00	24.61	13.24	9.18	10.13	0.28	1.47	8.06
1952	105.03	100.00	24.57	13.22	9.15	10.41	0.29	1.45	8.10
1953	105.49	100.00	24.56	13.24	9.13	10.63	0.30	1.38	8.18
1954	105.54	100.00	24.59	13.29	9.27	10.72	0.31	1.36	7.98
1955	105.35	100.00	24.55	13.27	9.30	10.62	0.31	1.32	8.06
1956	105.21	100.00	24.46	13.26	9.36	10.74	0.32	1.25	8.03
1957	105.11	100.00	24.31	13.31	8.48	10.84	0.32	1.18	7.81
1958	105.11	100.00	24.42	13.41	9.80	10.71	0.32	1.20	7.63

(continued)

TABLE A-10 (concluded)

| End of Year | Consumer Durables (10) | Private Land | | | Public Land (14) | Monetary Metals (15) | Net Foreign Assets (16) | Military Assets (17) |
		Agricultural (11)	Residential (12)	Nonresidential (13)				
1900	3.67	14.67	6.07	7.16	6.93	0.72	2.21	
1912	3.65	12.63	5.87	6.42	7.06	0.79	1.03	
1922	3.60	9.92	5.80	5.72	6.43	1.20	2.05	
1929	3.36	7.34	6.43	7.02	7.36	0.96	2.33	
1933	4.59	7.57	6.47	5.66	6.71	0.99	2.13	
1939	4.68	7.10	6.30	5.21	7.71	2.54	0.41	
1945	4.51	10.82	5.47	4.23	7.78	2.83	0.15	
1945	7.29	7.63	3.96	4.80	3.74	2.76	−0.34	12.72
1946	7.96	7.06	3.88	5.98	3.47	2.73	0.37	10.36
1947	8.71	6.71	3.77	4.53	3.39	2.89	1.25	8.25
1948	9.31	6.32	3.72	5.69	3.32	2.95	1.38	6.67
1949	9.98	6.16	3.69	5.02	3.33	2.88	1.42	5.65
1950	10.84	6.06	3.62	5.45	3.30	2.58	1.26	4.85
1951	11.12	5.84	3.62	5.46	3.35	2.47	1.24	4.60
1952	11.33	5.61	3.61	5.33	3.26	2.45	1.22	5.03
1953	11.68	5.39	3.60	5.27	3.09	2.26	1.27	5.49
1954	11.96	5.26	3.60	5.26	3.06	2.17	1.18	5.54
1955	12.48	5.03	3.60	5.20	3.04	2.08	1.10	5.35
1956	12.73	4.91	3.58	5.19	2.89	2.03	1.23	5.21
1957	12.85	4.80	3.57	5.18	2.84	2.04	1.48	5.11
1958	12.83	4.81	3.58	5.19	2.75	1.82	1.52	5.11

SOURCE: Based on figures in Table A-6. NOTE: Agricultural land includes forests.

TABLE A-11

PERCENTAGE DISTRIBUTION OF GROSS STOCK OF TANGIBLE ASSETS, CURRENT PRICES

| End of Year | Total | | Structures | | | Producer Durables | | Livestock | Inventories |
	Military Included (1)	Excluded (2)	Residential (3)	Private Nonresidential (4)	Public Civilian (5)	Private (6)	Public (7)	(8)	(9)
1945	116.37	100.00	28.52	18.36	10.00	9.36	0.67	1.06	4.67
1946	116.65	100.00	27.72	19.07	10.39	9.02	0.64	1.07	5.06
1947	114.80	100.00	28.21	18.63	10.51	9.06	0.60	1.00	5.02
1948	113.49	100.00	27.77	18.43	10.54	9.57	0.51	0.99	4.91
1949	111.81	100.00	27.40	18.31	10.20	10.55	0.39	0.88	4.57
1950	110.69	100.00	27.66	17.88	10.00	10.58	0.34	1.03	4.79
1951	110.37	100.00	27.21	17.59	9.97	10.96	0.33	1.09	5.06
1952	110.16	100.00	27.33	17.58	10.34	11.23	0.33	0.79	4.90
1953	109.71	100.00	27.23	17.68	10.27	11.63	0.34	0.61	4.92
1954	109.07	100.00	27.10	17.62	10.37	11.87	0.36	0.55	4.74
1955	108.89	100.00	27.27	17.54	10.40	11.72	0.37	0.49	4.73
1956	109.28	100.00	26.82	17.33	10.51	12.22	0.39	0.48	4.75
1957	109.24	100.00	26.03	17.79	10.37	12.35	0.41	0.56	4.49
1958	108.58	100.00	25.96	17.69	10.40	12.37	0.42	0.69	4.24

(continued)

TABLE A-11 (concluded)

End of Year	Consumer Durables (10)	Private Land Agricultural (11)	Residential (12)	Nonresidential (13)	Public Land (14)	Monetary Metals (15)	Net Foreign Assets (16)	Military Assets (17)
1945	11.77	5.75	2.46	2.60	2.23	2.79	−0.25	16.37
1946	11.83	5.16	2.36	2.19	2.33	2.90	0.25	16.65
1947	11.78	4.91	2.40	2.01	2.24	2.81	0.82	14.80
1948	12.18	4.96	2.38	1.94	2.09	2.85	0.89	13.49
1949	12.76	4.87	2.34	1.95	2.03	2.81	0.94	11.81
1950	13.09	4.99	2.38	1.61	2.14	2.65	0.81	10.69
1951	13.17	5.28	2.35	1.49	2.09	2.61	0.80	10.37
1952	13.19	5.05	2.37	1.46	1.95	2.71	0.78	10.16
1953	13.48	4.74	2.37	1.35	1.84	2.73	0.82	9.71
1954	13.58	4.74	2.36	1.29	1.80	2.87	0.76	9.07
1955	13.75	4.70	2.39	1.20	1.77	2.95	0.71	8.89
1956	13.91	4.60	2.37	1.13	1.70	3.05	0.76	9.28
1957	14.21	4.61	2.30	1.09	1.63	3.23	0.91	9.24
1958	14.56	4.60	2.30	0.96	1.55	3.34	0.92	8.58

SOURCE: Based on figures shown in Table A-7.   NOTE: Agricultural land includes forests.

TABLE A-12

PERCENTAGE DISTRIBUTION OF GROSS STOCK OF TANGIBLE ASSETS, CONSTANT (1947–49) PRICES

End of Year	Total		Structures			Producer Durables		Livestock	Inventories
	Military Included (1)	Excluded (2)	Residential (3)	Private Nonresidential (4)	Public Civilian (5)	Private (6)	Public (7)	(8)	(9)
1945	116.48	100.00	28.71	19.50	10.88	8.68	0.63	1.18	4.70
1946	116.26	100.00	28.46	19.27	10.71	8.81	0.63	1.10	5.04
1947	115.15	100.00	28.08	18.80	10.50	9.23	0.61	1.02	4.87
1948	113.25	100.00	27.63	18.36	10.34	9.74	0.52	0.97	5.02
1949	111.48	100.00	27.63	18.11	10.39	10.11	0.38	0.95	4.81
1950	110.29	100.00	27.45	17.68	10.36	10.46	0.34	0.95	4.90
1951	110.11	100.00	27.20	17.33	10.28	10.75	0.32	0.95	5.21
1952	109.94	100.00	27.10	17.05	10.30	11.07	0.33	0.93	5.24
1953	109.40	100.00	26.95	16.79	10.28	11.33	0.35	0.90	5.29
1954	108.76	100.00	26.84	16.63	10.31	11.46	0.35	0.88	5.16
1955	108.39	100.00	26.65	16.38	10.29	11.49	0.35	0.86	5.22
1956	108.58	100.00	26.47	16.18	10.28	11.56	0.37	0.81	5.20
1957	108.37	100.00	26.20	15.93	10.22	11.58	0.39	0.76	5.05
1958	107.85	100.00	26.11	15.81	10.27	11.57	0.39	0.77	4.90

(continued)

131

TABLE A-12 (concluded)

| End of Year | Consumer Durables (10) | Private Land | | | Public Land (14) | Monetary Metals (15) | Net Foreign Assets (16) | Military Assets (17) |
		Agricultural (11)	Residential (12)	Nonresidential (13)				
1945	10.87	4.77	2.48	3.78	2.34	1.72	−0.21	16.48
1946	11.23	4.44	2.43	3.76	2.18	1.72	0.23	16.26
1947	11.84	4.25	2.39	3.64	2.15	1.83	0.80	15.15
1948	12.46	4.02	2.37	3.61	2.12	1.87	0.88	13.25
1949	12.87	3.94	2.36	3.59	2.13	1.84	0.90	11.48
1950	13.53	3.89	2.36	3.50	2.12	1.66	0.81	10.29
1951	13.78	3.78	2.34	3.49	2.16	1.60	0.80	10.11
1952	14.08	3.63	3.33	3.45	2.11	1.58	0.79	9.94
1953	14.61	3.49	2.33	3.41	2.00	1.46	0.82	9.40
1954	15.12	3.39	2.36	3.39	1.97	1.40	0.76	8.76
1955	15.76	3.25	2.33	3.37	1.97	1.35	0.71	8.39
1956	16.27	3.18	2.32	3.36	1.88	1.32	0.80	8.58
1957	16.98	3.11	2.31	3.35	1.83	1.32	0.96	8.37
1958	17.53	3.09	2.30	3.34	1.77	1.17	0.97	7.85

SOURCE: Based on figures shown in Table A-8.   NOTE: Agricultural land includes forests.

TABLE A-13

ANNUAL PERCENTAGE RATES OF CHANGE IN MAIN COMPONENTS OF NET STOCK OF TANGIBLE ASSETS, CONSTANT (1947–49) PRICES

Year or Period	Total		Structures			Producer Durables		Livestock (8)	Inventories (9)
	Military		Residential (3)	Private Nonresidential (4)	Public Civilian (5)	Private (6)	Public (7)		
	Included (1)	Excluded (2)							
1912a	—	3.33	3.26	3.80	6.82	5.13	6.90	0.07	1.95
1922	—	2.40	2.58	1.77	3.01	2.74	−7.19	1.03	5.95
1929	—	4.12	5.42	3.20	6.72	3.09	20.27	−1.47	2.93
1933	—	−1.24	−0.55	−0.71	6.03	−3.83	4.37	2.32	−6.89
1939	—	0.14	−0.48	−1.41	4.49	0.36	2.32	−1.21	3.79
1945	—	0.30	−0.45	−1.56	0.76	2.64	24.15	1.32	3.80
1946	0.96	3.12	1.01	2.02	−1.33	10.33	−14.29	−4.03	9.95
1947	2.09	4.09	1.02	1.89	−0.12	14.92	−13.89	−4.90	−0.31
1948	2.82	4.34	1.03	2.45	0.98	13.26	−9.68	−1.47	7.08
1949	2.15	3.15	1.02	2.14	3.04	7.07	−3.57	1.49	−1.58
1950	3.47	4.26	3.63	2.58	3.66	7.06	0.00	2.94	5.69
1951	4.17	4.38	3.13	3.14	2.96	7.13	3.70	4.29	10.36
1952	3.58	3.20	2.99	3.05	3.31	5.66	7.14	1.37	3.63
1953	3.67	3.25	3.14	3.33	3.42	5.45	6.67	−1.35	4.23
1954	3.00	2.94	3.13	3.36	4.14	3.65	6.25	1.37	0.46
1955	4.02	4.17	4.00	4.02	4.57	3.35	2.94	1.35	5.31
1956	3.65	3.80	3.38	3.73	4.46	4.91	5.71	−2.00	3.29
1957	3.47	3.55	2.89	3.91	4.82	4.52	5.41	−2.72	0.74
1958	2.26	2.21	2.81	3.09	5.72	1.14	2.56	4.20	0.00
1945–58b	3.02	3.58	2.55	2.98	3.05	6.80	1.96	1.80	3.90

(continued)

TABLE A-13 (concluded)

Year or Period	Consumer Durables (10)	Private Land Agricultural (11)	Private Land Residential (12)	Private Land Nonresidential (13)	Public Land (14)	Monetary Metals (15)	Net Foreign Assets (16)	Military Assets (17)
1912[a]	3.49	2.06	3.29	2.41	3.30	4.16	c	—
1922	1.44	-0.05	2.35	1.22	2.24	6.67	c	—
1929	6.14	-0.49	5.66	7.20	3.26	0.89	6.11	—
1933	-4.18	-0.42	-1.00	-6.79	6.88	-0.64	-3.78	—
1939	3.05	-1.19	0.36	-1.28	0.39	17.30	-31.86	—
1945	1.03	1.52	-1.50	-2.65	0.49	2.65	-16.82	—
1946	12.52	-4.65	0.70	1.89	-4.41	2.16	c	-16.05
1947	14.06	-1.05	1.56	0.00	1.77	10.13	257.91	-17.10
1948	11.38	-1.76	2.72	3.09	2.44	6.17	14.49	-15.62
1949	9.98	-0.54	2.41	2.20	3.06	0.81	5.67	-12.73
1950	13.83	2.50	3.57	0.98	3.30	-6.46	6.92	-10.51
1951	7.09	0.70	2.99	3.48	6.07	0.04	3.01	-0.87
1952	5.08	-0.86	2.73	1.87	0.30	2.12	0.97	12.72
1953	6.48	-0.87	3.04	2.02	-2.10	-4.52	7.23	12.65
1954	5.27	0.35	3.06	2.70	1.84	-1.21	-3.97	3.97
1955	8.86	-0.35	4.11	3.15	3.61	0.00	-2.50	0.66
1956	5.80	1.41	3.41	3.57	-1.16	1.40	16.16	0.99
1957	4.55	1.21	2.94	3.28	1.47	3.76	23.76	1.63
1958	2.18	2.40	2.74	2.54	-0.87	-8.47	5.01	2.25
1945-58[b]	8.24	0.21	2.77	2.37	1.18	0.46	25.74	-4.88

SOURCE: Computed from figures shown in Table A-6.
NOTE: Agricultural land includes forests.
[a] From 1900 through 1912, calculated from value at beginning and end of period (except for last line, which is the average of annual rates of change).
[b] Average of annual rates of change.
c Negative balance in one year.

134

TABLE A-14

ANNUAL PERCENTAGE RATES OF CHANGE IN MAIN COMPONENTS OF GROSS STOCK OF TANGIBLE ASSETS, CONSTANT (1947–49) PRICES

| Year | Total | | Structures | | | Producer Durables | | Livestock (8) | Inventories (9) |
	Military Included (1)	Excluded (2)	Residential (3)	Private Nonresidential (4)	Public Civilian (5)	Private (6)	Public (7)		
1946	2.26	2.46	1.52	1.22	0.87	3.97	3.28	−4.03	3.95
1947	2.27	3.24	1.89	0.73	1.23	8.20	0.37	−4.90	−0.31
1948	2.15	3.29	2.56	1.45	2.27	9.58	−12.30	−1.47	7.08
1949	1.12	2.73	2.37	1.34	3.23	6.66	−25.42	1.49	−1.58
1950	2.61	3.72	3.04	0.84	3.44	7.34	−6.15	2.94	5.69
1951	3.58	3.74	2.80	1.70	2.90	6.63	−1.59	4.29	10.36
1952	2.82	2.97	2.57	1.31	3.14	6.01	5.85	1.37	3.63
1953	2.77	3.29	2.71	1.72	3.17	5.70	6.67	−1.35	4.23
1954	2.53	3.14	2.73	2.13	3.43	4.29	5.36	1.37	0.46
1955	3.65	4.02	3.27	2.55	3.79	4.35	5.08	1.35	5.31
1956	3.82	3.65	2.93	2.27	3.50	4.26	8.39	−2.00	3.29
1957	3.52	3.72	2.67	2.11	3.13	3.90	8.04	−2.72	0.74
1958	2.52	3.00	2.66	2.24	3.53	2.90	4.13	4.20	0.00

(continued)

135

TABLE A-14 (concluded)

Year	Consumer Durables (10)	Private Land Agricultural (11)	Residential (12)	Nonresidential (13)	Public Land (14)	Monetary Metals (15)	Net Foreign Assets (16)	Military Assets (17)
1946	5.84	-4.65	0.70	1.89	-4.41	2.16	a	1.05
1947	8.87	-1.05	1.56	0.00	1.77	10.13	257.91	-3.72
1948	9.35	-1.76	2.72	3.09	2.44	6.17	14.49	-9.18
1949	6.07	0.54	2.41	2.20	3.06	0.81	5.67	-11.02
1950	9.08	2.50	3.57	0.98	3.30	-6.46	6.92	-7.04
1951	5.65	0.70	2.99	3.48	6.07	0.04	3.01	1.97
1952	5.19	-0.86	2.73	1.87	0.30	2.12	0.97	1.28
1953	7.20	-0.87	3.04	2.02	-2.10	-4.52	7.23	-2.36
1954	-6.68	0.35	3.06	2.70	1.84	-1.21	-3.97	-3.85
1955	8.49	-0.35	4.11	3.15	3.61	0.00	-2.50	-0.39
1956	6.93	1.41	3.41	3.57	-1.16	1.40	16.16	5.88
1957	8.26	1.21	2.94	3.28	1.47	3.76	23.76	1.26
1958	6.34	2.40	2.74	2.54	-0.87	-8.47	5.01	-3.37

SOURCE: Computed from figures shown in Table A-8.

NOTE: Agricultural land includes forests.

a Increased from $-2.7 billion in 1945 to $3.0 billion in 1946.

TABLE A-15

TOTAL NET TANGIBLE WEALTH, BY SECTOR, CURRENT PRICES

(billions of dollars)

End of Year	All Sectors		Nonfarm Households (3)	Nonprofit Organizations (4)	Agriculture (5)	Unincorporated Business (6)	Corporations (7)
	Excluding Military (1)	Including Military (2)					
1900	87.9		28.0	1.5	24.5	7.2	21.9
1912	165.4		46.3	2.7	49.7	11.2	42.2
1922	334.5		100.7	5.2	69.5	24.8	94.0
1929	439.4		150.7	7.3	64.4	36.4	125.0
1933	330.5		109.3	6.2	41.0	25.0	94.8
1939	396.8		132.0	6.9	45.7	30.2	107.2
1945	571.4		191.9	8.1	86.3	41.9	138.9
1945	576.2	648.9	194.5	9.2	86.7	39.0	142.8
1946	700.9	775.4	231.3	12.3	99.0	49.4	184.0
1947	843.5	911.7	282.2	15.3	112.2	58.9	223.8
1948	928.4	991.7	311.5	16.6	119.1	65.6	254.4
1949	932.0	986.3	313.2	16.7	117.6	65.4	257.6
1950	1,067.1	1,121.5	368.2	18.8	136.3	73.8	296.2
1951	1,164.7	1,219.6	397.1	20.5	153.2	79.1	331.0
1952	1,214.3	1,277.1	419.8	22.3	150.7	81.0	347.9
1953	1,259.3	1,330.6	439.4	23.7	145.1	84.0	367.1
1954	1,306.4	1,381.1	458.4	25.5	147.8	86.5	380.7
1955	1,401.9	1,481.2	501.1	27.7	150.6	93.0	409.4
1956	1,518.1	1,602.4	541.9	30.3	158.4	99.8	452.5
1957	1,629.8	1,716.4	573.8	33.1	168.0	105.8	499.6
1958	1,702.8	1,791.7	602.6	35.8	182.6	108.6	510.7

(continued)

TABLE A-15 (concluded)

End of Year	State and Local Governments (8)	Federal Government Civilian (9)	Federal Government Military (10)	Total Government Excluding Military (11)	Total Government Including Military (12)	Total Private (13)	Net Foreign Assets (14)
1900	4.7	2.5		7.1		80.8	−2.3
1912	11.5	4.0		15.5		150.0	−2.1
1922	24.3	7.8		32.1		302.4	8.2
1929	34.3	8.9		43.2		396.2	12.4
1933	36.6	9.5		46.0		284.5	8.1
1939	42.0	31.1		73.1		323.6	1.7
1945	54.3	49.0		103.3		469.1	1.1
1945	57.3	46.7	72.7	104.1	176.8	472.2	[a]
1946	71.8	53.6	74.5	125.4	200.0	575.5	
1947	84.7	66.4	68.1	151.2	219.3	692.3	
1948	89.8	71.4	63.3	161.2	224.5	767.2	
1949	88.0	73.7	54.3	161.6	215.9	770.5	
1950	99.2	74.6	54.4	173.8	228.2	893.3	
1951	106.8	77.1	54.8	183.8	238.6	980.9	
1952	113.9	78.7	62.8	192.5	255.2	1,021.8	
1953	118.6	81.3	71.3	199.9	271.2	1,059.4	
1954	124.7	82.9	74.6	207.6	282.2	1,098.8	
1955	135.7	84.2	79.3	220.0	299.2	1,182.0	
1956	149.3	85.9	84.3	235.2	319.5	1,282.9	
1957	161.2	88.3	86.6	249.5	336.1	1,380.3	
1958	172.7	89.8	88.9	262.6	351.4	1,440.3	

SOURCE, BY COLUMN

(1) Sum of cols. 3 to 9.
(2) Col. 1 plus col. 10.
(3) Table A-50, col. 1.
(4) Table A-51, col. 1.
(5) Table A-53, col. 1.
(6) Table A-52, col. 1.
(7) Table A-54, col. 1.
(8) Table A-55, col. 1.
(9) Table A-56, col. 1.
(10) Table B-172, col. 6.
(11) Cols. 8 and 9.
(12) Cols. 10 and 11.
(13) Sum of cols. 3 to 7.
Includes col. 14 for 1900–45.
(14) Table A-45, col. 1.

a Allocated among sectors (for amounts, see Table A-5).

TABLE A-16

Total Net Tangible Wealth, by Sector, Constant (1947–49) Prices

(billions of dollars)

End of Year	All Sectors		Nonfarm Households (3)	Nonprofit Organizations (4)	Agriculture (5)	Unincorporated Business (6)	Corporations (7)
	Excluding Military (1)	Including Military (2)					
1900	314.6		113.6	5.9	79.9	23.7	75.9
1912	464.7		158.5	9.4	103.1	32.1	125.1
1922	588.2		192.0	10.6	108.3	44.0	165.7
1929	778.0		279.1	13.9	107.3	64.2	217.6
1933	742.2		261.5	14.2	102.8	54.0	196.4
1939	748.4		261.2	12.8	98.6	55.5	192.1
1945	748.4		258.1	11.1	110.2	57.5	190.4
1945	788.4	888.7	262.1	15.3	112.9	56.6	200.2
1946	812.9	897.1	270.6	15.3	111.3	58.3	216.2
1947	845.9	915.7	282.5	15.3	111.4	59.7	228.0
1948	882.6	941.5	296.4	15.6	114.9	61.9	240.1
1949	910.0	961.4	309.0	16.1	116.4	62.8	246.8
1950	949.1	995.1	329.4	16.9	121.2	65.0	258.1
1951	991.0	1,036.6	344.1	17.8	124.3	66.5	275.6
1952	1,022.3	1,073.7	357.6	18.5	125.4	67.0	286.6
1953	1,055.4	1,113.3	373.2	19.1	125.4	68.4	296.5
1954	1,086.3	1,146.5	389.1	20.1	126.5	69.3	302.8
1955	1,131.8	1,192.3	413.0	21.1	126.9	71.3	315.0
1956	1,174.6	1,235.8	432.2	22.0	127.0	73.4	331.2
1957	1,216.4	1,278.6	448.2	23.1	127.7	75.3	346.9
1958	1,244.5	1,308.1	461.2	24.3	131.5	75.9	348.8

(continued)

TABLE A-16 (concluded)

End of Year	State and Local Governments (8)	Federal Government Civilian (9)	Federal Government Military (10)	Total Government Excluding Military (11)	Total Government Including Military (12)	Total Private (13)	Net Foreign Assets (14)
1900	16.2	6.4		22.6		292.0	−6.9
1912	32.4	8.8		41.2		423.5	−4.8
1922	42.6	13.1		55.7		532.5	12.0
1929	62.6	15.2		77.8		700.2	18.2
1933	79.4	18.2		97.5		644.7	15.8
1939	83.2	42.0		125.2		623.2	3.1
1945	76.4	58.9		135.2		628.5	1.2
							[a]
1945	84.2	57.1	100.3	141.3	241.6	647.1	
1946	83.9	57.3	84.2	141.2	225.4	671.7	
1947	84.4	64.6	69.8	149.0	218.8	696.9	
1948	85.3	67.8	58.9	153.1	212.0	729.5	
1949	87.9	71.0	51.4	158.9	210.3	751.1	
1950	90.9	67.6	46.0	158.5	204.5	790.6	
1951	94.1	68.6	45.6	162.7	208.3	828.3	
1952	98.0	69.2	51.4	167.2	208.6	855.1	
1953	101.7	71.1	57.9	172.8	218.6	882.6	
1954	106.4	72.1	60.2	178.5	230.7	907.8	
1955	111.9	72.6	60.5	184.5	238.7	947.3	
1956	117.2	71.6	61.2	188.2	245.0	985.7	
1957	123.5	71.7	62.2	195.2	250.0	1,021.2	
1958	130.7	72.1	63.6	202.8	257.4	1,041.7	

SOURCE: Same as for Table A-15, using figures in constant (1947–49) prices, except that col. 10 data for 1945–58 are from col. 5 of Table B-172.

[a] Allocated among sectors (for amounts, see Table A-6).

TABLE A-17

TOTAL GROSS TANGIBLE WEALTH, BY SECTOR, CURRENT PRICES
(billions of dollars)

	All Sectors		Nonfarm Households	Nonprofit Organizations	Agriculture	Unincorporated Business	Corporations
End of Year	Excluding Military (1)	Including Military (2)	(3)	(4)	(5)	(6)	(7)
1945	917.9	1,068.1	336.2	17.6	115.5	61.2	243.7
1946	1,112.7	1,298.0	398.6	23.4	132.3	76.6	304.2
1947	1,328.3	1,524.9	482.7	29.2	151.9	91.2	358.1
1948	1,457.0	1,653.5	529.5	31.6	162.1	101.1	400.1
1949	1,460.7	1,633.1	532.0	31.2	161.9	101.6	406.0
1950	1,659.6	1,837.0	616.7	34.4	184.8	114.1	461.1
1951	1,796.6	1,932.9	661.8	36.7	205.9	122.9	506.0
1952	1,878.1	2,059.0	696.7	39.2	205.6	127.2	530.5
1953	1,952.0	2,141.7	728.6	41.3	202.4	132.6	559.0
1954	2,024.9	2,208.6	759.4	43.7	207.5	137.5	577.6
1955	2,169.0	2,361.7	823.6	46.9	213.8	147.7	619.7
1956	2,341.4	2,558.7	889.2	50.5	225.3	157.7	677.8
1957	2,509.1	2,741.0	946.6	54.1	238.1	168.2	742.8
1958	2,635.8	2,862.1	1,005.8	57.8	257.4	175.7	764.1

(continued)

TABLE A-17 (concluded)

End of Year	State and Local Governments (8)	Federal Government Civilian (9)	Federal Government Military (10)	Total Government Excluding Military (11)	Total Government Including Military (12)	Total Private (13)
1945	89.9	53.8	150.2	143.7	293.9	774.2
1946	114.1	63.5	185.3	177.6	362.8	935.1
1947	136.1	79.1	196.6	215.2	411.8	1,113.1
1948	147.9	84.7	196.5	232.6	429.1	1,224.4
1949	142.2	85.7	172.5	228.0	400.4	1,231.7
1950	160.5	88.0	177.4	248.5	425.9	1,411.1
1951	172.0	91.3	186.3	263.3	449.6	1,533.3
1952	184.3	94.5	190.9	278.8	469.7	1,599.3
1953	189.6	98.6	189.5	288.1	477.6	1,663.9
1954	198.2	101.0	183.7	299.3	483.0	1,725.6
1955	213.5	103.7	192.7	317.2	509.9	1,851.8
1956	234.2	106.8	217.3	341.0	558.3	2,000.4
1957	250.3	108.9	231.9	359.2	591.1	2,149.9
1958	265.5	109.5	226.3	375.0	601.3	2,260.8

SOURCE, BY COLUMN

(1) Sum of cols. 3 to 9.
(2) Cols. 1 and 10
(3) Table A-57, col. 1.
(4) Table A-58, col. 1.

(5) Table A-60, col. 1.
(6) Table A-59, col. 1.
(7) Table A-61, col. 1.

(8) Sum of cols. 3 to 9.
(9) Table A-62, col. 1.
(10) Table A-63, col. 1.
        Table B-172, col. 3.

(11) Cols. 8 and 9.
(12) Cols. 10 and 11.
(13) Sum of cols. 3 to 7.

TABLE A-18

TOTAL GROSS TANGIBLE WEALTH, BY SECTOR, CONSTANT (1947–49) PRICES
(billions of dollars)

| End of Year | All Sectors | | Nonfarm Households | Nonprofit Organizations | Agriculture | Unincorporated Business | Corporations |
| | Excluding Military | Including Military | | | | | |
	(1)	(2)	(3)	(4)	(5)	(6)	(7)
1945	1,262.5	1,470.6	453.7	29.1	151.3	89.0	339.6
1946	1,293.2	1,503.4	465.7	29.2	150.4	90.7	354.4
1947	1,335.8	1,538.2	483.8	29.2	151.6	92.4	356.4
1948	1,387.4	1,571.2	504.6	29.6	158.7	95.6	379.8
1949	1,425.3	1,588.8	524.4	30.3	159.3	96.7	388.0
1950	1,478.3	1,630.3	552.1	31.0	165.4	101.0	401.7
1951	1,533.6	1,688.6	573.6	31.9	169.7	103.9	421.6
1952	1,579.1	1,736.1	594.6	32.5	172.1	105.5	435.2
1953	1,631.1	1,784.4	620.8	33.3	174.1	108.0	447.8
1954	1,682.0	1,829.4	648.7	34.4	177.0	110.3	457.0
1955	1,749.4	1,896.3	685.4	35.6	179.4	113.2	473.0
1956	1,813.2	1,968.6	718.6	36.7	180.6	116.0	492.1
1957	1,880.4	2,037.9	755.0	37.8	182.3	119.5	509.3
1958	1,937.0	2,089.2	787.7	39.2	187.8	122.2	515.5

(continued)

TABLE A-18 (concluded)

End of Year	State and Local Governments (8)	Federal Government		Total Government		Total Private (13)
		Civilian (9)	Military (10)	Excluding Military (11)	Including Military (12)	
1945	132.5	67.3	208.1	199.8	407.9	1,060.3
1946	133.9	68.9	210.2	202.8	413.0	1,089.0
1947	136.0	77.4	202.4	213.4	415.8	1,120.9
1948	138.7	80.5	183.8	219.2	403.0	1,166.6
1949	143.0	82.6	163.6	225.6	389.2	1,197.8
1950	147.6	79.5	152.1	227.0	379.1	1,249.4
1951	152.0	80.9	155.1	232.9	388.0	1,298.8
1952	157.1	82.2	157.0	239.3	396.4	1,337.9
1953	162.4	84.7	153.3	247.1	400.4	1,382.1
1954	168.6	86.1	147.4	254.7	402.1	1,425.5
1955	175.7	87.1	146.9	262.8	409.7	1,485.0
1956	182.8	86.4	155.5	269.2	424.7	1,542.3
1957	190.9	85.7	157.4	276.6	434.0	1,602.3
1958	199.4	85.3	152.1	284.7	436.8	1,652.3

SOURCE: Same as for Table A-17, using figures in constant (1947–49) prices, except that col. 10 is from Table B-172, col. 2.

TABLE A-19

Percentage Distribution of Total Net Tangible Wealth, by Sector, Current Prices

| | All Sectors | | | | | | |
End of Year	Excluding Military (1)	Including Military (2)	Nonfarm Households (3)	Nonprofit Organizations (4)	Agriculture (5)	Unincorporated Business (6)	Corporations (7)
1900	100.00		31.88	1.67	27.88	8.24	24.89
1912	100.00		27.98	1.63	30.04	6.76	25.50
1922	100.00		30.11	1.57	20.77	7.43	28.09
1929	100.00		34.29	1.67	14.66	8.29	28.44
1933	100.00		33.07	1.89	12.41	7.57	28.67
1939	100.00		33.27	1.73	11.52	7.60	27.02
1945	100.00		33.69	1.42	15.08	7.32	24.26
1945	100.00	112.62	33.75	1.60	15.04	6.76	24.79
1946	100.00	110.63	33.00	1.75	14.05	7.04	26.26
1947	100.00	108.08	33.45	1.81	13.30	6.98	26.53
1948	100.00	106.81	33.56	1.79	12.82	7.06	27.40
1949	100.00	105.83	33.60	1.79	12.61	7.01	27.65
1950	100.00	105.10	34.51	1.76	12.77	6.92	27.77
1951	100.00	104.71	34.09	1.76	13.15	6.79	28.42
1952	100.00	105.17	34.57	1.84	12.41	6.67	28.65
1953	100.00	105.66	34.89	1.88	11.52	6.67	29.16
1954	100.00	105.76	35.09	1.95	11.31	6.62	29.14
1955	100.00	105.66	35.74	1.98	10.74	6.63	29.20
1956	100.00	105.55	35.70	2.00	10.43	6.57	29.81
1957	100.00	105.31	35.21	2.03	10.25	6.49	30.66
1958	100.00	105.22	35.40	2.10	10.73	6.38	30.00

(continued)

TABLE A-19 (concluded)

End of Year	State and Local Governments (8)	Federal Government Civilian (9)	Federal Government Military (10)	Total Government Excluding Military (11)	Total Government Including Military (12)	Total Private (13)	Net Foreign Assets (14)
1900	5.29	2.81		8.10		91.90	−2.67
1912	6.96	2.40		9.36		90.64	−1.27
1922	7.27	2.32		9.59		90.41	2.45
1929	7.81	2.02		9.83		90.17	2.82
1933	11.07	2.87		13.93		86.07	2.45
1939	10.59	7.84		18.43		81.57	0.44
1945	9.48	8.57		18.05		81.95	0.18
1945	9.95	8.11	12.62	18.06	30.68	81.94	a
1946	10.24	7.65	10.63	17.89	28.52	82.11	
1947	10.05	7.88	8.08	17.92	26.00	82.08	
1948	9.68	7.69	6.81	17.37	24.18	82.63	
1949	9.43	7.90	5.83	17.34	23.16	82.66	
1950	9.29	6.99	5.10	16.28	21.38	83.72	
1951	9.17	6.61	4.71	15.78	20.49	84.22	
1952	9.38	6.48	5.17	15.85	21.02	84.15	
1953	9.41	6.46	5.66	15.87	21.53	84.13	
1954	9.55	6.35	5.71	15.89	21.60	84.11	
1955	9.68	6.01	5.66	15.69	21.34	84.31	
1956	9.84	5.66	5.55	15.50	21.05	84.50	
1957	9.89	5.41	5.31	15.30	20.61	84.70	
1958	10.15	5.24	5.22	15.39	20.61	84.61	

SOURCE: Based on figures shown in Table A-15.
a Allocated among sectors.

TABLE A-20

Percentage Distribution of Total Net Tangible Wealth, by Sector, Constant (1947–49) Prices

| | All Sectors | | | | | | |
End of Year	Excluding Military (1)	Including Military (2)	Nonfarm Households (3)	Nonprofit Organizations (4)	Agriculture (5)	Unincorporated Business (6)	Corporations (7)
1900	100.00		36.09	1.88	25.39	7.52	24.12
1912	100.00		34.11	2.03	22.18	6.92	26.93
1922	100.00		32.64	1.81	18.41	7.47	28.16
1929	100.00		35.87	1.80	13.79	8.25	27.97
1933	100.00		35.23	1.91	13.85	7.28	26.46
1939	100.00		34.83	1.70	13.15	7.40	25.61
1945	100.00		33.79	1.45	14.43	7.53	24.93
1945	100.00	112.71	33.23	1.94	14.32	7.18	25.38
1946	100.00	110.35	33.26	1.88	13.69	7.16	26.58
1947	100.00	108.24	33.35	1.81	13.15	7.05	26.93
1948	100.00	106.63	33.37	1.75	12.93	6.97	27.61
1949	100.00	105.64	33.91	1.77	12.78	6.90	27.10
1950	100.00	104.84	34.68	1.78	12.76	6.84	27.18
1951	100.00	104.60	34.72	1.79	12.55	6.71	27.79
1952	100.00	105.02	34.98	1.81	12.27	6.56	28.04
1953	100.00	105.48	35.37	1.81	11.89	6.48	28.11
1954	100.00	105.55	35.85	1.85	11.65	6.39	27.92
1955	100.00	105.34	36.40	1.86	11.19	6.28	28.17
1956	100.00	105.20	36.72	1.87	10.79	6.24	28.54
1957	100.00	105.11	36.85	1.90	10.50	6.19	28.52
1958	100.00	105.11	37.01	1.95	10.55	6.09	28.37

(continued).

TABLE A-20 (concluded)

End of Year	State and Local Governments (8)	Federal Government		Total Government		Total Private (13)	Net Foreign Assets (14)
		Civilian (9)	Military (10)	Excluding Military (11)	Including Military (12)		
1900	5.16	2.03		7.19		92.81	−2.20
1912	6.97	1.89		8.87		91.13	−1.02
1922	7.24	2.23		9.47		90.53	2.04
1929	8.05	1.95		10.00		90.00	2.34
1933	10.69	2.45		13.14		86.86	2.13
1939	11.10	5.80		16.90		83.10	0.41
1945	10.00	7.71		17.70		82.30	0.16
1945	10.68	7.27	12.71	17.95	30.66	82.05	a
1946	10.30	7.13	10.35	17.43	27.79	82.56	
1947	9.95	7.77	8.24	17.72	25.97	82.28	
1948	9.56	7.81	6.63	17.37	24.00	82.61	
1949	9.56	7.98	5.64	17.54	23.18	82.46	
1950	9.58	7.12	4.84	16.70	21.55	83.30	
1951	9.50	6.92	4.60	16.42	21.05	83.58	
1952	9.59	6.77	5.02	16.35	21.37	83.65	
1953	9.51	6.82	5.48	16.33	21.81	83.67	
1954	9.63	6.71	5.55	16.34	21.89	83.66	
1955	9.66	6.44	5.34	16.10	21.44	83.90	
1956	9.73	6.11	5.20	15.84	21.04	84.16	
1957	10.15	5.89	5.11	16.04	21.16	83.96	
1958	10.25	5.79	5.11	16.03	21.14	83.97	

SOURCE: Based on figures shown in Table A-16.
a Allocated among sectors.

TABLE A-21

PERCENTAGE DISTRIBUTION OF TOTAL GROSS TANGIBLE WEALTH, BY SECTOR, CURRENT PRICES

End of Year	All Sectors		Nonfarm Households	Nonprofit Organizations	Agriculture	Unincorporated Business	Corporations
	Excluding Military (1)	Including Military (2)	(3)	(4)	(5)	(6)	(7)
1945	100.00	116.36	36.63	1.92	12.58	6.67	26.55
1946	100.00	116.65	35.82	2.10	11.89	6.88	27.34
1947	100.00	114.80	36.34	2.20	11.44	6.87	26.96
1948	100.00	113.49	36.34	2.17	11.13	6.94	27.46
1949	100.00	111.80	36.42	2.14	11.08	6.96	27.79
1950	100.00	110.69	37.16	2.07	11.14	6.88	27.78
1951	100.00	110.37	36.84	2.04	11.46	6.84	28.16
1952	100.00	110.16	37.10	2.09	10.95	6.77	28.25
1953	100.00	109.72	37.33	2.12	10.37	6.79	28.64
1954	100.00	109.07	37.50	2.16	10.25	6.79	28.52
1955	100.00	108.88	37.97	2.16	9.86	6.81	28.57
1956	100.00	109.28	37.98	2.16	9.62	6.74	28.95
1957	100.00	109.24	37.73	2.16	9.49	6.70	29.60
1958	100.00	108.59	38.16	2.19	9.77	6.67	28.99

(continued)

TABLE A-21 (concluded)

End of Year	State and Local Governments (8)	Federal Government		Total Government		Total Private (13)
		Civilian (9)	Military (10)	Excluding Military (11)	Including Military (12)	
1945	9.79	5.86	16.36	15.66	32.02	84.34
1946	10.25	5.71	16.65	15.96	32.61	84.04
1947	10.25	5.95	14.80	16.20	31.00	83.80
1948	10.15	5.81	13.49	15.96	29.45	84.04
1949	9.74	5.87	11.81	15.61	27.41	84.39
1950	9.67	5.30	10.69	14.97	25.66	85.03
1951	9.57	5.08	10.37	14.66	25.03	85.34
1952	9.81	5.03	10.16	14.85	25.01	85.16
1953	9.71	5.05	9.72	14.76	24.47	85.24
1954	9.79	4.99	9.07	14.78	23.85	85.22
1955	9.84	4.78	8.88	14.62	23.51	85.38
1956	10.00	4.56	9.28	14.56	23.84	85.44
1957	9.98	4.34	9.24	14.32	23.56	85.68
1958	10.07	4.15	8.59	14.23	22.81	85.77

SOURCE: Based on figures shown in Table A-17.

TABLE A-22

PERCENTAGE DISTRIBUTION OF TOTAL GROSS TANGIBLE WEALTH, BY SECTOR, CONSTANT (1947–49) PRICES

End of Year	All Sectors		Nonfarm Households	Nonprofit Organizations	Agriculture	Unincorporated Business	Corporations
	Excluding Military (1)	Including Military (2)	(3)	(4)	(5)	(6)	(7)
1945	100.00	116.48	35.93	2.30	11.99	7.05	26.90
1946	100.00	116.26	36.01	2.26	11.63	7.02	27.40
1947	100.00	115.15	36.22	2.19	11.35	6.91	27.35
1948	100.00	113.25	36.37	2.13	11.44	6.89	27.37
1949	100.00	111.48	36.82	2.13	11.19	6.79	27.24
1950	100.00	110.29	37.35	2.10	11.19	6.83	27.17
1951	100.00	110.11	37.40	2.08	11.07	6.77	27.49
1952	100.00	109.94	37.65	2.06	10.90	6.68	27.56
1953	100.00	109.40	38.06	2.04	10.68	6.62	27.45
1954	100.00	108.76	38.56	2.04	10.52	6.55	27.18
1955	100.00	108.39	39.17	2.03	10.25	6.47	27.05
1956	100.00	108.57	37.62	2.02	9.96	6.40	27.15
1957	100.00	108.37	40.14	2.01	9.69	6.35	27.11
1958	100.00	107.85	40.65	2.02	9.69	6.31	26.63

(continued)

TABLE A-22 (concluded)

End of Year	State and Local Governments (8)	Federal Government		Total Government		Total Private (13)
		Civilian (9)	Military (10)	Excluding Military (11)	Including Military (12)	
1945	10.50	5.33	16.48	15.83	32.31	84.17
1946	10.35	5.33	16.26	15.68	31.94	84.32
1947	10.18	5.79	15.15	15.97	31.13	84.03
1948	10.00	5.80	13.25	15.80	29.05	84.20
1949	10.04	5.80	11.48	15.84	27.32	84.16
1950	9.98	5.38	10.29	15.36	25.64	84.64
1951	9.91	5.28	10.11	15.19	25.30	84.81
1952	9.95	5.21	9.94	15.16	25.10	84.84
1953	9.96	5.19	9.40	15.15	24.55	84.85
1954	10.02	5.12	8.76	15.14	23.90	84.86
1955	10.04	4.98	8.39	15.02	23.41	84.08
1956	10.08	4.76	8.57	14.84	23.42	85.16
1957	10.15	4.56	8.37	14.70	23.07	85.30
1958	10.29	4.40	7.85	14.69	22.55	85.31

SOURCE: Based on figures shown in Table A-18.

TABLE A-23

ANNUAL PERCENTAGE RATES OF CHANGE IN TOTAL NET TANGIBLE WEALTH, BY SECTOR, CONSTANT (1947-49) PRICES

Year or Period	All Sectors		Nonfarm Households (3)	Nonprofit Organizations (4)	Agriculture (5)	Unincorporated Business (6)	Corporations (7)
	Excluding Military (1)	Including Military (2)					
1912	3.60		2.79	3.95	2.12	2.55	4.49
1922	2.40		1.95	1.22	0.51	3.41	3.06
1929	4.08		5.50	3.91	-0.14	5.23	3.97
1933	-1.17		-1.88	0.45	-1.06	-4.42	-2.82
1939	0.24		-0.02	-0.82	-0.70	0.46	-0.36
1945	0.30		-0.09	-2.49	1.90	0.59	-0.15
1946	3.12	0.95	3.24	0.00	-1.42	3.00	7.99
1947	4.09	2.09	4.40	0.00	0.09	2.40	5.46
1948	4.34	2.82	4.92	1.96	3.14	3.69	5.31
1949	3.15	2.15	4.25	3.21	1.31	1.45	2.79
1950	4.26	3.47	6.60	4.97	4.12	3.50	4.58
1951	4.38	4.17	4.46	5.33	2.56	2.31	6.78
1952	3.20	3.58	3.92	3.93	0.88	0.75	3.99
1953	3.25	3.67	4.36	3.24	0.00	2.09	3.45
1954	2.94	3.00	4.26	5.24	0.88	1.32	2.12
1955	4.17	4.02	6.14	4.98	0.32	2.89	4.03
1956	3.80	3.65	4.65	4.27	0.08	2.95	5.14
1957	3.55	3.47	3.70	3.35	0.55	2.59	4.74
1958	2.31	2.26	2.90	5.19	2.98	0.80	0.55

(continued)

TABLE A-23 (concluded)

Year or Period	State and Local Governments (8)	Federal Government		Total Government		Total Private (13)
		Civilian (9)	Military (10)	Excluding Military (11)	Including Military (12)	
1912	6.18	2.70		5.13		3.14
1922	2.77	4.07		3.29		2.30
1929	5.66	2.08		4.89		3.99
1933	6.11	4.64		5.80		−2.09
1939	0.79	14.96		4.26		−0.57
1945	−1.42	5.80		1.29		0.14
1946	−0.36	0.35	−16.05	−0.07	−6.71	3.80
1947	0.60	12.74	−17.10	5.52	−2.93	3.75
1948	1.07	4.95	−15.62	2.75	−3.11	4.68
1949	3.05	4.72	−12.73	3.79	−0.80	2.90
1950	3.41	−4.29	−10.51	−0.25	−2.76	5.26
1951	3.52	1.48	−0.87	2.21	1.86	4.77
1952	5.21	0.87	12.72	3.38	5.42	3.24
1953	2.32	2.75	12.65	3.35	5.05	3.22
1954	5.03	1.41	3.97	3.30	3.47	2.86
1955	5.17	0.69	0.50	3.36	2.64	4.35
1956	4.74	−1.38	1.16	2.33	2.04	4.05
1957	5.38	0.14	1.63	3.39	2.96	3.60
1958	5.83	0.56	2.25	3.89	3.50	2.01

Source: Computed from figures shown in Table A-16.

TABLE A-24

ANNUAL PERCENTAGE RATES OF CHANGE IN TOTAL GROSS TANGIBLE WEALTH, BY SECTOR, CONSTANT (1947–49) PRICES

Year or Period	All Sectors		Nonfarm Households (3)	Nonprofit Organizations (4)	Agriculture (5)	Unincorporated Business (6)	Corporations (7)
	Excluding Military (1)	Including Military (2)					
1946	2.46	2.26	2.64	0.38	−0.62	2.00	4.35
1947	3.24	2.27	3.90	0.00	0.08	1.80	3.10
1948	3.29	2.15	4.28	0.13	0.47	3.53	3.93
1949	2.73	1.12	3.94	0.23	0.04	1.13	2.18
1950	3.72	2.61	5.28	0.26	0.38	4.43	3.52
1951	3.74	3.58	3.88	0.27	0.26	2.83	4.96
1952	2.97	2.82	3.66	0.18	1.42	1.54	3.21
1953	3.29	2.77	4.42	0.24	1.17	2.43	2.89
1954	3.14	2.53	4.48	0.34	1.63	2.08	2.12
1955	4.02	3.65	5.67	0.35	1.36	2.70	3.53
1956	3.65	3.82	4.83	0.30	0.67	2.45	4.03
1957	3.72	3.52	5.06	0.32	0.96	2.98	3.54
1958	3.00	2.52	4.33	0.36	2.99	2.30	1.18

(continued)

155

TABLE A-24 (concluded)

Year or Period	State and Local Governments (8)	Federal Government		Total Government		Total Private (13)
		Civilian (9)	Military (10)	Excluding Military (11)	Including Military (12)	
1946	1.00	2.39	1.05	1.47	1.26	2.61
1947	2.60	12.37	-3.72	5.24	0.68	2.94
1948	2.02	3.93	-9.18	2.71	-3.08	4.08
1949	3.06	2.71	-11.02	2.93	-3.44	2.61
1950	3.21	-3.83	-7.04	0.63	-2.59	4.30
1951	3.00	1.85	1.97	2.59	2.35	3.95
1952	3.38	1.58	1.28	2.75	2.16	3.01
1953	3.36	3.00	-2.36	3.24	1.02	3.30
1954	3.84	1.62	-3.85	3.08	0.43	3.14
1955	4.22	1.17	-0.39	3.19	1.88	4.17
1956	4.02	-0.77	5.88	2.44	3.67	3.86
1957	4.41	-0.82	1.26	2.73	2.19	3.89
1958	4.46	-0.50	-3.37	2.93	0.64	3.01

SOURCE: Computed from figures shown in Table A-18.

TABLE A-25

TOTAL NET REPRODUCIBLE TANGIBLE WEALTH, BY SECTOR, CURRENT PRICES

(billions of dollars)

End of Year	All Sectors		Nonfarm Households (3)	Nonprofit Organizations (4)	Agriculture (5)	Unincorporated Business (6)	Corporations (7)
	Excluding Military (1)	Including Military (2)					
1900	59.3		20.8	1.2	10.0	6.1	18.2
1912	109.3		36.1	2.2	18.1	9.2	35.7
1922	233.4		80.1	4.2	27.9	20.7	80.9
1929	313.4		118.2	5.9	29.5	27.7	104.2
1933	241.3		85.8	5.1	18.2	20.5	81.1
1939	306.4		107.2	5.5	22.5	24.7	90.9
1945	442.3		159.6	6.5	41.8	35.3	119.7
1945	457.0	529.7	165.5	7.1	43.2	30.8	124.4
1946	556.2	630.7	199.0	9.4	52.0	38.4	159.4
1947	668.4	736.6	243.5	11.8	62.4	46.1	191.2
1948	736.2	799.9	268.7	12.8	67.1	51.5	214.7
1949	742.3	796.6	271.0	12.9	66.7	51.5	218.0
1950	851.9	906.4	320.5	14.6	77.9	58.1	251.1
1951	928.8	983.6	346.1	16.0	86.9	62.2	279.9
1952	972.7	1,035.4	364.7	17.4	83.8	63.9	295.0
1953	1,015.4	1,086.7	381.7	18.7	80.9	66.5	312.7
1954	1,052.7	1,127.3	396.2	20.0	81.4	68.2	324.0
1955	1,130.4	1,209.7	432.3	21.9	81.7	73.1	347.1
1956	1,226.2	1,310.5	466.3	24.0	84.4	78.8	384.9
1957	1,311.3	1,397.9	491.4	26.2	88.0	83.5	422.4
1958	1,367.6	1,456.5	513.2	28.3	95.0	85.8	433.0

(continued)

157

TABLE A-25 (concluded)

End of Year	State and Local Governments (8)	Federal Government		Total Government		Total Private (13)
		Civilian (9)	Military (10)	Excluding Military (11)	Including Military (12)	
1900	1.7	1.5		3.1		56.2
1912	5.0	3.0		8.0		101.3
1922	13.2	6.3		19.5		213.9
1929	21.1	6.8		27.9		285.5
1933	23.4	7.2		30.7		210.6
1939	27.4	28.3		55.7		250.7
1945	36.8	42.5		79.3		362.9
1945	43.1	42.9	72.7	86.0	158.7	371.1
1946	52.9	45.2	74.5	98.1	172.6	458.1
1947	63.3	50.1	68.2	113.4	181.6	555.0
1948	68.3	53.4	63.3	121.8	185.0	614.8
1949	67.4	54.7	54.3	122.2	176.5	620.1
1950	75.2	54.6	54.4	129.7	184.1	722.2
1951	82.6	55.2	54.8	137.8	192.6	791.0
1952	90.2	57.8	62.8	147.9	210.7	824.8
1953	94.6	60.5	71.3	155.1	226.4	860.3
1954	100.6	62.2	74.6	162.9	237.5	889.8
1955	110.9	63.3	79.3	174.3	253.5	956.1
1956	123.0	64.9	84.3	187.9	272.2	1,038.3
1957	133.8	66.1	86.6	199.9	286.5	1,111.4
1958	144.7	67.5	88.9	212.2	301.0	1,155.5

SOURCE, BY COLUMN,

(1) Sum of cols. 3 to 9.
(2) Cols. 1 and 10.
(3) Table A-50, sum of cols. 2, 5, and 6.
(4) Table A-51, cols. 2 and 4.
(5) Table A-53, col. 1, minus col. 4.

(6) Table A-52, sum of cols. 2, 3, 6, 7, and 8.
(7) Table A-54, sum of cols. 2, 3, 6, 7, and 8.
(8) Table A-55, col. 1, minus col. 4.
(9) Table A-56, cols. 2, 3, 5, 6, and 7.

(10) Table A-15, col. 10.
(11) Cols. 8 and 9.
(12) Cols. 10 and 11.
(13) Sum of cols. 3 to 7.

TABLE A-26

TOTAL NET REPRODUCIBLE TANGIBLE WEALTH, BY SECTOR, CONSTANT (1947–49) PRICES

(billions of dollars)

End of Year	All Sectors		Nonfarm Households (3)	Nonprofit Organizations (4)	Agriculture (5)	Unincorporated Business (6)	Corporations (7)
	Excluding Military (1)	Including Military (2)					
1900	221.9		85.0	5.0	38.2	19.5	63.1
1912	335.6		122.3	7.9	49.0	26.2	105.9
1922	428.5		149.9	8.9	55.4	36.7	143.1
1929	572.3		218.3	11.8	55.2	50.3	185.0
1933	546.5		206.0	11.9	51.3	44.7	169.2
1939	572.0		211.8	10.4	51.2	45.6	162.7
1945	591.1		212.4	9.0	56.7	48.7	164.6
1945	622.6	722.9	223.2	11.8	59.1	43.6	170.3
1946	644.1	728.3	231.5	11.8	60.4	45.2	183.9
1947	669.2	739.0	243.0	11.8	61.1	46.6	194.3
1948	702.5	761.4	255.9	12.0	65.6	48.9	204.8
1949	726.4	777.8	267.7	12.5	66.9	49.7	210.0
1950	762.0	808.0	286.5	13.2	70.3	51.9	220.4
1951	798.4	844.0	300.0	13.9	73.1	53.2	236.0
1952	827.7	879.1	312.1	14.4	74.7	53.8	245.5
1953	859.1	917.6	326.4	15.0	75.3	55.0	254.6
1954	887.0	947.3	340.5	15.8	76.2	55.8	260.2
1955	928.4	989.0	362.3	16.6	76.9	57.4	271.0
1956	965.2	1,026.4	379.7	17.4	76.2	59.1	284.4
1957	998.9	1,061.1	394.5	18.3	76.1	60.5	295.6
1958	1,022.4	1,086.0	405.4	19.2	78.5	60.8	297.1

(continued)

159

TABLE A-26 (concluded)

End of Year	State and Local Governments (8)	Federal Government		Total Government		Total Private (13)
		Civilian (9)	Military (10)	Excluding Military (11)	Including Military (12)	
1900	7.6	3.5		11.1		210.7
1912	17.7	6.5		24.3		311.4
1922	24.0	10.6		34.6		394.0
1929	40.0	11.6		51.6		520.7
1933	50.2	13.2		63.4		483.2
1939	53.9	36.4		90.3		481.7
1945	50.5	49.2		99.7		491.4
1945	63.8	50.8	100.3	114.6	214.9	508.0
1946	63.3	48.0	84.2	111.3	195.5	532.8
1947	63.6	48.8	69.8	112.4	182.2	556.8
1948	64.5	50.7	58.9	115.2	174.1	587.3
1949	66.9	52.6	51.4	119.5	170.9	606.8
1950	69.8	49.8	46.0	119.6	165.6	642.4
1951	72.8	49.5	45.6	122.6	168.2	675.8
1952	76.4	50.8	51.4	127.2	178.6	700.6
1953	80.0	52.8	57.9	132.8	190.7	726.3
1954	84.4	54.1	60.2	138.5	198.7	748.5
1955	89.6	54.6	60.6	144.2	204.8	784.2
1956	94.6	54.1	61.2	148.7	209.9	816.5
1957	100.4	53.5	62.2	153.9	216.1	845.0
1958	107.3	54.0	63.6	161.3	224.9	861.1

SOURCE: Same as for Table A-25, using figures in constant (1947–49) prices, except that col. 10 is from Table A-16, col. 10.

TABLE A-27

TOTAL GROSS REPRODUCIBLE TANGIBLE WEALTH, BY SECTOR, CURRENT PRICES
(billions of dollars)

	All Sectors						
End of Year	Excluding Military (1)	Including Military (2)	Nonfarm Households (3)	Nonprofit Organizations (4)	Agriculture (5)	Unincorporated Business (6)	Corporations (7)
1945	798.7	948.9	307.3	15.4	72.1	53.1	225.3
1946	967.9	1,153.2	366.3	20.6	85.8	65.6	279.4
1947	1,153.2	1,349.8	440.0	25.7	102.1	78.4	325.5
1948	1,265.2	1,461.7	486.7	27.8	110.2	87.0	360.4
1949	1,270.9	1,443.4	489.8	27.5	111.0	87.7	366.3
1950	1,444.5	1,621.9	569.0	30.2	126.4	98.4	416.0
1951	1,560.5	1,746.8	610.7	32.2	139.6	105.9	454.9
1952	1,636.6	1,827.5	641.7	34.4	138.7	110.1	477.5
1953	1,708.2	1,897.7	670.8	36.2	138.2	115.1	504.5
1954	1,771.2	1,954.9	697.3	38.2	141.1	119.2	520.9
1955	1,897.4	2,090.1	754.8	41.0	144.9	127.8	557.4
1956	2,049.7	2,267.0	813.6	44.1	151.3	136.7	610.2
1957	2,190.8	2,422.7	864.2	47.2	158.2	146.0	665.6
1958	2,300.7	2,527.0	916.4	50.3	169.8	153.0	686.4

(continued)

TABLE A-27 (concluded)

End of Year	State and Local Governments (8)	Federal Government		Total Government		Total Private (13)
		Civilian (9)	Military (10)	Excluding Military (11)	Including Military (12)	
1945	75.7	49.9	150.2	125.6	275.8	673.1
1946	95.2	55.0	185.3	150.2	335.5	817.7
1947	114.7	62.7	196.6	177.4	374.0	975.7
1948	126.4	66.8	196.5	193.2	389.7	1,072.0
1949	121.7	66.8	172.5	188.5	361.0	1,082.3
1950	136.5	67.9	177.4	204.4	381.8	1,240.0
1951	147.8	69.5	186.3	217.3	403.6	1,343.3
1952	160.6	73.7	190.9	234.3	425.2	1,402.4
1953	165.6	77.8	189.5	243.4	432.9	1,464.8
1954	174.1	80.4	183.7	254.5	438.2	1,516.7
1955	188.7	82.8	192.7	271.5	464.2	1,625.9
1956	207.9	85.8	217.3	293.7	511.0	1,756.0
1957	222.9	86.7	231.9	309.6	541.4	1,881.6
1958	237.5	87.4	226.3	324.8	551.1	1,975.9

SOURCE, BY COLUMN

(1) Sum of cols. 3 to 9.
(2) Col. 1 plus col. 10.
(3) Table A-57, cols. 2, 5 and 6.
(4) Table A-58, cols. 2 and 4.
(5) Table A-60, col. 1, minus col. 4.

(6) Table A-59, cols. 2, 3, 6, 7, 8.
(7) Table A-61, cols. 2, 3, 6, 7, 8.
(8) Table A-62, col. 1, minus col. 4.
(9) Table A-63, cols. 2, 3, 5, 6, 7.

(10) Table A-17, col. 10.
(11) Cols. 8 and 9.
(12) Cols. 10 and 11.
(13) Sum of cols. 3 to 7.

TABLE A-28

Total Gross Reproducible Tangible Wealth, by Sector, Constant (1947–49) Prices
(billions of dollars)

End of Year	All Sectors		Nonfarm Households	Nonprofit Organizations	Agriculture	Unincorporated Business	Corporations
	Excluding Military (1)	Including Military (2)	(3)	(4)	(5)	(6)	(7)
1945	1,096.7	1,304.7	414.8	25.6	97.5	76.0	309.7
1946	1,124.6	1,334.8	426.6	25.7	99.5	77.7	322.1
1947	1,159.1	1,361.6	444.4	25.7	101.3	79.3	331.6
1948	1,207.1	1,390.9	464.0	26.1	109.4	82.6	343.8
1949	1,241.2	1,404.8	483.1	26.6	109.8	84.5	351.1
1950	1,291.0	1,443.0	509.2	27.3	114.5	87.8	364.1
1951	1,340.8	1,495.8	529.4	28.0	118.4	90.6	381.9
1952	1,384.6	1,541.7	549.1	28.5	121.4	92.2	394.1
1953	1,434.7	1,588.0	574.1	29.2	124.0	94.6	405.8
1954	1,482.7	1,530.2	600.1	30.1	126.7	96.7	414.4
1955	1,546.0	1,692.9	634.8	31.1	129.3	99.4	429.0
1956	1,603.8	1,759.3	666.1	32.0	129.7	101.7	445.2
1957	1,663.0	1,820.4	701.3	33.0	130.7	104.7	458.0
1958	1,715.0	1,867.1	731.9	34.2	134.9	107.2	463.8

(continued)

TABLE A-28 (concluded)

End of Year	State and Local Governments (8)	Federal Government		Total Government		Total Private (13)
		Civilian (9)	Military (10)	Excluding Military (11)	Including Military (12)	
1945	112.1	61.0	208.1	173.1	381.2	923.6
1946	113.4	59.7	210.2	173.0	383.3	951.5
1947	115.3	61.6	202.4	176.9	379.3	982.3
1948	117.9	63.3	183.8	181.2	365.1	1,025.9
1949	122.0	64.2	163.6	186.2	349.7	1,055.0
1950	126.5	61.6	152.1	188.1	340.1	1,102.9
1951	130.7	61.8	155.1	192.5	347.5	1,148.3
1952	135.5	63.8	157.0	199.3	356.3	1,185.4
1953	140.7	66.4	153.3	207.1	360.4	1,227.6
1954	146.6	68.0	147.4	214.7	362.1	1,268.1
1955	153.4	69.0	146.9	222.5	369.3	1,323.5
1956	160.2	68.8	155.5	229.0	384.5	1,374.8
1957	167.8	67.5	157.4	235.3	392.7	1,427.7
1958	176.0	67.1	152.1	243.1	395.3	1,471.8

SOURCE: Same as for Table A-27, using figures in constant (1947–49) prices, except for col. 10 which is from Table A-18, col. 10.

TABLE A-29

PERCENTAGE DISTRIBUTION OF TOTAL REPRODUCIBLE NET WEALTH, BY SECTOR, CURRENT PRICES

End of Year	All Sectors		Nonfarm Households (3)	Nonprofit Organizations (4)	Agriculture (5)	Unincorporated Business (6)	Corporations (7)
	Excluding Military (1)	Including Military (2)					
1900	100.00		35.08	2.01	16.79	10.20	30.66
1912	100.00		33.01	2.00	16.59	8.43	32.67
1922	100.00		34.33	1.82	11.97	8.88	34.66
1929	100.00		37.72	1.90	9.41	8.84	33.24
1933	100.00		35.57	2.09	7.55	8.47	33.60
1939	100.00		34.98	1.80	7.33	8.06	29.65
1945	100.00		36.09	1.48	9.45	7.98	27.06
1945	100.00	115.91	36.22	1.55	9.45	6.74	27.22
1946	100.00	113.40	37.78	1.70	9.34	6.90	28.65
1947	100.00	110.20	36.43	1.76	9.33	6.90	28.61
1948	100.00	108.59	36.47	1.74	9.11	6.99	29.15
1949	100.00	107.32	36.51	1.74	8.98	6.94	29.37
1950	100.00	106.39	37.62	1.71	9.14	6.82	29.48
1951	100.00	105.90	37.26	1.72	9.35	6.69	30.14
1952	100.00	106.45	37.50	1.79	8.61	6.56	30.33
1953	100.00	107.02	37.59	1.84	7.97	6.54	30.79
1954	100.00	107.02	37.24	1.94	7.23	6.47	30.71
1955	100.00	107.00	38.20	1.93	7.22	6.46	30.78
1956	100.00	106.87	38.03	1.95	6.88	6.42	31.39
1957	100.00	106.60	37.48	1.99	6.71	6.37	32.21
1958	100.00	106.50	37.54	2.07	6.95	6.28	31.67

(continued)

TABLE A-29 (concluded)

End of Year	State and Local Governments (8)	Federal Government		Total Government		Total Private (13)
		Civilian (9)	Military (10)	Excluding Military (11)	Including Military (12)	
1900	2.78	2.48		5.26		94.74
1912	4.58	2.72		7.30		92.70
1922	5.66	2.69		8.35		91.65
1929	6.74	2.16		8.90		91.10
1933	9.71	3.00		12.71		87.29
1939	8.95	9.24		18.18		81.82
1945	8.32	9.62		17.94		82.06
1945	9.43	9.38	15.91	18.81	34.72	81.19
1946	9.51	8.13	13.40	17.63	31.03	82.37
1947	9.47	7.49	10.20	16.97	27.16	83.03
1948	9.28	7.25	8.59	16.53	25.12	83.47
1949	9.08	7.37	7.32	16.46	23.77	83.54
1950	8.82	6.40	6.39	15.23	21.61	84.77
1951	8.90	5.94	5.90	14.83	20.74	85.17
1952	9.27	5.94	6.45	15.21	21.66	84.79
1953	9.31	5.96	7.02	15.27	22.29	84.73
1954	9.81	5.60	7.02	15.42	22.43	84.58
1955	9.80	5.60	7.00	15.40	22.40	84.60
1956	10.03	5.29	6.87	15.33	22.20	84.67
1957	10.21	5.02	6.60	15.23	21.83	84.77
1958	10.58	4.90	6.50	15.49	21.98	84.52

SOURCE: Based on figures shown in Table A-25.

TABLE A-30

PERCENTAGE DISTRIBUTION OF TOTAL NET REPRODUCIBLE TANGIBLE WEALTH, BY SECTOR, CONSTANT (1947–49) PRICES

End of Year	All Sectors		Nonfarm Households (3)	Nonprofit Organizations (4)	Agriculture (5)	Unincorporated Business (6)	Corporations (7)
	Excluding Military (1)	Including Military (2)					
1900	100.00		38.30	2.24	17.23	8.79	28.43
1912	100.00		36.44	2.36	14.59	7.81	31.56
1922	100.00		34.98	2.08	12.92	8.56	33.38
1929	100.00		38.15	2.07	9.65	8.80	32.33
1933	100.00		37.70	2.18	9.39	8.18	30.96
1939	100.00		36.94	1.82	8.92	7.95	28.36
1945	100.00		35.93	1.52	9.60	8.23	27.86
1945	100.00	116.10	35.83	1.89	9.49	7.00	27.34
1946	100.00	113.06	35.90	1.83	9.37	7.01	28.51
1947	100.00	110.42	36.25	1.76	9.11	6.96	28.98
1948	100.00	108.32	36.14	1.70	9.27	6.90	29.56
1949	100.00	107.06	36.82	1.72	9.20	6.83	28.88
1950	100.00	106.03	37.57	1.73	9.22	6.80	28.92
1951	100.00	105.71	37.57	1.74	9.15	6.67	29.52
1952	100.00	106.20	37.71	1.74	9.02	6.50	29.67
1953	100.00	106.74	38.02	1.75	8.77	6.41	29.65
1954	100.00	106.80	38.44	1.78	8.60	6.29	29.38
1955	100.00	106.51	38.94	1.78	8.26	6.17	29.57
1956	100.00	106.33	39.26	1.80	7.87	6.11	29.84
1957	100.00	106.22	39.44	1.83	7.61	6.05	29.97
1958	100.00	106.22	39.60	1.88	7.67	5.94	29.44

(continued)

TABLE A-30 (concluded)

End of Year	State and Local Governments (8)	Federal Government Civilian (9)	Federal Government Military (10)	Total Government Excluding Military (11)	Total Government Including Military (12)	Total Private (13)
1900	3.43	1.59		5.02		94.98
1912	5.28	1.95		7.23		92.77
1922	5.60	2.48		8.07		91.91
1929	7.00	2.02		9.02		90.98
1933	9.18	2.42		11.60		88.40
1939	9.40	6.61		16.00		83.99
1945	8.54	8.33		16.87		83.13
1945	10.24	8.20	16.10	18.45	34.54	81.55
1946	9.82	7.56	13.06	17.38	30.44	82.62
1947	9.48	7.46	10.42	16.94	27.36	83.06
1948	9.05	7.38	8.32	16.43	24.75	83.57
1949	9.09	7.46	7.06	16.55	23.61	83.45
1950	9.03	6.73	6.03	15.75	21.79	84.25
1951	8.99	6.36	5.71	15.35	21.06	84.65
1952	9.08	6.27	6.20	15.35	21.56	84.65
1953	9.15	6.25	6.74	15.40	22.14	84.60
1954	9.32	6.18	6.80	15.50	22.30	84.50
1955	9.38	5.91	6.51	15.29	21.80	84.71
1956	9.51	5.61	6.33	15.12	21.45	84.88
1957	9.75	5.36	6.22	15.10	21.33	84.90
1958	10.19	5.28	6.22	15.46	21.68	84.54

SOURCE: Based on figures shown in Table A-26.

TABLE A-31

PERCENTAGE DISTRIBUTION OF TOTAL GROSS REPRODUCIBLE TANGIBLE WEALTH, BY SECTOR, CURRENT PRICES

End of Year	All Sectors		Nonfarm Households (3)	Nonprofit Organizations (4)	Agriculture (5)	Unincorporated Business (6)	Corporations (7)
	Excluding Military (1)	Including Military (2)					
1945	100.00	118.81	38.48	1.93	9.03	6.65	28.21
1946	100.00	119.14	37.84	2.13	8.86	6.78	28.87
1947	100.00	117.05	38.50	2.23	8.85	6.80	28.23
1948	100.00	115.53	38.47	2.20	8.71	6.88	28.49
1949	100.00	113.57	38.54	2.16	8.73	6.90	28.82
1950	100.00	112.28	39.39	2.09	8.75	6.81	28.80
1951	110.00	111.94	39.13	2.06	8.95	6.79	29.15
1952	100.00	111.66	39.21	2.10	8.47	6.73	29.18
1953	100.00	111.09	39.27	2.12	8.09	6.74	29.53
1954	100.00	110.37	39.37	2.16	7.97	6.73	29.41
1955	100.00	110.16	39.78	2.16	7.64	6.74	29.38
1956	100.00	110.60	39.69	2.15	7.38	6.67	29.77
1957	100.00	110.59	39.45	2.15	7.22	6.66	30.38
1958	100.00	109.84	39.83	2.19	7.38	6.65	29.83

(continued)

169

TABLE A-31 (concluded)

End of Year	State and Local Governments (8)	Federal Government		Total Government		Total Private (13)
		Civilian (9)	Military (10)	Excluding Military (11)	Including Military (12)	
1945	9.48	6.25	18.81	15.73	34.53	84.27
1946	9.84	5.68	19.14	15.52	34.66	84.48
1947	9.95	5.44	17.05	15.38	32.43	84.61
1948	9.99	5.28	15.53	15.27	30.80	84.73
1949	9.58	5.26	13.57	14.83	28.41	85.16
1950	9.45	4.70	12.28	14.15	26.43	85.84
1951	9.47	4.45	11.94	13.93	25.86	86.08
1952	9.81	4.50	11.66	14.32	25.98	85.69
1953	9.69	4.55	11.09	14.25	25.34	85.75
1954	9.83	4.54	10.37	14.37	24.74	85.63
1955	9.95	4.36	10.16	14.31	24.47	85.69
1956	10.14	4.19	10.60	14.33	24.93	85.67
1957	10.17	3.96	10.59	14.11	24.71	85.89
1958	10.32	3.80	9.84	14.12	23.95	85.88

SOURCE: Based on figures shown in Table A-27.

TABLE A-32

PERCENTAGE DISTRIBUTION OF TOTAL GROSS REPRODUCIBLE TANGIBLE WEALTH, BY SECTOR, CONSTANT (1947–49) PRICES

| | All Sectors | | | | | | |
End of Year	Excluding Military (1)	Including Military (2)	Nonfarm Households (3)	Nonprofit Organizations (4)	Agriculture (5)	Unincorporated Business (6)	Corporations (7)
1945	100.00	118.97	37.82	2.33	8.89	6.93	28.24
1946	100.00	118.70	37.94	2.29	8.85	6.91	28.64
1947	100.00	117.46	38.34	2.22	8.74	6.84	28.60
1948	100.00	115.23	38.44	2.16	9.06	6.84	28.48
1949	100.00	113.18	38.92	2.15	8.84	6.81	28.28
1950	100.00	111.78	39.45	2.11	8.87	6.80	28.20
1951	100.00	111.56	39.49	2.09	8.83	6.76	28.48
1952	100.00	111.34	39.66	2.06	8.77	6.66	28.47
1953	100.00	110.69	40.01	2.03	8.64	6.60	28.28
1954	100.00	109.94	40.47	2.03	8.55	6.52	27.95
1955	100.00	109.50	41.06	2.01	8.36	6.43	27.75
1956	100.00	109.69	41.53	2.00	8.09	6.34	27.76
1957	100.00	109.47	42.17	1.98	7.86	6.30	27.54
1958	100.00	108.87	42.68	1.99	7.86	6.25	27.04

(continued)

TABLE A-32 (concluded)

End of Year	State and Local Governments (8)	Federal Government		Total Government			Total Private (13)
		Civilian (9)	Military (10)	Excluding Military (11)	Including Military (12)		
1945	10.23	5.56	18.97	15.79	34.76		84.21
1946	10.08	5.31	18.70	15.39	34.08		84.61
1947	9.95	5.31	17.46	15.26	32.72		84.74
1948	9.77	5.25	15.23	15.01	30.24		84.99
1949	9.83	5.17	13.18	15.00	28.18		85.00
1950	9.79	4.77	11.78	14.57	26.35		85.43
1951	9.75	4.61	11.56	14.36	25.92		85.64
1952	9.79	4.61	11.34	14.39	25.73		85.61
1953	9.81	4.63	10.69	14.44	25.12		85.56
1954	9.89	4.59	9.94	14.48	24.42		85.52
1955	9.92	4.47	9.50	14.39	23.89		85.61
1956	9.99	4.29	9.69	14.28	23.97		85.72
1957	10.09	4.06	9.47	14.15	23.61		85.85
1958	10.26	3.91	8.87	14.18	23.05		85.82

Source: Based on figures shown in Table A-28.

TABLE A-33

ANNUAL PERCENTAGE RATES OF CHANGE IN NET REPRODUCIBLE TANGIBLE WEALTH, BY SECTOR, CONSTANT (1947–49) PRICES

Year or Period	All Sectors		Nonfarm Households (3)	Nonprofit Organizations (4)	Agriculture (5)	Unincorporated Business (6)	Corporations (7)
	Excluding Military (1)	Including Military (2)					
1912	3.53	—	3.10	3.99	2.09	2.49	4.40
1922	2.47	—	2.05	2.87	1.23	3.42	3.10
1929	4.22	—	5.51	4.09	−0.04	4.62	3.74
1933	−1.16	—	−1.46	0.19	−1.84	−3.02	−2.26
1939	0.76	—	0.50	−2.25	−0.05	0.33	−0.66
1945	0.55	—	0.24	−2.56	1.73	1.09	0.20
1946	3.50	0.74	3.72	0.08	2.16	3.64	7.95
1947	3.90	1.49	4.98	0.17	1.11	3.12	5.66
1948	4.95	3.01	5.27	2.03	7.43	4.76	5.48
1949	3.43	2.14	4.65	3.90	1.89	1.72	2.45
1950	4.90	3.89	7.01	5.28	5.16	4.37	5.02
1951	4.78	4.46	4.70	5.39	3.88	2.66	6.99
1952	3.73	4.16	4.04	4.03	2.25	1.07	4.11
1953	3.73	4.30	4.57	4.02	0.78	2.27	3.67
1954	3.27	3.31	4.34	5.13	1.25	1.33	2.22
1955	4.64	4.40	6.40	5.13	0.87	2.91	4.14
1956	3.99	3.80	4.79	4.64	−0.94	2.91	4.95
1957	3.49	3.38	3.89	5.24	−0.07	2.47	3.97
1958	2.34	2.34	2.78	5.25	3.19	0.53	0.49

(continued)

173

TABLE A-33 (concluded)

Year or Period	State and Local Governments (8)	Federal Government		Total Government		Total Private (13)
		Civilian (9)	Military (10)	Excluding Military (11)	Including Military (12)	
1912	7.29	5.30	—	6.70	—	3.54
1922	3.10	5.00	—	3.61	—	2.40
1929	7.60	1.23	—	5.88	—	4.05
1933-	5.80	3.37	—	5.28	—	-1.90
1939	1.20	18.42	—	6.07	—	-0.05
1945	-1.09	5.15	—	1.66	—	0.15
1946	-0.83	-5.51	-16.03	-2.91	-9.03	4.87
1947	0.65	1.58	-17.07	1.05	-6.75	4.51
1948	1.32	3.85	-15.69	2.42	-4.52	5.47
1949	3.70	3.83	-12.76	3.76	-1.83	3.32
1950	4.38	-5.40	-10.44	0.08	-3.10	5.86
1951	4.31	-0.56	-0.85	2.51	1.57	5.25
1952	4.82	2.63	12.56	3.93	6.28	3.64
1953	4.71	3.96	12.68	4.44	6.81	3.66
1954	5.50	2.44	4.10	4.31	4.24	3.07
1955	6.12	0.94	0.55	4.10	3.02	4.77
1956	5.55	-0.97	1.04	3.08	2.48	4.14
1957	6.13	-1.02	1.70	6.05	4.78	3.48
1958	3.11	0.92	2.25	2.37	2.33	1.91

SOURCE: Computed from figures in Table A-26.

TABLE A-34

ANNUAL PERCENTAGE RATES OF CHANGE IN GROSS REPRODUCIBLE TANGIBLE WEALTH, BY SECTOR, CONSTANT (1947–49) PRICES

Year	All Sectors		Nonfarm Households (3)	Nonprofit Organizations (4)	Agriculture (5)	Unincorporated Business (6)	Corporations (7)
	Excluding Military (1)	Including Military (2)					
1946	2.54	2.30	2.86	0.51	2.00	2.26	3.98
1947	3.07	2.00	4.16	0.16	1.84	2.09	2.95
1948	4.14	2.16	4.42	1.24	8.00	4.12	3.69
1949	2.82	0.99	4.12	2.23	0.31	2.29	2.11
1950	4.01	2.72	5.40	2.44	4.31	3.99	3.70
1951	3.86	3.66	3.96	2.57	3.44	3.14	4.90
1952	3.27	3.06	3.72	1.71	2.52	1.81	3.21
1953	3.61	3.01	4.55	2.39	2.11	2.59	2.95
1954	3.35	2.66	4.54	3.29	2.23	2.19	2.14
1955	4.27	3.85	5.78	3.42	2.04	2.75	3.51
1956	3.74	3.92	4.93	2.86	0.32	2.39	3.79
1957	3.69	3.48	5.28	3.03	0.79	2.96	2.88
1958	3.13	2.56	4.37	3.48	3.15	2.33	1.26

(continued)

TABLE A-34 (concluded)

Year	State and Local Governments (8)	Federal Government		Total Government		Total Private (13)
		Civilian (9)	Military (10)	Excluding Military (11)	Including Military (12)	
1946	1.10	-2.20	1.05	-0.06	0.55	3.03
1947	1.68	3.22	-3.72	2.21	-1.04	3.23
1948	2.29	2.83	-9.18	2.48	-3.75	4.44
1949	3.43	1.37	-11.02	2.71	-4.21	2.84
1950	3.68	-3.99	-7.04	1.04	-2.74	4.54
1951	3.34	0.28	1.97	2.33	2.17	4.12
1952	3.70	3.19	1.28	3.53	2.53	3.23
1953	3.82	4.16	-2.36	3.93	1.16	3.56
1954	4.22	2.42	-3.85	3.65	0.46	3.30
1955	4.65	1.48	-0.39	3.65	2.00	4.37
1956	4.41	0.32	5.88	2.94	4.11	3.87
1957	4.73	-1.93	1.26	2.72	2.13	3.85
1958	4.90	-0.53	-3.37	3.34	0.65	3.09

SOURCE: Computed from figures in Table A-28.

NET STOCK OF RESIDENTIAL STRUCTURES, BY SECTOR
(billions of dollars)

End of Year	All Sectors (1)	Nonfarm House-holds (2)	Unincor-porated Business (3)	Agri-culture (4)	Corpora-tions (5)	State and Local Govern-ments (6)	Federal Govern-ment (7)
			CURRENT PRICES				
1900	17.44	15.21	0.26	1.69	0.28		
1912	28.34	23.96	0.84	2.92	0.62		
1922	63.17	52.44	2.40	6.57	1.76		
1929	95.90	79.41	5.48	6.38	4.63		
1933	74.27	61.74	4.36	4.63	3.54		
1939	91.19	76.84	5.25	4.91	4.19		
1945	133.60	111.92	7.26	8.98	5.44		
1945	152.43	123.72	9.18	9.22	8.23	0.87	1.21
1946	178.53	145.28	10.26	11.00	9.49	1.35	1.15
1947	216.73	177.58	11.89	13.08	11.36	1.69	1.13
1948	234.24	192.31	12.95	13.63	12.60	1.76	0.99
1949	231.55	189.39	12.79	13.75	12.80	1.93	0.89
1950	267.39	220.58	14.07	14.91	14.66	2.33	0.84
1951	286.01	236.14	14.46	16.07	15.60	2.95	0.79
1952	301.66	249.61	14.71	16.58	16.40	3.62	0.74
1953	313.54	259.88	14.91	16.88	17.06	4.14	0.67
1954	324.78	270.18	14.83	17.26	17.53	4.41	0.57
1955	351.41	294.13	15.30	17.92	18.77	4.77	0.52
1956	375.53	315.54	15.80	18.53	20.04	5.14	0.48
1957	392.14	330.28	15.99	18.79	20.93	5.51	0.64
1958	411.34	346.81	16.26	19.28	21.95	6.03	1.01
			CONSTANT (1947–49) PRICES				
1900	75.64	65.79	1.09	7.55	1.21		
1912	109.43	93.44	3.16	10.42	2.41		
1922	138.02	115.96	5.14	13.03	3.89		
1929	199.62	165.48	11.05	13.44	9.65		
1933	191.91	159.49	10.76	12.52	9.14		
1939	189.12	158.28	10.41	11.80	8.63		
1945	184.28	155.23	9.85	11.65	7.55		
1945	211.14	171.80	12.52	12.68	11.29	1.19	1.67
1946	213.16	173.77	12.77	12.80	11.34	1.62	1.36
1947	216.82	177.24	12.12	13.08	11.51	1.72	1.15
1948	222.74	182.80	12.17	13.36	11.81	1.66	0.94
1949	228.19	187.29	12.23	13.61	12.37	1.84	0.85
1950	236.46	194.65	12.30	13.91	12.62	2.03	0.75
1951	243.94	201.42	12.08	14.22	13.10	2.46	0.66
1952	251.23	207.94	11.89	14.55	13.35	2.92	0.58
1953	259.09	215.09	11.76	14.78	13.66	3.27	0.53
1954	267.20	222.68	11.60	14.98	13.94	3.45	0.55
1955	277.88	232.97	11.46	15.14	14.30	3.57	0.44
1956	287.29	241.93	11.36	15.26	14.70	3.69	0.35
1957	295.60	249.60	11.23	15.38	15.07	3.87	0.45
1958	303.94	257.05	11.15	15.49	15.42	4.14	0.69

Notes to Table A-35 on next page

SOURCE, BY COLUMN

Current Prices

(1) Sum of cols. 2 to 7.

(2) 1900–45: *A Study of Saving* . . . , Vol. III, Table W-1, col. 4, minus unincorporated business and corporations share of residential structures from cols. 3 and 5 of this table.

1945–58: Table B-16, col. 8 plus Table B-164, col. 11.

(3) 1900–45: Derived by reverse cumulating net investment in individuals' share of multifamily dwellings back from 1945 figure to 1900, converted from 1947–49 to 1929 constant prices using figures from *Saving*, Vol. I, Table R-8, cols. 1 and 2. Current prices obtained by multiplying 1929 prices by year-end index, derived by averaging successive years, *ibid*, Vol. I, Table R-20, col. 2. Definition broader than before 1945.

1945–58: Table B-16, col. 9, plus Table B-54, col. 3, and Table B-146, col. 11.

(4) 1900–45: *Saving*, Vol. III, Table W-27, line 1.

1945–58: Table B-80, col. 8, plus proportionate share of accumulated value of dealer's commissions on sales of farm buildings from Table B-63, col. 11.

(5) 1900–45: *Saving*, Vol. III, Table W-30, line 1.

(1945–58: Table B-14, col. 3, minus Table B-16, col. 7 and Table B-54, col. 3.

(6) Table B-144, col. 11, plus Table B-147, col. 11.

(7) Table B-162, col. 11, plus Table B-165, col. 11.

Constant (1947–49) Prices

Same as for current prices. Current figures for 1900–45 from *A Study of Saving* . . . were converted to constant 1929 prices by dividing figures for given types of asset in *Saving*, Vol. III, Table W-1 by corresponding figure in Table W-3 for each base year used from 1900 to 1945. Constant prices were then converted to (1947–49) prices by using the deflators shown in Table B-188. Figures for 1945–58 are from tables cited above, using appropriate columns containing data in constant (1947–49) prices.

NET STOCK OF NONRESIDENTIAL STRUCTURES, BY SECTOR
(billions of dollars)

End of Year	All Sectors (1)	Institutions (2)	Unincorporated Business (3)	Agriculture (4)	Corporations (5)	State and Local Governments (6)	Federal Government (7)
			CURRENT PRICES				
1900	17.55	1.10	2.23	1.57	10.63	1.57	0.45
1912	34.18	2.04	3.84	2.72	19.70	4.83	1.05
1922	71.33	4.06	8.22	5.82	37.71	13.04	2.48
1929	93.92	5.57	11.24	5.86	47.87	20.54	2.84
1933	85.17	4.77	9.80	4.05	40.34	22.88	3.33
1939	97.29	5.37	11.45	4.09	42.63	26.86	6.89
1945	131.48	6.40	15.02	6.76	52.58	36.24	14.48
1945	133.20	6.97	8.21	7.10	55.61	41.55	13.76
1946	166.85	9.26	11.02	8.33	70.38	50.64	17.22
1947	197.94	11.54	13.25	9.86	82.19	60.49	20.61
1948	215.26	12.49	14.11	10.52	90.82	65.12	22.20
1949	214.55	12.44	13.73	10.82	91.45	63.77	22.34
1950	239.88	13.94	14.84	11.93	103.70	70.75	24.72
1951	259.37	15.15	15.83	13.18	112.05	77.27	25.89
1952	277.06	16.47	16.52	13.76	118.87	83.84	27.60
1953	292.17	17.55	17.32	14.07	127.06	87.42	28.75
1954	306.53	18.77	18.27	14.43	132.53	92.85	29.68
1955	332.22	20.40	20.06	15.09	143.59	102.29	30.79
1956	361.02	22.26	21.97	15.84	155.25	113.42	32.28
1957	398.10	24.25	24.01	16.40	176.60	123.27	33.57
1958	422.38	26.26	25.56	16.75	185.61	133.20	35.00
			CONSTANT (1947–49) PRICES				
1900	69.05	4.66	8.48	6.03	40.40	7.37	2.11
1912	114.14	7.51	12.61	8.33	64.72	17.23	3.74
1922	139.31	8.63	16.39	10.88	75.20	23.70	4.51
1929	183.07	11.23	22.06	11.28	93.97	39.12	5.41
1933	191.03	11.41	22.16	9.93	91.23	49.15	7.15
1939	188.89	10.19	21.87	8.92	81.40	52.93	13.58
1945	181.34	8.79	21.00	8.46	73.49	49.73	19.87
1945	196.72	11.60	13.04	9.54	79.80	61.71	21.03
1946	197.94	11.57	13.32	9.66	81.79	60.78	20.82
1947	199.87	11.54	13.27	9.95	83.73	60.77	20.77
1948	203.73	11.70	13.38	10.25	86.05	61.44	20.91
1949	208.81	12.06	13.41	10.55	87.99	63.43	21.37
1950	214.93	12.59	13.55	10.90	90.11	65.96	21.82
1951	221.70	13.17	13.76	11.29	93.01	68.33	22.14
1952	228.69	13.63	13.87	11.64	96.04	71.15	22.36
1953	236.36	14.11	14.19	11.90	99.47	74.20	22.49
1954	245.06	14.76	14.67	12.12	102.85	78.19	22.47
1955	255.56	15.45	15.42	12.30	107.04	83.00	22.35
1956	265.77	16.13	16.24	12.43	111.02	87.59	22.36
1957	277.26	16.95	16.96	12.55	115.45	92.98	22.37
1958	288.87	17.82	17.62	12.67	118.81	99.43	22.52

Notes to Table A-36 on next page

SOURCE, BY COLUMN

Current Prices

(1) Sum of cols. 2 to 7.
(2) 1900–45: *A Study of Saving* . . . , Vol. III, Table W-22, line I-2.
    1945–58: Table B-41, col. 3 plus Table B-42, col. 3.
(3) 1900–45: *Saving*, Vol. III, Table W-29, line I-2.
    1945–58: Table B-56, average of cols. 3 and 6, and col. 9, plus Table B-55, col. 1, plus Table B-42, col. 3. Definition broader than before 1945.
(4) 1900–45: *Saving*, Vol. III, Table W-27, line I-2.
    1945–58: Table B-80, col. 9, plus remaining share of dealers' commission on sale of farms from Table B-63, col. 11.
(5) 1900–45: *Saving*, Vol. III, Table W-30, line I-2, minus Table W-40, line I-1 to I-4.
    1945–58: Table B-123, col. 1, plus Table B-126, average of cols. 3 and 6, plus col. 9, plus Table B-125, col. 3, minus figures for unincorporated business in col. 3 of Table A-36, minus Table B-42, col. 3.
(6) 1900–45: *Saving*, Vol. III, Table W-42, line I-1 and I-2.
    1945–58: Table B-150, cols. 5 and 6.
(7) 1900–45: *Saving*, Vol. III, Table W-43, lines I-1 and I-2, plus Table W-40, line I-to I-4.
    1945–58: Table B-150, cols. 3 and 4.

Constant (1947–49) Prices
Same as for Table A-35, except that for col. 7 Table B-149 is used instead of Table B-150.

NET STOCK OF PRODUCER DURABLES, BY SECTOR
(billions of dollars)

End of Year	All Sectors (1)	Institutions (2)	Unincorporated Business (3)	Agriculture (4)	Corporations (5)	State and Local Governments (6)	Federal Government (7)
CURRENT PRICES							
1900	6.51	0.09	0.91	1.17	4.27	0.06	0.01
1912	13.75	0.15	1.42	2.24	9.77	0.15	0.02
1922	30.80	0.18	3.42	3.27	23.77	0.12	0.04
1929	38.38	0.37	4.56	3.87	29.01	0.51	0.06
1933	29.19	0.28	3.20	2.57	22.55	0.48	0.11
1939	34.24	0.15	3.84	3.51	25.96	0.48	0.30
1945	50.32	0.13	5.19	6.27	35.29	0.41	3.03
1945	48.61	0.13	5.31	5.79	34.12	0.62	2.64
1946	58.52	0.18	6.88	6.55	41.75	0.79	2.37
1947	73.67	0.25	9.21	8.39	52.81	1.05	1.96
1948	87.51	0.35	11.35	10.69	62.21	1.35	1.56
1949	96.87	0.48	12.83	12.47	68.22	1.63	1.24
1950	109.98	0.65	14.81	14.09	77.43	1.94	1.06
1951	123.60	0.83	16.63	15.68	87.19	2.27	1.00
1952	131.98	0.97	17.65	16.41	93.39	2.56	1.00
1953	140.77	1.10	18.82	16.64	100.35	2.86	1.00
1954	149.49	1.27	19.79	16.86	107.42	3.22	0.93
1955	156.62	1.47	21.76	17.23	111.60	3.71	0.85
1956	177.41	1.69	24.26	17.64	128.78	4.27	0.77
1957	193.14	1.90	26.44	18.01	141.25	4.85	0.69
1958	199.84	2.07	26.94	18.59	146.38	5.25	0.61
CONSTANT (1947–49) PRICES							
1900	20.46	0.30	2.96	3.13	13.85	0.19	0.03
1912	37.59	0.42	3.98	5.31	27.40	0.42	0.06
1922	50.07	0.30	5.53	5.54	38.45	0.19	0.06
1929	61.14	0.59	7.28	6.06	46.31	0.81	0.09
1933	52.77	0.50	5.81	4.46	40.92	0.88	0.20
1939	54.75	0.23	6.09	5.98	41.20	0.77	0.48
1945	67.30	0.17	6.87	8.95	46.75	0.55	4.01
1945	61.31	0.17	6.89	7.62	42.45	0.79	3.39
1946	66.70	0.21	7.89	7.93	46.99	0.90	2.71
1947	75.57	0.26	9.48	8.87	53.81	1.08	2.02
1948	84.81	0.34	10.97	10.11	60.52	1.31	1.51
1949	90.62	0.45	12.02	11.18	64.16	1.52	1.16
1950	96.84	0.58	13.20	12.09	68.16	1.73	0.94
1951	103.37	0.71	14.17	12.81	73.03	1.93	0.85
1952	109.43	0.81	14.87	13.25	77.48	2.16	0.84
1953	115.67	0.91	15.73	13.52	82.04	2.39	0.83
1954	119.75	1.03	16.27	13.51	85.47	2.65	0.76
1955	123.79	1.15	17.16	13.48	88.41	2.88	0.66
1956	129.89	1.24	18.06	13.14	93.70	3.13	0.57
1957	135.70	1.33	18.85	12.77	98.87	3.40	0.48
1958	137.35	1.42	18.69	12.67	100.55	3.60	0.42

Notes to Table A-37 on next page

SOURCE, BY COLUMN

Current Prices
(1) Sum of cols. 2 to 7.
(2) 1900–45: *A Study of Saving* . . . , Vol. III, Table W-25, line I-5.
      1945–58: Table B-43, col. 3.
(3) 1900–45: *Saving*, Vol. III, Table W-29, line I-5.
      1945–58: Table B-57, Col. 3, Table B-58, col. 3 and col. 6.
(4) 1900–45: *Saving*, Vol. III, Table W-27, line I-5.
      1945–58: Table B-81, cols. 3 and 6, Table B-82, col. 3, plus Table B-83, col. 3.
(5) 1900–45: *Saving*, Vol. III, Table W-30, line I-5, minus Table W-40, line I-5.
      1945–58: Table B-129, col. 1, plus Table B-57, col. 3, minus cols. 2 and 3 of Table A-37.
(6) 1900–45: *Saving*, Vol. III, Table W-42, line I-5.
      1945–58: Table B-155, cols. 3 and 4.
(7) 1900–45: *Saving*, Vol. III, Tables W-43 and W-40, line I-5 in each.
      1945–58: Table B-155, cols. 2 and 5.
Constant (1947–49) Prices
Same as for Table A-35, except that Tables B-128 and B-154, are used instead of Tables B-129 and B-155.

NET STOCK OF CONSUMER DURABLES, BY SECTOR
(billions of dollars)

End of Year	All Sectors (1)	Nonfarm Households (2)	Agriculture (3)
CURRENT PRICES			
1900	6.05	5.22	0.83
1912	13.58	11.72	1.86
1922	30.95	27.24	3.71
1929	42.23	38.42	3.81
1933	25.72	23.77	1.95
1939	32.51	29.96	2.55
1945	50.95	46.71	4.24
1945	46.24	40.98	5.26
1946	59.63	52.81	6.82
1947	73.38	65.00	8.38
1948	85.31	75.41	9.90
1949	91.20	80.69	10.51
1950	111.32	98.91	12.41
1951	122.45	108.85	13.60
1952	127.63	113.97	13.66
1953	134.77	120.57	14.20
1954	138.72	124.82	13.90
1955	150.77	136.92	13.85
1956	163.38	149.43	13.95
1957	173.61	159.61	14.00
1958	178.75	164.73	14.02
CONSTANT (1947–49) PRICES			
1900	21.65	18.67	2.98
1912	32.72	28.30	4.42
1922	37.75	33.23	4.52
1929	57.29	52.23	5.06
1933	49.82	46.03	3.79
1939	57.64	53.17	4.47
1945	61.30	56.15	5.15
1945	57.63	51.03	6.50
1946	64.74	57.34	7.40
1947	73.80	65.40	8.40
1948	82.16	72.63	9.53
1949	90.40	80.03	10.37
1950	102.85	91.41	11.44
1951	110.16	98.09	12.07
1952	115.80	103.66	12.14
1953	123.32	110.76	12.56
1954	129.83	117.33	12.50
1955	141.32	128.82	12.50
1956	149.49	137.18	12.31
1957	156.30	144.21	12.09
1958	159.67	147.67	12.00

SOURCE, BY COLUMN

Current Prices
(1)   Sum of cols. 2 and 3.
(2)   1900–45: *A Study of Saving* . . . , Vol. III, Table W-22, line I-6.
        1945–58: Table B-36, col. 1 plus Table B-37, col. 3.
(3)   1900–45: *Saving*, Vol. III, Table W-27, line I-6.
        1945–58: Table B-86, col. 1, minus col. 8, plus Table B-82, col. 6.
Constant (1947–49) Prices
Same as for Table A-35.

TABLE A-39

INVENTORIES, BY SECTOR
(billions of dollars)

End of Year	All Sectors (1)	Unincorporated Business (2)	Agriculture[a] (3)	Corporations (4)	State and Local Governments (5)	Federal Government (6)
			CURRENT PRICES			
1900	9.96	2.65	4.54	2.76	0.01	—
1912	16.68	3.12	8.24	5.30	0.02	—
1922	32.56	6.68	8.46	17.35	0.04	0.03
1929	37.97	6.43	9.48	22.00	0.06	—
1933	21.90	3.09	4.95	13.80	0.06	—
1939	30.45	4.15	7.30	18.00	0.06	0.94
1945	52.25	7.83	15.37	26.32	0.15	2.58
1945	52.62	7.97	15.68	26.32	0.07	2.58
1946	68.19	10.06	19.10	37.55	0.09	1.39
1947	79.98	11.59	22.50	44.69	0.10	1.10
1948	86.04	12.92	22.20	48.89	0.11	1.92
1949	79.59	11.97	18.93	45.31	0.10	3.28
1950	96.51	14.24	24.37	55.10	0.13	2.67
1951	110.43	15.07	28.14	64.85	0.13	2.24
1952	106.88	14.79	23.15	66.10	0.13	2.71
1953	107.76	15.21	18.91	67.91	0.14	5.59
1954	107.09	15.06	18.75	66.30	0.15	6.83
1955	113.30	15.81	17.38	72.97	0.16	6.98
1956	122.33	16.51	18.23	80.54	0.18	6.87
1957	126.78	16.82	20.57	83.27	0.19	5.93
1958	129.89	16.81	26.15	78.84	0.20	7.89
			CONSTANT (1947–49) PRICES			
1900	32.59	6.98	18.31	7.26	0.04	—
1912	37.75	6.45	20.29	10.96	0.05	—
1922	55.96	9.62	21.21	25.01	0.07	0.05
1929	63.30	9.95	19.20	34.04	0.11	—
1933	53.24	5.96	20.52	26.62	0.14	—
1939	61.44	7.23	19.91	31.35	0.18	2.77
1945	73.82	10.94	22.35	36.80	0.20	3.53
1945	74.20	11.12	22.74	36.70	0.10	3.54
1946	79.44	11.68	22.56	43.61	0.10	1.49
1947	78.57	11.69	20.71	45.09	0.10	0.98
1948	83.00	12.26	22.30	46.39	0.10	1.95
1949	82.10	11.96	21.08	45.27	0.11	3.68
1950	86.41	12.73	21.90	49.24	0.11	2.43
1951	94.46	13.15	22.57	56.59	0.12	2.03
1952	97.51	13.10	23.02	58.55	0.12	2.72
1953	100.91	13.27	22.43	59.26	0.13	5.82
1954	101.58	13.13	23.02	57.81	0.13	7.49
1955	106.22	13.25	23.36	61.11	0.14	8.36
1956	108.92	13.29	22.92	64.85	0.15	7.71
1957	109.23	13.36	23.21	66.14	0.16	6.36
1958	109.95	13.25	25.59	62.18	0.17	8.76

SOURCE, BY COLUMN

Current Prices

(1) Sum of cols. 2 to 6.
(2) 1900–45: *A Study of Saving* . . . , Vol. III, Table W-29, line I-7.
 1945–58: Table B-130, col. 3.
(3) 1900–45: *Saving*, Vol. III, Table W-27, sum of lines I-7 and I-8.
 1945–58: Table B-97, col. 1.
(4) 1900–45: *Saving*, Vol. III, Table W-30, line I-7, minus Table W-40, line I-7.
 1945–58: Table B-130, col. 2.
(5) 1900–45: *Saving*, Vol. III, Table W-42, line I-7.
 1945–58: Table B-156, col. 4.
(6) 1900–45: *Saving*, Vol. III, Table W-40, line I-7.
 1945–58: Table B-156, col. 2.

Constant (1947–49) Prices

Same as for Table A-35, except that Table B-131 is used instead of Table B-130.

ᵃ Including livestock.

TABLE A-40

RESIDENTIAL LAND, BY SECTOR
(billions of dollars)

End of Year	All Sectors (1)	Nonfarm Households (2)	Unincorporated Business (3)	Corporations (4)
	CURRENT PRICES			
1900	4.40	4.22	0.07	0.11
1912	6.99	6.51	0.21	0.27
1922	15.41	13.94	0.60	0.87
1929	24.06	20.65	1.37	2.04
1933	18.66	15.91	1.09	1.66
1939	22.90	19.45	1.31	2.14
1945	31.09	26.22	1.82	3.05
1945	22.58	18.46	2.30	1.82
1946	26.31	21.66	2.56	2.09
1947	31.92	26.47	2.96	2.49
1948	34.61	28.65	3.19	2.77
1949	34.19	28.23	3.13	2.83
1950	39.55	32.89	3.43	3.23
1951	42.17	35.22	3.52	3.43
1952	44.42	37.24	3.58	3.60
1953	46.18	38.80	3.63	3.75
1954	47.80	40.35	3.61	3.84
1955	51.79	43.95	3.74	4.10
1956	55.40	47.17	3.86	4.37
1957	57.90	49.41	3.92	4.57
1958	60.67	51.91	3.99	4.77
	CONSTANT (1947–49) PRICES			
1900	18.97	18.23	0.27	0.47
1912	27.18	25.34	0.79	1.05
1922	33.96	30.76	1.29	1.91
1929	49.94	42.95	2.76	4.23
1933	48.00	41.04	2.69	4.27
1939	46.99	39.99	2.60	4.40
1945	42.97	36.30	2.46	4.21
1945	31.25	25.64	3.12	2.49
1946	31.47	25.91	3.06	2.50
1947	31.98	26.42	3.02	2.53
1948	32.84	27.24	3.00	2.60
1949	33.62	27.92	2.99	2.72
1950	34.83	29.03	2.98	2.82
1951	35.87	30.05	2.94	2.88
1952	36.86	31.04	2.90	2.92
1953	37.98	32.12	2.87	2.99
1954	39.13	33.27	2.82	3.04
1955	40.74	34.83	2.80	3.11
1956	42.15	36.18	2.78	3.19
1957	43.37	37.35	2.76	3.26
1958	44.56	38.48	2.74	3.34

Current Prices

(1) Sum of cols. 2 to 4.

(2) 1900–45: *A Study of Saving* . . . , Vol. III, Table W-22, line I-3, minus col. 3 of Table A-40.

1945–58: Fifteen per cent of Table B-16, col. 8 (see Table B-12, notes to col. 2).

(3) 1900–45: Land underlying multifamily dwellings owned by individuals (assumed to be 25 per cent) as estimated in Table A-35, note to col. 3.

1945–58: Sum of land underlying multifamily structures in Table B-16, col. 9, plus Table B-54, col. 5, minus col. 3.

(4) 1900–45: *Saving*, Vol. III, Table W-30, line I-3.

1945–58: Table B-14, col. 5, minus col. 3, minus cols. 2 and 3 of Table A-40.

Constant (1947–49) Prices

Same as for Table A-35.

TABLE A-41

NONRESIDENTIAL LAND, EXCLUDING FORESTS AND SUBSOIL ASSETS, BY SECTOR
(billions of dollars)

End of Year	All Sectors (1)	Nonfarm Households (2)	Institutions (3)	Unincorporated Business[a] (4)	Agriculture (5)	Corporations[a] (6)	State and Local Governments (7)	Federal Government (8)
CURRENT PRICES								
1900	26.53	3.00	0.28	1.12	14.55	3.58	3.00	1.00
1912	51.24	3.70	0.51	1.76	31.57	6.20	6.50	1.00
1922	77.49	6.65	1.01	3.52	41.54	12.17	11.10	1.50
1929	89.47	11.78	1.39	7.34	34.93	18.73	13.20	2.10
1933	62.44	7.55	1.19	3.48	22.80	12.04	13.15	2.23
1939	65.70	5.33	1.34	4.16	23.24	14.23	14.60	2.80
1945	96.95	6.00	1.60	4.77	44.51	16.12	17.45	6.50
1945	89.62	7.75	2.12	4.48	43.47	11.30	14.20	6.30
1946	104.74	7.90	2.82	6.80	46.53	14.79	18.90	7.00
1947	116.74	9.45	3.49	7.31	49.78	17.02	21.40	8.30
1948	123.88	11.45	3.77	7.73	51.93	18.60	21.50	8.90
1949	121.56	11.30	3.75	7.48	50.90	18.53	20.50	9.10
1950	137.81	11.85	4.17	7.97	58.40	19.92	24.00	11.50
1951	150.85	12.70	4.50	8.37	66.31	21.37	24.20	13.40
1952	154.31	14.70	4.84	8.68	66.89	22.60	23.70	12.90
1953	153.57	15.95	5.12	9.08	64.22	23.20	24.00	12.00
1954	161.00	18.45	5.44	9.73	66.41	24.47	24.10	12.40
1955	171.41	21.00	5.87	10.48	68.94	26.72	24.80	13.60
1956	184.96	24.35	6.37	11.44	73.96	29.14	26.30	13.40
1957	202.02	29.25	6.90	12.35	79.94	32.58	27.40	13.60
1958	216.48	32.80	7.45	13.22	87.58	34.63	28.00	12.80
CONSTANT (1947–49) PRICES								
1900	80.70	10.35	0.96	3.87	41.68	12.36	8.61	2.87
1912	106.63	10.83	1.49	5.15	54.07	18.15	14.68	2.26
1922	113.72	11.31	1.71	5.98	52.91	20.69	18.61	2.51
1929	137.58	17.83	2.10	11.11	52.05	28.34	22.56	3.59
1933	131.85	14.39	2.26	6.63	51.48	22.94	29.19	4.96
1939	126.39	9.36	2.35	7.31	47.43	25.00	29.32	5.62
1945	127.07	8.02	2.14	6.38	53.48	21.55	25.86	9.64
1945	121.16	10.13	3.53	7.27	53.80	16.93	20.40	9.10
1946	117.73	10.22	3.51	7.40	50.91	17.49	20.50	7.70
1947	117.39	10.38	3.49	7.31	50.28	17.23	20.70	8.00
1948	117.87	10.71	3.54	7.33	49.27	17.62	20.80	8.60
1949	119.61	10.93	3.63	7.29	49.57	17.89	21.00	9.30
1950	122.17	11.23	3.77	7.32	50.87	17.68	21.10	10.20
1951	125.35	11.42	3.91	7.37	51.29	18.16	21.30	11.90
1952	125.70	11.78	4.01	7.33	50.72	18.56	21.60	11.70
1953	124.97	12.14	4.12	7.44	50.17	18.50	21.70	10.90
1954	126.95	12.46	4.28	7.63	50.24	19.14	22.00	11.20
1955	129.66	12.69	4.45	7.98	50.07	20.07	22.30	12.10
1956	131.85	12.96	4.62	8.39	50.87	21.02	22.60	11.40
1957	135.10	13.38	4.84	8.75	51.58	22.05	23.10	11.40
1958	137.53	13.66	5.06	9.09	52.92	22.60	23.40	10.80

SOURCE, BY COLUMN

Current Prices
(1) Sum of cols. 2 to 8.
(2) 1900–45: *A Study of Saving* . . . , Vol. III, Table W-22, line I-4, minus Table W-25, line I-4.
     1945–58: Table B-17, col. 3.
(3) 1900–45: *Saving*, Vol. III, Table W-25, line I-4.
     1945–58: Table B-41, col. 5 plus Table B-42, col. 5.
(4) 1900–45: *Saving*, Vol. III, Table W-29, line I-4.
     1945–58: Table B-59, col. 5, plus Table B-125, one-third of col. 5.
(5) 1900–45: *Saving*, Vol. III, Table W-27, lines I-3 and I-4.
     1945–58: Table B-91, col. 2.
(6) 1900–45: *Saving*, Vol. III, Table W-30, line I-4.
     1945–58: Table B-124, col. 6, plus Table B-125, one-third of col. 5, minus col. 4 of Table A-41.
(7) 1900–45: *Saving*, Vol. III, Table W-42, lines I-3 and I-4.
     1945–58: Table B-151, col. 6.
(8) 1900–45: *Saving*, Vol. III, Table W-43, lines I-3 and I-4.
     1945–58: Table B-151, col. 2.
Constant (1947–49) Prices
Same as for Table A-35, except that Table B-152 is used instead of Table B-151.
  ᵃ Includes forests for bench-mark years 1900–45.

TABLE A-42

Forests, by Sector
(billions of dollars)

End of Year	All Sectors (1)	Unincorporated Business (2)	Corporations (3)
	CURRENT PRICES		
1945	3.09	0.79	2.30
1946	3.80	0.95	2.85
1947	6.09	1.54	4.55
1948	7.57	1.87	5.70
1949	8.33	2.08	6.25
1950	11.87	2.97	8.90
1951	14.31	3.56	10.75
1952	13.29	3.34	9.95
1953	11.95	3.00	8.95
1954	12.61	3.16	9.45
1955	15.02	3.77	11.25
1956	14.69	3.69	11.00
1957	15.03	3.78	11.25
1958	13.73	3.43	10.30
	CONSTANT (1947–49) PRICES		
1945	6.40	1.60	4.80
1946	6.44	1.59	4.85
1947	6.48	1.63	4.85
1948	6.52	1.62	4.90
1949	6.56	1.66	4.90
1950	6.60	1.65	4.95
1951	6.64	1.14	5.00
1952	6.68	1.68	5.00
1953	6.72	1.67	5.05
1954	6.76	1.71	5.05
1955	6.80	1.70	5.10
1956	6.84	1.69	5.15
1957	6.88	1.73	5.15
1958	6.92	1.72	5.20

SOURCE, BY COLUMN

Current Prices
(1) Sum of cols. 2 and 3.
(2) Table B-132, col. 1, minus col. 4.
(3) Table B-132, col. 4.

Constant (1947–49) Prices
(1) Sum of cols. 2 and 3.
(2) Table B-132, col. 2 minus col. 5.
(3) Table B-132, col. 5.

TABLE A-43

SUBSOIL ASSETS, BY SECTOR
(billions of dollars)

End of Year	All Sectors (1)	Unincorporated Business (2)	Corporations (3)
CURRENT PRICES			
1945	6.20	0.60	5.60
1946	7.10	0.70	6.40
1947	9.40	1.00	8.40
1948	12.80	1.30	11.50
1949	11.90	1.20	10.70
1950	12.50	1.30	11.20
1951	14.30	1.50	12.80
1952	14.70	1.50	13.20
1953	16.30	1.80	14.50
1954	16.90	1.80	15.10
1955	17.90	1.90	16.00
1956	19.00	2.00	17.00
1957	20.70	2.20	18.50
1958	19.90	2.10	17.80
CONSTANT (1947–49) PRICES			
1945	9.70	1.00	8.70
1946	10.00	1.00	9.00
1947	10.20	1.10	9.10
1948	10.90	1.10	9.80
1949	11.40	1.20	10.20
1950	11.70	1.20	10.50
1951	12.60	1.30	11.30
1952	12.80	1.30	11.50
1953	13.40	1.40	12.00
1954	13.60	1.40	12.20
1955	13.70	1.40	12.30
1956	14.00	1.50	12.50
1957	14.10	1.50	12.60
1958	14.20	1.50	12.70

SOURCE, BY COLUMN

Current Prices
(1) Sum of cols. 2 and 3.
(2) Table B-135, col. 2.
(3) Table B-135, col. 1.

Constant (1947–49) Prices
(1) Sum of cols. 2 and 3.
(2) Table B-135, col. 4.
(3) Table B-135, col. 3.

TABLE A-44

MONETARY METALS, BY SECTOR
(billions of dollars)

End of Year	All Sectors (1)	Nonfarm House-holds (2)	Unincor-porated Business (3)	Agri-culture (4)	Corpora-tions (5)	State and Local Govern-ments (6)	Federal Govern-ment (7)
			CURRENT PRICES				
1900	1.81	0.38		0.16	0.25	0.01	1.01
1912	2.78	0.40		0.15	0.32	0.01	1.90
1922	4.63	0.45		0.12	0.32	0.01	3.73
1929	5.05	0.39	n.a.	0.10	0.67	0.01	3.88
1933	5.04	0.33		0.07	0.84	a	3.80
1939	20.75	0.40		0.09	0.07	0.01	20.18
1945	23.69	1.01		0.18	0.05	0.01	22.44
1945	23.91	0.84	0.13	0.16	0.12		22.66
1946	24.39	0.89	0.14	0.17	0.13		23.06
1947	26.66	0.92	0.15	0.18	0.13		25.28
1948	28.20	0.95	0.15	0.18	0.15		26.77
1949	28.45	0.95	0.16	0.19	0.16		26.99
1950	26.79	1.01	0.17	0.18	0.16		25.27
1951	26.83	1.06	0.19	0.20	0.15	n.a.	25.23
1952	27.39	1.14	0.18	0.20	0.17		25.70
1953	26.30	1.20	0.19	0.19	0.20		24.52
1954	26.04	1.21	0.20	0.19	0.22		24.22
1955	26.08	1.27	0.21	0.20	0.21		24.19
1956	26.48	1.33	0.22	0.21	0.21		24.51
1957	27.46	1.50	0.25	0.24	0.25		25.22
1958	25.41	1.62	0.27	0.25	0.27		23.00
			CONSTANT (1947–49) PRICES				
1900	2.49	0.52		0.22	0.35	0.02	1.38
1912	4.00	0.58		0.21	0.45	0.02	2.74
1922	7.43	0.72		0.19	0.51	0.02	5.99
1929	7.90	0.61	n.a.	0.16	1.05	0.02	6.06
1933	7.76	0.51		0.10	1.29	0.01	5.85
1939	20.13	0.38		0.09	0.07	0.02	19.57
1945	23.02	0.98		0.17	0.05	0.02	21.80
1945	21.74	0.37	0.06	0.07	0.05		21.19
1946	22.21	0.39	0.06	0.07	0.06		21.63
1947	24.47	0.40	0.07	0.08	0.06		23.86
1948	25.99	0.42	0.07	0.08	0.07		25.35
1949	26.18	0.42	0.07	0.08	0.07		25.54
1950	24.49	0.44	0.08	0.08	0.07		23.82
1951	24.50	0.46	0.08	0.09	0.07	n.a.	23.80
1952	25.03	0.50	0.08	0.09	0.08		24.28
1953	23.89	0.52	0.08	0.08	0.09		23.12
1954	23.61	0.53	0.09	0.08	0.10		22.81
1955	23.60	0.55	0.09	0.09	0.09		22.78
1956	23.93	0.58	0.10	0.09	0.09		23.07
1957	24.83	0.66	0.11	0.10	0.11		23.85
1958	22.67	0.71	0.12	0.11	0.12		21.61

SOURCE, BY COLUMN

Current Prices

(1) Sum of cols. 2 to 7.
(2) 1900–45: *A Study of Saving* . . . , Vol. III, Table W-22, line **9.**
      1945–58: Table B-183, col. 7.
(3) Table B-183, col. 5.
(4) 1900–45: *Saving*, Vol. III, Table W-27, line 9.
      1945–58: Table B-183, col. 6.
(5) 1900–45: *Saving*, Vol. III, Table W-30, line 9.
      1945–58: Table B-183, cols. 3 and 4.
(6) 1900–45: *Saving*, Vol. III, Table W-42, line 9.
(7) 1900–45: *Saving*, Vol. III, Table W-43, line 9.
      1945–58: Table B-182, col. 2, plus Table B-183, col. 2.

Constant (1947–49) Prices

Same as for Table A-35, except that Table B-184 is used instead of Table B-183.

ª Less than $5 million.
  n.a. = not available.

TABLE A-45

NET FOREIGN ASSETS, BY SECTOR
(billions of dollars)

End of Year	All Sectors (1)	Nonfarm Households (2)	Corporations (3)	Federal Government (4)
CURRENT PRICES				
1900	−2.34			
1912	−2.10			
1922	8.20			
1929	12.40	n.a.	n.a.	n.a.
1933	8.10			
1939	1.73			
1945	1.05			
1945	−2.29	2.70	−2.58	−2.41
1946	2.81	2.77	−1.41	1.45
1947	10.93	2.75	0.13	8.05
1948	12.90	2.75	1.11	9.04
1949	13.79	2.63	1.36	9.80
1950	13.39	2.95	1.90	8.54
1951	14.41	3.12	2.83	8.46
1952	14.73	3.11	3.63	7.99
1953	15.94	3.00	4.14	8.80
1954	15.44	3.37	3.83	8.24
1955	15.39	3.87	4.23	7.29
1956	17.87	4.12	6.14	7.61
1957	22.81	3.78	10.40	8.63
1958	24.34	4.69	10.20	9.45
CONSTANT (1947–49) PRICES				
1900	−6.92			
1912	−4.76			
1922	12.01			
1929	18.17	n.a.	n.a.	n.a.
1933	15.81			
1939	3.05			
1945	1.20			
1945	−2.67	3.16	−3.01	−2.82
1946	2.97	2.92	−1.48	1.53
1947	10.64	2.68	0.13	7.83
1948	12.17	2.59	1.05	8.53
1949	12.86	2.45	1.27	9.14
1950	11.98	2.64	1.70	7.64
1951	12.33	2.67	2.42	7.24
1952	12.45	2.63	3.07	6.75
1953	13.35	2.52	3.46	7.37
1954	12.81	2.80	3.18	6.83
1955	12.51	3.14	3.44	5.93
1956	14.52	3.35	4.99	6.18
1957	17.98	2.98	8.20	6.80
1958	18.87	3.63	7.91	7.33

SOURCE, BY COLUMN

Current Prices
 (1) 1900–45: *A Study of Saving* . . . , Vol. III, Table W-1, col. 25. 1945–58: sum of cols 2, 3, and 4.
 (2) Table B-187, line 4 minus line 10.
 (3) Table B-187, line 3 minus line 9.
 (4) Table B-187, line 5 minus line 11.

Constant (1947–49) Prices
 (1) 1900–45: *Saving*, Vol. III, Table W-3, col. 26, adjusted by Table B-188, line 12. 1945–58: Sum of cols. 2 to 4.
 (2–4) Corresponding figure in current prices adusted by gross national product deflator.
 n.a. = not available.

TABLE A-46

GROSS STOCK OF RESIDENTIAL STRUCTURES, BY SECTOR
(billions of dollars)

End of Year	All Sectors (1)	Nonfarm House-holds (2)	Unincor-porated Business (3)	Agri-culture (4)	Corpora-tions (5)	State and Local Govern-ments (6)	Federal Govern-ment (7)
			CURRENT PRICES				
1945	261.79	210.89	17.11	18.64	12.80	0.96	1.39
1946	308.42	248.78	19.48	22.33	14.93	1.48	1.42
1947	374.65	304.31	22.84	26.46	17.64	1.89	1.51
1948	404.57	328.46	25.01	27.43	20.29	2.02	1.36
1949	400.22	323.32	24.78	27.58	21.06	2.22	1.26
1950	459.19	374.69	27.49	29.77	23.27	2.69	1.28
1951	488.80	399.17	28.70	31.79	24.50	3.38	1.26
1952	513.32	419.83	29.66	32.57	25.89	4.13	1.24
1953	531.53	435.03	30.47	33.02	27.14	4.75	1.12
1954	548.65	450.01	30.75	33.72	28.07	5.11	0.99
1955	591.51	485.44	32.22	34.98	32.35	5.61	0.91
1956	627.91	517.77	33.64	36.25	33.33	6.12	0.80
1957	653.12	539.13	34.51	36.77	35.11	6.64	0.96
1958	684.13	566.34	35.66	37.72	35.73	7.34	1.34
			CONSTANT (1947–49) PRICES				
1945	362.63	292.87	23.34	25.60	17.56	1.31	1.95
1946	368.14	297.58	23.30	25.94	17.85	1.78	1.69
1947	375.14	303.69	23.28	26.46	18.27	1.93	1.51
1948	384.74	312.22	23.50	26.90	18.93	1.90	1.29
1949	393.82	319.80	23.69	27.30	19.67	2.12	1.24
1950	405.84	330.69	23.91	27.73	20.02	2.34	1.15
1951	417.19	340.59	23.95	28.13	20.61	2.83	1.08
1952	427.91	349.90	23.98	28.57	21.14	3.34	0.98
1953	439.52	360.13	24.04	28.91	21.76	3.75	0.93
1954	451.49	370.99	24.07	29.27	22.35	4.00	0.81
1955	466.30	384.99	24.12	29.56	22.72	4.19	0.72
1956	479.90	397.40	24.18	29.86	23.45	4.40	0.61
1957	492.73	408.84	24.26	30.09	24.14	4.67	0.73
1958	505.81	420.16	24.44	30.30	24.89	5.03	0.99

Constant (1947–49) Prices

(1)   Sum of cols. 2 to 7.

(2)   Components of expenditures in Table B-15, col. 2, cumulated for life of component, beginning with 1945, adding later expenditures and dropping retirements plus Table B-164, col. 2. Life of components used: structures, 80 years; additions and alterations, 40 years; speculative builders' margin, 80 years; dealers commission, 40 years.

(3)   Components of expenditures in Table B-52, col. 2, cumulated for life of component, beginning with 1945, adding later expenditures and dropping retirements, plus Table B-53, col. 2, plus Table B-146, col. 2. Life of components used: structures, 65 years; additions and alternations, 32 years; dealers' commission, 32 years.

(4)   Expenditures in Table B-60, col. 2, cumulated for 60 years. Earlier figures from *A Study of Saving . . .* , Vol. I, Table A-7, col. 2 (converted to 1947–49 prices), and from worksheets.

(5)   Cumulation of gross expenditures in Table B-5, col. 2, Table B-7, col. 2, and Table B-8, col. 2, minus cols. 2 and 3 of this table.

(6)   Cumulation of gross expenditures in Table B-144, col. 2, for 50 years. Earlier figures in *Construction Volume and Costs, 1915–1956,* Statistical Supplement to *Construction Review* (Department of Commerce), p. 10, plus cumulation of gross expenditures in Table B-147, col. 2, on 20-year basis.

(7)   Cumulation of gross expenditures in Table B-162, col. 2 on 50-year basis, plus gross cumulated expenditures from Table B-165, col. 2, on 20-year basis.

Current Prices

Cumulated gross stock in constant (1947–49) dollars, multiplied by appropriate year-end deflator for each component included in aggregate gross cumulation; e.g., in col. 2, deflator used is from col. 3 of Table B-9.

TABLE A-47

GROSS STOCK OF NONRESIDENTIAL STRUCTURES, BY SECTOR

(billions of dollars)

End of Year	All Sectors (1)	Institu- tions (2)	Unincor- porated Business (3)	Agri- culture (4)	Corpora- tions (5)	State and Local Govern- ments (6)	Federal Govern- ment (7)
			CURRENT	PRICES			
1945	260.24	15.15	18.45	15.84	119.06	73.22	18.52
1946	327.74	20.23	24.35	18.48	149.08	91.92	23.68
1947	387.05	25.26	29.07	21.54	171.64	110.62	28.92
1948	422.08	27.20	30.82	22.65	187.80	121.85	31.76
1949	416.44	26.75	29.98	22.97	187.78	116.60	32.36
1950	463.46	29.28	32.21	24.86	210.44	130.42	36.25
1951	495.15	31.03	34.15	27.10	223.71	140.63	38.53
1952	524.28	33.00	35.52	27.92	233.72	152.43	41.69
1953	445.54	34.63	36.71	28.26	245.46	156.29	44.19
1954	566.70	36.37	38.26	28.74	253.39	163.75	46.19
1955	606.06	38.77	41.20	29.72	270.71	176.86	48.80
1956	651.81	41.40	43.86	30.98	289.52	194.39	51.66
1957	706.58	44.00	47.25	31.81	323.23	207.60	52.69
1958	740.33	46.71	50.04	32.23	337.32	220.57	53.46
			CONSTANT (1947–49)	PRICES			
1945	383.38	25.21	29.23	21.29	170.53	108.93	28.19
1946	387.41	25.29	29.38	21.44	173.14	109.56	28.60
1947	391.35	25.26	29.09	21.73	175.00	111.12	29.15
1948	398.18	25.49	29.23	22.07	177.94	113.54	29.91
1949	406.24	25.95	22.28	29.28	180.53	117.11	30.98
1950	414.49	26.45	29.45	22.77	182.63	121.14	32.05
1951	423.37	26.98	29.73	23.20	185.82	124.64	33.00
1952	431.80	27.32	29.85	23.62	188.42	128.74	33.85
1953	441.61	27.84	30.08	23.91	192.03	133.14	34.61
1954	453.19	28.59	30.67	24.13	196.29	138.35	35.16
1955	466.76	29.37	31.62	24.22	201.47	144.43	35.65
1956	479.72	30.03	32.50	24.32	206.49	150.37	36.01
1957	491.81	30.75	33.40	24.36	211.06	156.99	35.25
1958	505.27	31.69	34.51	24.37	215.69	164.40	34.61

SOURCE, BY COLUMN

Constant (1947–49) Prices

(1) Sum of cols. 2 to 7.
(2) Cumulation of gross expenditures in Table B-38, col. 2, assuming an average life of 50 years, plus Table B-39, col. 2, average life of 45 years.
(3) Cumulation of gross expenditures in Table B-39, col. 2 (45 yrs.), Table B-45, col. 1 (40 yrs.), col. 2 (40 yrs.), col. 3 (40 yrs.), col. 4 (25 yrs.), col. 5 (40 yrs.).
(4) Cumulation of gross expenditures in Table B-61, col. 2, on basis of a 45-year life, plus apportioned share of cumulated gross expenditures of dealers' commission for sales of farms, from Table B-63, col. 2 (50 yrs.).
(5) Cumulated gross expenditures in Table B-101, col. 2 (40 yrs.), Table B-102, col. 2 (40 yrs.), Table B-103, col. 2 (40 yrs.), Table B-104, col. 2 (50 yrs.), Table B-105, col. 2 (45 yrs.), average of Table B-107, col. 2, and Table B-108, col. 2 (25 yrs.); Table B-109, col. 2 (40 yrs.), minus col. 3 of this Table (A-47), minus cumulated gross expenditures in Table B-39, col. 2 (45 yrs.).
(6) Cumulated gross expenditures of components in Table B-137 (calendar-year portion), col. 2 (30 yrs. for highways, 50 yrs. for other construction), plus Table B-138, col. 2 (30 yrs.), plus components of Table B-141, col. 2 (30 yrs. for highways, 50 yrs. for other construction).
(7) Cumulated gross expenditures of components in Table B-158, col. 2 (50 yrs. for nonresidential buildings; 30 yrs. for highways; 80 yrs. for conservation and development) and components of Table B-160, col. 2 (50 yrs. for all construction except RFC, which is 15 yrs.).

Current Prices

See current prices note to Table A-46.

TABLE A-48

GROSS STOCK OF PRODUCER DURABLES, BY SECTOR
(billions of dollars)

End of Year	All Sectors (1)	Unincor- porated Business (2)	Institu- tions (3)	Agricul- ture (4)	Corpora- tions (5)	State and Local Govern- ments (6)	Federal Govern- ment (7)
			CURRENT PRICES				
1945	92.08	9.41	0.28	9.25	66.97	1.40	4.77
1946	107.51	11.57	0.36	10.68	77.75	1.69	5.46
1947	128.26	14.76	0.46	13.67	91.40	2.07	5.90
1948	146.88	18.12	0.59	17.47	103.26	2.46	4.98
1949	159.80	20.79	0.73	20.54	112.00	2.80	2.94
1950	181.23	24.33	0.95	23.28	127.00	3.22	2.45
1951	202.70	27.81	1.18	26.23	141.64	3.62	2.22
1952	217.09	29.96	1.38	27.87	151.65	3.92	2.31
1953	233.80	32.47	1.58	29.27	163.76	4.38	2.34
1954	247.56	34.91	1.87	30.63	172.94	5.05	2.16
1955	262.28	38.36	2.27	32.51	181.16	6.02	1.96
1956	295.38	42.50	2.73	34.42	206.56	7.23	1.94
1957	320.22	47.12	3.21	35.80	223.73	8.50	1.86
1958	337.19	50.22	3.59	38.08	234.27	9.34	1.69
			CONSTANT (1947–49) PRICES				
1945	117.50	12.22	0.36	12.11	84.88	1.80	6.13
1946	122.10	13.27	0.41	12.85	87.39	1.93	6.25
1947	131.47	15.18	0.48	14.46	93.14	2.13	6.08
1948	142.28	17.52	0.57	16.52	100.47	2.38	4.82
1949	149.45	19.47	0.69	18.41	105.51	2.62	2.75
1950	159.69	21.67	0.84	20.05	112.09	2.86	2.18
1951	169.88	23.69	1.01	21.42	118.79	3.08	1.89
1952	180.04	25.23	1.15	22.47	125.95	3.30	1.94
1953	190.39	27.16	1.31	23.71	132.61	3.66	1.94
1954	198.60	28.74	1.52	24.57	137.87	4.14	1.76
1955	207.29	30.28	1.77	25.47	143.56	4.68	1.53
1956	216.37	31.66	2.00	25.67	150.33	5.29	1.42
1957	225.08	33.61	2.25	25.40	156.56	5.96	1.30
1958	231.70	34.86	2.46	25.94	160.88	6.40	1.16

SOURCE, BY COLUMN

Constant (1947–49) Prices
(1) Sum of cols. 2 to 7.
(2) Cumulated gross expenditures from Table B-49, col. 2 (assuming an average life of 15 years), Table B-50, col. 2 (6 yrs.), Table B-51, col. 2 (3 yrs.).
(3) Cumulated gross expenditures from Table B-40, col. 2 (12 yrs.).
(4) Cumulated gross expenditures from Table B-64, col. 2 (15 yrs.), Table B-65, col. 2 (15 yrs.), Table B-67, col. 2 (10 yrs.), Table B-68, col. 2 (5 yrs.), Table B-69, col. 2 (10 yrs.).
(5) Cumulated gross expenditures from Table B-111 for each column from 2 to 20 with varying average lengths of life (see Table B-112, note to cols. 2 to 13) and Table B-119, col. 2 (excluding passenger cars), Table B-50, col. 2 (6 yrs.), Table B-120, col. 2 (6 yrs.), Table B-51, col. 2 (3 yrs.), minus cols. 2 and 3 of this table (A-48).
(6) Cumulated gross expenditures from Table B-139, calendar-year basis, col. 2 (12 yrs.), plus Table B-142, col. 2 (12 yrs.).
(7) Cumulated gross expenditures from Table B-159, col. 2 (12 yrs.), and Table B-161, col. 2 (12 yrs., except RFC which is 6 yrs.).

Current Prices
See current prices note to Table A-46.

TABLE A-49

GROSS STOCK OF CONSUMER DURABLES, BY SECTOR
(billions of dollars)

End of Year	All Sectors (1)	Nonfarm Households (2)	Agriculture (3)
	CURRENT PRICES		
1945	108.03	95.53	12.50
1946	131.67	116.64	15.03
1947	156.52	138.79	17.73
1948	177.50	157.26	20.24
1949	186.38	165.56	20.82
1950	217.24	193.32	23.92
1951	236.60	210.49	26.11
1952	247.69	220.72	26.97
1953	263.16	234.59	28.57
1954	275.06	246.04	29.02
1955	298.18	268.08	30.10
1956	325.66	294.46	31.20
1957	356.57	323.56	33.01
1958	383.77	348.41	35.36
	CONSTANT (1947–49) PRICES		
1945	137.24	121.52	15.72
1946	145.26	128.64	16.62
1947	158.14	140.27	17.87
1948	172.92	151.38	21.54
1949	183.40	162.91	20.49
1950	200.05	178.10	21.95
1951	211.37	188.36	23.01
1952	222.33	198.70	23.63
1953	238.33	213.41	24.92
1954	254.25	228.60	25.65
1955	275.84	249.24	26.60
1956	294.96	268.11	26.85
1957	319.32	291.75	27.57
1958	339.57	311.03	28.54

SOURCE, BY COLUMN

Constant (1947–49) Prices
(1) Sum of cols. 2 and 3.
(2) Cumulated gross expenditures from Table B-19, for each column from 2 through 12 (for average lengths of life see Table B-31), plus Table B-32, col. 2 (9 years).
(3) Cumulated gross expenditures from Table B-72, for each column from 2 through 12 (for average lengths of life see Table B-31 and Table B-66, note to col. 3).
Current Prices
See current prices note to Table A-46.

NET STOCK OF TANGIBLE ASSETS OF NONFARM HOUSEHOLDS
(billions of dollars)

End of Year	Total (1)	Residential Structures (2)	Residential Land (3)	Nonresidential Land (4)	Consumer Durables (5)	Monetary Metals (6)	Net Foreign Assets (7)
			CURRENT PRICES				
1900	28.03	15.21	4.22	3.00	5.22	0.38	
1912	46.29	23.96	6.51	3.70	11.72	0.40	
1922	100.72	52.44	13.94	6.65	27.24	0.45	
1929	150.65	79.41	20.65	11.78	38.42	0.39	n.a.
1933	109.30	61.74	15.91	7.55	23.77	0.33	
1939	131.98	76.84	19.45	5.33	29.96	0.40	
1945	191.86	111.92	26.22	6.00	46.71	1.01	
1945	194.45	123.72	18.46	7.75	40.98	0.84	2.70
1946	231.31	145.28	21.66	7.90	52.81	0.89	2.77
1947	282.17	177.58	26.47	9.45	65.00	0.92	2.75
1948	311.52	192.31	28.65	11.45	75.41	0.95	2.75
1949	313.19	189.39	28.23	11.30	80.69	0.95	2.63
1950	368.19	220.58	32.89	11.85	98.91	1.01	2.95
1951	397.09	236.14	35.22	12.70	108.85	1.06	3.12
1952	419.77	249.61	37.24	14.70	113.97	1.14	3.11
1953	439.40	259.88	38.80	15.95	120.57	1.20	3.00
1954	458.38	270.18	40.35	18.45	124.82	1.21	3.37
1955	501.14	294.13	43.95	21.00	136.92	1.27	3.87
1956	541.94	315.54	47.17	24.35	149.43	1.33	4.12
1957	573.83	330.28	49.41	29.25	159.61	1.50	3.78
1958	602.56	346.81	51.91	32.80	164.73	1.62	4.69
			CONSTANT (1947–49) PRICES				
1900	113.56	65.79	18.23	10.35	18.67	0.52	
1912	158.49	93.44	25.34	10.83	28.30	0.58	
1922	191.98	115.96	30.76	11.31	33.23	0.72	
1929	279.10	165.48	42.95	17.83	52.23	0.61	n.a.
1933	261.46	159.49	41.04	14.39	46.03	0.51	
1939	261.18	158.28	39.99	9.36	53.17	0.38	
1945	256.68	155.23	36.36	8.02	56.15	0.98	
1945	262.13	171.80	25.64	10.13	51.03	0.37	3.16
1946	270.55	173.77	25.91	10.22	57.34	0.34	2.92
1947	282.52	177.24	26.42	10.38	65.40	0.40	2.68
1948	296.39	182.80	27.24	10.71	72.63	0.42	2.59
1949	309.04	187.29	27.92	10.93	80.03	0.42	2.45
1950	329.40	194.65	29.03	11.23	91.41	0.44	2.64
1951	344.11	201.42	30.05	11.42	98.09	0.46	2.67
1952	357.55	207.94	31.04	11.78	103.66	0.52	2.52
1953	373.15	215.09	32.12	12.14	110.76	0.52	2.52
1954	389.07	222.68	33.27	12.46	117.33	0.53	2.80
1955	413.00	232.87	34.84	12.69	128.82	0.55	3.14
1956	432.18	241.93	36.18	12.96	137.18	0.58	3.35
1957	448.18	249.60	37.35	13.38	144.21	0.66	2.98
1958	461.20	257.05	38.48	13.66	147.67	0.71	3.63

SOURCE, CURRENT AND CONSTANT PRICES, BY COLUMN

(1)	Sum of cols. 2 to 7.	(5)	Table A-38, col. 2.
(2)	Table A-35, col. 2.	(6)	Table A-44, col. 2.
(3)	Table A-40, col. 2.	(7)	Table A-45, col. 2.
(4)	Table A-41, col. 2.		

n.a. = not available.

NET STOCK OF TANGIBLE ASSETS OF NONPROFIT INSTITUTIONS
(billions of dollars)

End of Year	Total (1)	Nonresidential Structures (2)	Nonresidential Land (3)	Producer Durables (4)
CURRENT PRICES				
1900	1.47	1.10	0.28	0.09
1912	2.69	2.04	0.51	0.15
1922	5.25	4.06	1.01	0.18
1929	7.33	5.57	1.39	0.37
1933	6.24	4.77	1.19	0.28
1939	6.86	5.37	1.34	0.15
1945	8.13	6.40	1.60	0.13
1945	9.22	6.97	2.12	0.13
1946	12.26	9.26	2.82	0.18
1947	15.28	11.54	3.49	0.25
1948	16.61	12.49	3.77	0.35
1949	16.67	12.44	3.75	0.48
1950	18.76	13.94	4.17	0.65
1951	20.48	15.15	4.50	0.83
1952	22.28	16.47	4.84	0.97
1953	23.77	17.55	5.12	1.10
1954	25.48	18.77	5.44	1.27
1955	27.74	20.40	5.87	1.47
1956	30.32	22.26	6.37	1.69
1957	33.05	24.25	6.90	1.90
1958	35.78	26.26	7.45	2.07
CONSTANT (1947–49) PRICES				
1900	5.92	4.66	0.96	0.30
1912	9.42	7.51	1.49	0.42
1922	10.64	8.63	1.71	0.30
1929	13.92	11.23	2.10	0.59
1933	14.17	11.41	2.26	0.50
1939	12.77	10.19	2.35	0.23
1945	11.10	8.79	2.14	0.17
1945	15.30	11.60	3.53	0.17
1946	15.29	11.57	3.51	0.21
1947	15.29	11.54	3.49	0.26
1948	15.58	11.70	3.54	0.34
1949	16.14	12.06	3.63	0.45
1950	16.94	12.59	3.77	0.58
1951	17.79	13.17	3.91	0.71
1952	18.45	13.63	4.01	0.81
1953	19.14	14.11	4.12	0.91
1954	20.07	14.76	4.28	1.03
1955	21.05	15.45	4.45	1.15
1956	21.99	16.13	4.62	1.24
1957	23.12	16.95	4.84	1.33
1958	24.30	17.82	5.06	1.42

SOURCE, CURRENT AND CONSTANT PRICES, BY COLUMN

(1) Sum of cols. 2 to 4.   (3) Table A-41, col. 3.
(2) Table A-36, col. 2.   (4) Table A-37, col. 2.

NET STOCK OF TANGIBLE ASSETS OF UNINCORPORATED BUSINESS
(billions of dollars)

End of Year	Total (1)	Structures Residential (2)	Structures Nonresidential (3)	Land Residential (4)	Land Nonresidential (5)	Producer Durables (6)	Inventories (7)	Monetary Metals (8)	Forests[a] (9)	Subsoil Assets (10)
				CURRENT PRICES						
1900	7.24	0.26	2.23	0.07	1.12	0.91	2.65			
1912	11.19	0.84	3.84	0.21	1.76	1.42	3.12			
1922	24.84	2.40	8.22	0.60	3.52	3.42	6.68			
1929	36.42	5.48	11.24	1.37	7.34	4.56	6.43			
1933	25.02	4.36	9.80	1.09	3.48	3.20	3.09			
1939	30.16	5.25	11.45	1.31	4.16	3.84	4.15			
1945	41.89	7.26	15.02	1.82	4.77	5.19	7.83			
1945	38.97	9.18	8.21	2.30	4.48	5.31	7.97	0.13	0.79	0.60
1946	49.37	10.26	11.02	2.56	6.80	6.88	10.06	0.14	0.95	0.70
1947	58.90	11.89	13.25	2.96	7.31	9.21	11.59	0.15	1.54	1.00
1948	65.57	12.95	14.11	3.19	7.73	11.35	12.92	0.15	1.87	1.30
1949	65.37	12.79	13.73	3.13	7.48	12.83	11.97	0.16	2.08	1.20
1950	73.80	14.07	14.84	3.43	7.97	14.81	14.24	0.17	2.97	1.30
1951	79.13	14.46	15.83	3.52	8.37	16.63	15.07	0.19	3.56	1.50
1952	80.95	14.71	16.52	3.58	8.68	17.65	14.79	0.18	3.34	1.50
1953	83.96	14.91	17.32	3.63	9.08	18.82	15.21	0.19	3.00	1.80
1954	86.45	14.83	18.27	3.61	9.73	19.79	15.06	0.20	3.16*	1.80
1955	93.03	15.30	20.06	3.74	10.48	21.76	15.81	0.21	3.77	1.90
1956	99.75	15.80	21.97	3.86	11.44	24.26	16.51	0.22	3.69	2.00
1957	105.76	15.99	24.01	3.92	12.35	26.44	16.82	0.25	3.78	2.20
1958	108.58	16.26	25.56	3.99	13.22	26.94	16.81	0.27	3.43	2.10
				CONSTANT (1947–49) PRICES						
1900	23.65	1.09	8.48	0.27	3.87	2.96	6.98			
1912	32.14	3.16	12.61	0.79	5.15	3.98	6.45			
1922	43.95	5.14	16.39	1.29	5.98	5.53	9.62			
1929	64.21	11.05	22.06	2.76	11.11	7.28	9.95			
1933	54.01	10.76	22.16	2.69	6.63	5.81	5.96			
1939	55.51	10.41	21.87	2.60	7.31	6.09	7.23			
1945	57.50	9.85	21.00	2.46	6.38	6.87	10.94			
1945	56.62	12.52	13.04	3.12	7.27	6.89	11.12	0.06	1.60	1.00
1946	58.27	12.27	13.32	3.06	7.40	7.89	11.68	0.06	1.59	1.00
1947	59.69	12.12	13.27	3.02	7.31	9.48	11.69	0.07	1.63	1.10
1948	61.90	12.17	13.38	3.00	7.33	10.97	12.26	0.07	1.62	1.10
1949	62.83	12.23	13.41	2.99	7.29	12.02	11.96	0.07	1.66	1.20
1950	65.01	12.30	13.55	2.98	7.32	13.20	12.73	0.08	1.65	1.20
1951	66.49	12.08	13.76	2.94	7.37	14.17	13.15	0.08	1.64	1.30
1952	67.02	11.89	13.87	2.90	7.33	14.87	13.10	0.08	1.68	1.30
1953	68.41	11.76	14.19	2.87	7.44	15.73	13.27	0.08	1.67	1.40
1954	69.32	11.60	14.67	2.82	7.63	16.27	13.13	0.09	1.71	1.40
1955	71.26	11.46	15.42	2.80	7.98	17.16	13.25	0.09	1.70	1.40
1956	73.41	11.36	16.24	2.78	8.39	18.06	13.29	0.10	1.69	1.50
1957	75.25	11.23	16.96	2.76	8.75	18.85	13.36	0.11	1.73	1.50
1958	75.86	11.15	17.62	2.74	9.09	18.69	13.25	0.12	1.72	1.50

SOURCE, CURRENT AND CONSTANT PRICES, BY COLUMN

(1)	Sum of cols. 2 to 10.	(6)	Table A-37, col. 3.
(2)	Table A-35, col. 3.	(7)	Table A-39, col. 2.
(3)	Table A-36, col. 3.	(8)	Table A-44, col. 3.
(4)	Table A-40, col. 3.	(9)	Table A-42, col. 2.
(5)	Table A-41, col. 4.	(10)	Table A-43, col. 2.

a Forest land for bench-mark years, 1900–45, included in nonresidential land.

TABLE A-53
Net Stock of Tangible Assets of Agriculture
(billions of dollars)

End of Year	Total (1)	Structures Residential (2)	Structures Non-residential (3)	Land (4)	Producer Durables (5)	Consumer Durables (6)	Inventories (7)	Livestock (8)	Monetary Metals (9)
				CURRENT PRICES					
1900	24.51	1.69	1.57	14.55	1.17	0.83	1.42	3.12	0.16
1912	49.70	2.92	2.72	31.57	2.24	1.86	2.59	5.65	0.15
1922	69.47	6.57	5.82	41.54	3.27	3.71	3.09	5.37	0.12
1929	64.42	6.38	5.86	34.93	3.87	3.81	2.97	6.51	0.10
1933	41.03	4.63	4.05	22.80	2.57	1.95	1.78	3.17	0.07
1939	45.69	4.91	4.09	23.24	3.51	2.55	2.17	5.13	0.09
1945	86.30	8.98	6.76	44.51	6.27	4.24	5.63	9.74	0.18
1945	86.68	9.22	7.10	43.47	5.79	5.26	5.96	9.74	0.16
1946	98.50	11.00	8.33	46.53	6.55	6.82	7.18	11.92	0.17
1947	112.17	13.08	9.86	49.78	8.39	8.38	9.24	13.26	0.18
1948	119.05	13.63	10.52	51.93	10.69	9.90	7.77	14.43	0.18
1949	117.57	13.75	10.82	50.90	12.47	10.51	6.04	12.89	0.19
1950	136.29	14.91	11.93	58.40	14.09	12.41	7.27	17.10	0.18
1951	153.18	16.07	13.18	66.31	15.68	13.60	8.61	19.53	0.20
1952	150.65	16.58	13.76	66.89	16.41	13.66	8.37	14.78	0.20
1953	145.11	16.88	14.07	64.22	16.64	14.20	7.16	11.75	0.19
1954	147.80	17.26	14.43	66.41	16.86	13.90	7.54	11.21	0.19
1955	150.61	17.92	15.09	68.94	17.23	13.85	6.68	10.70	0.20
1956	158.36	18.53	15.84	73.96	17.64	13.95	7.10	11.13	0.21
1957	167.95	18.79	16.40	79.94	18.01	14.00	6.50	14.07	0.24
1958	182.62	19.28	16.75	87.58	18.59	14.02	8.04	18.11	0.25
				CONSTANT (1947–49) PRICES					
1900	79.90	7.55	6.03	41.68	3.13	2.98	4.75	13.56	0.22
1912	103.05	10.42	8.33	54.07	5.31	4.42	6.60	13.69	0.21
1922	108.28	13.03	10.88	52.91	5.54	4.52	6.03	15.18	0.19
1929	107.25	13.44	11.28	52.05	6.06	5.06	5.51	13.69	0.16
1933	102.80	12.52	9.93	51.48	4.46	3.79	5.51	15.01	0.10
1939	98.60	11.80	8.92	47.43	5.98	4.47	5.95	13.96	0.09
1945	110.21	11.65	8.46	53.48	8.95	5.15	7.25	15.10	0.17
1945	112.94	12.67	9.54	53.80	7.62	6.50	7.86	14.88	0.07
1946	111.33	12.80	9.66	50.91	7.93	7.40	8.31	14.25	0.07
1947	111.37	13.08	9.95	50.28	8.87	8.40	7.12	13.59	0.08
1948	114.90	13.36	10.25	49.27	10.11	9.53	8.88	13.42	0.08
1949	116.44	13.61	10.55	49.57	11.18	10.37	7.47	13.61	0.08
1950	121.19	13.91	10.90	50.87	12.09	11.44	7.86	14.04	0.08
1951	124.34	14.22	11.29	51.29	12.81	12.07	8.01	14.56	0.09
1952	125.41	14.55	11.64	50.72	13.25	12.14	8.27	14.75	0.09
1953	125.44	14.78	11.90	50.17	13.52	12.56	7.80	14.63	0.08
1954	126.45	14.98	12.12	50.24	13.51	12.50	8.18	14.84	0.08
1955	126.94	15.14	12.30	50.07	13.48	12.50	8.39	14.97	0.09
1956	127.02	15.26	12.43	50.87	13.14	12.31	8.25	14.67	0.09
1957	127.68	15.38	12.55	51.58	12.77	12.09	8.95	14.26	0.10
1958	131.45	15.49	12.67	52.92	12.67	12.00	10.65	14.94	0.11

SOURCE, CURRENT AND CONSTANT PRICES, BY COLUMN

(1) Sum of cols. 2 to 9.
(2) Table A-35, col. 4.
(3) Table A-36, col. 4.
(4) Table A-41, col. 5.
(5) Table A-37, col. 4.
(6) Table A-38, col. 3.
(7) Table A-39, col. 3, minus col. 8 of Table A-53.
(8) Current prices, Table A-5, col. 8.
    Constant prices, Table A-6, col. 8.
(9) Table A-44, col. 4.

TABLE A-54

NET STOCK OF TANGIBLE ASSETS OF CORPORATIONS

(billions of dollars)

End of Year	Structures			Land		Producer Durables (6)	Inven- tories (7)	Monetary Metals (8)	Forests[a] (9)	Subsoil Assets (10)	Net Foreign Assets (11)
	Total (1)	Residential (2)	Nonresi- dential (3)	Residential (4)	Nonresi- dential (5)						
	CURRENT PRICES										
1900	21.88	0.28	10.63	0.11	3.58	4.27	2.76	0.25			
1912	42.18	0.62	19.70	0.27	6.20	9.77	5.30	0.32			
1922	93.95	1.76	37.71	0.87	12.17	23.77	17.35	0.32			
1929	124.95	4.63	47.87	2.04	18.73	29.01	22.00	0.67			
1933	94.77	3.54	40.34	1.66	12.04	22.55	13.80	0.84			
1939	107.22	4.19	42.63	2.14	14.23	25.96	18.00	0.07			
1945	138.85	5.44	52.58	3.05	16.12	35.29	26.32	0.05			
1945	142.84	8.23	55.61	1.82	11.30	34.12	26.32	0.12	2.30	5.60	−2.58
1946	184.02	9.49	70.38	2.09	14.79	41.75	37.55	0.13	2.85	6.40	−1.41
1947	223.77	11.36	82.19	2.49	17.02	52.81	44.69	0.13	4.55	8.40	0.13
1948	254.35	12.60	90.82	2.77	18.60	62.21	48.89	0.15	5.70	11.50	1.11
1949	257.61	12.80	91.45	2.83	18.53	68.22	45.31	0.16	6.25	10.70	1.36
1950	296.20	14.66	103.70	3.23	19.92	77.43	55.10	0.16	8.90	11.20	1.90
1951	331.02	15.60	112.05	3.43	21.37	87.19	64.85	0.15	10.75	12.80	2.83
1952	347.91	16.40	118.87	3.60	22.60	93.39	66.10	0.17	9.95	13.20	3.63
1953	367.12	17.06	127.06	3.75	23.20	100.35	67.91	0.20	8.95	14.50	4.14
1954	380.69	17.53	132.53	3.84	24.47	107.42	66.30	0.22	9.45	15.10	3.83
1955	409.44	18.77	143.59	4.10	26.72	111.60	72.97	0.21	11.25	16.00	4.23
1956	452.47	20.04	155.25	4.37	29.14	128.78	80.54	0.21	11.00	17.00	6.14
1957	499.60	20.93	176.60	4.57	32.58	141.25	83.27	0.25	11.25	18.50	10.40
1958	510.75	21.95	185.61	4.77	34.63	146.38	78.84	0.27	10.30	17.80	10.20

(continued)

TABLE A-54 (concluded)

CONSTANT (1947–49) PRICES

End of Year	Total (1)	Structures		Land		Producer Durables (6)	Inventories (7)	Monetary Metals (8)	Forests[a] (9)	Subsoil Assets (10)	Net Foreign Assets (11)
		Residential (2)	Nonresidential (3)	Residential (4)	Nonresidential (5)						
1900	75.90	1.21	40.40	0.47	12.36	13.85	7.26	0.35			
1912	125.14	2.41	64.72	1.05	18.15	27.40	10.96	0.45			
1922	165.66	3.89	75.20	1.91	20.69	38.45	25.01	0.51			
1929	217.59	9.65	93.97	4.23	28.34	46.31	34.04	1.05			
1933	196.41	9.14	91.23	4.27	22.94	40.92	26.62	1.29			
1939	192.05	8.63	81.40	4.40	25.00	41.20	31.35	0.07			
1945	192.40	7.55	73.49	4.21	21.55	46.75	36.80	0.05			
1945	200.19	11.29	79.80	2.49	16.93	42.45	36.70	0.05	4.80	8.70	−3.02
1946	216.15	11.34	81.79	2.50	17.49	46.99	43.61	0.06	4.85	9.00	−1.48
1947	228.04	11.51	83.73	2.53	17.23	53.81	45.09	0.06	4.85	9.10	0.13
1948	240.81	11.81	86.05	2.60	17.62	60.52	46.39	0.07	4.90	9.80	1.05
1949	246.84	12.37	87.99	2.72	17.89	64.16	45.27	0.07	4.90	10.20	1.27
1950	258.05	12.82	90.11	2.82	17.68	68.16	49.24	0.07	4.95	10.50	1.70
1951	275.56	13.10	93.01	2.88	18.16	73.03	56.59	0.07	5.00	11.30	2.42
1952	286.55	13.35	96.04	2.92	18.56	77.48	58.55	0.08	5.00	11.50	3.07
1953	296.52	13.66	99.47	2.99	18.50	82.04	59.26	0.09	5.05	12.00	3.46
1954	302.78	13.94	102.85	3.04	19.14	85.47	57.81	0.09	5.05	12.20	3.18
1955	314.97	14.30	107.04	3.11	20.07	88.41	61.11	0.10	5.10	12.30	3.44
1956	331.21	14.70	111.02	3.19	21.02	93.70	64.85	0.09	5.15	12.50	4.99
1957	346.90	15.07	115.45	3.26	22.05	98.87	66.14	0.11	5.15	12.60	8.20
1958	348.83	15.42	118.81	3.34	22.60	100.55	62.18	0.12	5.20	12.70	7.91

SOURCE, CURRENT AND CONSTANT PRICES, BY COLUMN

(1) Sum of cols. 2 to 11.
(2) Table A-35, col. 5.
(3) Table A-36, col. 5.
(4) Table A-40, col. 4.
(5) Table A-41, col. 6.
(6) Table A-37, col. 5.
(7) Table A-39, col. 4.
(8) Table A-44, col. 5.
(9) Table A-42, col. 3.
(11) Table A-45, col. 3.
(10) Table A-43, col. 3.

[a] Forest land for bench-mark years, 1900–45, included in nonresidential land.

208

Net Stock of Tangible Assets of State and Local Governments
(billions of dollars)

End of Year	Total (1)	Structures Residential (2)	Structures Nonresidential (3)	Land (4)	Producer Durables (5)	Inventories (6)	Monetary Metals (7)
			CURRENT PRICES				
			a				
1900	4.65		1.57	3.00	0.06	0.01	0.01
1912	11.51		4.83	6.50	0.15	0.02	0.01
1922	24.31		13.04	11.10	0.12	0.04	0.01
1929	34.31		20.54	13.20	0.51	0.06	0.01
1933	36.57		22.88	13.15	0.48	0.06	b
1939	42.01		26.86	14.60	0.48	0.06	0.01
1945	54.26		36.24	17.45	0.41	0.15	0.01
1945	57.31	0.87	41.55	14.20	0.62	0.07	
1946	71.77	1.35	50.64	18.90	0.69	0.09	
1947	84.73	1.69	60.49	21.40	1.05	0.10	
1948	89.84	1.76	65.12	21.50	1.35	0.11	
1949	87.93	1.93	63.77	20.50	1.63	0.10	
1950	99.15	2.33	70.75	24.00	1.94	0.13	
1951	106.82	2.95	77.27	24.20	2.27	0.13	
1952	113.85	3.62	83.84	23.70	2.56	0.13	
1953	118.56	4.14	87.42	24.00	2.86	0.14	
1954	124.73	4.41	92.85	24.10	3.22	0.15	
1955	135.73	4.77	102.29	24.80	3.71	0.16	
1956	149.31	5.14	113.42	26.30	4.27	0.18	
1957	161.22	5.51	123.27	27.40	4.85	0.19	
1958	172.68	6.03	133.20	28.00	5.25	0.02	
			CONSTANT (1947–49) PRICES				
			a				
1900	16.23		7.37	8.61	0.19	0.04	0.02
1912	32.40		17.23	14.68	0.42	0.05	0.02
1922	42.59		23.70	18.61	0.19	0.07	0.02
1929	62.62		39.12	22.56	0.81	0.11	0.02
1933	79.37		49.15	29.19	0.88	0.14	0.01
1939	83.22		52.93	29.32	0.77	0.18	0.02
1945	76.36		49.73	25.86	0.55	0.20	0.02
1945	84.19	1.19	61.71	20.40	0.79	0.10	
1946	83.90	1.62	60.78	20.50	0.90	0.10	
1947	84.37	1.72	60.77	20.70	1.08	0.10	
1948	85.31	1.66	61.44	20.80	1.31	0.10	
1949	87.90	1.84	63.43	21.00	1.52	0.11	
1950	90.93	2.03	65.96	21.10	1.73	0.11	
1951	94.14	2.46	68.33	21.30	1.93	0.12	
1952	98.95	2.92	71.15	21.60	2.16	0.12	
1953	101.69	3.27	74.20	21.70	2.39	0.13	
1954	106.42	3.45	78.19	22.00	2.65	0.13	
1955	111.89	3.57	83.00	22.30	2.88	0.14	
1956	117.16	3.69	87.59	22.60	3.13	0.15	
1957	123.51	3.87	92.98	23.10	3.40	0.16	
1958	130.74	4.14	99.43	23.40	3.60	0.17	

SOURCE, CURRENT AND CONSTANT PRICES, BY COLUMN
(1) Sum of Cols. 2 to 7.   (4) Table A-41, col. 7.   (6) Table A-39, col. 5.
(2) Table A-35, col. 6.   (5) Table A-37, col. 6.   (7) Table A-44, col. 6.
(3) Table A-36, col. 6.
a Not available separately; included in nonresidential structures, Table A-36.
b Less than $5 million.

NET STOCK OF TANGIBLE NONMILITARY ASSETS OF FEDERAL GOVERNMENT
(billions of dollars)

End of Year	Total (1)	Structure Residential (2)	Nonresidential (3)	Land (4)	Producer Durables (5)	Inventories (6)	Monetary Metals (7)	Net Foreign Assets (8)
			CURRENT PRICES					
1900	2.47	0.45 a		1.00	0.01	—	1.01	
1912	3.97	1.05		1.00	0.02	—	1.90	
1922	7.77	2.48		1.50	0.04	0.03	3:73	
1929	8.88	2.84		2.10	0.06	—	3.88	
1933	9.47	3.33		2.23	0.11	—	3.80	
1939	31.10	6.89		2.80	0.30	0.94	20.18	
1945	49.03	14.48		6.50	3.03	2.58	22.44	
1945	46.74	1.21	13.76	6.30	2.64	2.58	22.66	−2.41
1946	53.64	1.15	17.22	7.00	2.37	1.39	23.06	1.45
1947	66.43	1.13	20.61	8.30	1.96	1.10	25.28	8.05
1948	71.38	0.99	22.20	8.90	1.56	1.92	26.77	9.04
1949	73.64	0.89	22.34	9.10	1.24	3.28	26.99	9.80
1950	74.60	0.84	24.72	11.50	1.06	2.67	25.27	8.54
1951	77.01	0.79	25.89	13.40	1.00	2.24	25.23	8.46
1952	78.64	0.74	27.60	12.90	1.00	2.71	25.70	7.99
1953	81.33	0.67	28.75	12.00	1.00	5.59	24.52	8.80
1954	82.87	0.57	29.68	12.40	0.93	6.83	24.22	8.24
1955	84.22	0.52	30.79	13.60	0.85	6.98	24.19	7.29
1956	85.92	0.48	32.28	13.40	0.77	6.87	24.51	7.61
1957	88.28	0.64	33.57	13.60	0.69	5.93	25.22	8.63
1958	89.76	1.01	35.00	12.80	0.61	7.89	23.00	9.45
			CONSTANT (1947–49) PRICES					
1900	6.39	2.11 a		2.87	0.03	—	1.38	
1912	8.80	3.74		2.26	0.06	—	2.74	
1922	14.12	4.51		3.51	0.06	0.05	5.99	
1929	15.15	5.41		3.59	0.09	—	6.06	
1933	18.16	7.15		4.96	0.20	—	5.85	
1939	42.02	13.58		5.62	0.48	2.77	19.57	
1945	58.85	19.87		9.64	4.01	3.53	21.80	
1945	57.10	1.67	21.03	9.10	3.39	3.54	21.19	−2.82
1946	57.25	1.37	20.82	7.70	2.71	1.49	21.63	1.53
1947	64.61	1.15	20.77	8.00	2.02	0.98	23.86	7.83
1948	67.79	0.94	20.91	8.60	1.51	1.95	25.35	8.53
1949	71.04	0.85	21.37	9.30	1.16	3.68	25.54	9.14
1950	67.60	0.75	21.82	10.20	0.94	2.43	23.82	7.64
1951	68.62	0.66	22.14	11.90	0.85	2.03	23.80	7.24
1952	69.23	0.58	22.36	11.70	0.84	2.72	24.28	6.75
1953	71.00	0.53	22.49	10.90	0.83	5.82	23.12	7.37
1954	72.11	0.55	22.47	11.20	0.76	7.49	22.81	6.83
1955	72.62	0.44	22.35	12.10	0.66	8.36	22.78	5.93
1956	71.64	0.35	22.36	11.40	0.57	7.71	23.07	6.18
1957	71.71	0.45	22.37	11.40	0.48	6.36	23.05	6.80
1958	72.13	0.69	22.52	10.80	0.42	8.76	21.61	7.33

SOURCE, CURRENT AND CONSTANT PRICES, BY COLUMN

(1) Sum of cols. 2 to 8.   (4) Table A-41, col. 8.   (7) Table A-44, col. 7.
(2) Table A-35, col. 7.   (5) Table A-37, col. 7.   (8) Table A-45, col. 4.
(3) Table A-36, col. 7.   (6) Table A-39, col. 6.
a Not available separately; included in nonresidential structures, Table A-36.

TABLE A-57

GROSS STOCK OF TANGIBLE ASSETS OF NONFARM HOUSEHOLDS
(billions of dollars)

End of Year	Total (1)	Residential Structures (2)	Land		Consumer Durables (5)	Monetary Metals (6)	Net Foreign Assets (7)
			Residential (3)	Nonresi- dential (4)			
CURRENT PRICES							
1945	336.17	210.89	18.46	7.75	95.53	0.84	2.70
1946	398.64	248.78	21.66	7.90	116.64	0.89	2.77
1947	482.69	304.31	26.47	9.45	138.79	0.92	2.75
1948	529.52	328.46	28.65	11.45	157.26	0.95	2.75
1949	531.99	323.32	28.23	11.30	165.56	0.95	2.63
1950	616.71	374.69	32.89	11.85	193.32	1.01	2.95
1951	661.76	399.17	35.22	12.70	210.49	1.06	3.12
1952	696.74	419.83	37.24	14.70	220.72	1.14	3.11
1953	728.57	435.03	38.80	15.95	234.59	1.20	3.00
1954	759.43	450.01	40.35	18.45	246.04	1.21	3.37
1955	823.61	485.44	43.95	21.00	268.08	1.27	3.87
1956	889.20	517.77	47.17	24.35	294.46	1.33	4.12
1957	946.63	539.13	49.41	29.25	323.56	1.50	3.78
1958	1,005.77	566.34	51.91	32.80	348.41	1.62	4.69
CONSTANT (1947–49) PRICES							
1945	453.69	293.87	25.64	10.13	121.52	0.37	3.16
1946	465.62	297.58	25.91	10.22	128.64	0.39	2.92
1947	483.84	303.69	26.42	10.38	140.27	0.40	2.68
1948	504.56	312.22	27.24	10.71	151.38	0.42	2.59
1949	524.43	319.80	27.92	10.93	162.91	0.42	2.45
1950	552.13	330.69	29.03	11.23	178.10	0.44	2.64
1951	573.55	340.59	30.05	11.42	188.36	0.46	2.67
1952	594.55	349.90	31.04	11.78	198.70	0.50	2.63
1953	620.84	360.13	32.12	12.14	213.41	0.52	2.52
1954	648.65	370.99	33.27	12.46	228.60	0.53	2.80
1955	685.44	384.99	34.83	12.69	249.24	0.55	3.14
1956	718.58	397.40	36.18	12.96	268.11	0.58	3.35
1957	754.96	408.84	37.35	13.38	291.75	0.66	2.98
1958	787.67	420.16	38.48	13.66	311.03	0.71	3.63

SOURCE, CURRENT AND CONSTANT PRICES, BY COLUMN

(1)	Sum of cols. 2 to 7.	(5)	Table A-49, col. 2.
(2)	Table A-46, col. 2.	(6)	Table A-50, col. 6.
(3)	Table A-50, col. 3.	(7)	Table A-50, col. 7.
(4)	Table A-50, col. 4.		

TABLE A-58

GROSS STOCK OF TANGIBLE ASSETS OF NONPROFIT INSTITUTIONS

End of Year	Total (1)	Nonresidential Structures (2)	Nonresidential Land (3)	Producer Durables (4)
		CURRENT PRICES		
1945	17.55	15.15	2.12	0.28
1946	23.41	20.23	2.82	0.36
1947	29.21	25.26	3.49	0.46
1948	31.56	27.20	3.77	0.59
1949	31.23	26.75	3.75	0.73
1950	34.40	29.28	4.17	0.95
1951	36.71	31.03	4.50	1.18
1952	39.22	33.00	4.84	1.38
1953	41.33	34.63	5.12	1.58
1954	43.68	36.37	5.44	1.87
1955	46.91	38.77	5.87	2.27
1956	50.50	41.40	6.37	2.73
1957	54.11	44.00	6.90	3.21
1958	57.75	46.71	7.45	3.59
		CONSTANT (1947–49) PRICES		
1945	29.10	25.21	3.53	0.36
1946	29.21	25.29	3.51	0.41
1947	29.23	25.26	3.49	0.48
1948	29.60	25.49	3.54	0.57
1949	30.27	25.95	3.63	0.69
1950	31.06	26.45	3.77	0.84
1951	31.90	26.98	3.91	1.01
1952	32.48	27.32	4.01	1.15
1953	33.27	27.84	4.12	1.31
1954	34.39	28.59	4.28	1.52
1955	35.59	29.37	4.45	1.77
1956	36.65	30.03	4.62	2.00
1957	37.84	30.75	4.84	2.25
1958	39.21	31.69	5.06	2.46

SOURCE, CURRENT AND CONSTANT PRICES, BY COLUMN

(1) Sum of cols. 2 to 4.   (3) Table A-51, col. 3.
(2) Table A-47, col. 2.   (4) Table A-48, col. 3.

TABLE A-59

GROSS STOCK OF TANGIBLE ASSETS OF UNINCORPORATED BUSINESS

(billions of dollars)

End of Year	Total (1)	Structures		Land		Producer Durables (6)	Inventories (7)	Monetary Metals (8)	Forests (9)	Subsoil Assets (10)
		Residential (2)	Nonresidential (3)	Residential (4)	Nonresidential (5)					
				CURRENT PRICES						
1945	61.24	17.11	18.45	2.30	4.48	9.41	7.97	0.13	0.79	0.60
1946	76.61	19.48	24.35	2.56	6.80	11.57	10.06	0.14	0.95	0.70
1947	91.22	22.84	29.07	2.96	7.31	14.76	11.59	0.15	1.54	1.00
1948	101.11	25.01	30.82	3.19	7.73	18.12	12.92	0.15	1.87	1.30
1949	101.57	24.78	29.98	3.13	7.48	20.79	11.97	0.16	2.08	1.20
1950	114.11	27.49	32.21	3.43	7.97	24.33	14.24	0.17	2.97	1.30
1951	122.87	28.70	34.15	3.52	8.37	27.81	15.07	0.19	3.56	1.50
1952	127.21	29.66	35.52	3.58	8.68	29.96	14.78	0.18	3.34	1.50
1953	132.56	30.47	36.71	3.63	9.08	32.47	15.21	0.19	3.00	1.80
1954	137.48	30.75	38.26	3.61	9.73	34.91	15.06	0.20	3.16	1.80
1955	147.69	32.22	41.20	3.74	10.48	38.36	15.81	0.21	3.77	1.90
1956	157.72	33.64	43.86	3.86	11.44	42.50	16.51	0.22	3.69	2.00
1957	168.20	34.51	47.25	3.92	12.35	47.12	16.82	0.25	3.78	2.20
1958	175.74	35.66	50.04	3.99	13.22	50.22	16.81	0.27	3.43	2.10

(continued)

TABLE A-59 (concluded)

| | | Structures | | Land | | | | | | |
End of Year (1)	Total (1)	Residential (2)	Nonresidential (3)	Residential (4)	Nonresidential (5)	Producer Durables (6)	Inventories (7)	Monetary Metals (8)	Forests (9)	Subsoil Assets (10)
				CONSTANT (1947–49) PRICES						
1945	88.96	23.34	29.23	3.12	7.27	12.22	11.12	0.06	1.60	1.00
1946	90.74	23.30	29.38	3.06	7.40	13.27	11.68	0.06	1.59	1.00
1947	92.37	23.28	29.09	3.02	7.31	15.18	11.69	0.07	1.63	1.10
1948	95.63	23.50	29.23	3.00	7.33	17.52	12.26	0.07	1.62	1.10
1949	97.61	23.69	29.28	2.99	7.29	19.47	11.96	0.07	1.66	1.20
1950	100.99	23.91	29.28	2.98	7.32	21.67	12.73	0.08	1.65	1.20
1951	103.85	23.95	29.73	2.94	7.37	23.69	13.15	0.08	1.64	1.30
1952	105.45	23.98	29.85	2.90	7.33	25.23	13.10	0.08	1.68	1.30
1953	108.01	24.04	30.08	2.87	7.44	27.16	13.27	0.08	1.67	1.40
1954	110.26	24.07	30.67	2.82	7.63	28.74	13.13	0.09	1.71	1.40
1955	113.24	24.12	31.62	2.80	7.98	30.28	13.25	0.09	1.70	1.40
1956	116.09	24.18	32.50	2.78	8.39	31.66	13.29	0.10	1.69	1.50
1957	119.48	24.26	33.40	2.76	8.75	33.61	13.36	0.11	1.73	1.50
1958	122.23	24.44	34.51	2.74	9.09	34.86	13.25	0.12	1.72	1.50

SOURCE, CURRENT AND CONSTANT PRICES, BY COLUMN

(1) Sum of cols. 2 to 10.
(2) Table A-46, col. 3.
(3) Table A-47, col. 3.

(4) Table A-52, col. 4.
(5) Table A-52, col. 5.
(6) Table A-48, col. 2.

(7) Table A-52, col. 7.
(8) Table A-52, col. 8.

(9) Table A-52, col. 9.
(10) Table A-52, col. 10.

TABLE A-60

(billions of dollars)

| End of Year | Total (1) | Structures | | Land (4) | Producer Durables (5) | Consumer Durables (6) | Inventories (7) | Livestock (8) | Monetary Metals (9) |
		Residential (2)	Nonresidential (3)						
						CURRENT PRICES			
45	115.54	18.64	15.84	43.47	9.25	12.50	5.96	9.72	0.16
46	132.32	22.33	18.48	46.53	10.68	15.03	7.18	11.92	0.17
47	151.86	26.46	21.54	49.78	13.67	17.73	9.24	13.26	0.18
48	162.10	27.43	22.65	51.93	17.47	20.24	7.77	14.43	0.18
49	161.93	27.58	22.97	50.90	20.54	20.82	6.04	12.89	0.19
50	184.78	29.77	24.86	58.40	23.92	23.92	7.27	17.10	0.18
51	205.88	31.79	27.10	66.31	26.23	26.11	8.61	19.53	0.20
52	205.57	32.57	27.92	66.89	27.87	26.97	8.37	14.78	0.20
53	202.44	33.02	28.26	64.22	29.27	28.57	7.16	11.75	0.19
54	207.46	33.72	28.74	66.41	30.63	29.02	7.54	11.21	0.19
55	213.83	34.98	29.72	68.94	32.51	30.10	6.68	10.70	0.20
56	225.25	36.25	30.98	73.96	34.42	31.20	7.10	11.13	0.21
57	238.14	36.77	31.81	79.94	35.80	33.01	6.50	14.07	0.24
58	257.37	37.72	32.23	87.58	38.08	35.36	8.04	18.11	0.25
					CONSTANT (1947–49) PRICES				
45	151.33	25.60	21.29	53.80	12.11	15.72	7.86	14.88	0.07
46	150.39	25.94	21.44	50.91	12.85	16.62	8.31	14.25	0.07
47	151.59	26.46	21.73	50.28	14.46	17.87	7.12	13.59	0.08
48	158.68	26.90	22.07	49.27	16.52	21.54	8.88	13.42	0.08
49	159.32	27.30	22.39	49.57	18.41	20.49	7.47	13.61	0.08
50	165.35	27.73	22.77	50.87	20.05	21.95	7.86	14.04	0.08
51	169.71	28.13	23.20	51.29	21.42	23.01	8.01	14.56	0.09
52	172.12	28.57	23.62	50.72	22.47	23.63	8.27	14.75	0.09
53	174.13	28.91	23.91	50.17	23.71	24.92	7.80	14.63	0.08
54	176.96	29.27	24.14	50.24	24.57	25.64	8.18	14.84	0.08
55	179.37	29.56	24.22	50.07	25.47	26.60	8.39	14.97	0.09
56	180.58	29.86	24.32	50.87	25.67	26.85	8.25	14.67	0.09
57	182.31	30.09	24.36	51.58	25.40	27.57	8.95	14.26	0.10
58	187.77	30.30	24.37	52.92	25.94	28.54	10.65	14.94	0.11

SOURCE, CURRENT AND CONSTANT PRICES, BY COLUMN
(1)	Sum of cols. 2 to 9.	(6)	Table A-49, col. 3.
(2)	Table A-46, col. 4.	(7)	Table A-53, col. 7.
(3)	Table A-47, col. 4.	(8)	Table A-53, col. 8.
(4)	Table A-53, col. 4.	(9)	Table A-53, col. 9.
(5)	Table A-48, col. 4.		

215

TABLE A-61

GROSS STOCK OF TANGIBLE ASSETS OF CORPORATIONS
(billions of dollars)

End of Year	Total (1)	Structures Residential (2)	Nonresidential (3)	Land Residential (4)	Nonresidential (5)	Producer Durables (6)	Inventories (7)	Monetary Metals (8)	Forests (9)	Subsoil Assets (10)	Net Foreign Assets (11)
				CURRENT PRICES							
1945	243.71	12.80	119.06	1.82	11.30	66.97	26.32	0.12	2.30	5.60	−2.58
1946	304.16	14.93	149.08	2.09	14.79	77.75	37.55	0.13	2.85	6.40	−1.41
1947	358.09	17.64	171.64	2.49	17.02	91.40	44.69	0.13	4.55	8.40	0.13
1948	400.07	20.29	187.80	2.77	18.60	103.26	48.89	0.15	5.70	11.50	1.11
1949	405.98	21.06	187.78	2.83	18.53	112.00	45.31	0.16	6.25	10.70	1.36
1950	461.12	23.27	210.44	3.23	19.92	127.00	55.10	0.16	8.90	11.20	1.90
1951	506.03	24.50	223.71	3.43	21.37	141.64	64.85	0.15	10.75	12.80	2.83
1952	530.51	25.89	233.72	3.60	22.60	151.65	66.10	0.17	9.95	13.20	3.63
1953	559.01	27.14	245.46	3.75	23.20	163.76	67.91	0.20	8.95	14.50	4.14
1954	577.61	28.07	253.39	3.84	24.47	172.94	66.30	0.22	9.45	15.10	3.83
1955	619.70	32.35	270.71	4.10	26.72	181.16	72.97	0.21	11.25	16.00	4.23
1956	677.77	33.33	289.52	4.33	29.14	206.56	80.54	0.21	11.00	17.00	6.14
1957	742.25	35.11	323.23	4.43	32.58	223.73	83.27	0.25	11.25	18.50	10.40
1958	764.13	35.73	337.32	4.77	34.63	234.27	78.84	0.27	10.30	17.80	10.20

(continued)

TABLE A-61 (concluded)

CONSTANT (1947–49) PRICES

End of Year	Total (1)	Structures		Land		Producer Durables (6)	Inventories (7)	Monetary Metals (8)	Forests (9)	Subsoil Assets (10)	Net Foreign Assets (11)
		Residential (2)	Nonresidential (3)	Residential (4)	Nonresidential (5)						
1945	339.63	17.56	170.53	2.49	16.93	84.88	36.70	0.05	4.80	8.70	−3.01
1946	354.41	17.85	173.14	2.50	17.49	87.39	43.61	0.06	4.85	9.00	−1.48
1947	365.40	18.27	175.00	2.53	17.23	93.14	45.09	0.06	4.85	9.10	0.13
1948	379.77	18.93	177.94	2.60	17.62	100.47	46.39	0.07	4.90	9.80	1.05
1949	388.03	19.67	180.53	2.72	17.89	105.51	45.27	0.07	4.90	10.20	1.27
1950	401.70	20.02	182.63	2.82	17.68	112.09	49.24	0.07	4.95	10.50	1.70
1951	421.64	20.61	185.82	2.88	18.16	118.79	56.59	0.07	5.00	11.30	2.42
1952	435.19	21.14	188.42	2.92	18.56	125.95	58.55	0.08	5.00	11.50	3.07
1953	447.75	21.76	192.03	2.99	18.50	132.61	59.26	0.09	5.05	12.00	3.46
1954	457.03	22.35	196.29	3.04	19.14	137.87	57.81	0.09	5.05	12.20	3.18
1955	472.97	22.72	201.47	3.11	20.07	143.56	61.11	0.10	5.10	12.30	3.44
1956	492.06	23.45	206.49	3.19	21.02	150.33	64.85	0.09	5.15	12.50	4.99
1957	509.27	24.14	211.06	3.26	22.05	156.56	66.14	0.09	5.15	12.60	8.20
1958	515.51	24.89	215.69	3.34	22.60	160.88	62.18	0.11	5.20	12.70	7.91

SOURCE, CURRENT AND CONSTANT PRICES, BY COLUMN

(1)	Sum of cols. 2 to 11.	(4)	Table A-54, col. 4.
(2)	Table A-46, col. 5.	(5)	Table A-54, col. 5.
(3)	Table A-47, col. 5.	(6)	Table A-48, col. 5.

(7)	Table A-54, col. 7.
(8)	Table A-54, col. 8.
(9)	Table A-54, col. 9.

(10)	Table A-54, col. 10.
(11)	Table A-54, col. 11.

TABLE A-62

GROSS STOCK OF TANGIBLE ASSETS OF STATE AND LOCAL GOVERNMENTS
(billions of dollars)

End of Year	Total (1)	Structures Residential (2)	Structures Nonresidential (3)	Land (4)	Producer Durables (5)	Inventories (6)
			CURRENT PRICES			
1945	89.85	0.96	73.22	14.20	1.40	0.07
1946	114.08	1.48	91.92	18.90	1.69	0.09
1947	136.08	1.89	110.62	21.40	2.07	0.10
1948	147.94	2.02	121.85	21.50	2.46	0.11
1949	142.22	2.22	116.60	20.50	2.80	0.10
1950	160.50	2.69	130.46	24.00	3.22	0.13
1951	171.96	3.38	140.63	24.20	3.62	0.13
1952	184.31	4.13	152.43	23.70	3.92	0.13
1953	189.56	4.75	156.29	24.00	4.38	0.14
1954	198.16	5.11	163.75	24.10	5.05	0.15
1955	213.45	5.61	176.86	24.80	6.02	0.16
1956	234.22	6.12	194.39	26.30	7.23	0.18
1957	250.33	6.64	207.60	27.40	8.50	0.19
1958	265.45	7.34	220.57	28.00	9.34	0.20
			CONSTANT (1947–49) PRICES			
1945	132.54	1.31	108.93	20.40	1.80	0.10
1946	133.87	1.78	109.56	20.50	1.93	0.10
1947	135.98	1.93	111.12	20.70	2.13	0.10
1948	138.72	1.90	113.54	20.80	2.38	0.10
1949	142.96	2.12	117.11	21.00	2.62	0.11
1950	147.55	2.34	121.14	21.10	2.86	0.11
1951	151.97	2.83	124.64	21.30	3.08	0.12
1952	157.10	3.34	128.74	21.60	3.30	0.12
1953	162.38	3.75	133.14	21.70	3.66	0.13
1954	168.62	4.00	138.35	22.00	4.14	0.13
1955	175.74	4.19	144.43	22.30	4.68	0.14
1956	182.81	4.40	150.37	22.60	5.29	0.15
1957	190.88	4.67	156.99	23.10	5.96	0.16
1958	199.40	5.03	164.40	23.40	6.40	0.17

SOURCE, CURRENT AND CONSTANT PRICES, BY COLUMN

(1) Sum of cols. 2 to 16.   (4) Table A-55, col. 4.
(2) Table A-46, col. 6.   (5) Table A-48, col. 6.
(3) Table A-47, col. 6.   (6) Table A-55, col. 6.

TABLE A-63

GROSS STOCK OF TANGIBLE NONMILITARY ASSETS FOR FEDERAL GOVERNMENT
(billions of dollars)

End of Year	Total (1)	Structures		Land (4)	Producer Durables (5)	Inventories (6)	Monetary Metals (7)	Net Foreign Assets (8)
		Residential (2)	Nonresidential (3)					
				CURRENT PRICES				
1945	53.81	1.39	18.52	6.30	4.77	2.58	22.66	−2.41
1946	63.46	1.42	23.68	7.00	5.46	1.39	23.06	1.45
1947	79.06	1.51	28.92	8.30	5.90	1.10	25.28	8.05
1948	84.73	1.36	31.76	8.90	4.98	1.92	26.77	9.04
1949	85.73	1.26	32.36	9.10	2.94	3.28	26.99	9.80
1950	87.96	1.28	36.25	11.50	2.45	2.67	25.27	8.54
1951	91.34	1.26	38.53	13.40	2.22	2.24	25.23	8.46
1952	94.54	1.24	41.69	12.90	2.31	2.71	25.70	7.99
1953	98.56	1.12	44.19	12.00	2.34	5.59	24.52	8.80
1954	101.03	0.99	46.19	12.40	2.16	6.83	24.22	8.24
1955	103.73	0.91	48.80	13.60	1.96	6.98	24.19	7.29
1956	106.79	0.80	51.66	13.40	1.94	6.87	24.51	7.61
1957	108.89	0.96	52.69	13.60	1.86	5.93	25.22	8.63
1958	109.63	1.34	53.46	12.80	1.69	7.89	23.00	9.45
				CONSTANT (1947–49) PRICES				
1945	67.28	1.95	28.19	9.10	6.13	3.54	21.19	−2.82
1946	68.89	1.69	28.60	7.70	6.25	1.49	21.63	1.53
1947	77.41	1.51	29.15	8.00	6.08	0.98	23.86	7.83
1948	80.45	1.29	29.91	8.60	4.82	1.95	25.35	8.53
1949	82.63	1.24	30.98	9.30	2.75	3.68	25.54	9.14
1950	79.47	1.15	32.05	10.20	2.18	2.43	23.82	7.64
1951	80.94	1.08	33.00	11.90	1.89	2.03	23.80	7.24
1952	82.22	0.98	33.85	11.70	1.94	2.72	24.28	6.75
1953	84.69	0.93	34.61	10.90	1.94	5.82	23.12	7.37
1954	86.06	0.81	35.16	11.20	1.76	7.49	22.81	6.83
1955	87.07	0.72	35.65	12.10	1.53	8.36	22.78	5.93
1956	86.40	0.61	36.01	11.40	1.42	7.71	23.07	6.18
1957	85.69	0.73	35.25	11.40	1.30	6.36	23.85	6.80
1958	85.25	0.99	34.61	10.80	1.16	8.76	21.61	7.33

SOURCE, CURRENT AND CONSTANT PRICES, BY COLUMN

(1) Sum of cols. 2 to 8. (5) Table A-48, col. 7.
(2) Table A-46, col. 7. (6) Table A-56, col. 6.
(3) Table A-47, col. 7. (7) Table A-56, col. 7.
(4) Table A-56, col. 4. (8) Table A-56, col. 8.

TABLE A-64

RATIO OF NET TO GROSS STOCK OF MAIN TYPES OF REPRODUCIBLE TANGIBLE WEALTH, CURRENT PRICES
(per cent)

End of Year	Structures				Producer Durables			Military Assets (8)	Consumer Durables (9)
	Total (1)	Residential (2)	Private Nonresidential (3)	Public Civilian (4)	Total (5)	Private (6)	Public (7)		
1945	54.71	58.23	46.22	60.28	52.77	52.78	52.92	48.42	42.81
1946	54.30	57.88	46.66	58.71	54.37	55.16	44.12	40.21	45.28
1947	54.45	57.85	47.21	58.12	57.44	58.74	37.72	34.66	46.88
1948	54.36	57.90	47.66	56.86	59.60	60.67	39.11	32.19	48.07
1949	54.62	57.86	48.02	57.81	60.64	61.02	49.93	31.48	48.93
1950	54.98	58.23	48.66	57.28	60.67	60.94	52.94	30.67	51.24
1951	55.43	58.51	49.43	57.58	60.98	61.12	55.94	29.42	51.76
1952	55.77	58.77	50.17	57.41	60.80	60.90	57.19	32.87	51.53
1953	56.23	58.99	50.98	57.95	60.22	60.29	57.41	37.62	51.21
1954	56.60	59.19	51.58	58.36	60.38	60.46	57.27	40.63	50.43
1955	57.09	59.41	52.37	58.97	59.78	59.80	57.16	41.12	50.57
1956	57.56	59.80	53.08	59.22	60.05	60.23	54.93	38.78	50.17
1957	58.11	59.87	54.06	60.29	60.29	60.54	53.47	37.34	48.69
1958	58.49	60.04	54.51	61.38	59.28	59.47	53.22	39.28	46.57

SOURCE, BY COLUMN

(1) Table A-5, sum of cols. 3, 4, 5, divided by Table A-7, sum of cols. 3, 4, 5.
(2) Same procedure as above, using col. 3 in both tables.
(3) Same procedure using col. 4 in both Tables.
(4) Same procedure using col. 5 in both Tables.
(5) Table A-5, sum of cols. 6 and 7, divided by Table A-7, sum of cols. 6 and 7.
(6) Same procedure using col. 6 in both tables.
(7) Same procedure using col. 7 in both tables.
(8) Table A-5, col. 17, divided by Table A-7, col. 17.
(9) Table A-5, col. 10, divided by Table A-7, col. 10.

TABLE A-65

RATIO OF NET TO GROSS STOCK OF REPRODUCIBLE TANGIBLE ASSETS, BY SECTOR, CURRENT PRICES

(per cent)

| END OF YEAR | Nonfarm Households | | Nonprofit Institutions | | Unincorporated Business | | | Agriculture | | | |
| | Residential Structures (1) | Consumer Durables (2) | Nonresidential Structures (3) | Producer Durables (4) | Structures | | Producer Durables (7) | Structures | | Producer Durables (10) | Consumer Durables (11) |
					Residential (5)	Nonresidential (6)		Residential (8)	Nonresidential (9)		
1945	58.7	42.9	46.0	46.4	53.7	44.5	56.4	49.5	44.8	62.6	42.1
1946	58.4	45.3	45.8	50.0	52.7	45.3	59.5	49.3	45.1	61.3	45.4
1947	58.4	46.8	45.7	54.3	52.1	45.6	62.4	49.4	45.8	61.4	47.3
1948	58.5	48.0	45.9	59.3	51.8	45.8	62.6	49.7	46.4	61.2	48.9
1949	58.6	48.7	46.5	65.8	51.6	45.8	61.7	49.9	47.1	60.7	50.5
1950	58.9	51.2	47.6	68.4	51.2	46.1	60.9	50.1	48.0	58.9	51.9
1951	59.2	51.7	48.8	70.3	50.4	46.4	59.8	50.6	48.6	59.8	52.1
1952	59.5	51.6	49.9	70.3	49.6	46.5	58.9	50.9	49.3	58.9	50.6
1953	59.7	51.4	50.7	69.6	48.9	47.2	58.0	51.1	49.8	56.9	49.7
1954	60.0	50.7	51.6	67.9	48.2	47.8	56.7	51.2	50.2	55.0	47.9
1955	60.6	51.1	52.6	64.8	47.5	48.7	56.7	51.2	50.8	53.0	46.0
1956	60.9	50.7	53.8	61.9	47.0	50.1	57.1	51.1	51.1	51.2	44.7
1957	61.3	49.3	55.1	59.2	46.3	50.8	56.1	51.1	51.6	50.3	42.4
1958	61.2	47.3	56.2	57.7	45.6	51.1	53.6	51.1	52.0	48.8	39.6

(continued)

221

TABLE A-65 (concluded)

END OF YEAR	CORPORATIONS Structures			STATE AND LOCAL GOVERNMENTS Structures			FEDERAL GOVERNMENT Structures		
	Residential (12)	Nonresidential (13)	Producer Durables (14)	Residential (15)	Nonresidential (16)	Producer Durables (17)	Residential (18)	Nonresidential (19)	Producer Durables (20)
1945	64.3	46.7	50.9	90.6	57.0	44.3	87.1	74.3	55.3
1946	63.6	47.2	53.7	91.2	56.8	40.8	81.0	72.7	43.4
1947	64.4	47.9	57.8	89.4	55.5	50.7	74.8	71.3	33.2
1948	62.1	48.4	60.2	87.1	53.8	54.9	72.8	69.9	31.3
1949	60.8	48.7	60.9	86.9	54.0	58.2	70.6	69.0	42.2
1950	63.0	49.3	61.0	86.6	55.4	60.2	65.6	68.2	43.3
1951	63.7	50.1	61.6	87.3	55.3	62.7	62.7	67.2	45.0
1952	63.3	50.9	61.6	87.7	55.3	65.3	59.7	66.2	43.3
1953	62.9	54.4	61.3	87.2	55.7	65.3	59.8	65.1	42.7
1954	62.5	52.3	62.1	86.3	56.9	63.8	57.6	64.3	43.1
1955	58.0	53.6	61.6	85.0	58.3	61.6	57.1	63.1	43.4
1956	60.1	54.0	62.3	84.0	58.3	59.1	60.0	62.5	39.7
1957	59.6	54.4	63.1	83.0	59.4	57.1	66.7	63.7	37.1
1958	61.4	55.1	62.5	82.2	60.4	56.2	75.4	65.5	36.1

SOURCE, BY COLUMN

(1 and 2) Table A-50, cols. 2 and 5, divided by Table A-57, cols. 2 and 5, respectively.

(3 and 4) Table A-51. cols. 2 and 4, divided by Table A-58, cols. 2 and 4, respectively.

(5, 6, and 7) Table A-52, cols. 2, 3, and 6 divided by Table A-59, cols. 2, 3, and 6, respectively.

(8, 9, 10, and 11) Table A-53, cols. 2, 3, 5, and 6, divided by Table A-60, cols. 2, 3, 5, and 6, respectively.

(12, 13, and 14) Table A-54, cols. 2, 3, and 6, divided by Table A-61, cols. 2, 3, and 6, respectively.

(15, 16, and 17) Table A-55, cols. 2, 3, and 5, divided by Table A-62, cols. 2, 3, and 5, respectively.

(18, 19, and 20) Table A-56, cols. 2, 3, and 5, divided by Table A-63, cols. 2, 3, and 5, respectively.

Appendix B

Tables

TABLE B-1

EXPENDITURES ON PRIVATE NONFARM RESIDENTIAL BUILDING
(millions of dollars)

YEAR	Construction Expenditures New Dwelling Units			Nonhouse-keeping (4)	Change in Value of Work in Place on Uncompleted Projects (5)	Settlement Costs on New Housing (6)	Expenditures on Additions and Alterations (7)	Speculative Builders' Margin (8)	Total Expenditures on New Residential Structures (9)	Transactions in Existing Structures		Total Expenditure on New and Existing Residential Structures (12)
	Total (1)	1- to 4-Family (2)	Multifamily (3)							Dealers' Commissions (10)	Settlement Costs (11)	
1946	3,300	3,150	150	145	−721	50	1,307	246	4,327	773	264	5,364
1947	5,450	5,124	326	125	−853	81	1,960	409	7,172	706	242	8,720
1948	7,500	6,900	600	155	−12	112	2,467	563	10,785	737	252	11,774
1949	7,257	6,426	831	185	−320	106	2,200	472	9,900	749	256	10,905
1950	11,525	10,666	859	175	−1,671	171	2,410	800	13,400	949	323	14,672
1951	9,849	9,370	479	190	314	148	2,490	717	13,708	965	328	15,001
1952	9,870	9,440	430	185	147	148	2,787	736	13,873	1,001	340	15,214
1953	10,555	10,049	506	267	455	159	2,955	799	15,190	1,082	367	16,639
1954	12,070	11,579	491	296	−805	182	3,013	938	15,694	1,119	379	17,192
1955	14,990	14,487	503	339	−280	225	3,376	1,195	19,845	1,252	424	21,521
1956	13,535	12,980	555	447	370	205	3,695	1,090	18,252	1,258	426	19,936
1957	12,615	12,098	517	501	147	192	3,903	1,079	18,437	1,166	395	19,998
1958	13,405	12,855	550	620	−485	205	3,859	1,166	18,770	1,055	358	20,183

SOURCE, BY COLUMN

(1) 1946–57: *U.S. Income and Output Supplement to the Survey of Current Business,* Nov. 1958, Table V-3, p. 190.
1958: *Construction Review,* January 1959, p. 16:

(2 and 3) 1946–55: Col. 1 split between 1- to 4-family (col. 2) and multifamily (col. 3) by following procedure: Total construction expenditures on new dwelling units (col. 1) were divided by number of new dwelling units started (Table B-189, col. 1) to obtain average expenditures on all new dwelling units. (This average is affected by the fact that the expenditure figures measure value of work put in place while the number figures refer only to dwelling units started, but this difference is only of slight significance for the final calculation.) The average expenditure on all new dwelling units was then multiplied by the ratio of the average valuation of multifamily units (dwellings of 5 or more units) to the average valuation of all dwelling units as derived from data on urban building authorized (Table B-190, col. 6), to obtain average expenditures on multi-family units which was translated into total expenditures (col. 3 of this table) by multiplication with number figures (Table B-189, col. 6).
1956–58: Split estimated by simple arithmetic average of percentage split in preceding 3 years.

(4) 1946–58: Same sources as col. 1.

(5) 1946–58: Federal Reserve Board flow-of-funds figures (for 1946–53 see Board of Governors of the Federal Reserve System, *Flow of Funds in the United States, 1939–1953,* Table 71). Represents net investment (or disinvestment) during the year by the construction industry in the inventory of work in process. Estimated at 1.5 per cent of col. 2 and 1 per cent of cols. 3 and 4.

(6) 1946–58: Same sources as col. 1.

(7) 1946–58: From Table B-3, col. 5.

(8) 1946–58: Sum of cols. 1, 4 to 8.

(9) 1946–58:

(10) 1956–58: Table B-4, col. 4, plus allowance of $35 million a year for dealers' commissions on sales of existing multifamily structures, which implies an average turnover ratio of such properties of about 12 per cent, an average commission rate of 1.5 per cent, and average value of properties of this type of about $20 billion in this period (cf. Raymond W. Goldsmith, *A Study of Saving in the United States* (3 vols, Princeton University Press, 1955–56), Vol. III, Table W-1, and related worksheets).

(11) 1946–58: One-third of Table B-4, col. 4, on assumption that average settlement costs of 1- to 4-family structures amount to 1.5 per cent compared to average commission of 4.5 per cent; plus allowance of $18 million per year for settlement cost of multi-family structures, which implies average settlement cost of 0.75 per cent.

(12) 1946–58: Sum of cols. 9, 10 and 11.

TABLE B-2

EXPENDITURES ON PRIVATE NONFARM ONE- TO FOUR-FAMILY HOMES
(millions of dollars)

Year	New Dwelling Units (1)	Change in Value of Work in Place on Uncompleted Projects (2)	Settlement Costs on New Housing (3)	Expenditures on Additions and Alterations (4)	Speculative Builders Margin (5)	Transactions in Existing Structures		Total (8)
						Dealers' Commissions (6)	Settlement Costs (7)	
1946	3,150	−659	47	1,268	246	738	246	5,036
1947	5,124	−785	77	1,998	409	671	224	7,718
1948	6,900	−11	104	2,393	563	702	234	10,885
1949	6,426	−276	96	2,134	472	714	238	9,804
1950	10,666	−1,524	160	2,328	800	914	305	13,649
1951	9,370	293	141	2,415	717	930	310	14,176
1952	9,440	138	142	2,703	736	966	322	14,447
1953	10,049	423	151	2,866	799	1,047	349	15,684
1954	11,579	−754	174	2,923	938	1,084	361	16,305
1955	14,487	−265	217	3,275	1,195	1,217	406	20,532
1956	12,980	343	195	3,584	1,166	1,223	408	19,823
1957	12,098	136	181	3,786	1,079	1,131	377	18,788
1958	12,855	−445	193	3,743	1,166	1,020	340	18,872

SOURCE, BY COLUMN

(1) From Table B-1, col. 2.
(2) Table B-1, col. 5 divided among 1- to 4-family, multifamily and nonhousekeeping structures according to the share of each in total residential construction expenditures (Table B-1, cols. 1 to 4).
(3) Estimated at $1\frac{1}{2}$ per cent of col. 1.
(4) Roughly estimated at 97 per cent of Table B-1, col. 7.
(5) From Table B-1, col. 9.
(6) From Table B-4, col. 4.
(7) One-third of col. 6. See note to Table B-1, col. 11.
(8) Sum of cols. 1–7.

TABLE B-3

SPECULATIVE BUILDERS' MARGIN ON ONE- TO FOUR-FAMILY NONFARM HOMES

Year	1- to 4-Family Home Construction Expenditures ($ million) (1)	Homes Built by Speculative Builders (per cent) (2)	Expenditures on Homes Built by Speculative Builders ($ million) (3)	Builders' Profit of Total Expenditures (per cent) (4)	Speculative Builders' Margin ($ million) (5)
1946	3,150	46	1,449	17	246
1947	5,124	47	2,408	17	409
1948	6,900	48	3,312	17	563
1949	6,426	49	3,149	15	472
1950	10,666	50	5,333	15	800
1951	9,370	51	4,779	15	717
1952	9,440	52	4,909	15	736
1953	10,049	53	5,326	15	799
1954	11,579	54	6,253	15	938
1955	14,487	55	7,968	15	1,195
1956	12,980	56	7,269	15	1,090
1957	12,615	57	7,191	15	1,079
1958	13,405	58	7,775	15	1,166

SOURCE, BY COLUMN

(1) From Table B-1, col. 2.
(2) Estimated on basis of data given in *Structure of the Residential Building Industry in 1949*, Bureau of Labor Statistics, Bull. No. 1170, p. 21.
(3) Col. 1 multiplied by col. 2.
(4) Based on Siskind's Estimates (*New and Maintenance Construction, Construction in the 1947 Interindustry Relations Study*, Bureau of Labor Statistics, Report No. 2, pp. 39–40). The figure includes builders' profit on land (beyond actual development expenditures) which, on average, may amount to approximately one-third of total margin. This profit is in the nature of a capital gain and its inclusion in builders' margin is conceptually disputed.
(5) Col. 3 multiplied by col. 4.

TABLE B-4

Dealers' Commissions on Sales of One- to Four-Family Nonfarm Homes

Year	Index of Real Estate Activity (1)	Index of Real Estate Prices (1947–49 = 100) (2)	Index of Value of Real Estate Activity (3)	Dealers' Commissions Total ($ million) (4)	Dealers' Commissions Depreciable ($ million) (5)
1946	128.9	81.8	105.4	738	606
1947	108.1	88.6	95.8	671	551
1948	100.8	99.5	100.3	702	577
1949	91.1	112.0	102.0	714	587
1950	114.1	114.4	130.5	914	750
1951	106.2	125.0	132.8	930	764
1952	106.1	130.1	138.0	966	794
1953	106.3	140.6	149.5	1,047	860
1954	105.3	147.0	154.8	1,084	890
1955	117.2	148.4	173.9	1,217	1,000
1956	111.2	157.1	174.7	1,223	1,005
1957	100.6	160.5	161.5	1,131	929
1958	90.5	161.0	145.7	1,020	838

SOURCE, BY COLUMN

(1) *Real Estate Analyst*, Jan. 1, 1955, as revised and brought up to date by Roy Wenzlick & Co., p. 5. 1951–58: *ibid.*, Feb. 28, 1958.

(2) Housing price index from *A Study of Saving* . . . , Vol. I, Table R-32, linked in 1947 to index of average property valuation of existing homes as given in annual reports of the Federal Housing Administration (Housing and Home Finance Agency, e.g., *7th Annual Report*, p. 240).

(3) Col. 1 multiplied by col. 2.

(4) Indexes of col. 3 applied to base value of $700 million derived as follows:

(1) Value in current prices of 1- to 4-family homes (including builders' profits, alterations, and additions, and land) at the end of 1948 (assumed to be roughly equivalent to the average for period 1947–49) computed from figures given in *A Study of Saving* . . . , Vol. III, Table W-1 and related worksheets.

(2) It was assumed that average value of real estate activity giving rise to dealers' commissions in 1947–49 was equal to 8 per cent of average value of 1- to 4-family homes. This estimate was based, in addition to other scattered evidence, on findings by the Survey of Consumer Finances that about one-half of homeowners sampled had acquired their houses since Pearl Harbor, indicating a median turnover period of a little over seven years (*Federal Reserve Bulletin*, 1949, p. 1041) and by Ernest M. Fisher's tentative conclusion (*Urban Real Estate Markets: Characteristics and Financing*, New York, NBER, 1951, p. 43) that "The average term of ownership is less than ten years". Both figures may be somewhat lower than average market turnover period involving commission to a real estate dealer in the postwar period as they include acquisitions by means other than purchase and the first refers to a period of particularly high real estate activity.

(3) Finally, it was assumed on the basis of the standard commission rate of 5 per cent that dealers' profits averaged 4.5 per cent of the total value of real estate activity for any given year to allow for lower rate of commission on some transactions.

(5) Indexes in col. 3 applied to base value of $575 million, derived the same way as base value for col. 4, except that estimated share of land in total real estate activity was excluded since land is not considered a depreciable asset.

TABLE B-5

NET INVESTMENT IN ONE- TO FOUR-FAMILY NONFARM HOMES
(millions of dollars)

	Expenditures		Depreciation			Net Investment		
Year	Original Cost (1)	1947–49 Prices (2)	Original Cost (3)	1947–49 Prices (4)	Replacement Cost (5)	Original Cost (6)	1947–49 Prices (7)	Replacement Cost (8)
1946	4,860	6,311	1,736	4,450	3,426	3,124	1,861	1,434
1947	7,461	8,006	1,832	4,539	4,231	5,629	3,467	3,230
1948	10,718	10,227	1,974	4,651	4,874	8,744	5,576	5,844
1949	9,635	9,437	2,130	4,779	4,880	7,505	4,658	4,755
1950	13,430	12,471	2,304	4,918	5,297	11,126	7,553	8,133
1951	13,955	12,030	2,508	5,073	5,884	11,447	6,962	8,071
1952	14,224	11,938	2,718	5,218	6,215	11,500	6,721	8,003
1953	15,435	12,732	2,939	5,366	6,503	12,469	7,362	8,932
1954	16,147	13,340	3,176	5,526	6,649	12,871	7,814	9,398
1955	20,242	16,337	3,445	5,710	7,074	16,797	10,627	13,168
1956	19,532	15,095	3,741	5,907	7,644	15,791	9,188	11,888
1957	18,519	14,052	4,028	6,091	8,028	14,491	7,961	10,491
1958	18,629	14,007	4,310	6,286	8,360	14,319	7,721	10,269

SOURCE, BY COLUMN

(1) Depreciable expenditures. Sum of Table B-2, cols. 1 to 5, Table B-4, col. 5 and estimate of settlement costs on existing 1- to 4-family homes (one-third of Table B-4, col. 5).
(2) Col. 1 divided by Table B-9, col. 1.
(3) Components of col. 1 depreciated on a straight-line basis assuming an average life of eighty years for new structures (Table B-2, cols. 1 to 3), and speculative builders' margin (Table B-2, col. 5) and forty years for additions and alterations (Table B-2, col. 4) and dealers' commissions and settlement costs on existing homes (see notes to col. 1). Expenditure figures for years before 1946, required for the calculation of depreciation, obtained from A Study of Saving . . . , Vol. I, Tables R-25 to R-28, R-30 to R-32, and related worksheets.
(4) Same method as for col.3 but based on expenditure figures of col. 2. Expenditures in 1947–49 prices for years before 1946 obtained by deflating expenditures in original cost (see notes to col. 3) by price index derived by extrapolating Table B-9, col. 1, from 1946 by index given in Saving, Vol. I, Table R-20, col. 1.
(5) Col. 4 multiplied by Table B-9, col. 1.
(6) Col. 1 minus col. 3.
(7) Col. 2 minus col. 4.
(8) Col. 1 minus col. 5.

TABLE B-6

EXPENDITURES ON PRIVATE NONFARM MULTIFAMILY DWELLINGS
(millions of dollars)

Year	New Dwelling Units (1)	Change in Value of Work in Place on Uncompleted Projects (2)	Settlement Costs on New Housing (3)	Expenditures on Additions and Alterations (4)	Transactions in Existing Structures		Total (7)
					Dealers' Commissions (5)	Settlement Costs (6)	
1946	150	−32	2	39	35	18	212
1947	326	−49	3	59	35	18	392
1948	600	−1	6	74	35	18	732
1949	831	−36	8	66	35	18	922
1950	859	−122	9	72	35	18	871
1951	479	15	5	75	35	18	627
1952	430	6	4	84	35	18	577
1953	506	21	5	89	35	18	674
1954	491	−32	5	90	35	18	607
1955	503	−9	5	101	35	18	653
1956	555	15	6	111	35	18	740
1957	517	6	5	117	35	18	698
1958	550	−20	6	116	35	18	705

SOURCE, BY COLUMN

(1) From Table B-1, col. 3.
(2) Table B-1, col. 5 respectively divided among one- to four-family, multifamily, and nonhousekeeping structures according to the share of each in total residential construction expenditures (Table B-1, cols. 1 to 4).
(3) Estimated at 1 per cent of col. 1.
(4) Roughly estimated at 3 per cent of Table B-1, col. 7.
(5 and 6) See notes to Table B-1, cols. 10 and 11.
(7) Sum of cols. 1–6.

TABLE B-7

NET INVESTMENT IN MULTIFAMILY DWELLINGS
(millions of dollars)

	Expenditures		Depreciation			Net Investment		
Year	Original Cost (1)	1947–49 Prices (2)	Original Cost (3)	1947–49 Prices (4)	Replacement Cost (5)	Original Cost (6)	1947–49 Prices (7)	Replacement Cost (8)
1946	204	262	178	419	327	26	−157	−123
1947	384	418	182	424	390	202	−6	−6
1948	724	699	193	431	446	531	268	278
1949	914	872	206	441	462	708	431	452
1950	863	788	220	453	497	643	335	366
1951	619	525	234	463	545	385	62	74
1952	569	467	243	469	572	326	−2	−3
1953	666	530	255	476	599	411	54	67
1954	599	472	265	482	611	334	−10	−12
1955	645	493	276	489	639	369	4	6
1956	732	534	289	495	678	443	39	54
1957	679	481	301	502	708	378	−21	−29
1958	711	495	314	509	730	397	−14	−19

SOURCE, BY COLUMN

(1)   Depreciable expenditures. Sum of Table B-6, cols. 1 to 4 and estimate of depreciable dealers' commissions and settlement costs on transactions in existing multifamily structures at $30 million a year and $15 million a year, respectively (see notes to Table B-1, cols. 10 and 11).
(2)   Col. 1 divided by Table B-9, col. 2.
(3)   Components of col. 1 depreciated on a straight-line basis assuming an average life of sixty-five years for new structures (Table B-6, cols. 1 to 3) and thirty-two years for additions and alterations (Table B-6, col. 4) and dealers' commissions and settlements costs on existing homes (see notes to col. 1). Expenditure figures for years before 1946, required for the calculation of depreciation, obtained from *A Study of Saving* . . . , Vol. I, Tables R-25 to R-28, R-30 to R-32, and related worksheets. In the absence of data and in view of the small amounts involved, dealers' commissions and settlements costs on existing structures were omitted for years before 1946.
(4)   Same method as for col. 3, but based on expenditure figures of col. 2. Expenditures in 1947–49 prices for years before 1946 obtained by deflating expenditures in original cost (see notes to col. 3) by price index derived by extrapolating Table B-9, col. 2 from 1946 by index given in *A Study of Saving* . . . , Vol. I, Table R-20, col. 2.
(5)   Col. 4 multiplied by Table B-9, col. 2.
(6)   Col. 1 minus col. 3.
(7)   Col. 2 minus col. 4.
(8)   Col. 1 minus col. 5.

TABLE B-8

NET INVESTMENT IN NONHOUSEKEEPING STRUCTURES
(millions of dollars)

	Expenditures		Depreciation			Net Investment		
Year	Original Cost (1)	1947–49 Prices (2)	Original Cost (3)	1947–49 Prices (4)	Replacement Cost (5)	Original Cost (6)	1947–49 Prices (7)	Replacement Cost (8)
1946	116	149	108	238	186	8	−89	−70
1947	107	117	109	238	218	−2	−121	−111
1948	157	152	112	238	246	45	−86	−89
1949	179	171	115	238	249	64	−67	−70
1950	152	139	118	238	261	34	−99	−109
1951	198	168	121	238	281	77	−70	−83
1952	190	156	125	238	290	65	−82	−100
1953	281	223	130	238	299	151	−15	−18
1954	280	221	136	240	304	144	−19	−24
1955	336	257	142	242	316	194	15	20
1956	463	338	151	245	336	312	93	127
1957	512	363	162	249	351	350	114	161
1958	606	422	174	255	366	432	167	240

SOURCE, BY COLUMN

(1) Table B-1, col. 4 plus portion of Table B-1, cols. 5 and 6. (See notes to Tables B-2 and B-6).
(2) Col. 1 divided by Table B-9, col. 2.
(3) Col. 1, depreciated, assuming an average life of forty years. Expenditure figures required for the calculation of depreciation for the period 1906–14 estimated to be 4 per cent of expenditures on new nonfarm dwelling units (*A Study of Saving* . . . , Vol. I, Table R-27, col. 2), which is a rough average of the relationship of nonhousekeeping expenditures to new nonfarm dwelling units in the 1920's and after World War II. Expenditure figures for the period 1915–45 from *Construction and Building Materials, Statistical Supplement*, Department of Commerce, May 1954, p. 6.
(4) Col. 2, depreciated, assuming an average life of forty years. Expenditures in 1947–49 prices for years before 1946 obtained by deflating expenditures in original cost (see notes to col. 3) by price index derived by extrapolating Table B-9, col. 2 from 1946 by index given in *Saving*, Vol. I, Table R-20, col. 2.
(5) Col. 4 multiplied by Table B-9, col. 2.
(6) Col. 1 minus col. 3.
(7) Col. 2 minus col. 4.
(8) Col. 1 minus col. 5.

NOTE: Nonhousekeeping structures include buildings containing nonhousekeeping quarters, such as transient hotels, dormitories, clubhouses, and tourist courts and cabins.

Cost Indexes of Residential Construction
(1947–49 = 100.0)

	Annual Averages		Year-End Figures	
Year	1- to 4-Family (1)	Multifamily and Nonhousekeeping (2)	1- to 4-Family (3)	Multifamily and Nonhousekeeping (4)
1945	70.1	71.3	72.0	73.3
1946	77.0	78.0	83.6	83.6
1947	93.2	91.7	100.2	98.1
1948	104.8	103.5	105.2	106.4
1949	102.1	104.8	101.1	104.6
1950	107.7	109.6	113.3	115.0
1951	116.0	118.0	117.2	119.8
1952	119.1	122.0	120.0	123.7
1953	121.2	125.8	120.8	126.8
1954	120.3	126.8	121.3	127.8
1955	123.9	130.6	126.2	133.6
1956	129.4	137.0	130.4	139.1
1957	131.8	141.1	132.3	142.3
1958	133.0	143.5	134.9	145.9

Source, by Column

(1 and 3) Boeckh's building cost index for residences. Annual average figures (col. 1) *Construction Volume and Costs*, Department of Commerce, 1915–56, p. 28. Year-end figures (col. 3; average of December of current year and January of succeeding year) from *ibid.*, pp. 30–31; *Survey of Current Business*, Statistical Supplement, 1949, p. 36; and *Construction Review*, May 1959, p. 30.

(2 and 4) Boeckh's building cost index for apartments, hotels, and office buildings from same sources used for cols. 1 and 3.

TABLE B-10

Value of Private Nonfarm Housekeeping Units, Excluding Land
(millions of dollars)

End of Year	Original Cost			1947–49 Dollars			Current Prices		
	Total (1)	1- to 4-Family (2)	Multi-family (3)	Total (4)	1- to 4-Family (5)	Multi-family (6)	Total (7)	1- to 4-Family (8)	Multi-family (9)
1945	80,046	72,849	7,197	190,149	174,237	15,912	137,114	125,451	11,663
1946	83,196	75,973	7,223	191,853	176,098	15,755	160,390	147,219	13,171
1947	89,004	81,602	7,425	195,314	179,565	15,749	195,370	179,924	15,446
1948	98,302	90,346	7,956	201,158	185,141	16,017	211,772	194,768	17,042
1949	106,515	97,851	8,664	206,246	189,799	16,448	209,090	191,886	17,204
1950	118,284	108,977	9,307	214,135	197,352	16,783	242,899	223,599	19,300
1951	130,113	120,424	9,692	221,154	204,309	16,845	259,629	239,449	20,180
1952	141,942	131,924	10,018	227,872	211,029	16,843	274,128	253,294	20,834
1953	154,849	144,420	10,429	235,292	218,395	16,897	285,246	263,821	21,425
1954	168,054	157,291	10,763	243,096	226,209	16,887	295,978	274,397	21,581
1955	185,220	174,088	11,132	253,727	236,836	16,891	321,454	298,887	22,567
1956	201,364	189,879	11,575	262,954	246,024	16,930	351,654	320,815	23,549
1957	216,310	204,370	11,940	270,890	253,985	16,905	359,151	335,095	24,056
1958	231,017	218,689	12,328	278,596	261,706	16,890	377,684	353,042	24,642

(Notes to Table B–10 on next page)

SOURCE, BY COLUMN

(1)　　　Sum of cols. 2 and 3.
(2 and 3)　Derived by addition of cumulated net investment, original cost (Tables B-5 and B-7) to estimated value for 1945, obtained by cumulating expenditures less depreciation for number of years preceding 1945 corresponding to the assumed length of life of the component of construction involved.
(4)　　　Sum of cols. 5 and 6.
(5 and 6)　Same procedure as for cols. 2 and 3 but applied to expenditures in 1947–49 prices.
(7)　　　Sum of cols. 8 and 9.
(8 and 9)　Cumulated depreciated capital expenditures in 1947–49 prices multiplied by year-end index from Table B-9, cols. 3 and 4.

TABLE B-11

RATIO OF AVERAGE VALUES OF LAND TO STRUCTURES
(amounts in dollars)

End of Year	New Homes				Existing Homes			
	Property Value (1)	Property Less Land (2)	Land (3)	Land as Per Cent of Structure Value (4)	Property Value (5)	Property Less Land (6)	Land (7)	Land as Per Cent of Structure Value (8)
1940	5,199	4,537	662	15	5,179	4,231	948	22
1946	6,597	5,836	761	13	6,269	5,436	833	15
1947	7,817	6,924	893	13	7,190	6,275	915	15
1948	7,965	7,916	1,049	13	8,075	7,105	970	14
1949	8,753	8,735	1,018	13	9,093	7,995	1,098	14
1950	8,594	7,559	1,035	14	9,298	8,148	1,150	14
1951	9,307	8,215	1,092	13	10,147	8,925	1,222	14
1952	10,245	9,018	1,227	14	10,567	9,271	1,296	14
1953	10,357	9,066	1,291	14	11,419	9,958	1,461	15
1954	11,120	9,664	1,456	15	11,934	10,343	1,591	15
1955	12,118	10,492	1,626	15	12,047	10,340	1,707	17
1956	13,399	11,551	1,848	16	12,756	10,825	1,931	18
1957	14,464	12,316	2,148	17	13,028	10,987	2,041	19
1958	14,394	12,171	2,223	18	13,069	10,919	2,150	20

SOURCE: Housing and Home Finance Agency, *Annual Reports*, 1948, pp. 194, 202; 1951, pp. 264, 272; 1953, pp. 228, 240; 1954, pp. 186, 196; 1955 from Housing and Home Finance Agency. 1956–58 from *Annual Reports* of the Federal Housing Administration e.g., 1957, p. 68; 1958, p. 66.

TABLE B-12

VALUE OF PRIVATE NONFARM HOUSEKEEPING UNITS,
INCLUDING VALUE OF UNDERLYING LAND
(millions of dollars)

End of Year	1947–49 Prices			Current Prices		
	Total (1)	1- to 4- Family (2)	Multifamily (3)	Total (4)	1- to 4- Family (5)	Multifamily (6)
1945	220,263	200,373	19,890	158,848	144,269	14,579
1946	222,357	202,663	19,694	185,766	169,302	16,464
1947	226,186	206,500	19,686	226,221	206,913	19,308
1948	232,933	212,912	20,021	245,286	223,983	21,303
1949	238,829	218,269	20,560	242,174	220,669	21,505
1950	247,934	226,955	20,979	281,264	257,139	24,125
1951	256,011	234,955	21,056	300,591	275,366	25,225
1952	263,737	242,683	21,054	317,331	291,288	26,043
1953	272,275	251,154	21,121	330,175	303,394	26,781
1954	281,249	260,140	21,109	342,533	315,557	26,976
1955	293,475	272,361	21,114	371,929	343,720	28,209
1956	304,091	282,928	21,163	398,373	368,937	29,436
1957	313,214	292,083	21,131	415,429	385,359	30,070
1958	322,075	300,962	21,113	436,801	405,998	30,803

SOURCE, BY COLUMN

(1) Sum of cols. 2 and 3.
(2) Table B-10, col. 5, plus underlying land estimated to be 15 per cent of structure value on basis of Housing and Home Finance Agency data given in Table B-11.
(3) Table B-10, col. 6 plus underlying land estimated on basis of data given in *A Study of Saving* . . . , Vol. II, Table B-50.
(4) Sum of cols. 5 and 6.
(5) Table B-10, col. 8 plus underlying land (see notes to col. 2).
(6) Table B-10, col. 9 plus underlying land (see notes to col. 3).

TABLE B-13

VALUE OF PRIVATE NONFARM NONHOUSEKEEPING REAL ESTATE
(millions of dollars)

End of Year	Nonhousekeeping Structures			Nonhousekeeping Real Estate	
	Original Cost (1)	1947–49 Prices (2)	Current Prices (3)	1947–49 Prices (4)	Current Prices (5)
1945	2,193	4,572	3,351	5,715	4,189
1946	2,201	4,483	3,748	5,604	4,685
1947	2,199	4,362	4,279	5,452	5,349
1948	2,244	4,276	4,550	5,345	5,688
1949	2,308	4,209	4,403	5,261	5,504
1950	2,342	4,110	4,726	5,138	5,908
1951	2,419	4,040	4,840	5,050	6,050
1952	2,484	3,958	4,896	4,948	6,120
1953	2,635	3,943	5,000	4,929	6,250
1954	2,779	3,924	5,015	4,905	6,269
1955	2,973	3,939	5,263	4,924	6,579
1956	3,285	4,032	5,609	5,040	7,011
1957	3,635	4,146	5,900	5,183	7,375
1958	4,067	4,313	6,293	5,391	7,866

SOURCE, BY COLUMN

(1) Derived by addition of cumulated net investment, original cost, (Table B-8, col. 6) to estimated value for 1945, obtained by cumulating expenditures less depreciation for forty years preceding 1945, the assumed length of life of nonhousekeeping structures.

(2) Same procedure as for col. 1 but derived from Table B-8, col. 7.

(3) Col. 2 multiplied by Table B-9, col. 4.

(4 and 5) Cols. 2 and 3, respectively, plus value of underlying land estimated on basis of data given in *A Study of Saving. . .* , Vol. II, Table B-50, col. 2.

TABLE B-14
VALUE OF PRIVATE NONFARM RESIDENTIAL REAL ESTATE
(millions of dollars)

End of Year	Residential Structures			Residential Real Estate	
	Original Cost (1)	1947–49 Prices (2)	Current Prices (3)	1947–49 Prices (4)	Current Prices (5)
1945	82,239	194,721	140,465	225,978	163,037
1946	85,397	196,436	164,138	227,961	190,451
1947	91,226	199,676	199,649	231,638	231,570
1948	100,546	205,434	216,322	238,278	250,974
1949	108,823	210,456	213,493	244,090	247,678
1950	120,626	218,245	247,625	253,072	287,172
1951	132,535	225,194	264,469	261,061	306,641
1952	144,426	231,830	279,024	268,685	323,451
1953	157,484	239,235	290,246	277,204	336,425
1954	170,833	247,020	300,993	286,154	348,802
1955	188,193	257,666	326,717	298,399	378,940
1956	198,740	266,986	357,250	309,131	405,748
1957	205,089	275,036	365,051	318,397	422,804
1958	235,084	282,909	383,977	327,466	444,667

SOURCE, BY COLUMN
(1)   Table B-10, col. 1 plus Table B-13, col. 1.
(2)   Table B-10, col. 4 plus Table B-13, col. 2.
(3)   Table B-10, col. 7 plus Table B-13, col. 3.
(4)   Table B-12, col. 1 plus Table B-13, col. 4.
(5)   Table B-12, col. 4 plus Table B-13, col. 5.

TABLE B-15
NET INVESTMENT BY INDIVIDUALS IN ONE- TO FOUR-FAMILY NONFARM HOMES
(millions of dollars)

Year	Expenditures		Depreciation			Net Investment		
	Original Cost (1)	1947–49 Prices (2)	Original Cost (3)	1947–49 Prices (4)	Replacement Cost (5)	Original Cost (6)	1947–49 Prices (7)	Replacement Cost (8)
1946	4,763	6,186	1,704	4,372	3,366	3,059	1,814	1,397
1947	7,312	7,846	1,798	4,457	4,153	5,514	3,389	3,159
1948	10,504	10,025	1,935	4,568	4,788	8,569	5,455	5,716
1949	9,442	9,247	2,088	4,693	4,792	7,354	4,554	4,650
1950	13,161	12,220	2,259	4,829	5,200	10,902	7,391	7,961
1951	13,677	11,791	2,459	4,979	5,777	11,218	6,812	7,900
1952	13,934	11,699	2,665	5,121	6,100	11,269	6,578	7,834
1953	15,127	12,481	2,882	5,266	6,382	12,245	7,215	8,745
1954	15,726	13,073	3,112	5,423	6,524	12,614	7,650	9,202
1955	19,837	16,011	3,376	5,603	6,942	16,461	10,408	12,895
1956	19,141	14,792	3,666	5,796	7,500	15,475	8,996	11,641
1957	18,148	13,769	3,949	5,976	7,876	14,199	7,793	10,272
1958	18,257	13,726	4,225	6,153	8,184	14,032	7,573	10,073

SOURCE: Same procedure as for Table B-5. Expenditures by individuals on 1- to 4-family homes determined by multiplying the components of Table B-5, col. 1, by percentages given in A Study of Saving . . . , Vol. I, Table R-29, col. 1 (interpolating between decadal percentages; 1900 figure carried through 1958).

TABLE B-16

VALUE OF INDIVIDUALS' SHARE OF PRIVATE NONFARM HOUSEKEEPING UNITS, EXCLUDING LAND
(millions of dollars)

End of Year	Original Cost			1947–49 Prices			Current Prices		
	Total (1)	1- to 4- Family (2)	Multi-family (3)	Total (4)	1- to 4- Family (5)	Multi-family (6)	Total (7)	1- to 4- Family (8)	Multi-family (9)
1945	75,737	71,415	4,322	180,763	170,910	9,853	130,276	123,054	7,222
1946	78,768	74,474	4,294	182,409	172,724	9,685	152,493	144,397	8,096
1947	84,326	79,988	4,338	185,678	176,103	9,581	185,854	176,455	9,399
1948	93,060	88,557	4,512	191,142	181,558	9,584	201,207	191,010	10,197
1949	100,667	95,911	4,756	195,774	186,122	9,652	198,265	188,169	10,096
1950	111,787	106,813	4,974	203,196	193,513	9,683	230,396	219,260	11,136
1951	123,121	118,031	5,090	209,932	200,325	9,607	246,290	234,781	11,509
1952	134,482	129,300	5,182	216,410	206,903	9,507	260,044	248,284	11,760
1953	146,852	141,543	5,309	223,549	214,118	9,431	270,613	258,654	11,959
1954	159,565	154,159	5,406	231,096	221,768	9,328	280,928	269,005	11,923
1955	176,137	170,620	5,517	241,413	232,176	9,237	305,347	293,006	12,341
1956	191,723	186,066	5,657	250,331	241,172	9,159	327,229	314,489	12,740
1957	206,049	200,276	5,773	258,023	248,965	9,058	342,271	329,381	12,890
1958	220,118	214,222	5,896	265,498	256,537	8,961	359,144	346,070	13,074

SOURCE, BY COLUMN

(1)   Sum of cols. 2 and 3.
(2 and 3)   Derived by addition of cumulated net investment, original cost (Tables B-15 and B-52) to estimated value for 1945, obtained by cumulating expenditures less depreciation for number of years preceding 1945 corresponding to the assumed length of life of the component of construction involved.
(4)   Sum of cols. 5 and 6.
(5 and 6)   Same procedure as for cols. 2 and 3 but applied to expenditures in 1947–49 prices.
(7)   Sum of cols. 8 and 9.
(8 and 9)   Cumulated depreciated capital expenditures in 1947–49 prices multiplied by year-end index from Table B-9, cols. 3 and 4.

TABLE B-17

VALUE OF VACANT LOTS

Year	Number (millions) (1)	Average Value (dollars) (2)	Aggregate Value	
			Current Prices (3)	1947–49 Prices (4)
			($ billions)	
1945	10.13	765	7.75	10.13
1946	10.22	775	7.90	10.22
1947	10.38	910	9.45	10.38
1948	10.71	1,070	11.45	10.71
1949	10.93	1,035	11.30	10.93
1950	11.23	1,055	11.85	11.23
1951	11.42	1,110	12.70	11.42
1952	11.78	1,250	14.70	11.78
1953	12.14	1,315	15.95	12.14
1954	12.46	1,480	18.45	12.46
1955	12.69	1,655	21.00	12.69
1956	12.96	1,880	24.35	12.96
1957	13.38	2,185	29.25	13.38
1958	13.66	2,400	32.80	13.66

SOURCE, BY COLUMN

(1) 1955: From "Real Estate Assessments in the United States" (Bureau of Census Release, May 31, 1957), p. 9. Since the figures refer to early 1956 they have been regarded as applicable to the end of 1955, rather than the end of 1956.
Other years: Based on 1955 figures and change in nonfarm population.

(2) 1955: Obtained by division of col. 3 by col. 1.
Other years: Estimates based on changes in average value of land underlying new one-family homes with insured mortgages (see *Annual Reports* of Federal Housing Administration).

(3) 1955: Derived from ratio between market and assessed value of all vacant lots, as determined by Bureau of Census (*1957 Census of Governments*, Vol. V., pp. 6, 27).
Other years: Obtained by multiplication of cols. 1 and 2, rounding to nearest $10 million.

(4) 1945–58: Obtained by multiplying col. 1 by 1947–49 average of col. 2 ($1,000), rounding to nearest $10 million.

TABLE B-18

Nonfarm Individuals' Expenditures on Main Types of Consumer Durable Goods, Original Cost
(millions of dollars)

Year	Total (1)	Furniture (2)	Household Appliances (3)	China, Glassware, Tableware, and Utensils (4)	Household Furnishings (5)	Radio, TV, and Musical Instruments (6)	Books and Maps (7)	Passenger Cars (8)	Passenger Car Accessories (9)	Jewelry and Watches (10)	Ophthalmic Products and Orthopedic Appliances (11)	Miscellaneous (12)
1946	12,990	1,963	1,581	1,103	1,915	998	519	2,153	391	1,315	346	706
1947	17,537	2,238	2,788	1,182	2,151	1,253	470	4,531	438	1,283	351	852
1948	19,161	2,429	3,031	1,273	2,370	1,293	514	5,325	437	1,255	377	857
1949	21,095	2,420	2,814	1,273	2,344	1,534	567	7,313	441	1,218	409	762
1950	26,631	2,778	3,566	1,386	2,706	2,224	613	10,301	582	1,240	440	795
1951	25,080	2,872	3,493	1,477	2,950	2,042	702	8,365	552	1,321	492	814
1952	24,778	3,081	3,464	1,462	2,664	2,155	717	7,807	566	1,432	527	903
1953	27,731	3,297	3,674	1,547	2,639	2,405	766	9,776	577	1,485	557	1,008
1954	27,859	3,372	3,738	1,579	2,441	2,538	746	9,717	531	1,557	551	1,089
1955	35,114	3,896	4,375	1,735	2,838	2,602	828	14,539	643	1,710	638	1,310
1956	33,994	4,144	4,567	1,781	3,115	2,685	941	12,112	620	1,795	761	1,473
1957	35,317	4,078	4,472	1,783	3,136	2,806	963	13,225	662	1,778	820	1,594
1958	32,564	4,018	4,406	1,757	3,090	2,764	995	10,665	538	1,837	847	1,647

SOURCE, BY COLUMN

(1) Sum of cols. 2 to 12.

(2 to 7 and 10 to 12) Expenditures by individuals on durable goods from *U.S. Income and Output*, pp. 150, 151; and *Survey of Current Business*, July 1959, p. 17, split between nonfarmers and farmers according to ratio given in Table B-70, col. 5.

(8) From Table B-27, col. 6.

(9) Table B-30, col. 3, divided between nonfarmers and farmers according to 1946 ratios given in Table B-70, col. 5.

NOTE: Miscellaneous, as in all other consumer durable goods tables, includes wheel goods, durable toys, sports equipment. boats, and pleasure aircraft.

TABLE B-19

NONFARM INDIVIDUALS' EXPENDITURES ON MAIN TYPES OF CONSUMER DURABLE GOODS, CONSTANT (1947–49) PRICES
(millions of dollars)

Year	Total (1)	Furniture (2)	Household Appliances (3)	China, Glassware, Tableware, and Utensils (4)	Household Furnishings (5)	Radio, TV, and Musical Instruments (6)	Books and Maps (7)	Passenger Cars (8)	Passenger Car Accessories (9)	Jewelry and Watches (10)	Ophthalmic Products and Orthopedic Appliances (11)	Miscellaneous (12)
1946	15,544	2,304	1,947	1,268	2,333	1,392	617	2,725	434	1,356	384	784
1947	18,438	2,373	2,910	1,224	2,248	1,296	510	4,968	442	1,246	369	852
1948	18,894	2,324	2,940	1,264	2,335	1,229	509	5,341	437	1,281	377	857
1949	20,319	2,391	2,783	1,240	2,380	1,562	530	6,703	432	1,243	393	762
1950	25,702	2,734	3,588	1,367	2,462	2,441	568	9,365	626	1,305	427	819
1951	22,583	2,580	3,289	1,326	2,294	2,184	639	7,261	531	1,283	443	753
1952	22,470	2,832	3,296	1,289	2,148	2,483	615	6,549	534	1,418	475	831
1953	25,209	3,042	3,539	1,352	2,140	2,846	633	8,215	555	1,456	497	934
1954	25,922	3,140	3,719	1,378	1,975	3,180	617	8,413	511	1,557	492	940
1955	32,531	3,707	4,524	1,519	2,180	3,428	671	12,290	618	1,781	570	1,243
1956	31,388	3,858	5,030	1,460	2,346	3,580	758	9,912	576	1,862	655	1,351
1957	31,752	3,821	5,019	1,415	2,259	3,616	709	10,276	599	1,879	707	1,452
1958	29,352	3,766	5,041	1,369	2,226	3,557	687	8,031	483	1,975	727	1,490

SOURCE, BY COLUMN

(1) Sum of cols. 2 to 12;   (2 to 12) Table B-18 deflated by price indexes shown in Table B-33.

241

TABLE B-20

Depreciation on Nonfarm Individuals' Holdings of Main Types of Consumer Durable Goods, Original Cost
(millions of dollars)

Year	Total (1)	Furniture (2)	Household Appliances (3)	China, Glassware, Tableware, and Utensils (4)	Household Furnishings (5)	Radio, TV, and Musical Instruments (6)	Books and Maps (7)	Passenger Cars (8)	Passenger Car Accessories (9)	Jewelry and Watches (10)	Ophthalmic Products and Orthopedic Appliances (12)	Miscellaneous (12)
1946	5,972	886	626	545	1,048	413	338	920	151	489	290	266
1947	7,206	986	767	617	1,176	494	384	1,364	208	568	315	327
1948	8,779	1,112	960	696	1,328	590	426	2,012	278	647	336	394
1949	10,538	1,245	1,146	781	1,488	697	468	2,835	344	721	358	455
1950	12,565	1,383	1,355	870	1,655	844	506	3,987	417	793	383	512
1951	14,738	1,527	1,594	963	1,790	1,008	544	4,991	474	868	412	567
1952	16,409	1,674	1,823	1,053	1,961	1,163	581	5,634	503	944	448	625
1953	18,215	1,835	2,045	1,148	2,111	1,346	622	6,371	530	1,026	486	695
1954	19,996	2,037	2,281	1,249	2,243	1,562	666	7,003	553	1,110	518	774
1955	22,239	2,220	2,579	1,350	2,377	1,790	707	8,040	568	1,196	550	862
1956	24,491	2,417	2,935	1,436	2,512	1,989	756	9,039	581	1,280	598	948
1957	26,454	2,614	3,293	1,500	2,621	2,151	805	9,836	597	1,354	660	1,023
1958	27,990	2,810	3,583	1,554	2,706	2,302	850	10,333	603	1,419	730	1,100

Source, by Column

(1) Sum of cols. 2 to 12.

(2 to 7 and 9 to 12) Depreciation calculated from Table B-18 applying rates given in Tables B-31. Expenditures for years before 1946 which were required for estimating depreciation were obtained for the period 1934–45 by the same methods and sources as the later figures. For years before 1934, figures taken from *A Study of Saving...*, Vol. I, Table Q-5, and related worksheets.

(8) Depreciation calculated from Table B-18 applying rates given in Table B-31. Expenditures for years before 1946 derived as in Table B-27, col. 6.

TABLE B-21

DEPRECIATION ON NONFARM INDIVIDUALS' HOLDINGS OF MAIN TYPES OF CONSUMER DURABLE GOODS, CONSTANT (1947–49) PRICES
(millions of dollars)

Year	Total (1)	Furniture (2)	Household Appliances (3)	China, Glassware, Tableware, and Utensils (4)	Household Furnishings (5)	Radio, TV, and Musical Instruments (6)	Books and Maps (7)	Passenger Cars (8)	Passenger Car Accessories (9)	Jewelry and Watches (10)	Ophthalmic Products and Orthopedic Appliances (11)	Miscellaneous (12)
1946	9,382	1,537	1,083	789	1,706	703	440	1,635	151	638	333	367
1947	10,431	1,618	1,207	843	1,790	781	482	2,027	200	708	354	421
1948	11,675	1,712	1,358	897	1,878	851	510	2,584	265	778	365	477
1949	12,976	1,809	1,489	953	1,960	928	531	3,237	323	845	375	526
1950	14,616	1,908	1,651	1,010	2,033	1,049	545	4,164	391	909	386	570
1951	16,076	1,991	1,837	1,065	2,092	1,188	556	4,927	439	970	401	610
1952	17,092	2,067	1,995	1,113	2,131	1,326	562	5,338	457	1,031	422	650
1953	18,227	2,160	2,138	1,168	2,165	1,518	572	5,779	478	1,095	448	706
1954	19,538	2,259	2,299	1,230	2,190	1,770	591	6,304	498	1,161	469	767
1955	21,271	2,364	2,579	1,292	2,220	2,056	612	7,081	505	1,232	493	837
1956	23,072	2,516	2,951	1,332	2,240	2,314	640	7,826	509	1,307	531	906
1957	24,737	2,642	3,343	1,351	2,241	2,539	661	8,519	520	1,377	580	964
1958	25,845	2,779	3,664	1,366	2,236	2,772	673	8,729	519	1,445	636	1,029

SOURCE, BY COLUMN

(1) Sum of cols. 2 to 12.

(2 to 12) Depreciation calculated from Table B-19 applying rates given in Table B-31. Expenditures in constant dollars for years before 1946, required for the calculation of depreciation allowances, obtained by deflating expenditures in original cost (see note to Table B-20) by appropriate price indexes. For all types of consumer durables, except books and maps, where the Bureau of Labor Statistics index of retail prices of newspapers was carried back to 1942, the 1946 value as shown in Table B-33 was extrapolated by figures given in *A Study of Saving . . .*, Vol. I, Table Q-16. Index for china, glassware, table-

ware and utensils, which is combined in *A Study of Saving . . .*, Vol. I, with index of jewelry and watches, derived by extrapolating the 1946 value of Table B-33, col. 3, by the Bureau of Labor Statistics index of dinnerware for the period 1942–45. Index for the earlier years obtained by extrapolating the 1942 value by Shavell's index of china, glassware, tableware, and utensils (*Survey of Current Business*, May 1943, p. 17). Index for jewelry and watches obtained by carrying the Sears Roebuck and Company index back to 1940 and extrapolating, on the basis of the 1939–41 relationship, by Shavell's index of jewelry and watches (*op. cit.*).

243

TABLE B-22

DEPRECIATION ON NONFARM INDIVIDUALS' HOLDINGS OF MAIN TYPES OF CONSUMER DURABLE GOODS, REPLACEMENT COST
(millions of dollars)

Year	Total (1)	Furniture (2)	Household Appliances (3)	China, Glassware, Tableware, and Utensils (4)	Household Furnishings (5)	Radio, TV, and Musical Instruments (6)	Books and Maps (7)	Passenger Cars (8)	Passenger Cars Accessories (9)	Jewelry and Watches (10)	Ophthalmic Products and Orthopedic Appliances (11)	Miscellaneous (12)
1946	7,827	1,310	879	686	1,401	504	370	1,292	136	619	300	330
1947	9,941	1,526	1,156	814	1,713	755	444	1,849	198	729	336	421
1948	11,853	1,789	1,400	903	1,906	895	515	2,576	265	762	365	477
1949	13,412	1,831	1,505	979	2,015	911	568	3,532	329	826	390	526
1950	15,136	1,939	1,641	1,024	2,234	956	589	4,580	364	858	398	553
1951	17,992	2,216	1,951	1,186	2,690	1,111	611	5,676	457	990	445	659
1952	19,118	2,249	2,097	1,262	2,642	1,151	655	6,363	484	1,041	468	706
1953	20,298	2,341	2,219	1,337	2,669	1,283	692	6,877	497	1,119	488	762
1954	21,289	2,426	2,310	1,409	2,707	1,412	715	7,281	518	1,155	525	831
1955	23,182	2,485	2,494	1,475	2,890	1,561	755	8,377	525	1,186	552	882
1956	25,437	2,652	2,680	1,625	2,975	1,736	794	9,563	548	1,260	616	988
1957	28,084	2,838	2,979	1,702	3,124	1,970	898	10,964	575	1,303	673	1,058
1958	29,542	2,965	3,202	1,753	3,104	2,154	975	11,592	578	1,344	741	1,134

SOURCE, BY COLUMN

(1) Sum of cols. 2 to 12.   (2 to 12) Table B-21, cols. 2 to 12, multiplied by respective price indexes from Table B-33.

TABLE B-23

NONFARM INDIVIDUALS' NET INVESTMENT IN MAIN TYPES OF CONSUMER DURABLE GOODS, ORIGINAL COST

(millions of dollars)

Year	Total (1)	Furniture (2)	Household Appliances (3)	China, Glassware, Tableware, and Utensils (4)	Household Furnishings (5)	Radio, TV, and Musical Instruments (6)	Books and Maps (7)	Passenger Cars (8)	Passenger Car Accessories (9)	Jewelry and Watches (10)	Ophthalmic Products and Orthopedic Appliances (11)	Miscellaneous (12)
1946	7,018	1,077	955	558	867	585	181	1,233	240	826	56	440
1947	10,331	1,252	2,021	565	975	759	86	3,167	230	715	36	525
1948	10,382	1,317	2,071	577	1,042	703	88	3,313	159	608	41	463
1949	10,557	1,175	1,668	492	856	837	99	4,478	97	497	51	307
1950	13,926	1,396	2,211	516	1,051	1,380	107	6,314	165	447	57	283
1951	10,344	1,345	1,899	514	1,160	1,034	158	3,374	78	455	80	247
1952	8,369	1,407	1,641	409	703	992	136	2,173	63	488	79	278
1953	9,516	1,462	1,629	399	528	1,059	144	3,405	47	459	71	313
1954	7,863	1,335	1,457	330	198	976	80	2,714	−22	447	33	315
1955	12,875	1,676	1,796	385	461	812	121	6,499	75	514	88	448
1956	9,503	1,727	1,632	345	603	696	185	3,073	39	515	163	525
1957	8,863	1,464	1,179	283	515	655	158	3,389	65	424	160	571
1958	4,574	1,208	823	203	384	462	145	332	−65	418	117	547

SOURCE, BY COLUMN

(1) Sum of cols. 2 to 12. (2 to 12) Table B-18, cols. 2 to 12, minus Table B-20, cols. 2 to 12, respectively.

TABLE B-24

Nonfarm Individuals' Net Investment in Main Types of Consumer Durable Goods, Constant (1947–49) Prices

(millions of dollars)

Year	Total (1)	Furniture (2)	Household Appliances (3)	China, Glassware, Tableware, and Utensils (4)	Household Furnishings (5)	Radio, TV, and Musical Instruments (6)	Books and Maps (7)	Passenger Cars (8)	Passenger Car Accessories (9)	Jewelry and Watches (10)	Ophthalmic Products and Orthopedic Appliances (11)	Miscellaneous (12)
1946	6,162	767	864	479	627	689	177	1,090	283	718	51	417
1947	8,007	755	1,703	381	458	515	28	2,941	242	538	15	431
1948	7,219	612	1,582	367	457	378	−1	2,757	172	503	12	380
1949	7,343	582	1,294	287	320	634	−1	3,466	109	398	18	236
1950	11,086	826	1,937	357	429	1,392	23	5,201	235	396	41	249
1951	6,507	589	1,452	261	202	996	83	2,334	92	313	42	143
1952	5,378	765	1,301	176	17	1,157	53	1,211	77	387	53	181
1953	6,982	882	1,401	184	−25	1,328	61	2,436	77	361	49	228
1954	6,384	881	1,420	148	−215	1,410	26	2,109	13	396	23	173
1955	11,260	1,343	1,945	227	−40	1,372	59	5,209	113	549	77	406
1956	8,316	1,342	2,079	128	106	1,266	118	2,086	67	555	124	445
1957	7,015	1,179	1,676	64	18	1,077	48	1,757	79	502	127	488
1958	3,507	987	1,377	3	−10	785	14	−698	−36	530	91	464

Source, by Column

(1) Sum of cols. 2 to 12.   (2 to 12) Table B-19, cols. 2 to 12, minus Table B-21, cols. 2 to 12, respectively.

TABLE B-25

NONFARM INDIVIDUALS' NET INVESTMENT IN MAIN TYPES OF CONSUMER DURABLE GOODS, REPLACEMENT COST

(millions of dollars)

Year	Total (1)	Furniture (2)	Household Appliances (3)	China, Glassware, Tableware, and Utensils (4)	Household Furnishings (5)	Radio, TV, and Musical Instruments (6)	Books and Maps (7)	Passenger Cars (8)	Passenger Car Accessories (9)	Jewelry and Watches (10)	Ophthalmic Products and Orthopedic Appliances (11)	Miscellaneous (12)
1946	5,163	653	702	417	514	494	149	861	255	696	46	376
1947	7,596	712	1,632	368	438	498	26	2,682	240	554	15	431
1948	7,308	640	1,631	370	464	398	-1	2,749	172	493	12	380
1949	7,683	589	1,309	294	329	623	-1	3,781	112	392	19	236
1950	11,495	839	1,925	362	472	1,268	24	5,721	218	382	42	242
1951	7,089	656	1,542	291	260	932	91	2,689	95	331	47	155
1952	5,680	832	1,367	200	22	1,004	62	1,444	82	391	59	197
1953	7,433	956	1,455	210	-30	1,122	74	2,899	80	366	55	246
1954	6,570	946	1,428	170	-266	1,126	31	2,436	13	402	26	258
1955	11,932	1,411	1,881	260	-52	1,041	73	6,162	118	524	86	428
1956	8,557	1,492	1,887	156	140	949	147	2,549	72	535	145	485
1957	7,185	1,240	1,493	81	12	836	65	2,261	87	475	147	488
1958	3,022	1,053	1,204	4	-14	610	20	-927	-40	493	106	513

SOURCE, BY COLUMN

(1) Sum of cols. 2 to 12;   (2 to 12)   Table B-18, cols. 2 to 12, minus Table B-22, cols. 2 to 12, respectively.

TABLE B-26

EXPENDITURES ON NEW PASSENGER CARS
(millions of dollars)

Year	Consumers' Expenditures on New Passenger Cars Plus Net Purchases of Used Cars (1)	Business Expenditures on Passenger Cars (2)	Total Expenditures on New Cars Plus Net Purchases of Used Cars (3)	Dealers' Margin on Used Cars (4)	Expenditures on New Cars (5)
1946	2,436	995	3,431	800	2,631
1947	4,587	1,889	6,476	937	5,539
1948	5,724	2,167	7,891	1,094	6,797
1949	8,077	2,838	10,915	981	9,934
1950	10,729	3,221	13,950	1,232	12,718
1951	9,444	2,669	12,113	1,314	10,799
1952	8,872	2,314	11,186	1,673	9,513
1953	11,822	2,598	14,420	1,635	12,785
1954	11,347	2,383	13,730	1,540	12,190
1955	15,800	3,318	19,118	1,676	17,442
1956	13,260	2,785	16,045	1,563	14,479
1957	14,575	3,061	17,636	1,652	15,984
1958	12,046	2,530	14,576	1,674	12,902

SOURCE, BY COLUMN

(1) 1946–57, *U.S. Income and Output*, p. 150.
 1954–58, *Survey of Current Business*, July 1959.
(2) 1946–54, *U.S. Income and Output*, p. 192 (cf. Table B-27, cols. 3 to 5).
 1955–58, Estimated on the basis of col. 1.
(3) Sum of cols. 1 and 2.
(4) From Table B-28, col. 1.
(5) Col. 3 minus col. 4.

TABLE B-27

EXPENDITURES ON NEW PASSENGER CARS, BY SECTOR
(millions of dollars)

Year	All Sectors (1)	Business			Individuals		
		Total (2)	Unincor- porated (3)	Corporate (4)	Total (5)	Nonfarm (6)	Farm (7)
1946	2,631	315	210	105	2,316	2,153	163
1947	5,539	665	443	222	4,874	4,531	343
1948	6,797	816	544	272	5,981	5,325	656
1949	9,934	1,192	795	397	8,742	7,313	1,429
1950	12,718	1,526	1,017	509	11,192	10,301	891
1951	10,799	1,296	864	432	9,503	8,365	1,138
1952	9,513	1,142	761	381	8,371	7,807	564
1953	12,785	1,534	1,023	511	11,251	9,776	1,475
1954	12,190	1,463	975	488	10,727	9,717	1,010
1955	17,442	2,093	1,395	698	15,349	14,539	810
1956	14,479	1,737	1,158	579	12,742	12,112	630
1957	15,984	1,918	1,279	639	14,066	13,225	841
1958	12,092	1,548	1,032	516	11,354	10,665	689

SOURCE, BY COLUMN

(1) From Table B-26, col. 5.
(2) Sum of cols. 3 and 4.
(3 to 5) 8, 4, and 88 per cent, respectively, of col. 1 on basis of data (from R. L. Polk & Co.) on total passenger cars in use and Survey of Consumer Finances figures on cars purchased by consumers. Thus, allocation to business (12 per cent) is considerably lower than that assumed by the Department of Commerce (nearly 30 per cent, cf, Table B-26, col. 2), which is regarded as excessive.
(6) Col. 5 minus col. 7.
(7) Agricultural Marketing Service estimates.

TABLE B-28

DEALERS' MARGIN ON USED CARS
(millions of dollars)

Year	All Groups (1)	*Used Cars Bought by:*		Nonfarm Consumers (4)
		Farmers (2)	Business (3)	
1946	800	32	46	722
1947	937	45	54	838
1948	1,094	107	59	928
1949	981	81	54	846
1950	1,232	115	67	1,050
1951	1,314	85	74	1,155
1952	1,673	77	96	1,500
1953	1,635	108	92	1,435
1954	1,540	77	88	1,375
1955	1,676	117	94	1,465
1956	1,566	102	88	1,376
1957	1,652	112	92	1,448
1958	1,674	101	94	1,479

SOURCE, BY COLUMN

(1) 1946–49: *A Study of Saving* . . . , Vol. I, Table P-15, col. 10.
　　1950–58: Sum of cols. 2 to 4.
(2) 1946–58: Assumed at 20 per cent of gross expenditures on used cars by farmers.
(3) 1946–49: Estimated at 6 per cent of total margin on nonfarm purchases of used cars (col. 1 minus col. 2) on assumption that business share in used cars is about half as large as in new cars.
　　1950–58: Derived from col. 4, assuming that col. 3 is 6 per cent of the sum of cols. 3 and 4.
(4) 1946–49: Col. 1 minus sum of cols. 2 and 3.
　　1950–58: From Table B-29, col. 4.

TABLE B-29

DEALERS' MARGIN ON USED CARS SOLD TO HOUSEHOLDS

Year	Used Cars Purchased (millions) (1)	Average Price Per Used Car (dollars) (2)	Margin Per Car (3)	Aggregate Dealers' Margin ($ millions) (4)
1946	3.5	630	126	440
1947	4.5	780	156	700
1948	5.6	880	176	985
1949	6.9	760	152	1,050
1950	7.5	700	140	1,050
1951	7.3	790	158	1,155
1952	7.9	950	190	1,500
1953	7.8	920	184	1,435
1954	8.6	800	160	1,375
1955	9.3	780	156	1,465
1956	8.9	800	160	1,375
1957	8.0	905	181	1,450
1958	8.7	850	170	1,480

SOURCE, BY COLUMN

(1) 1946–50: Survey of Consumer Finances data as shown in *Automobile Facts and Figures*, Automobile Manufacturers Association, 1954, p. 14.

1951–58: *Federal Reserve Bulletin*, various issues, e.g. 1957, p. 641.

(2) 1946–49: *Ibid*, 1951, p. 761.

1950–58: *Ibid*, 1952, p. 863, July 1958, p. 775.

(3) 1946–58: Assumed to be 20 per cent of col. 2, the ratio employed in *A Study of Saving . . .*, Vol. I, Table P-15, for the period before 1946.

(4) 1946–58: Col. 1 multiplied by col. 3 and rounded.

TABLE B-30

CONSUMER PURCHASES OF PASSENGER CAR ACCESSORIES
(millions of dollars)

Year	Tires, Tubes, Parts, and Accessories (1)	Tires, Tubes, Batteries, and Other Replacement Items (2)	Parts and Accessories, Original Equipment (3)
1946	1,492	1,044	448
1947	1,674	1,172	502
1948	1,669	1,168	501
1949	1,684	1,179	505
1950	2,223	1,556	667
1951	2,106	1,474	632
1952	2,161	1,513	648
1953	2,205	1,544	661
1954	2,027	1,419	608
1955	2,454	1,718	736
1956	2,368	1,658	710
1957	2,528	1,770	758
1958	2,054	1,438	616

SOURCE, BY COLUMN

(1) 1946–57: From *U.S. Income and Output*, pp. 150–151.

1958: Estimated using ratio of accessories to passenger car expenditures in preceding years.

(2 and 3) 70 and 30 per cent, respectively, of col. 1. Ratios based on data from *1947 Census of Manufactures*.

251

TABLE B-31

Life Expectancy of Consumer Durable Goods

Commodity	Expected Useful Life (years)
1. Furniture	15
2. Household appliances	12
3. China, glassware, tableware, and utensils	10
4. Other durable household furnishings	10
5. Radio and TV receivers, records, and musical instruments	10
6. Books and maps	6
7. Passenger cars	15
8. Passenger car accessories	5
9. Jewelry and watches	15
10. Ophthalmic products and orthopedic appliances	4
11. Miscellaneous (wheel goods, durable toys, sport equipment, boats, and pleasure aircraft)	10

SOURCE, BY COLUMN

(1) Based on Reavis Cox and R. F. Breyer, *The Economic Implications of Consumer Plant and Equipment*, Retail Credit Institute of America, 1944, pp. 56–58.

(2 to 4) Based on J. Frederick Dewhurst and Associates, *America's Needs and Resources*, Twentieth Century Fund, 1955, p. 198.

(5 and 6) From Lenore A. Epstein, "Consumers' Tangible Assets," *Studies in Income and Wealth*, Vol. 12 (New York, NBER, 1950), p. 442.

(7) New passenger cars, because of availability of information on pattern of depreciation, were not subject to straight-line depreciation used for all other commodities (except, also, passenger car accessories), but on the basis of data given in *Automobile Facts and Figures*, Automobile Manufacturers Association, 1954, p. 33, assumed to depreciate as follows:

Year of Service	15-Year Life (per cent)	Year of Service	15-Year Life (per cent)
1st	10	9th	4.25
2nd	16	10th	3.5
3rd	14	11th	3
4th	12	12th	2.5
5th	10	13th	2
6th	8	14th	1.5
7th	6.5	15th	1
8th	5.25	16th	0.5

(8) Based on data in *Bulletin F* of Department of Treasury, Bureau of Internal Revenue.

(9) Based on Cox and Breyer, *op. cit.*, and Epstein, *op. cit.*, estimates.

(10) Epstein, *op. cit.*

(11) Based on data in *Bulletin F*.

NONFARM CONSUMERS' SAVING THROUGH DEALERS' MARGIN ON USED CARS
(millions of dollars)

Year	Expenditure		Depreciation			Net Investment		
	Original Cost (1)	1947–49 Prices (2)	Original Cost (3)	1947–49 Prices (4)	Replacement Cost (5)	Original Cost (6)	1947–49 Prices (7)	Replacement Cost (8)
1946	722	924	520	777	607	202	147	115
1947	838	867	604	814	787	234	53	51
1948	928	851	695	832	908	233	19	20
1949	846	898	759	847	798	87	51	48
1950	1,050	1,210	822	914	793	228	296	257
1951	1,155	1,180	916	1,006	985	239	174	170
1952	1,500	1,273	1,053	1,079	1,271	447	194	229
1953	1,435	1,259	1,191	1,143	1,303	244	116	132
1954	1,375	1,386	1,264	1,203	1,193	111	183	182
1955	1,465	1,515	1,321	1,286	1,244	144	229	221
1956	1,376	1,387	1,359	1,342	1,331	17	45	45
1957	1,448	1,375	1,382	1,359	1,431	66	16	17
1958	1,479	1,319	1,414	1,361	1,526	65	−42	−47

SOURCE, BY COLUMN

(1) From Table B-28, col. 4.
(2) Col. 1 deflated by Table B-33, col. 12.
(3) Col. 1 depreciated assuming the following depreciation pattern:

Year of Service	9-Year Life	Year of Service	9-Year Life
1st	16.0%	6th	6.5%
2nd	27.0	7th	4.5
3rd	18.0	8th	3.0
4th	13.0	9th	2.0
5th	9.0	10th	1.0

The estimate of a 9-year remaining life is based on facts that nearly three-fourths of new car sales give rise to used car turn-ins (Automobile Facts and Figures, Automobile Manufacturers Association, 1953, p. 15); that the median age of the cars turned in is about three years (ibid., p. 16); and that the cars thus turned in constitute nearly one-half of total used car sales as estimated on the basis of Survey of Consumer Finances (ibid., p. 14). The average age of other used cars sold by dealers is unknown but is assumed considerably higher than the three years of the used cars turned in by new car buyers. The assumption of an average age of nine years appears reasonable, although it may somewhat understate remaining life. Expenditures for years before 1946 required for the calculation of depreciation, from A Study of Saving..., Vol. I, Table P-16, col. 4.

(4) Same procedure as for col. 3, except expenditure figures from col. 2 and expenditures in 1947–49 prices for years before 1946 obtained by deflating expenditures in original cost (see col. 3) by index derived by linking A Study of Saving..., Vol. I, Table P-10, col. 12, to 1946 value of Table B-33, col. 12.
(5) Col. 4 multiplied by Table B-33, col. 12.
(6) Col. 1 minus col. 3.
(7) Col. 2 minus col. 4.
(8) Col. 1 minus col. 5.

TABLE B-33
INDEXES OF PRICES OF CONSUMER DURABLE GOODS
(1947–49 = 100.0)

A. ANNUAL AVERAGES

Year	Furniture (1)	Household Appliances (2)	China, Glassware, Tableware, and Utensils (3)	Household Furnishings (4)	Radio, TV, and Musical Instruments (5)	Books and Maps (6)	Passenger Car Accessories (7)	Jewelry and Watches (8)	Ophthalmic Products etc. (9)	Miscellaneous (10)	Passenger Cars Bought by Nonfarm Individuals	
											New (11)	Used (12)
1946	85.2	81.2	86.5	82.1	71.7	84.1	90.0	97.0	90.0	90.0	79.0	78.1
1947	94.3	95.8	96.5	95.7	96.7	92.2	99.0	103.0	95.0	100.0	91.2	96.7
1948	104.5	103.1	100.6	101.5	105.2	100.9	100.0	98.0	100.0	100.0	99.7	109.1
1949	101.2	101.1	102.9	102.8	98.2	106.9	102.0	97.8	104.0	100.0	109.1	94.2
1950	101.6	99.4	101.5	109.9	91.1	108.0	93.0	94.4	103.0	97.1	110.0	86.8
1951	111.3	106.2	111.2	128.6	93.5	109.9	104.0	102.1	111.0	108.1	115.2	97.9
1952	108.8	105.1	113.3	124.0	86.8	116.6	106.0	101.0	111.0	108.6	119.2	117.8
1953	108.4	103.8	114.5	123.3	84.5	121.0	104.0	102.2	112.0	107.9	119.0	114.0
1954	107.4	100.5	114.9	123.6	79.8	121.0	104.0	99.5	112.0	108.3	115.5	99.2
1955	105.1	96.7	114.2	130.2	75.9	123.4	104.0	96.3	112.0	105.4	118.3	96.7
1956	105.4	90.8	122.0	132.8	75.0	124.1	107.6	96.4	116.1	109.0	122.2	99.2
1957	107.4	89.1	126.0	139.4	77.6	135.9	110.5	94.6	116.0	109.8	128.7	105.3
1958	106.7	87.4	128.3	138.8	77.7	144.8	111.3	93.0	116.5	110.5	132.8	112.1

(continued)

TABLE B-33 (concluded)

Year	Furniture (1)	Household Appliances (2)	China, Glassware, Tableware, and Utensils (3)	Household Furnishings (4)	Radio, TV, and Musical Instruments (5)	Books and Maps (6)	Passenger Car Accessories (7)	Jewelry and Watches (8)	Ophthalmic Products etc. (9)	Miscellaneous (10)	Passenger Cars Bought by Nonfarm Individuals	
											New (11)	Used (12)
				B. YEAR-END FIGURES								
1945	81.2	76.8	83.1	76.7	70.6	82.0	89.0	97.0	90.0	88.0	73.6	72.2
1946	92.0	90.3	93.5	94.1	83.1	89.8	96.0	104.0	92.0	97.0	85.1	87.4
1947	100.3	101.6	98.7	99.3	104.6	94.6	97.0	99.0	98.0	98.0	95.4	102.9
1948	105.4	104.8	103.8	103.5	103.2	106.6	104.0	100.0	103.0	102.0	104.4	101.6
1949	98.6	99.0	101.4	103.2	93.2	107.4	95.0	94.5	104.0	98.0	109.6	90.5
1950	109.8	104.5	105.9	125.4	95.7	108.5	98.0	97.7	106.0	101.1	112.6	92.4
1951	110.6	106.4	114.0	126.3	88.8	112.8	106.0	102.2	112.0	110.2	117.2	107.8
1952	107.9	104.2	113.4	123.5	85.8	121.1	104.0	101.1	111.0	107.5	119.1	115.9
1953	107.7	102.9	116.0	123.2	82.4	120.8	105.0	103.1	114.0	109.0	117.2	106.6
1954	106.6	98.2	113.6	127.4	76.8	122.4	104.0	96.0	112.0	106.4	116.9	98.0
1955	104.4	92.6	118.6	131.2	75.0	123.7	105.0	96.3	114.0	106.7	120.3	98.0
1956	107.3	89.9	125.4	136.9	76.1	125.2	109.5	96.1	116.5	109.9	125.5	102.3
1957	107.3	88.0	128.4	140.9	79.0	144.2	111.1	94.1	116.2	110.0	130.8	108.7
1958	106.7	86.9	128.2	137.7	78.1	145.2	111.5	91.5	116.5	110.4	138.5	120.3

(Notes to Table B-33 on next page)

SOURCE, BY COLUMN

A. *Annual Averages*

Figures from the following sources converted to a 1947–49 base:

(1) Bureau of Labor Statistics index of retail prices of furniture 1946–51: *Consumer Prices in the United States*, Bureau of Labor Statistics, 1949–52, Bull. No. 1165, p. 62. 1952–54: *Preliminary Indexes of Retail Prices of Selected Items and Specified Groups*, Bureau of Labor Statistics, May 1955, p. 7.

1955–58: *Consumer Price Index*, Bureau of Labor Statistics, various issues, e.g., July 1956, p. 4.

(2) 1946–58: Weighted average of Bureau of Labor Statistics indexes of retail prices of sewing machines, washing machines, vacuum cleaners, electric refrigerators, and gas cooking stoves. Weights as of January 1950 from *Consumer Prices* . . . (*op. cit.*, p. 33). Figures for various items from sources listed for col. 1. (1946 based only on index for stoves, since no data were available for the other categories.)

(3) 1946–58: Unweighted average of Sears Roebuck index of catalog prices of housewares (unpublished data) and index based on Bureau of Labor Statistics figures, obtained for the period 1951–55 by weighting Bureau of Labor Statistics indexes for dinnerware and aluminum pans by weights given in *Consumer Prices* . . . , and for the period 1946–50 by extrapolating by the index for dinnerware (since index for aluminum pans was not available.) Bureau of Labor Statistics figures from sources given for col. 1.

(4) 1946–58: Weighted average (January 1950 weights) of Bureau of Labor Statistics indexes of retail prices of sofa beds, bed springs, inner-spring mattresses, wool rugs, and felt-base rugs. Figures from sources listed for col. 1.

(5) 1946–50: December 1950 figures extrapolated by Sears Roebuck index of catalog prices of radios, television sets, phonographs, and musical instruments (unpublished data).

1951–58: Weighted average of Bureau of Labor Statistics indexes of retail prices of radios and television sets. For 1950 and 1951, Bureau of Labor Statistics, January 1950 weights were used; for 1952 to 1955, December 1952 weights. All data from sources listed for col. 1.

(6) 1946–58: Bureau of Labor Statistics index for retail prices of newspapers from sources given for col. 1 (1947 and 1948 interpolated on basis of daily and Sunday newspapers delivered).

(7 to 10) 1946–58: Sears Roebuck indexes (unpublished data) of catalog prices of automobile accessories and motor scooters, excluding tires and tubes (col. 7), jewelry, silverware, clocks, and optical goods (col. 8), drugs, sickroom supplies, and hearing aids (col. 9), and sporting goods, luggage, bicycles, and boats (col. 10).

(11) 1946–51: Bureau of Labor Statistics index of retail prices of new automobiles from sources given for col. 1 (1946 figure interpolated on basis of wholesale prices of new automobiles from Bureau of Labor Statistics releases).

1952–58: Extrapolated from 1951 by implicit price deflators of business passenger cars (see Table B-118). Adjustment made because Bureau of Labor Statistics index of retail prices of wne automobiles, in that period, apparently does not fully reflect overallowances given by new car dealers for trade-ins and thus does not adequately represent the effective price of new cars.

(12) 1946–58: Based on Federal Reserve estimates of the average price of used cars (*Federal Reserve Bulletin*, various issues, e.g., 1956, p. 816).

B. Year-End Figures

For the Bureau of Labor Statistics indexes, averages are of December and following March data; for Sears Roebuck, averages are of fall and following spring indexes.

(1 to 10) 1946–58: Derived by same procedure as annual averages. In addition to the sources mentioned, data also from *Consumers' Prices in the United States 1942–48*, Bureau of Labor Statistics, Bull. No. 966, pp. 72–79.

(11) 1946–57: Obtained by arithmetic averaging of annual averages.

1958: Extrapolated from annual average 1958 by Bureau of Labor Statistics index of retail prices of new automobiles, given in *Consumer Price Index*, May 1959, p. 5.

(12) 1946–57: Obtained by arithmetic averaging of annual averages.

1958: Same procedure as for col. 11, except Bureau of Labor Statistics index of retail prices of used automobiles applied.

257

TABLE B-34

Value of Nonfarm Individuals' Holdings of Main Types of Consumer Durable Goods, Original Cost

(millions of dollars)

End of Year	Total (1)	Furniture (2)	Household Appliances (3)	China, Glassware, Tableware, and Utensils (4)	Household Furnishings (5)	Radio, TV, and Musical Instruments (6)	Books and Maps (7)	Passenger Cars (8)	Passenger Car Accessories (9)	Jewelry and Watches (10)	Ophthalmic Products, and Orthopedic Appliances (11)	Miscellaneous (12)
1945	31,516	7,468	3,205	2,787	5,562	1,919	1,090	2,984	330	4,245	584	1,342
1946	38,534	8,545	4,160	3,345	6,429	2,504	1,271	4,217	570	5,071	640	1,782
1947	48,865	9,797	6,181	3,910	7,404	3,263	1,357	7,384	800	5,786	676	2,307
1948	59,247	11,114	8,252	4,487	8,446	3,966	1,445	10,697	959	6,394	717	2,770
1949	69,804	12,289	9,920	4,979	9,302	4,803	1,544	15,175	1,056	6,891	768	3,077
1950	83,730	13,684	12,131	5,495	10,353	6,183	1,651	21,489	1,221	7,338	825	3,360
1951	94,074	15,029	14,030	6,009	11,513	7,217	1,809	24,863	1,299	7,793	905	3,607
1952	102,443	16,436	15,671	6,418	12,216	8,209	1,945	27,036	1,362	8,281	984	3,885
1953	111,959	17,898	17,300	6,817	12,744	9,268	2,089	30,441	1,409	8,740	1,055	4,198
1954	119,822	19,233	18,757	7,147	12,942	10,244	2,169	33,155	1,387	9,187	1,088	4,513
1955	132,697	20,909	20,553	7,532	13,403	11,056	2,290	39,654	1,462	9,701	1,176	4,961
1956	142,200	22,636	22,185	7,877	14,006	11,752	2,475	42,727	1,501	10,216	1,339	5,486
1957	151,063	24,100	23,364	8,160	14,521	12,407	2,633	46,116	1,566	10,640	1,499	6,057
1958	155,637	25,308	24,187	8,363	14,905	12,869	2,778	46,448	1,501	11,058	1,616	6,604

Source, by Column: (1) Sum of cols. 2 to 12; (2 to 12) Derived by addition of cumulated net investment, original cost (Table B-23), to estimated value for 1945, obtained by cumulating expenditures less depreciation for number of years preceding 1945, corresponding to the assumed length of life of asset involved.

TABLE B-35

Value of Nonfarm Individuals' Holdings of Main Types of Consumer Durable Goods, Constant (1947–49) Prices
(millions of dollars)

End of Year	Total (1)	Furniture (2)	Household Appliances (3)	China, Glassware, Tableware, and Utensils (4)	Household Furnishings (5)	Radio, TV, and Musical Instruments (6)	Books and Maps (7)	Passenger Cars (8)	Passenger Car Accessories (9)	Jewelry and Watches (10)	Ophthalmic Products, and Orthopedic Appliances (11)	Miscellaneous (12)
1945	49,190	12,464	5,553	3,942	8,727	3,254	1,403	5,698	435	5,239	671	1,805
1946	55,352	13,231	6,416	4,421	9,354	3,943	1,580	6,788	718	5,957	722	2,222
1947	63,359	13,986	8,119	4,802	9,812	4,458	1,608	9,729	960	6,495	737	2,653
1948	70,578	14,598	9,701	5,169	10,269	4,836	1,607	12,486	1,132	6,998	749	3,033
1949	77,921	15,180	10,995	5,456	10,589	5,470	1,606	15,952	1,241	7,396	767	3,269
1950	89,007	16,006	12,932	5,813	11,018	6,862	1,629	21,153	1,476	7,792	808	3,518
1951	95,514	16,595	14,384	6,074	11,220	7,858	1,712	23,487	1,568	8,105	850	3,661
1952	100,892	17,360	15,685	6,250	11,237	9,015	1,765	24,698	1,645	8,492	903	3,842
1953	107,874	18,242	17,086	6,434	11,212	10,343	1,826	27,134	1,722	8,853	952	4,070
1954	114,258	19,123	18,506	6,582	10,997	11,753	1,852	29,243	1,735	9,249	975	4,243
1955	125,518	20,466	20,451	6,809	10,957	13,125	1,911	34,452	1,848	9,798	1,052	4,649
1956	133,834	21,808	22,530	6,937	11,062	14,391	2,029	36,538	1,915	10,353	1,176	5,094
1957	140,849	22,987	24,206	7,001	11,081	15,468	2,077	38,295	1,994	10,855	1,303	5,582
1958	144,356	23,974	25,583	7,004	11,071	16,253	2,091	37,597	1,958	11,385	1,394	6,046

Source, by Column: (1) Sum of cols. 2 to 12; (2 to 12) Same procedure as for Table B-34, but applied to expenditures in 1947–49 dollars (see Table B-24),

259

TABLE B-36

Value of Nonfarm Individuals' Holdings of Main Types of Consumer Durable Goods, Current Prices

(millions of dollars)

End of Year	Total (1)	Furniture (2)	Household Appliances (3)	China, Glassware, Tableware, and Utensils (4)	Household Furnishings (5)	Radio, TV, and Musical Instruments (6)	Books and Maps (7)	Passenger Cars (8)	Passenger Car Accessories (9)	Jewelry and Watches (10)	Ophthalmic Products, and Orthopedic Appliances (11)	Miscellaneous (12)
1945	39,657	10,121	4,264	3,276	6,694	2,297	1,150	4,194	387	5,082	604	1,588
1946	51,079	12,173	5,794	4,134	8,802	3,277	1,419	5,777	689	6,195	664	2,155
1947	62,908	14,028	8,249	4,740	9,743	4,663	1,521	9,281	931	6,430	722	2,600
1948	73,325	15,386	10,167	5,365	10,628	4,991	1,713	13,035	1,177	6,998	771	3,094
1949	78,788	14,967	10,885	5,532	10,928	5,098	1,725	17,483	1,179	6,989	798	3,204
1950	96,686	17,575	13,514	6,156	13,817	6,567	1,767	23,818	1,446	7,613	856	3,557
1951	106,071	18,354	15,305	6,924	14,121	6,978	1,931	27,527	1,662	8,283	952	4,034
1952	110,756	18,731	16,344	7,088	13,878	7,735	2,137	29,415	1,711	8,858	1,002	4,130
1953	117,490	19,647	17,581	7,463	13,813	8,523	2,206	31,801	1,808	9,127	1,085	4,436
1954	121,813	20,385	18,173	7,477	14,010	9,026	2,267	34,185	1,804	8,879	1,092	4,515
1955	133,944	21,367	18,938	8,075	14,376	9,844	2,364	41,446	1,940	9,435	1,199	4,960
1956	145,859	23,400	20,254	8,699	15,145	10,952	2,540	45,855	2,097	9,949	1,370	5,598
1957	155,957	24,665	21,301	8,989	15,613	12,220	2,995	50,090	2,215	10,215	1,514	6,140
1958	160,737	25,580	22,232	8,979	15,245	12,694	3,036	52,072	2,183	10,417	1,624	6,675

SOURCE, BY COLUMN: (1) Sum of cols. 2 to 12. (2 to 12) Cumulated depreciated capital expenditures in 1947–49 prices (Table B-35), multiplied by appropriate price index from Table B-33 (year-end figures).

TABLE B-37

(millions of dollars)

End of Year	Original Cost (1)	1947–49 Prices (2)	Current Prices (3)
1945	1,190	1,836	1,326
1946	1,392	1,983	1,733
1947	1,626	2,036	2,095
1948	1,859	2,055	2,088
1949	1,946	2,106	1,906
1950	2,174	2,402	2,219
1951	2,413	2,576	2,777
1952	2,860	2,770	3,210
1953	3,104	2,886	3,076
1954	3,215	3,069	3,008
1955	3,359	3,298	2,975
1956	3,376	3,343	3,574
1957	3,442	3,359	3,651
1958	3,507	3,317	3,990

SOURCE, BY COLUMN

(1) Derived by addition of cumulated net investment, original cost, to estimated value for 1945, obtained by cumulating dealers' margin less depreciation for nine years, the assumed life span of dealers' margin. See Table B-32.
(2) Same procedure as for col. 1 but applied to expenditures in 1947–49 prices. See Table B-32, col. 7.
(3) Col. 2 multiplied by Table B-33, col. 12, year-end index.

TABLE B-38

NET INVESTMENT BY NONPROFIT NONFINANCIAL INSTITUTIONS IN BUILDINGS, EXCLUDING SOCIAL AND RECREATIONAL BUILDINGS

(amounts in millions of dollars)

Year	Expenditures		Depreciation			Net Investment			Construction Cost Index (1947-49 = 100.0) (9)
	Original Cost (1)	1947-49 Prices (2)	Original Cost (3)	1947-49 Prices (4)	Replacement Cost (5)	Original Cost (6)	1947-49 Prices (7)	Replacement Cost (8)	
1946	284	415	148	444	304	136	-29	-20	68.5
1947	410	448	154	445	407	256	3	3	91.5
1948	630	604	163	447	466	467	157	164	104.3
1949	831	797	176	454	474	655	343	357	104.3
1950	1,047	984	193	462	492	854	522	555	106.4
1951	1,216	1,075	214	473	535	1,002	602	681	113.1
1952	1,144	972	235	482	567	909	490	577	117.7
1953	1,215	990	257	491	602	958	499	613	122.7
1954	1,459	1,161	282	503	632	1,177	658	827	125.7
1955	1,577	1,220	310	518	670	1,267	702	907	129.3
1956	1,632	1,208	340	533	720	1,292	679	917	135.1
1957	1,918	1,359	373	546	770	1,545	813	1,148	141.1
1958	2,037	1,404	410	562	815	1,627	842	1,222	145.1

SOURCE, BY COLUMN

(1) *Construction Volume and Costs*, Department of Commerce, 1915–56, p. 3; plus various issues of *Construction Review*, e.g., Mar. 1957, p. 12. Sum of religious, educational, hospital, and institutional building.

(2) Col. 1 deflated by col. 9.

(3) Col. 1 depreciated assuming an average life of fifty years. Expenditures for years before 1946 required for calculation of depreciation from *Construction Volume . . . , loc. cit*, and *A Study of Saving . . .* , Vol. I, Table R-17, col. 1.

(4) Col. 2 depreciated assuming an average life of fifty years. Expenditures in 1947–49 prices obtained by deflating expendi-

tures in original cost (col. 3) by index for the period 1915–45 from same source as for later years (see col. 9); for years before 1915, index extrapolated by figures given in *A Study of Saving . . .* , Vol. I, Table R-20, col. 5.

(5) Col. 4 multiplied by col. 9.

(6) Col. 1 minus col. 3.

(7) Col. 2 minus col. 4.

(8) Col. 1 minus col. 5.

(9) American Appraisal Company index from same source as for col. 1. Figures are annual averages.

TABLE B-39

Net Investment by Nonprofit Nonfinancial Institutions in
Social and Recreational Buildings
(millions of dollars)

Year	Expenditures Original Cost (1)	Expenditures 1947–49 Prices (2)	Depreciation Original Cost (3)	Depreciation 1947–49 Prices (4)	Depreciation Replacement Cost (5)	Net Investment Original Cost (6)	Net Investment 1947–49 Prices (7)	Net Investment Replacement Cost (8)
1946	41	60	25	67	46	16	−7	−5
1947	33	36	26	67	61	7	−31	−28
1948	74	71	27	67	70	47	4	4
1949	88	84	28	68	71	60	16	17
1950	83	78	30	68	72	53	10	11
1951	54	48	31	69	78	23	−21	−24
1952	41	35	32	68	80	9	−33	−39
1953	55	45	33	68	83	22	−23	−28
1954	76	60	34	68	85	42	−8	−9
1955	79	61	36	68	88	43	−7	−9
1956	92	68	37	68	92	55	0	0
1957	103	73	39	68	96	64	15	7
1958	142	97	42	69	100	100	28	41

Source, by Column

(1)   From Table B-46, col. 5;   (2)   Col. 1 divided by Table B-105, col. 9;   (3 and 4)   One-third of Table B-105, cols. 3 and 4, respectively;   (5)   Col. 4 multiplied by Table B-105, col. 9;   (6)   Col. 1 minus col. 3;   (7)   Col. 2 minus col. 4;   (8)   Col. 1 minus col. 5.

TABLE B-40

Net Investment by Nonprofit Nonfinancial Institutions in Equipment

(amounts in millions of dollars)

Year	Expenditures		Depreciation			Net Investment			Price Deflator (1947–49 = 100.0)
	Original Cost (1)	1947–49 Prices (2)	Original Cost (3)	1947–49 Prices (4)	Replacement Cost (5)	Original Cost (6)	1947–49 Prices (7)	Replacement Cost (8)	(9)
1946	57	70	21	32	26	36	38	31	81.0
1947	82	88	25	37	35	57	51	47	93.3
1948	126	125	33	44	44	93	81	82	101.0
1949	166	157	43	52	55	123	105	111	105.7
1950	209	193	57	64	69	152	129	140	108.1
1951	243	207	74	77	91	169	130	152	117.6
1952	229	193	91	90	107	138	103	122	118.5
1953	243	202	108	103	124	135	99	119	120.3
1954	292	240	129	118	143	163	122	149	121.5
1955	315	253	153	137	171	162	116	144	124.7
1956	327	247	179	157	208	148	90	119	132.4
1957	384	273	208	177	249	176	96	135	140.7
1958	407	281	237	196	283	170	85	124	144.6

Source, by Column

(1) Estimated roughly at 20 per cent of expenditures on construction by nonprofit institutions (see Table B-38) as in *A Study of Saving* . . . , Vol. I, Table P-1, col. 4.

(2) Col. 1 deflated by col. 9.

(3) Col. 1 depreciated assuming an average life of twelve years. Expenditures for years before 1946 required for calculation of depreciation obtained by same procedure and from same sources as figures for later years (see col. 1).

(4) Col. 2 depreciated assuming an average life of twelve years. Expenditures in 1947–49 prices for years before 1946, obtained by deflating expenditures in original cost (col. 3) by index derived from same source as col. 9.

(5) Col. 4 multiplied by col. 9.

(6) Col. 1 minus col. 3

(7) Col. 2 minus col. 4.

(8) Col. 1 minus col. 5.

(9) Implicit price deflator of producer durable goods from *U.S. Income and Output*, pp. 225, 229; and *Survey of Current Business*, July 1959, p. 40, converted to a 1947–49 base.

TABLE B-41

End of Year	Buildings			Land		Real Estate	
	Original Cost (1)	1947–49 Prices (2)	Current Prices (3)	1947–49 Prices (4)	Current Prices (5)	1947–49 Prices (6)	Current Prices (7)
1945	3,917	10,106	6,074	2,527	1,518	12,633	7,592
1946	4,053	10,077	8,062	2,519	2,016	12,596	10,078
1947	4,309	10,080	10,080	2,520	2,520	12,600	12,600
1948	4,776	10,237	10,923	2,559	2,731	12,796	13,654
1949	5,431	10,580	10,908	2,645	2,727	13,225	13,635
1950	6,285	11,102	12,290	2,776	3,072	13,878	15,362
1951	7,287	11,704	13,460	2,926	3,365	14,630	16,825
1952	8,196	12,194	14,730	3,048	3,682	15,242	18,412
1953	9,154	12,693	15,790	3,173	3,948	15,866	19,738
1954	10,331	13,351	16,982	3,338	4,246	16,689	21,228
1955	11,598	14,053	18,550	3,513	4,638	17,566	23,188
1956	12,890	14,728	20,324	3,682	5,081	18,410	25,405
1957	14,435	15,541	22,239	3,885	5,560	18,426	27,799
1958	16,062	16,383	24,149	4,096	6,037	20,479	30,186

SOURCE, BY COLUMN

(1) Derived by addition of cumulated net investment, original cost, to estimated value for 1945, obtained by cumulating expenditures less depreciation for fifty years preceding 1945, corresponding to the assumed length of life of institutional buildings (see Table B-38, col. 6).

(2) Same procedure as for col. 1, but applied to expenditures in 1947–49 prices (see Table B-38, col. 2).

(3) Col. 2 multiplied by December–January average of construction cost index (see Table B-38, note to col. 3).

(4 and 5) Estimated at 25 per cent of value of institutional construction (see *A Study of Saving* . . . , Vol. III, Table W-25).

(6) Col. 2 plus col. 4.

(7) Col. 3 plus col. 5.

TABLE B-42

VALUE OF SOCIAL AND RECREATIONAL BUILDINGS OWNED BY
NONPROFIT NONFINANCIAL INSTITUTIONS
(millions of dollars)

End of Year	Buildings			Land		Real Estate	
	Original Cost (1)	1947–49 Prices (2)	Current Prices (3)	1947–49 Prices (4)	Current Prices (5)	1947–49 Prices (6)	Current Prices (7)
1945	620	1,498	900	999	601	2,497	1,501
1946	636	1,491	1,193	999	796	2,485	1,989
1947	643	1,460	1,460	974	974	2,434	2,434
1948	690	1,464	1,562	976	1,043	2,440	2,605
1949	750	1,480	1,526	987	1,019	2,467	2,545
1950	803	1,490	1,649	994	1,100	2,484	2,749
1951	826	1,469	1,689	980	1,127	2,449	2,816
1952	835	1,436	1,735	958	1,158	2,394	2,893
1953	857	1,413	1,758	942	1,173	2,355	2,931
1954	899	1,405	1,787	937	1,193	2,343	2,990
1955	942	1,398	1,845	932	1,233	2,330	3,078
1956	997	1,398	1,928	932	1,288	2,330	3,216
1957	1,062	1,384	1,980	923	1,321	2,307	3,301
1958	1,161	1,412	2,082	942	1,388	2,354	3,470

SOURCE: Cols. 1 to 7, same procedure as for Table B-41, but based on figures of Table B-39. Land estimates revised to maintain constant proportion (66.7%) of structures.

TABLE B-43

VALUE OF NONPROFIT NONFINANCIAL INSTITUTIONAL EQUIPMENT
(millions of dollars)

End of Year	Original Cost (1)	1947–49 Prices (2)	Current Prices (3)
1945	111	171	132
1946	147	209	182
1947	204	260	253
1948	297	341	353
1949	420	446	477
1950	572	575	649
1951	741	705	833
1952	879	808	965
1953	1,014	907	1,097
1954	1,177	1,029	1,267
1955	1,339	1,145	1,472
1956	1,487	1,235	1,687
1957	1,663	1,331	1,899
1958	1,883	1,416	2,065

SOURCE, BY COLUMN

(1) Derived by addition of cumulated net investment, original cost, to estimated value for 1945, obtained by cumulating expenditures less depreciation for twelve years preceding 1945, corresponding to the assumed length of life of institutional equipment (see Table B-40, Col. 6).

(2) Same procedure as for col. 1, but applied to expenditures in 1947–49 prices (see Table B-40, Col. 7).

(3) Col. 2 multiplied by year-end average of price deflator. See Table B-40, col. 9. For 1945–57, year-end index obtained by averaging deflator for current year and succeeding year. Year-end 1958 is average of 4th quarter 1958 and 1st quarter 1959.

TABLE B-44

SHARE OF UNINCORPORATED BUSINESS IN TOTAL BUSINESS PLANT AND EQUIPMENT EXPENDITURES, USING *A Study of Saving* ... ALLOCATIONS
(amounts in millions of dollars)

Year	Plant and Equipment		Commercial Structures			Industrial Structures			Miscellaneous Nonresidential		
	Total (1)	Unincorporated (2)	Total (3)	Share of Unincorporated (4)	Unincorporated (5)	Total (6)	Share of Unincorporated (7)	Unincorporated (8)	Total (9)	Share of Unincorporated (10)	Unincorporated (11)
1946	14,521	2,293	1,132	40%	453	1,689	5%	84	111	40%	44
1947	20,008	3,074	856	40	342	1,702	5	85	75	40	30
1948	22,615	3,587	1,253	40	501	1,397	5	70	117	40	47
1949	20,120	3,346	1,027	40	411	972	5	49	136	40	54
1950	22,429	3,917	1,288	40	515	1,062	5	53	133	40	53
1951	27,811	4,368	1,371	40	548	2,117	5	106	284	40	114
1952	28,478	4,257	1,137	40	455	2,320	5	116	288	40	115
1953	30,029	4,956	1,791	40	716	2,229	5	111	282	40	113
1954	29,164	4,947	2,212	40	885	2,030	5	102	321	40	128
1955	33,962	5,953	3,218	40	1,287	2,399	5	120	178	40	71
1956	40,195	6,692	3,631	40	1,452	3,084	5	154	195	40	78
1957	42,429	6,970	3,564	40	1,426	3,557	5	178	206	40	82
1958	35,162	5,879	3,561	40	1,424	2,443	5	122	252	40	101

(continued)

TABLE B-44 (concluded)

Year	Petroleum and Gas Well Drilling				Mining Development			Equipment, Excluding Passenger Cars			Passenger Cars, New and Used	
	Public Utility (12)	Total (13)	Share of Unincorporated (14)	Unincorporated (15)	Total (16)	Share of Unincorporated (17)	Unincorporated (18)	Total (19)	Share of Unincorporated (20)	Unincorporated (21)	Total (22)	Unincorporated (23)
1946	1,426	783	14.7%	115	122	5%	6	8,897	15%	1,335	361	256
1947	2,407	925	15.0	139	178	5	9	13,146	15	1,972	719	497
1948	3,108	1,249	15.0	187	208	5	10	14,447	15	2,167	883	605
1949	3,401	1,262	15.0	189	154	5	8	11,908	15	1,786	1,260	849
1950	3,442	1,501	15.0	225	182	5	9	13,184	15	1,978	1,637	1,084
1951	3,793	1,828	15.0	274	202	5	10	15,840	15	2,376	1,393	940
1952	4,088	1,870	15.0	280	184	5	9	16,166	15	2,425	1,271	857
1953	4,536	2,187	15.0	328	186	5	9	17,093	15	2,564	1,725	1,115
1954	4,405	2,311	15.0	347	155	5	8	16,091	15	2,414	1,639	1,063
1955	4,704	2,487	15.0	373	185	5	9	17,353	15	2,603	3,438	1,490
1956	5,233	2,732	15.0	405	200	5	10	22,284	15	3,343	2,836	1,250
1957	5,823	2,697	15.0	405	209	5	10	23,321	15	3,498	3,052	1,371
1958	5,743	2,760	15.0	414	207	5	10	17,883	15	2,682	2,313	1,126

SOURCE, BY COLUMN

(1) Sum of cols. 3, 6, 9, 12, 13, 16, 19, and 22.
(2) Sum of cols. 5, 8, 11, 15, 18, 21, and 23.
(3) Table B-102, col. 1.
(4) Figures for 1946–1949 from *A Study of Saving* . . . , Vol. I, Table R-29, col. 3 continued through 1958.
(5) Col. 3 multiplied by col. 4.
(6) Table B-101, col. 1.
(7) Same procedure as for col. 4 except figures from *A Study of Saving* . . . , Vol. I, Table R-29, col. 4.
(8) Col. 6 multiplied by col. 7.
(9) Table B-103, col. 1.
(10) Same as col. 4.
(11) Col. 9 multiplied by col. 10.
(12) Table B-104, col. 1.
(13) Average of Table B-107, col. 1 and Table B-108, col. 1.
(14) Same procedure as for col. 4 except per cents are complements of *A Study of Saving* . . . , Vol. I, Table C-16, col. 3.
(15) Col. 13 multiplied by col. 14.
(16) Table B-109, col. 1.
(17) Same procedure as for col. 4 except that per cents are complements of *A Study of Saving* . . . , Vol. I, Table C-16, col. 4.
(18) Col. 16 multiplied by col. 17.
(19) Table B-99, col. 1 minus col. 15, minus Table B-40, col. 1.
(20) Same procedure as for col. 4 except figures from *A Study of Saving* . . . , Vol. I, Table P-12.
(21) Col. 19 multiplied by col. 20.
(22) Sum of Tables B-50, col. 1, B-120, col. 1, and B-51, col. 1.
(23) Sum of Tables B-50, col. 1, and B-51, col. 1.

UNINCORPORATED BUSINESS EXPENDITURES FOR
NONRESIDENTIAL CONSTRUCTION, CONSTANT (1947–49) PRICES
(millions of dollars)

Year	Commercial Structures (1)	Industrial Structures (2)	Miscellaneous Nonresidential (3)	Petroleum and Gas Well Drilling (4)	Mining Development (5)
1946	637	107	64	147	8
1947	370	91	33	148	10
1948	483	67	45	182	10
1949	396	48	52	183	8
1950	492	50	50	210	9
1951	492	90	101	222	8
1952	396	96	98	242	7
1953	599	90	92	260	6
1954	714	85	102	293	7
1955	1,011	98	55	326	7
1956	1,092	115	58	315	8
1957	1,028	125	58	285	7
1958	992	86	70	292	7

SOURCE, BY COLUMN

(1)   Table B-44, col. 5, divided by component weighted average of indexes in Table B-106, cols. 2 and 3.
(2)   Table B-44, col. 8 divided by Table B-106, col. 1.
(3)   Table B-44, col. 11 divided by Table B-106, col. 3.
(4)   Table B-44, col. 15 divided by Table B-106, col. 1.
(5)   Table B-44, col. 18 divided by Table B-106, col. 1.

TABLE B-46

EXPENDITURES ON SOCIAL AND RECREATIONAL BUILDINGS,
BY MAJOR OWNERSHIP GROUP
(millions of dollars)

Year	Total Expenditures (1)	Business Expenditures			Institutional Expenditures (5)
		Total (2)	Corporate (3)	Noncorporate (4)	
1946	125	84	42	42	41
1947	99	66	33	33	33
1948	224	150	75	75	74
1949	262	174	87	87	88
1950	247	164	82	82	83
1951	164	110	55	55	54
1952	125	84	42	42	41
1953	163	108	54	54	55
1954	228	152	76	76	76
1955	239	160	80	80	79
1956	274	182	91	91	92
1957	311	208	104	104	103
1958	424	282	141	141	142

SOURCE, BY COLUMN

(1)   *Construction Volume and Costs,* 1915–56, Department of Commerce, p. 2; *Survey of Current Business,* July 1959, p. 29.
(2)   Sum of cols. 3 and 4.
(3 to 5)   Rough division, one-third of col. 1 being allocated to each group.

TABLE B-47

NET INVESTMENT BY UNINCORPORATED BUSINESS IN INDUSTRIAL, COMMERCIAL, AND MISCELLANEOUS NONRESIDENTIAL BUILDINGS
(millions of dollars)

Year	Industrial			Commercial			Miscellaneous Nonresidential		
	Original Cost (1)	1947-49 Prices (2)	Replacement Cost (3)	Original Cost (4)	1947-49 Prices (5)	Replacement Cost (6)	Original Cost (7)	1947-49 Prices (8)	Replacement Cost (9)
1946	49	17	13	254	163	116	31	34	23
1947	50	4	3	136	-104	-96	17	3	3
1948	34	-17	-17	287	10	10	33	14	15
1949	12	-34	-35	188	-78	-81	39	21	22
1950	16	-29	-30	283	18	19	37	18	19
1951	68	13	15	305	16	18	96	68	77
1952	76	20	24	202	-80	-92	94	63	74
1953	69	15	18	452	122	146	89	55	68
1954	59	12	14	604	230	285	102	63	79
1955	75	25	30	981	516	657	42	14	18
1956	106	42	56	1,114	582	774	47	16	21
1957	126	52	74	1,056	503	698	49	15	21
1958	68	13	18	1,021	449	645	66	26	37

SOURCE, BY COLUMN

(1 to 3) Derived by same procedure used in Table B-101, cols. 6 to 8, from expenditures by unincorporated business on industrial structures (1946–58 from Table B-44, col. 8); years before 1946 obtained by multiplying expenditures by all owners (see notes to Table B-101, col. 3) by *A Study of Saving . . .*, Vol. I, Table R-29, col. 4, using linear interpolation between decadal percentages.

(4 to 6) Derived by same procedure used in Table B-102, cols. 6 to 8, from expenditures by unincorporated business on commercial structures (1946–58 from Table B-44, col. 5);

years before 1946 obtained by multiplying expenditures by all owners (see notes to Table B-102, col. 3) by *A Study of Saving . . .*, Vol. I, Table R-29, col. 3.

(7 to 9) Derived by same procedure used in Table B-103, cols. 6 to 8, from expenditures by unincorporated business on miscellaneous nonresidential buildings (1946–58 from Table B-44, col. 11); years before 1946 obtained by multiplying expenditures by all owners (see notes to Table B-103, col. 3) by *A Study of Saving . . .*, Vol. I, Table R-29, col. 3.

TABLE B-48

NET INVESTMENT BY UNINCORPORATED BUSINESS IN UNDERGROUND MINING CONSTRUCTION
(millions of dollars)

| | PETROLEUM AND GAS WELL DRILLING | | | | | | MINING DEVELOPMENT | | |
| | Estimate A[a] | | | Estimate B[b] | | | | | |
YEAR	Original Cost (1)	1947–49 Prices (2)	Replacement Cost (3)	Original Cost (4)	1947–49 Prices (5)	Replacement Cost (6)	Original Cost (7)	1947–49 Prices (8)	Replacement Cost (9)
1946	60	51	40	98	99	77	2	−1	−1
1947	78	52	48	121	99	93	5	1	1
1948	117	79	82	173	133	139	6	1	1
1949	111	78	79	162	129	131	4	−1	−1
1950	137	99	105	194	154	162	5	0	0
1951	165	105	124	227	158	186	5	−1	−1
1952	174	108	143	249	172	207	4	−2	−2
1953	202	130	160	267	182	225	4	−3	−2
1954	217	151	181	287	209	251	3	−2	−3
1955	247	172	210	328	235	288	4	−2	−2
1956	253	154	206	335	211	283	5	−1	−2
1957	226	122	173	298	168	238	4	−1	−1
1958	222	122	173	292	170	237	4	−1	−1

SOURCE: Derived by same procedure as cols. 6 to 8 of Table B-107, B-108, and B-109, respectively, from expenditures by unincorporated business, obtained by multiplying expenditures by all owners (see col. 3 of Tables B-107, B-108, and B-109) by the complement of the per cents given in *A Study of Saving . . .* , Vol. I, Table C-16, col. 3, for petroleum and gas well drilling, and Table C-16, col. 4, for mining development (linear interpolation between given ratios; 1947 ratios continued through 1958).
  a Based on Department of Commerce figures (see Table B-107).
  b Based on Department of Commerce and other expenditure esti-
  ⦁ mates (see Table B-108).

271

TABLE B-49

Net Investment by Unincorporated Business Through
Purchase of Equipment, Excluding Passenger Cars
(millions of dollars)

Year	Expenditures		Depreciation			Net Investment		
	Original Cost (1)	1947–49 Prices (2)	Original Cost (3)	1947–49 Prices (4)	Replacement Cost (5)	Original Cost (6)	1947–49 Prices (7)	Replacement Cost (8)
1946	1,335	1,648	514	792	642	821	856	693
1947	1,972	2,114	608	889	829	1,364	1,225	1,143
1948	2,167	2,146	734	1,012	1,022	1,316	1,134	1,145
1949	1,786	1,690	851	1,113	1,176	829	577	610
1950	1,978	1,830	957	1,196	1,293	1,021	634	685
1951	2,376	2,020	1,077	1,279	1,504	1,299	741	872
1952	2,425	2,046	1,204	1,357	1,608	1,221	689	817
1953	2,564	2,131	1,339	1,444	1,737	1,225	687	827
1954	2,414	1,987	1,476	1,534	1,864	938	453	550
1955	2,603	2,087	1,608	1,612	2,010	995	475	593
1956	3,343	2,525	1,761	1,694	2,243	1,582	831	1,100
1957	3,498	2,486	1,946	1,798	2,530	1,552	688	968
1958	2,682	1,855	2,116	1,892	2,736	566	−37	−54

Source, by Column

(1)   Table B-44, col. 21.
(2)   Col. 1 divided by implicit price deflator of producer durable goods, shown in Table B-40, col. 9.
(3)   Col. 1 depreciated assuming an average life of fifteen years, which is approximately the weighted average of lengths of life used in computing depreciation on various types of producer durable goods (see notes to Table B-112). Expenditures for years before 1946 obtained by same procedure as figures for later years (see col. 1).
(4)   Col. 2 depreciated assuming an average life of fifteen years. Expenditures in 1947–49 prices for years before 1946, obtained by deflating expenditures in original cost (see col. 3) by index derived from same source as Table B-40, col. 9.
(5)   Col. 4 multiplied by Table B-40, col. 9.
(6)   Col. 1 minus col. 3.
(7)   Col. 2 minus col. 4.
(8)   Col. 1 minus col. 5.

TABLE B-50

NET INVESTMENT BY UNINCORPORATED BUSINESS THROUGH PURCHASE
OF PASSENGER CARS
(millions of dollars)

	Expenditures		Depreciation			Net Investment		
Year	Original Cost (1)	1947–49 Prices (2)	Original Cost (3)	1947–49 Prices (4)	Replace-ment Cost (5)	Original Cost (6)	1947–49 Prices (7)	Replace-ment Cost (8)
1946	210	252	83	124	103	127	128	107
1947	443	477	100	125	116	343	352	327
1948	544	536	161	175	178	383	361	366
1949	795	752	269	278	293	526	474	502
1950	1,017	959	418	418	443	599	541	574
1951	864	780	574	561	621	290	219	243
1952	761	652	691	659	769	70	−7	−8
1953	1,023	897	785	727	829	238	170	194
1954	975	871	870	790	884	105	81	91
1955	1,395	1,197	956	855	996	439	342	399
1956	1,158	967	1,017	893	1,070	141	74	88
1957	1,279	1,014	1,064	913	1,151	215	101	128
1958	1,032	793	1,121	944	1,228	−89	−151	−196

SOURCE BY COLUMN

(1)   From Table B-27, col. 3.
(2)   1946–56, col. 1 divided by Table B-118, col. 14; 1957–58, by 126.0 and 130.0, respectively.
(3)   Col. 1 depreciated assuming an average life of six years. Expenditures for years before 1946 from *A Study of Saving. . .*, Vol. I, Table P-13, col. 1.
(4)   Same method as for col. 3, but expenditures figures of col. 2 used. Expenditures in 1947–49 prices for years before 1946, obtained by deflating expenditures in original cost (see col. 3) by index derived by extrapolating Table B-118, col. 14, from 1946 by *A Study of Saving. . .*, Vol. I, Table P-10, col. 12.
(5)   1946–56, col. 4 multiplied by Table B-118, col. 14; 1957–58, by 126.0 and 130.0, respectively.
(6)   Col. 1 minus col. 3.
(7)   Col. 2 minus col. 4.
(8)   Col. 1 minus col. 5.

TABLE B-51

Business Saving Through Dealers' Margin on Used Cars
(millions of dollars)

Year	Dealers' Margin Original Cost (1)	Dealers' Margin 1947–49 Prices (2)	Depreciation Original Cost (3)	Depreciation 1947–49 Prices (4)	Depreciation Replacement Cost (5)	Saving Original Cost (6)	Saving 1947–49 Prices (7)	Saving Replacement Cost (8)
1946	46	55	30	41	34	16	14	12
1947	54	58	39	48	45	15	10	9
1948	59	58	48	54	55	11	4	4
1949	54	51	54	56	59	—	−5	−5
1950	67	63	58	57	60	9	6	7
1951	74	67	63	59	65	11	8	9
1952	96	82	72	66	77	24	16	19
1953	92	81	83	74	84	9	7	8
1954	88	79	90	79	88	−2	—	—
1955	94	81	92	81	94	2	—	—
1956	88	73	91	79	95	−3	−6	−7
1957	92	73	91	77	97	1	−4	−5
1958	94	72	91	74	96	3	−2	−2

Source, by Column

(1) From Table B-28, col. 3.
(2) 1946–56, col. 1 divided by Table B-118, col. 14; 1957–58, by 126.0 and 130.0, respectively.
(3) Col. 1 depreciated assuming an average life of three years. Expenditures for years before 1946 from *A Study of Saving* . . . , Vol. I, Table P-16, col. 3.
(4) Same method as for col. 3 except expenditure figures of col. 2 used. Expenditures in 1947–49 prices for years before 1946 obtained by deflating expenditures in original cost (col. 3) by index derived by extrapolating Table B-118, col. 14, back from 1946 by *A Study of Saving* . . . , Vol. I, Table P-10, col. 12.
(5) 1946–56, col. 4 multiplied by Table B-118, col. 14; 1957–58, by 126.0 and 130.0, respectively.
(6) Col. 1 minus col. 3.
(7) Col. 2 minus col. 4.
(8) Col. 1 minus col. 5.

TABLE B-52

Net Investment in Multifamily Dwellings: Unincorporated Business Share
(millions of dollars)

Year	Expenditures Original Cost (1)	1947–49 Prices (2)	Depreciation Original Prices (3)	1947–49 Cost (4)	Replacement Cost (5)	Net Investment Original Cost (6)	1947–49 Prices (7)	Replacement Cost (8)
1946	83	107	111	275	214	−28	−168	−131
1947	157	171	113	275	253	44	−104	−96
1948	290	280	116	277	287	174	3	3
1949	365	348	121	280	294	244	68	71
1950	345	314	127	283	310	218	31	35
1951	248	209	132	285	337	116	−76	−89
1952	228	187	136	287	350	92	−100	−122
1953	267	212	140	288	363	127	−76	−96
1954	240	189	143	290	367	97	−101	−127
1955	258	198	147	291	381	111	−93	−123
1956	292	213	152	291	399	140	−78	−107
1957	272	193	156	294	414	116	−101	−142
1958	284	198	161	295	424	123	−97	−140

Source: Same procedure as for Table B-7. Expenditures by individuals on multi-family dwellings, determined by multiplying the components of Table B-7, col. 1, by percentages given in *A Study of Saving* . . . , Vol. I, Table R-29, col. 2. (interpolating between decadal percentages; 1948 figure carried through 1958).

TABLE B-53

Net Investment by Unincorporated Business in Nonhousekeeping Structures
(millions of dollars)

Year	Expenditures Original Cost (1)	1947–49 Prices (2)	Depreciation Original Cost (3)	1947–49 Prices (4)	Replacement Cost (5)	Net Investment Original Cost (6)	1947–49 Prices (7)	Replacement Cost (8)
1946	48	62	65	149	116	−17	−87	−68
1947	44	48	66	148	136	−22	−100	−92
1948	63	61	66	146	151	−3	−85	−88
1949	72	69	67	145	152	5	−76	−80
1950	61	56	68	143	157	−7	−87	−96
1951	79	67	69	141	166	10	−74	−87
1952	76	62	70	140	171	6	−78	−95
1953	112	89	71	139	175	41	−50	−63
1954	112	88	73	138	175	39	−50	−63
1955	134	103	76	137	179	58	−34	−45
1956	185	135	79	137	188	106	−2	−3
1957	205	145	82	137	193	123	8	12
1958	242	169	87	138	198	155	31	44

Source: Same procedure as for Table B-8. Expenditures by unincorporated business on nonhousekeeping units determined by multiplying Table B-8, col. 1, by percentages given in *A Study of Saving* . . . , Vol. I, Table R-29, col. 2 (interpolating between decadal percentages; 1948 figure carried through 1958).

VALUE OF UNINCORPORATED BUSINESS SHARE OF
PRIVATE NONFARM HOUSEKEEPING REAL ESTATE
(millions of dollars)

End of Year	Nonhousekeeping Structures			Nonhousekeeping Real Estate	
	Original Cost (1)	1947–49 Prices (2)	Current Prices (3)	1947–49 Prices (4)	Current Prices (5)
1945	1,257	2,669	1,956	3,336	2,445
1946	1,240	2,582	2,159	3,228	2,699
1947	1,218	2,482	2,435	3,103	3,044
1948	1,215	2,397	2,550	2,996	3,188
1949	1,220	2,321	2,428	2,901	3,035
1950	1,213	2,234	2,569	2,792	3,211
1951	1,223	2,160	2,588	2,700	3,235
1952	1,229	2,082	2,575	2,602	3,219
1953	1,270	2,032	2,577	2,540	3,221
1954	1,309	1,982	2,533	2,478	3,166
1955	1,367	1,948	2,603	2,435	3,254
1956	1,473	1,946	2,707	2,409	3,350
1957	1,596	1,954	2,781	2,443	3,476
1958	1,751	1,985	2,896	2,481	3,622

SOURCE, BY COLUMN

(1) Derived by addition of cumulated net investment, original cost (Table B-53, col. 6), to estimated value for 1945, obtained by cumulating expenditures less depreciation for forty years preceding 1945, the assumed length of life of nonhousekeeping structures.
(2) Same procedure as for col. 1, but derived from Table B-53, col. 7.
(3) Col. 2 multiplied by Table B-9, col. 4.
(4 and 5) Cols. 2 and 3, respectively, plus value of underlying land, estimated on basis of data given in A Study of Saving . . . , Vol. II, Table B-50, col. 2.

TABLE B-55

VALUE OF UNINCORPORATED BUSINESS STRUCTURES, CURRENT PRICES
(millions of dollars)

End of Year	Total (1)	Industrial (2)	Commercial (3)	Miscellaneous Nonresidential (4)
1945	6,473	882	5,233	358
1946	13,256	1,113	7,112	503
1947	16,135	1,287	8,527	632
1948	11,011	1,341	8,981	689
1949	10,618	1,260	8,670	688
1950	11,295	1,356	9,181	758
1951	11,940	1,477	9,597	866
1952	12,399	1,519	9,894	986
1953	12,987	1,542	10,361	1,084
1954	13,738	1,524	11,026	1,188
1955	15,067	1,639	12,177	1,251
1956	16,524	1,762	13,433	1,329
1957	17,968	1,992	14,575	1,401
1958	19,192	2,018	15,693	1,481

SOURCE, BY COLUMN

(1) Sum of cols. 2, 3, and 4; (2 to 4) Cumulated depreciated capital expenditures in 1947–49 prices, multiplied by appropriate price deflator from Table B-106 (year-end figures used).

TABLE B-55A

VALUE OF UNINCORPORATED BUSINESS STRUCTURES,
CONSTANT(1947–49) PRICES
(millions of dollars)

End of Year	Total (1)	Industrial (2)	Commercial (3)	Miscellaneous Nonresidential (4)
1945	10,334	1,271	8,468	595
1946	10,548	1,288	8,631	629
1947	10,451	1,292	8,527	632
1948	10,458	1,275	8,537	646
1949	10,367	1,241	8,459	667
1950	10,374	1,212	8,477	685
1951	10,471	1,225	8,493	753
1952	10,474	1,245	8,413	816
1953	10,666	1,260	8,535	871
1954	10,971	1,272	8,765	934
1955	11,526	1,297	9,281	948
1956	12,166	1,339	9,863	964
1957	12,736	1,391	10,366	979
1958	13,224	1,404	10,815	1,005

SOURCE, BY COLUMN

(1)   Sum of cols. 2, 3, and 4.   (2 to 4)   Same procedure as for Table B-121, cols. 2 to 5, but applied to expenditures in 1947–49 prices (see Table B-47).

TABLE B-55B

VALUE OF UNINCORPORATED BUSINESS STRUCTURES, ORIGINAL COST
(millions of dollars)

End of Year	Total (1)	Industrial (2)	Commercial (3)	Miscellaneous Nonresidential (4)
1945	4,667	565	3,839	263
1946	5,001	614	4,093	294
1947	5,204	664	4,229	311
1948	5,558	698	4,516	344
1949	5,797	710	4,704	383
1950	6,133	726	4,987	420
1951	6,602	794	5,292	516
1952	6,974	870	5,494	610
1953	7,584	939	5,946	699
1954	8,349	998	6,550	801
1955	9,447	1,073	7,531	843
1956	10,684	1,179	8,645	890
1957	11,945	1,305	9,701	939
1958	13,100	1,373	10,722	1,005

SOURCE, BY COLUMN

(1)   Sum of cols. 2, 3, and 4.   (2 to 4)   Derived by addition of cumulated net investment, original cost, to estimated value for 1945, obtained by cumulating expenditures less depreciation for number of years preceding 1945 corresponding to the assumed length of life of asset involved (see Tables B-101 to B-104, and B-47).

TABLE B-56

VALUE OF UNINCORPORATED BUSINESS SHARE OF UNDERGROUND MINING CONSTRUCTION

(millions of dollars)

| | PETROLEUM AND GAS WELL DRILLING | | | | | | MINING DEVELOPMENT | | |
| | Estimate A[a] | | | Estimate B[b] | | | | | |
END OF YEAR	Original Cost (1)	1947–49 Prices (2)	Current Prices (3)	Original Cost (4)	1947–49 Prices (5)	Current Prices (6)	Original Cost (7)	1947–49 Prices (8)	Current Prices (9)
1945	524	1,028	713	524	1,028	713	83	175	121
1946	584	1,079	932	622	1,127	974	85	174	150
1947	662	1,131	1,126	743	1,226	1,221	90	175	174
1948	779	1,210	1,273	916	1,359	1,430	96	176	185
1949	890	1,288	1,307	1,078	1,488	1,510	100	175	178
1950	1,027	1,387	1,552	1,272	1,642	1,837	105	175	196
1951	1,192	1,492	1,799	1,498	1,800	2,171	110	174	210
1952	1,366	1,600	1,952	1,748	1,972	2,409	114	172	210
1953	1,518	1,730	2,118	2,015	2,154	2,636	118	169	207
1954	1,785	1,881	2,253	2,302	2,363	2,831	121	167	200
1955	2,032	2,053	2,595	2,630	2,598	3,284	125	165	209
1956	2,285	2,207	2,904	2,965	2,809	3,697	130	164	216
1957	2,511	2,329	3,335	3,263	2,977	4,263	134	163	233
1958	2,733	2,451	3,522	3,555	3,147	4,522	138	162	233

SOURCE, BY COLUMN

(1, 4, and 7) Derived by addition of cumulated net investment, original cost, to estimated value for 1945, obtained by cumulating expenditures less depreciation for number of years preceding 1945 corresponding to the assumed length of life of asset involved (see Table B-48).

(2, 5, and 8) Same procedure as for col. 1, but applied to expenditures in 1947–49 prices.

(3, 6, and 9) Cumulated depreciated capital expenditures in 1947–49 prices multiplied by price index (year-end figures used; see Table B-106).

[a] Based on unincorporated business share of Department of Commerce figures.

[b] Based on unincorporated business share of Department of Commerce and other expenditure estimates (see Table 48).

TABLE B-57

VALUE OF DEALERS' MARGIN ON USED CARS PURCHASED BY BUSINESS
(millions of dollars)

End of Year	Original Cost (1)	1947–49 Prices (2)	Current Prices (3)
1945	42	60	46
1946	58	74	65
1947	73	84	82
1948	84	88	91
1949	84	83	88
1950	93	89	96
1951	104	97	110
1952	128	113	130
1953	137	120	136
1954	135	120	137
1955	137	120	142
1956	134	114	140
1957	135	110	141
1958	138	108	146

SOURCE, BY COLUMN

(1) Derived by addition of cumulated net investment, original cost, to estimated value for 1945, obtained by cumulating dealers' margin less expenditures for three years, the assumed life span of dealers' margin.

(2) Same procedure as for col. 1, but applied to expenditures in 1947–49 prices (see Table B-51, cols. 2 and 4).

(3) Cumulated depreciated capital expenditures in 1947–49 prices, multiplied by price index (see Table B-58, note to col. 6).

TABLE B-58

VALUE OF UNINCORPORATED BUSINESS SHARE OF EQUIPMENT AND CARS
(millions of dollars)

End of Year	Business Equipment			Passenger Cars		
	Original Cost (1)	1947–49 Prices (2)	Current Prices (3)	Original Cost (4)	1947–49 Prices (5)	Current Prices (6)
1945	4,425	6,667	5,134	105	163	125
1946	5,246	7,523	6,561	232	291	256
1947	6,610	8,748	8,503	575	643	625
1948	7,926	9,882	10,218	958	1,004	1,040
1949	8,755	10,459	11,181	1,484	1,478	1,565
1950	9,776	11,093	12,524	2,083	2,019	2,189
1951	11,075	11,834	13,976	2,373	2,238	2,545
1952	12,296	12,523	14,952	2,443	2,231	2,572
1953	13,521	13,210	15,971	2,681	2,401	2,713
1954	14,459	13,663	16,819	2,786	2,482	2,834
1955	15,454	14,218	18,284	3,225	2,824	3,338
1956	17,036	15,049	20,557	3,366	2,898	3,565
1957	18,588	15,737	22,457	3,581	2,999	3,839
1958	19,154	15,710	22,934	3,492	2,848	3,862

SOURCE, BY COLUMN

(1) Derived by addition of cumulated net investment, original cost, to estimated value for 1945 (see Table B-49).

(2) Same procedure as for col. 1, but applied to expenditures in 1947–49 prices.

(3) Col. 2 multiplied by year-end index for producers' durable equipment obtained by averaging yearly index for successive years (see Table B-40, col. 9).

(4) Same procedure as for col. 1, using figures in Table B-50.

(5) Same as for col. 2.

(6) Col. 5 multiplied by year-end index for passenger cars derived by averaging successive years of index in Table B-118, col. 14. 1957 and 1958 extrapolated by using passenger car index from Table B-33, part B, col. 11.

TABLE B-59
VALUE OF UNINCORPORATED BUSINESS LAND
(millions of dollars)

End of Year	1947–49 Prices				Current Prices			
	Total (1)	Industrial (2)	Commercial (3)	Miscellaneous Nonresidential (4)	Total (5)	Industrial (6)	Commercial (7)	Miscellaneous Nonresidential (8)
1945	6,269	224	5,648	397	3,884	155	3,490	239
1946	6,404	227	5,757	420	5,726	196	4,744	336
1947	6,447	227	5,688	422	6,337	227	5,688	422
1948	6,349	224	5,694	431	6,686	236	5,990	460
1949	6,305	218	5,642	445	6,464	222	5,783	459
1950	6,324	213	5,654	457	6,869	239	6,124	506
1951	6,389	216	5,665	502	7,239	260	6,401	578
1952	6,374	219	5,611	544	7,524	267	6,599	658
1953	6,496	222	5,693	581	7,905	271	6,911	723
1954	6,693	224	5,846	623	8,414	268	7,354	792
1955	7,050	228	6,190	632	9,244	288	8,122	834
1956	7,458	236	6,579	643	10,156	310	8,960	886
1957	7,811	244	6,914	653	11,007	351	9,722	934
1958	8,131	247	7,214	670	11,810	355	10,467	988

SOURCE, BY COLUMN

(1) Sum of cols. 2 to 4.

(2 and 6) Estimated at 15 per cent of the total value of unincorporated business industrial real estate.

(3, 4, 7, and 8) Estimated at 40 per cent of the total value of unincorporated business commercial real estate (see Tables B-55 and B-55A, cols. 3 and 4).

(5) Sum of cols. 6 to 8.

TABLE B-60

FARMERS' NET INVESTMENT IN DWELLINGS
(millions of dollars)

Year	Expenditures Original Cost (1)	Expenditures 1947–49 Prices (2)	Depreciation Original Cost (3)	Depreciation 1947–49 Prices (4)	Depreciation Replacement Cost (5)	Net Investment Original Cost (6)	Net Investment 1947–49 Prices (7)	Net Investment Replacement Cost (8)
1946	409	538	148	423	321	261	115	88
1947	683	711	156	429	412	527	282	271
1948	738	710	167	437	454	571	273	284
1949	695	695	178	444	444	517	251	251
1950	763	748	189	451	460	574	297	303
1951	863	768	202	457	514	661	311	354
1952	890	783	215	464	527	675	319	363
1953	809	707	228	471	539	581	236	270
1954	769	675	240	477	544	529	198	225
1955	750	644	251	482	561	499	162	189
1956	730	607	263	487	585	467	120	145
1957	744	606	274	491	603	470	115	141
1958	750	605	285	495	613	465	110	137

SOURCE, BY COLUMN

(1) 1946–57, *U.S. Income and Output*, Dept. of Commerce, p. 190.
1958 estimated on basis of average proportion of dwellings to total farm construction for 1955–57.
(2) Col. 1 divided by Table B-79, col. 1.
(3) Col. 1 depreciated assuming an average life of sixty years. Expenditure figures for years before 1946 obtained by raising the figures given in *A Study of Saving . . .* , Vol. I, Table A-7, col. 3 and related worksheets by 50 per cent. This step-up, which is based upon *A Study of Saving . . .* , Vol. II, Table B-62, was not applied to expenditures after 1945, as the Agricultural Marketing Service (formerly the Bureau of Agricultural Economics) raised fairly substantially the level of its figures for 1946 and later years in order to bring them into line with postwar surveys of farm construction activity.
(4) Col. 2 depreciated assuming an average life of sixty years. Expenditure figures in 1947–49 prices for years before 1946 obtained by deflating expenditures in original cost, as derived by the procedure described in col. 3 above, by price index obtained for the period 1910–45 from same source as index for later years (see Table B-79, col. 1; for years before 1910, index extrapolated by *A Study of Saving . . .* , Vol. I, Table A-30, col. 1).
(5) Col. 4 multiplied by Table B-79, col. 1.
(6) Col. 1 minus col. 3.
(7) Col. 2 minus col. 4.
(8) Col. 1 minus col. 5.

TABLE B-61

FARMERS' NET INVESTMENT IN SERVICE BUILDINGS
(millions of dollars)

Year	Expenditures		Depreciation			Net Investment		
	Original Cost (1)	1947–49 Prices (2)	Original Cost (3)	1947–49 Prices (4)	Replacement Cost (5)	Original Cost (6)	1947–49 Prices (7)	Replacement Cost (8)
1946	447	575	202	466	362	445	109	85
1947	714	753	213	471	447	501	282	267
1948	806	779	227	478	494	579	301	312
1949	793	780	242	485	493	551	295	300
1950	872	843	258	493	510	614	350	362
1951	983	882	275	502	580	708	380	403
1952	1,015	860	295	511	603	720	349	412
1953	922	778	313	519	615	609	259	307
1954	876	742	330	524	618	546	218	258
1955	850	707	345	528	635	505	179	215
1956	830	663	360	530	663	470	133	167
1957	846	653	374	531	688	472	122	158
1958	850	646	389	532	700	461	114	150

SOURCE: Derived from same source and by same procedure as Table B-60, except expenditures depreciated assuming an average life of forty-five years. Construction cost index from Table B-79, col. 2.

TABLE B-62

COMMISSIONS PAID TO REAL ESTATE DEALERS IN CONNECTION WITH SALE OF FARMS

(cols. 4–9, millions of dollars)

Year	Land in Farms	Rate of Voluntary Sales (1947–49 = 100)	Land Prices	Value of Sales	Dealers Commissions		Depreciated Commissions on Farm Structures		
					Total	Depreciable	Original Cost	1947–49 Prices	Replacement Cost
	(1)	(2)	(3)	(4)	(5)	(6)	(7)	(8)	(9)
1946	99	136	90	121	108	30	23	23	18
1947	100	116	98	114	101	28	21	13	13
1948	100	96	102	98	87	24	16	6	6
1949	100	88	100	88	78	22	14	5	5
1950	101	93	115	108	96	26	17	8	9
1951	101	89	127	114	101	27	18	6	7
1952	101	81	127	104	93	25	15	4	4
1953	101	71	124	89	79	21	11	0	0
1954	102	76	130	99	88	23	13	2	2
1955	102	76	138	104	93	23	13	1	2
1956	102	75	145	106	94	23	12	1	1
1957	102	75	155	114	101	23	11	−1	−1
1958	102	75	165	121	108	25	13	1	1

SOURCE, BY COLUMN

(1) Based on census-year figures given in *Agricultural Statistics*, 1954, p. 430. Estimates for intercensal years obtained by linear interpolation and extrapolation. Figures so obtained were converted to June 30 basis by two-year moving average.

(2) Derived from data on the number of farms changing ownership by voluntary sales and trades given in *Agricultural Finance Review*, Nov. 1955, p. 112. March 1 data assumed to apply to end of preceding year.

(3) Index of average value per acre of farm real estate from *Current Developments in the Farm Real Estate Market* (Agricultural Research Service), various issues, e.g.; AR 43–32 (CO-43), March 1956, 1956, p. 17 (converted from 1912–14 = 100 base). November of preceding year and March 1 data averaged to apply to end of preceding year.

(4) Col. 1 multiplied by product of cols. 2 and 3.

(5) Col. 4 multiplied by $89 million, estimated average commissions for the years 1947–49. This figure obtained as follows:

a. Value of land and buildings (Department of Agriculture figures) is $75.1 billion.

b. Average annual number of farms, per thousand, changing hands as a result of voluntary sales and trades and of administrators' and executors' sales is 56.7 (*Agricultural Finance Review*, November 1955, p. 112).

c. About 52 per cent of all sales of farm real estate are made through agents and dealers (*Current Developments in the Farm Real Estate Market*, AR 43-14, CD-40, March 1955, p. 11).

d. Average rate of dealers' commissions is estimated, on basis of information from the Agricultural Marketing Service, at 4 per cent.

(6) Col. 5 multiplied by per cent of value of buildings to total value of land and buildings (Department of Agriculture, unpublished figures).

(7) Original cost dealers' commissions depreciated on basis of 50-year life.

(8) Constant cost dealers' commissions obtained by deflating by average-year index for farm buildings depreciated on basis of 50-year life.

(9) Original cost dealers' commissions minus replacement cost depreciations.

TABLE B-63

NET INVESTMENT AND ACCUMULATED VALUES OF DEALERS' COMMISSIONS FOR SALE OF FARMS
(millions of dollars)

Year	Expenditures		Depreciation			Net Investment			Accumulated Values		
	Original Cost (1)	1947–49 Prices (2)	Original Cost (3)	1947–49 Prices (4)	Replacement Cost (5)	Original Cost (6)	1947–49 Prices (7)	Replacement Cost (8)	Original Cost (9)	1947–49 Prices (10)	Replacement Cost (11)
1945	—	—	—	—	—	—	—	—	208	440	325
1946	30	39	7	16	12	23	23	23	231	463	399
1947	28	29	7	16	15	21	13	13	252	476	473
1948	24	23	8	17	18	16	6	6	268	482	493
1949	22	22	8	17	17	14	5	5	282	487	496
1950	26	25	9	17	17	17	8	9	299	495	531
1951	27	24	9	18	20	18	6	7	317	501	571
1952	25	22	10	18	21	15	4	4	332	505	587
1953	21	18	10	18	21	11	—	—	343	505	588
1954	23	20	10	18	21	13	2	2	356	507	594
1955	23	19	10	18	21	13	1	2	369	508	613
1956	23	19	11	19	22	12	—	1	381	509	634
1957	23	18	12	19	24	11	−1	−1	392	508	646
1958	25	20	12	19	24	13	1	1	405	509	655

SOURCE: See notes to Table B-62.

TABLE B-64

FARMERS' NET INVESTMENT IN FARM MACHINERY
(millions of dollars)

Year	Expenditures		Depreciation			Net Investment		
	Original Cost (1)	1947–49 Prices (2)	Original Cost (3)	1947–49 Prices (4)	Replacement Cost (5)	Original Cost (6)	1947–49 Prices (7)	Replacement Cost (8)
1946	444	582	293	429	327	151	153	117
1947	795	921	355	471	406	440	450	389
1948	1,159	1,152	432	536	539	727	616	620
1949	1,256	1,110	509	605	684	747	506	572
1950	1,279	1,110	585	666	767	694	444	512
1951	1,383	1,112	660	720	896	723	392	487
1952	1,368	1,060	734	766	989	634	294	379
1953	1,225	940	805	807	1,052	420	133	173
1954	1,120	857	868	843	1,102	252	14	18
1955	1,099	841	922	876	1,145	177	−35	−46
1956	998	731	963	898	1,227	235	−167	229
1957	976	681	999	901	1,291	−23	−220	−315
1958	1,308	874	1,041	911	1,363	267	−37	−55

SOURCE, BY COLUMN

(1) *The Farm Income Situation*, Agricultural Marketing Service, various issues, e.g., *FIS*-159, p. 36, and unpublished figures for later years.

(2) Col. 1 divided by Table B-79, col. 3.

(3) Col. 1 depreciated assuming an average life of fifteen years. Expenditures for years before 1946 from same source as figures for later years (see col. 1).

(4) Same method as for col. 3, but based on expenditure figures of col. 2. Expenditures in 1947–49 prices for years before 1946 obtained by deflating expenditures in original cost (see notes to col. 3) by price index derived from same source as index for later years (see Table B-79, col. 3).

(5) Col. 4 multiplied by Table B-79, col. 3.

(6) Col. 1 minus col. 3.

(7) Col. 2 minus col. 4.

(8) Col. 1 minus col. 5.

TABLE B-65

FARMERS' NET INVESTMENT IN TRACTORS
(millions of dollars)

	Expenditures		Depreciation			Net Investment		
Year	Original Cost (1)	1947–49 Prices (2)	Original Cost (3)	1947–49 Prices (4)	Replacement Cost (5)	Original Cost (6)	1947–49 Prices (7)	Replacement Cost (8)
1946	241	315	174	267	204	67	48	37
1947	449	501	195	290	260	254	211	189
1948	661	658	230	326	327	431	332	334
1949	769	696	275	367	404	491	329	362
1950	769	692	320	403	448	449	289	321
1951	807	675	363	433	517	444	242	290
1952	755	638	402	456	539	353	182	216
1953	722	623	439	479	555	283	144	167
1954	570	487	472	501	587	98	−14	−17
1955	689	577	502	517	618	187	60	79
1956	525	422	526	525	655	−1	−103	−128
1957	522	390	542	522	699	−20	−132	−177
1958	675	483	567	526	738	108	−43	−63

SOURCE, BY COLUMN

(1) *The Farm Income Situation*, Agricultural Marketing Service, various issues, e.g., *FIS*-159, p. 36, unpublished figures for later years.

(2) Col. 1 divided by Table B-79, col. 4.

(3) Col. 1 depreciated assuming an average life of fifteen years. Expenditures for years before 1946 from same source as figures for later years (see col. 1).

(4) Same method as for col. 3, but based on expenditure figures of col. 2. Expenditures in 1947–49 prices for years before 1946 obtained by deflating expenditures in original cost (see notes to col. 3) by cost index derived for period 1935–45 from same source as Table B-79, col. 4, for period before 1935, index extrapolated on basis of *A Study of Saving* . . . , Vol. I, Table A-30, col. 4.

(5) Col. 4 multiplied by Table B-79, col. 4.

(6) Col. 1 minus col. 3.

(7) Col. 2 minus col. 4.

(8) Col. 1 minus col. 5.

TABLE B-66

FARMERS' NET INVESTMENT IN USED PASSENGER CARS

(millions of dollars)

	Expenditures		Depreciation			Net Investment		
Year	Original Cost (1)	1947–49 Prices (2)	Original Cost (3)	1947–49 Prices (4)	Replacement Cost (5)	Original Cost (6)	1947–49 Prices (7)	Replacement Cost (8)
1946	97	120	82	125	101	15	−5	−4
1947	142	149	87	127	121	55	22	21
1948	112	100	92	125	140	20	−25	−28
1949	−218	−235	88	63	58	−130	−298	−276
1950	375	427	80	72	63	295	355	362
1951	75	71	96	130	137	−21	−59	−62
1952	223	186	109	125	150	114	61	73
1953	122	100	122	134	163	0	−34	−41
1954	106	87	123	120	147	17	−33	−41
1955	364	295	135	144	177	229	151	187
1956	335	265	168	188	237	167	77	98
1957	315	232	201	205	279	114	27	36
1958	325	229	212	216	306	113	13	19

SOURCE, BY COLUMN

(1) Agricultural Marketing Service estimates (unpublished). Figures represent net purchases of used cars, i.e., gross purchases less value of all cars traded in by farmers. (In determining farmers' expenditures for used cars, Agricultural Marketing Service in its recent estimates subtracts only trade-ins for purchases of used cars; trade-ins for purchases of new cars are subtracted from its series on farmers' purchases of new cars. In col. 1 all of these trade-ins have been netted against purchases of used cars.)

(2) Col. 1 deflated by Table B-79, col. 6.

(3) Col. 1 depreciated assuming the following pattern:

Year of Service	9-Year Life
1st	16.0
2nd	27.0
3rd	18.0
4th	13.0
5th	9.0
6th	6.5
7th	4.5
8th	3.0
9th	2.0
10th	1.0

See Table B-32, col. 3, for basis of estimate of depreciation pattern. Expenditures for years before 1946 from same source as figures for later years (see col. 1).

(4) Same method as for col. 3 but based on expenditure figures of col. 2. Expenditures in 1947–49 prices for years before 1946 obtained by deflating expenditures in original cost (see col. 3) by cost index derived by extrapolating from the 1946 value of Table B-79, col. 6, by *A Study of Saving* . . . , Vol. I, Table A-30, col. 6.

(5) Col. 4 multiplied by Table B-79, col. 6.

(6) Col. 1 minus col. 3.

(7) Col. 2 minus col. 4.

(8) Col. 1 minus col. 5.

FARMERS' NET INVESTMENT IN NEW TRUCKS
(millions of dollars)

Year	Expenditures Original Cost (1)	1947–49 Prices (2)	Depreciation Original Cost (3)	1947–49 Prices (4)	Replacement Cost (5)	Net Investment Original Cost (6)	1947–49 Prices (7)	Replacement Cost (8)
1946	135	163	42	64	53	93	99	82
1947	330	357	59	79	73	271	278	257
1948	369	361	89	106	108	280	255	261
1949	390	370	123	136	143	267	234	247
1950	404	385	157	166	174	247	219	230
1951	348	311	188	190	213	160	121	135
1952	245	208	213	209	246	132	−1	−1
1953	320	272	240	231	272	80	41	48
1954	327	277	271	257	304	56	20	23
1955	225	189	298	280	333	−73	−91	−108
1956	224	183	314	290	354	−90	−107	−130
1957	281	214	316	284	373	−35	−70	−92
1958	349	255	312	272	373	37	−17	−24

SOURCE, BY COLUMN

(1) Agricultural Marketing Service (unpublished) estimates. Figures represent gross purchases of new trucks, i.e., before deduction of old trucks traded in.
(2) Col. 1 deflated by Table B-79, col. 7.
(3) Col. 1 depreciated assuming an average life of ten years. Expenditures for years before 1946 from same source as figures for later years (see col. 1).
(4) Col. 2 depreciated assuming an average life of ten years. Expenditures in 1947–49 prices for years before 1946 obtained by deflating expenditures in original cost (see col. 3) by cost index derived by extrapolating from the 1946 value of Table B-79, col. 7, by *A Study of Saving . . .* , Vol. I, Table A-30, col. 7.
(5) Col. 4 multiplied by Table B-79, col. 7.
(6) Col. 1 minus col. 3.
(7) Col. 2 minus col. 4.
(8) Col. 1 minus col. 5.

TABLE B-68

FARMERS' NET INVESTMENT IN USED TRUCKS
(millions of dollars)

Year	Expenditures Original Cost (1)	1947–49 Prices (2)	Depreciation Original Cost (3)	1947–49 Prices (4)	Replacement Cost (5)	Net Investment Original Cost (6)	1947–49 Prices (7)	Replacement Cost (8)
1946	81	98	93	102	84	−12	−4	−3
1947	133	144	102	)	102	31	34	31
1948	166	162	111	119	122	55	43	44
1949	150	142	117	126	133	33	16	17
1950	116	111	126	130	136	−10	−19	−20
1951	133	119	133	134	150	0	−15	−17
1952	151	128	130	134	158	21	−16	−7
1953	117	99	126	126	148	−9	−27	−31
1954	125	106	126	116	137	−1	−10	−12
1955	181	152	127	117	139	−46	45	−58
1956	208	170	99	126	154	109	44	−54
1957	207	158	71	134	176	136	54	−31
1958	182	133	44	140	192	138	−7	−10

(Notes to **Table B-68** on next page)

Notes to Table B-68

(1) Agricultural Marketing Service (unpublished) estimates. Figures represent net purchases of used trucks, i.e., gross purchases less value of all trucks traded-in (see note to Table B-67, col. 1). The sum of farmers' expenditures for new and used trucks is published in *The Farm Income Situation*, Agricultural Marketing Service, e.g., *FIS*-155, p. 56.
(2) Col. 1 deflated by Table B-79, col. 7.
(3) Col. 1 depreciated assuming an average life of five years. Expenditures for years before 1946 from same source as figures for later years (see col. 1).
(4) Col. 2 depreciated assuming an average life of five years. Expenditures in 1947–49 prices for years before 1946 obtained by deflating expenditures in original cost (see col. 3) by cost index derived by extrapolating from the 1946 value of Table B-79, col. 7, by *A Study of Saving...*, Vol. I, Table A-30, col. 8.
(5) Col. 4 multiplied by Table B-79, col. 7.
(6) Col. 1 minus col. 3.
(7) Col. 2 minus col. 4.
(8) Col. 1 minus col. 5.

TABLE B-69

FARM CAPITAL EXPENDITURES CHARGED TO CURRENT EXPENSE
(millions of dollars)

Year	Expenditures Original Cost (1)	1947–49 Prices (2)	Depreciation Original Cost (3)	1947–49 Prices (4)	Replacement Cost (5)	Net Investment Original Cost (6)	1947–49 Prices (7)	Replacement Cost (8)
1946	72	82	65	91	80	7	−9	−8
1947	79	84	68	91	86	11	−7	−7
1948	78	78	71	91	92	7	−13	−14
1949	76	73	73	90	94	3	−17	−18
1950	73	69	76	89	94	−3	−20	−21
1951	73	65	78	88	99	−5	−23	−26
1952	67	56	79	85	101	−12	−29	−34
1953	71	61	79	82	96	−8	−21	−25
1954	71	63	77	78	88	−6	−15	−17
1955	72	65	75	73	81	−3	−8	−9
1956	73	66	73	70	78	0	−4	−5
1957	73	65	73	68	76	0	−3	−3
1958	75	67	72	66	74	3	1	1

(1) 1946–55 *U.S. Income and Output*, pp. 226–227; 1956–58 *Survey of Current Business*, July 1959, p. 41.
(2) Col. 1 deflated by Table B-79, col. 8.
(3) Col. 1 depreciated assuming an average life of ten years. Expenditures for years before 1946 from same source as figures for later years (see col. 1).
(4) Col. 2 depreciated assuming an average life of ten years. Expenditures in 1947–49 prices for years before 1946 obtained by dividing expenditures in original cost (see col. 3) by price index derived from same source as Table B-79, col. 8.
(5) Col. 4 multiplied by Table B-79, col. 8.
(6) Col. 1 minus col. 3.
(7) Col. 2 minus col. 4.
(8) Col. 1 minus col. 5.

TABLE B-70

FARMERS' SHARE IN DISPOSABLE INCOME
(amounts in millions of dollars)

Year	Net Income of Farm Population from All Sources (1)	Direct Taxes (2)	Farmers' Disposable Income (3)	Personal Disposable Income (4)	Farmers' Share in Personal Disposable Income (5)
1946	21,400	1,083	20,317	160,569	12.7%
1947	22,400	1,462	20,938	170,113	12.3
1948	24,900	1,073	23,827	189,300	12.6
1949	19,900	940	18,911	189,654	10.0
1950	21,000	985	19,774	207,665	9.5
1951	23,700	1,315	22,385	227,481	9.8
1952	23,400	1,501	21,899	238,714	9.2
1953	21,100	1,559	19,641	252,474	7.8
1954	20,200	1,239	18,961	256,885	7.4
1955	19,800	1,232	18,568	274,448	6.8
1956	20,100	1,262	18,838	290,454	6.5
1957	19,700	1,166	18,534	305,149	6.1
1958	21,400	1,420	19,980	310,500	6.4

SOURCE, BY COLUMN

(1) 1946–58: *Economic Report of the President*, Jan. 1959, p. 212.
(2) Covers only motor vehicle license and permit taxes paid (*Agricultural Finance Review*, Department of Agriculture, Sept. 1960, p. 160, as revised and brought up to date by Department of Agriculture) and income taxes (Department of Agriculture estimates). Taxes on farm property have already been deducted in calculation of net income of farm operators. No annual estimates exist of other taxes—e.g., estate and gift taxes—paid by farmers, but the amounts are undoubtedly small. Retail sales taxes paid by farmers are disregarded, since they are also excluded from col. 4.
(3) 1946–58: Col. 1 minus col. 2.
(4) 1946–57: *U.S. Income and Output*, p. 145.
1958: *Economic Report of The President*, Jan. 1959, p. 154.
(5) 1946–58: Col. 3 divided by col. 4.

TABLE B-71

Farmers' Expenditures on Main Types of Consumer Durable Goods, Original Cost
(millions of dollars)

Year	Total (1)	Furniture (2)	Household Appliances (3)	China, Glassware, Tableware, and Utensils (4)	Household Furnishings (5)	Radio, TV, and Musical Instruments (6)	Books and Maps (7)	Passenger Cars (8)	Passenger Car Accessories (9)	Jewelry and Watches (10)	Ophthalmic Products, and Orthopedic Appliances (11)	Miscellaneous (12)
1946	1,738	285	230	160	279	145	75	163	57	191	50	103
1947	2,171	314	391	166	302	176	66	343	64	180	49	120
1948	2,651	350	437	184	342	186	74	656	64	181	54	123
1949	2,975	269	313	141	261	170	63	1,429	64	135	45	85
1950	2,671	292	374	145	284	233	64	935	85	130	46	83
1951	3,018	312	380	160	320	222	76	1,180	80	144	54	90
1952	2,322	312	351	148	270	218	73	579	82	145	53	91
1953	3,053	279	311	131	223	203	65	1,499	84	126	47	85
1954	2,508	265	295	124	212	203	60	1,016	77	125	44	87
1955	2,177	284	319	127	207	190	60	630	93	125	47	95
1956	2,199	288	318	124	217	187	65	630	90	125	33	102
1957	2,330	265	290	116	204	182	63	841	96	116	53	104
1958	2,546	275	301	120	211	189	68	1,007	78	126	58	113

SOURCE, BY COLUMN

(1) Sum of cols. 2 to 12.

(2 to 7) and (10 to 12) Expenditures by individuals on durable goods from *U.S. Income and Output*, pp. 150–151, and *Survey of Current Business*, July 1959, p. 17, split between nonfarmers and farmers according to ratios given in Table B-70, col. 5.

(8) 1946–57: Agricultural Marketing Service estimates. 1958: estimated on basis of percentage change in auto-motive expenditures from *Economic Report of the President*, January 1959, p. 148. Figures represent gross purchases of new cars, i.e., before value of cars traded in are deducted.

(9) Table B-30, col. 3, divided between nonfarmers and farmers according to 1946 ratio given in Table B-70, col. 5.

TABLE B-72

FARMERS' EXPENDITURES ON MAIN TYPES OF CONSUMER DURABLE GOODS, CONSTANT (1947–49) PRICES
(millions of dollars)

Year	Total (1)	Furniture (2)	Household Appliances (3)	China, Glassware, Tableware, and Utensils (4)	Household Furnishings (5)	Radio, TV, and Musical Instruments (6)	Books and Maps (7)	Passenger Cars (8)	Passenger Car Accessories (9)	Jewelry and Watches (10)	Ophthalmic Products and Orthopedic Appliances (11)	Miscellaneous (12)
1946	2,073	335	283	184	340	202	89	211	63	197	56	113
1947	2,279	333	408	172	316	182	72	384	65	175	52	120
1948	2,606	335	424	183	337	177	73	651	64	185	54	123
1949	2,827	266	310	137	254	173	59	1,299	63	138	43	85
1950	2,580	287	376	143	258	256	59	843	91	137	45	85
1951	2,694	280	358	144	249	237	69	1,008	77	140	49	83
1952	2,084	287	334	131	218	251	63	447	77	144	48	84
1953	2,613	257	300	115	181	240	54	1,140	81	124	42	79
1954	2,216	247	294	108	172	254	50	773	74	125	39	80
1955	2,131	270	330	111	159	250	49	611	89	130	42	90
1956	2,007	273	350	102	163	249	52	464	84	130	46	94
1957	2,019	247	325	92	147	235	46	576	87	123	46	95
1958	2,159	258	344	94	152	243	47	661	70	138	50	102

SOURCE, BY COLUMN

(1) Sum of cols. 2 to 12; (2 to 12) Table B-71 deflated by respective price indexes from Table B-33, except passenger cars index from Table B-79.

TABLE B-73

DEPRECIATION ON FARMERS' HOLDINGS OF MAIN TYPES OF CONSUMER DURABLE GOODS, ORIGINAL COST
(millions of dollars)

Year	Total (1)	Furniture (2)	Household Appliances (3)	China, Glassware, Tableware and Utensils (4)	Household Furnishings (5)	Radio, TV, and Musical Instruments (6)	Books and Maps (7)	Passenger Cars (8)	Passenger Car Accessories (9)	Jewelry and Watches (10)	Ophthalmic Products, and Orthopedic Appliances (11)	Miscellaneous (12)
1946	757	111	83	72	138	54	45	97	20	63	39	35
1947	906	129	103	82	157	66	52	125	29	76	43	44
1948	1,112	149	131	94	179	80	58	195	39	87	46	54
1949	1,393	167	154	105	199	93	63	356	49	97	49	61
1950	1,645	181	175	114	217	109	66	502	61	104	49	67
1951	1,867	195	200	123	235	126	68	617	69	112	49	73
1952	2,009	208	223	131	250	140	70	670	70	119	50	78
1953	2,176	221	241	137	258	155	69	758	77	126	50	84
1954	2,331	233	257	142	264	171	68	847	80	132	49	88
1955	2,419	244	277	147	268	187	66	868	82	137	49	94
1956	2,454	254	301	147	266	202	66	849	84	141	48	96
1957	2,447	262	324	143	258	182	65	840	87	142	49	95
1958	2,481	270	325	142	247	189	64	863	87	141	51	102

SOURCE, BY COLUMN

(1) Sum of cols. 2 to 12.

(2 to 12) Depreciation calculated from Table B-71 applying rates given in Table B-31. Expenditures for years before 1946, which were required for estimating depreciation, obtained for the period 1934–45 by the same method, and sources as the later figures. For years before 1934 figures taken from *A Study of Saving . . .*, Vol. I, Table A-24, and related worksheets. Expenditures for passenger cars for all years before 1946 are Agricultural Marketing Service estimates. See Table B-71, col. 8.

TABLE B-74

Depreciation on Farmers' Holdings of Main Types of Consumer Durable Goods, Constant (1947–49) Prices
(millions of dollars)

End of Year	Total (1)	Furniture (2)	Household Appliances (3)	China, Glassware, Tableware, and Utensils (4)	Household Furnishings (5)	Radio, TV, and Musical Instruments (6)	Books and Maps (7)	Passenger Cars (8)	Passenger Car Accessories (9)	Jewelry and Watches (10)	Ophthalmic Products, and Orthopedic Appliances (11)	Miscellaneous (12)
1946	1,174	190	143	104	223	92	58	164	26	81	45	48
1947	1,292	208	161	112	237	104	65	186	22	93	48	56
1948	1,460	226	183	120	250	114	70	246	32	104	51	64
1949	1,682	240	199	127	261	124	72	383	41	113	52	70
1950	1,866	249	213	132	267	136	71	503	51	119	50	75
1951	2,008	255	231	132	270	149	71	590	59	125	48	78
1952	2,077	260	246	135	269	161	68	618	62	130	47	81
1953	2,160	264	255	137	264	175	64	665	65	140	46	85
1954	2,241	268	263	137	258	194	61	715	67	144	45	89
1955	2,278	270	280	137	252	214	58	715	68	147	44	93
1956	2,279	272	305	136	240	226	57	688	69	149	43	94
1957	2,263	272	330	135	222	231	54	665	70	149	43	92
1958	2,261	273	331	135	220	237	51	662	70	149	43	90

Source, by Column

(1) Sum of cols. 2 to 12.

(2 to 12) Depreciation calculated from Table B-72 applying rates given in Table B-31. Expenditures in constant prices for years before 1946, required for the calculation of deprecia- tion, obtained by deflating expenditures in original cost (see note to Table B-73) by appropriate price indexes described in notes to Table B-21.

TABLE B-75

DEPRECIATION ON FARMERS' HOLDINGS OF MAIN TYPES OF CONSUMER DURABLE GOODS, REPLACEMENT COST

(millions of dollars)

Year	Total (1)	Furniture (2)	Household Appliances (3)	China, Glassware, Tableware and Utensils (4)	Household Furnishings (5)	Radio, TV, and Musical Instruments (6)	Books and Maps (7)	Passenger Cars (8)	Passenger Car Accessories (9)	Jewelry and Watches (10)	Ophthalmic Products, and Orthopedic Appliances (11)	Miscellaneous (12)
1946	978	162	116	90	183	66	49	127	23	79	40	43
1947	1,232	196	154	108	227	101	60	166	22	96	46	56
1948	1,488	236	189	121	254	120	71	248	32	102	51	64
1949	1,739	243	201	130	268	122	77	421	42	111	54	70
1950	1,935	253	212	134	293	124	77	558	47	112	52	73
1951	2,289	284	245	147	347	139	78	723	61	128	53	84
1952	2,453	283	259	153	334	140	79	868	66	131	52	88
1953	2,611	286	265	157	326	148	77	997	68	143	52	92
1954	2,729	288	264	157	319	155	74	1,113	70	143	50	96
1955	2,794	284	271	156	328	162	72	1,150	71	141	49	98
1956	2,855	287	277	166	319	170	71	1,153	74	144	50	102
1957	2,913	292	294	170	309	179	73	1,227	77	141	50	101
1958	2,997	291	289	173	305	184	74	1,315	78	139	50	99

SOURCE, BY COLUMN: (1) Sum of cols. 2 to 12; (2 to 12) Table B-74, cols. 2 to 12, multiplied by price indexes from Table B-33.

297

TABLE B-76

Farmers' Net Investment in Main Types of Consumer Durable Goods, Original Cost
(millions of dollars)

Year	Total (1)	Furniture (2)	Household Appliances (3)	China, Glassware, Tableware and Utensils (4)	Household Furnishings (5)	Radio, TV, and Musical Instruments (6)	Books and Maps (7)	Passenger Cars (8)	Passenger Car Accessories (9)	Jewelry and Watches (10)	Ophthalmic Products, and Orthopedic Appliances (11)	Miscellaneous (12)
1946	981	174	147	88	141	91	30	66	37	128	11	68
1947	1,265	185	288	84	145	110	14	218	35	104	6	76
1948	1,439	201	306	90	163	106	16	461	25	94	8	69
1949	1,581	102	159	36	62	77	—	1,073	15	38	−5	24
1950	1,026	111	199	31	67	124	−2	433	24	26	−3	16
1951	1,135	117	180	37	85	96	−8	563	11	32	5	17
1952	310	104	128	17	20	78	3	−91	9	26	3	13
1953	883	58	70	−6	−35	48	−4	741	7	—	−3	1
1954	182	32	38	−18	−52	32	−8	169	3	−7	−6	−1
1955	−62	40	42	−20	−61	3	−6	−58	11	−12	−2	−1
1956	−255	34	17	−23	−49	−15	−1	−219	6	−16	5	6
1957	−117	3	−34	−27	−54	0	−2	1	9	−26	4	9
1958	65	5	−24	−22	−36	0	4	144	−9	−15	7	11

Source, by Column: (1) Sum of cols. 2 to 12; (2 to 12) Table B-71, cols. 2 to 12, minus Table B-73, cols. 2 to 12, respectively.

TABLE B-77

FARMERS' NET INVESTMENT IN MAIN TYPES OF CONSUMER DURABLE GOODS, CONSTANT (1947–49) PRICES
(millions of dollars)

Year	Total (1)	Furniture (2)	Household Appliances (3)	China, Glassware, Tableware and Utensils (4)	Household Furnishings (5)	Radio, TV, and Musical Instruments (6)	Books and Maps (7)	Passenger Cars (8)	Passenger Car Accessories (9)	Jewelry and Watches (10)	Ophthalmic Products, and Orthopedic Appliances (11)	Miscellaneous (12)
1946	899	145	140	80	117	110	31	47	37	116	11	65
1947	987	125	247	60	79	78	7	198	43	82	4	64
1948	1,141	109	241	63	87	63	3	405	32	81	3	59
1949	1,145	26	111	10	−7	9	−13	916	12	25	−9	15
1950	714	38	163	11	−9	20	−12	340	40	18	−5	10
1951	686	25	127	12	−21	8	−2	418	18	15	1	5
1952	−3	27	88	−4	−51	90	−5	−171	15	14	1	3
1953	453	−7	45	−22	−83	65	−10	475	16	−16	−4	−6
1954	−25	−21	31	−29	−86	60	−11	58	7	−19	−6	−9
1955	−147	0	50	−26	−93	36	−9	−104	21	−17	−2	−3
1956	−272	1	45	−34	−77	23	−5	−224	15	−19	3	0
1957	−245	−25	−5	−43	−75	4	−8	−89	17	−26	3	3
1958	−102	−15	13	−41	−68	6	−4	−1	—	−11	7	12

SOURCE, BY COLUMN: (1) Sum of cols. 2 to 12; (2 to 12) Table B-72, cols. 2 to 12, minus Table B-74, cols. 2 to 12, respectively.

TABLE B-78

Farmers' Net Investment in Main Types of Consumer Durable Goods, Replacement Cost

(millions of dollars)

Year	Total (1)	Furniture (2)	Household Appliances (3)	China, Glassware, Tableware and Utensils (4)	Household Furnishings (5)	Radio, TV, and Musical Instruments (6)	Books and Maps (7)	Passenger Cars (8)	Passenger Car Accessories (9)	Jewelry and Watches (10)	Ophthalmic Products, and Orthopedic Appliances (11)	Miscellaneous (12)
1946	759	123	114	70	96	79	26	36	34	12	9	60
1947	939	118	237	58	75	75	6	177	42	84	3	64
1948	1,163	114	248	63	88	66	3	408	32	79	3	39
1949	1,236	26	112	11	−7	48	−14	1,008	22	24	−9	15
1950	736	39	162	11	−9	109	−13	77	38	18	−6	10
1951	729	28	135	13	−27	83	−2	457	19	16	1	6
1952	−131	29	92	−5	−64	78	−6	89	16	14	1	3
1953	442	−7	46	−26	−103	55	−12	502	16	−17	−5	−07
1954	−221	−23	31	−33	−107	48	−14	−97	7	−18	−6	−09
1955	−445	—	48	−29	−121	28	−12	−340	22	−16	−2	−03
1956	−368	1	41	−42	−102	17	−6	−523	16	−19	3	—
1957	−529	27	−4	−54	−105	3	−10	−386	19	−25	3	3
1958	−451	−16	12	−53	−94	5	−6	−308	—	−13	8	14

Source, by Column: (1) Sum of cols. 2 to 12; (2 to 12) Table B-71, cols. 2 to 12, minus Table B-75, cols. 2 to 12, respectively.

TABLE B-79

PRICE INDEXES OF AGRICULTURAL DURABLE GOODS
(1947–49 = 100.0)

Year	Construction		Farm Machinery (3)	Tractors (4)	Automobiles		Trucks (7)	Farm Supplies (8)
	Dwellings (1)	Service Buildings (2)			New (5)	Used (6)		
1946	76.0	77.7	76.3	76.5	77.4	80.6	82.6	87.8
1947	96.0	94.8	86.3	89.6	89.3	95.3	92.3	94.6
1948	104.0	103.4	100.6	100.4	100.7	112.2	102.2	100.6
1949	100.0	101.7	113.1	110.0	110.0	92.6	105.4	104.8
1950	102.0	103.4	115.2	111.2	110.9	87.8	104.9	105.3
1951	112.4	115.5	124.4	119.5	117.1	105.2	112.0	112.5
1952	113.6	118.0	129.1	118.3	129.6	120.0	117.9	119.3
1953	114.4	118.5	130.3	115.9	131.5	122.0	117.6	116.7
1954	114.0	118.0	130.7	117.1	131.4	122.2	118.2	112.5
1955	116.4	120.2	130.7	119.5	132.5	123.2	119.1	110.4
1956	120.2	125.1	136.6	124.4	135.8	126.3	122.1	110.8
1957	122.8	129.6	143.3	133.9	146.1	135.9	131.4	111.6
1958	123.9	131.5	149.6	139.7	152.4	141.7	137.1	112.5

SOURCE, BY COLUMN

(1 and 2) 1946–58: Agricultural Marketing Service, Department of Agriculture, index (unpublished) of farm construction cost.

(3) 1946–58: *Agricultural Prices*, Agricultural Marketing Service, Jan. 31, 1956, p. 44; March 1959; June 1959 (index converted to 1947–49 base).

(4) 1946–55: Index constructed from average prices paid by farmers given in *Agricultural Prices*, Nov. 30, 1955, p. 18; Jan. 31, 1956. p. 43.

1956: From *ibid.*, Jan. 15, 1957, p. 37.

1957–58: Extrapolated by motor vehicles index.

(5 to 7) 1946–54: Derived from Agricultural Marketing Service (unpublished) estimates of current and deflated expenditures.

1955: Extrapolated from 1954 by index of prices paid by farmers for motor vehicles given in *Agricultural Prices*, Jan. 1956, p. 44.

1956–58: Same method as for 1955 using index in *ibid.*, Jan. 15, 1957, p. 38, and unpublished figures.

(8) 1946–58: Same source as for col. 3.

TABLE B-80

VALUE OF FARM BUILDINGS

(millions of dollars)

Year	Original Cost			1947–49 Prices			Current Prices		
	Total (1)	Dwellings (2)	Service Buildings (3)	Total (4)	Dwellings (5)	Service Buildings (6)	Total (7)	Dwellings (8)	Service Buildings (9)
1945	9,495	4,960	4,535	21,765	12,416	9,349	15,995	9,039	6,956
1946	10,201	5,221	4,980	21,989	12,531	9,458	18,930	10,777	8,153
1947	11,229	5,748	5,481	22,553	12,813	9,740	22,465	12,813	9,652
1948	12,379	6,319	6,060	23,127	13,086	10,041	23,650	13,348	10,302
1949	13,447	6,836	6,611	23,673	13,337	10,336	24,075	13,470	10,605
1950	14,635	7,410	7,225	24,432	13,634	10,686	26,305	14,615	11,690
1951	16,004	8,071	7,933	25,011	13,945	11,066	28,683	15,758	12,925
1952	17,399	8,746	8,653	25,679	14,264	11,415	29,754	16,261	13,493
1953	18,589	9,327	9,262	26,174	14,500	11,674	30,358	16,559	13,799
1954	19,664	9,856	9,808	26,590	14,698	11,892	31,095	16,932	14,163
1955	20,668	10,355	10,313	26,931	14,860	12,071	32,399	17,588	14,811
1956	21,605	10,822	10,783	27,184	14,980	12,204	33,734	18,186	15,548
1957	22,547	11,292	11,255	27,421	15,095	12,326	34,544	18,446	16,098
1958	23,473	11,757	11,716	27,645	15,205	12,440	35,376	18,930	16,446

SOURCE, BY COLUMN

(1) Sum of cols. 2 and 3.

(2 and 3) Derived by addition of cumulated net investment, original cost, to estimated value for 1945, obtained by cumulating expenditures less depreciation for number of years preceding 1945, corresponding to the assumed length of life of asset involved (see Tables B-60 and B-61).

(4) Sum of cols. 5 and 6.

(5 and 6) Same procedure as for cols 2 and 3, but expenditures in 1947–49 prices used.

(7) Sum of cols. 8 and 9.

(8 and 9) Cumulated depreciated capital expenditures in 1947–49 prices, multiplied by appropriate price index of Table B-79 (figures averaged to obtain year-end index).

302

TABLE B-81

VALUE OF FARM MACHINERY AND TRACTORS
(millions of dollars)

End of Year	Farm Machinery			Tractors		
	Original Cost (1)	1947–49 Prices (2)	Current Prices (3)	Original Cost (4)	1947–49 Prices (5)	Current Prices (6)
1945	2,911	4,195	3,146	1,626	2,478	1,829
1946	3,062	4,348	3,535	1,693	2,526	2,097
1947	3,502	4,798	4,481	1,947	2,737	2,600
1948	4,229	5,414	5,782	2,378	3,069	3,229
1949	4,976	5,920	6,761	2,869	3,398	3,758
1950	5,660	6,364	7,624	3,320	3,687	4,255
1951	6,393	6,756	8,567	3,764	3,929	4,672
1952	7,027	7,050	9,144	4,117	4,111	4,814
1953	7,447	7,183	9,243	4,400	4,255	4,957
1954	7,699	7,197	9,406	4,498	4,241	5,017
1955	7,876	7,162	9,576	4,685	4,301	5,247
1956	9,911	6,995	9,793	4,684	4,198	5,424
1957	7,888	6,775	9,925	4,664	4,066	5,562
1958	8,155	6,738	10,275	4,772	4,023	5,730

SOURCE, BY COLUMN

(1 and 4) Derived by addition of cumulated net investment, original cost, to estimated value for 1945, obtained by cumulating expenditures less depreciation for number of years preceding 1945 corresponding to the assumed length of life of asset involved (see Tables B-64 and B-65).

(2 and 5) Same procedure as for cols. 1 and 4, but expenditures in 1947–49 prices used.

(3 and 6) Cumulated depreciated capital expenditures in 1947–49 prices multiplied by appropriate price index from Table B-79 (figures averaged to obtain year-end index).

TABLE B-82

VALUE OF FARM TRUCKS AND PASSENGER CARS
(millions of dollars)

End of Year	Trucks (new and used)			Passenger Cars (new and used)		
	Original Cost (1)	1947–49 Prices (2)	Current Prices (3)	Original Cost (4)	1947–49 Prices (5)	Current Prices (6)
1945	385	469	399	554	875	676
1946	466	564	493	635	917	778
1947	768	876	852	908	1,137	1,108
1948	1,103	1,174	1,219	1,389	1,517	1,590
1949	1,413	1,424	1,498	2,332	2,135	2,359
1950	1,640	1,624	1,760	3,060	2,830	3,166
1951	1,803	1,730	1,990	3,644	3,189	3,904
1952	1,853	1,723	2,030	3,667	3,079	3,988
1953	1,924	1,717	2,048	4,408	3,520	4,596
1954	1,979	1,747	2,074	4,594	3,545	4,654
1955	1,860	1,701	2,051	4,765	3,592	4,780
1956	1,879	1,638	2,077	4,713	3,445	4,807
1957	1,980	1,622	2,179	4,828	3,383	4,992
1958	2,155	1,598	2,237	5,085	3,395	5,247

SOURCE: Same procedure as for Table B-81, using basic figures from Tables B-66, B-67, B-68, B-76, B-77, and B-78.

TABLE B-83

VALUE OF FARM CAPITAL EXPENDITURES CHARGED TO CURRENT EXPENSE
(millions of dollars)

End of Year	Original Cost (1)	1947–49 Prices (2)	Current Prices (3)
1945	368	479	419
1946	375	470	429
1947	386	463	452
1948	393	450	462
1949	396	433	455
1950	393	413	450
1951	388	390	452
1952	376	361	426
1953	368	340	390
1954	362	325	362
1955	359	317	351
1956	359	313	348
1957	359	310	348
1958	362	311	351

SOURCE, BY COLUMN

(1) Derived by addition of cumulated net investment, original cost, to estimated value for 1945 (see Table B-69).
(2) Same procedure as for col. 1, but applied to expenditures in 1947–49 prices.
(3) Col. 2 multiplied by year-end index of farm supplies, obtained by averaging successive years from Table B-79, col. 8.

TABLE B-84
VALUE OF FARMERS' HOLDINGS OF MAIN TYPES OF CONSUMER DURABLE GOODS, ORIGINAL COST
(millions of dollars)

End of Year	Total (1)	Furniture (2)	Household Appliances (3)	China, Glassware, Tableware, and Utensils (4)	Household Furnishings (5)	Radio, TV, and Musical Instruments (6)	Books and Maps (7)	Passenger Cars (8)	Passenger Car Accessories (9)	Jewelry and Watches (10)	Ophthalmic Products and Orthopedic Appliances (11)	Miscellaneous (12)
1945	4,041	965	415	363	724	249	142	335	43	554	77	174
1946	5,002	1,139	542	451	865	340	172	401	80	682	88	242
1947	6,267	1,324	830	535	1,010	450	186	619	115	786	94	318
1948	7,786	1,525	1,136	625	1,173	556	202	1,080	130	870	102	387
1949	9,387	1,627	1,295	661	1,235	633	202	2,153	155	918	97	411
1950	10,413	1,738	1,494	692	1,302	757	200	2,586	179	944	94	427
1951	11,564	1,855	1,674	729	1,387	853	208	3,149	190	976	99	444
1952	11,874	1,959	1,802	746	1,497	931	211	3,058	199	1,002	102	457
1953	12,751	2,017	1,872	740	1,372	979	207	3,799	206	1,002	99	458
1954	12,933	2,049	1,910	722	1,320	1,011	199	3,968	209	995	93	457
1955	12,871	2,089	1,952	702	1,259	1,014	193	3,910	220	983	91	458
1956	12,616	2,123	1,969	679	1,210	999	192	3,691	226	967	96	464
1957	12,499	2,126	1,935	652	1,156	999	190	3,692	235	941	100	473
1958	12,564	2,131	1,911	630	1,120	999	194	3,836	226	926	107	484

SOURCE, BY COLUMN: (1) Sum of cols. 2 to 12; (2 to 12) Derived by addition of cumulated net investment, original cost (Table B-76), to estimated value for 1945, obtained by cumulating expenditures less depreciation for number of years preceding 1945 corresponding to the assumed length of life of asset.

TABLE B-85

Value of Farmers' Holdings of Main Types of Consumer Durable Goods, Constant (1947–49) Prices

(millions of dollars)

End of Year	Total (1)	Furniture (2)	Household Appliances (3)	China, Glassware, Tableware, and Utensils (4)	Household Furnishings (5)	Radio, TV, and Musical Instruments (6)	Books and Maps (7)	Passenger Cars (8)	Passenger Car Accessories (9)	Jewelry and Watches (10)	Ophthalmic Products, and Orthopedic Appliances (11)	Miscellaneous (12)
1945	6,205	1,603	718	511	1,134	422	184	579	56	678	88	232
1946	7,104	1,748	858	591	1,251	532	215	626	93	794	99	297
1947	8,091	1,873	1,105	651	1,330	610	222	824	136	876	103	361
1948	9,237	1,982	1,346	714	1,417	673	225	1,229	168	957	106	420
1949	10,382	2,008	1,457	724	1,410	722	212	2,145	190	982	97	435
1950	11,096	2,046	1,620	735	1,401	842	200	2,485	230	1,000	92	445
1951	11,782	2,071	1,747	747	1,380	930	198	2,903	248	1,015	93	450
1952	11,789	2,098	1,835	743	1,329	1,020	193	2,732	263	1,029	94	453
1953	12,242	2,091	1,880	721	1,246	1,085	183	3,207	279	1,013	90	447
1954	12,217	2,070	1,911	692	1,160	1,145	172	3,265	286	994	84	438
1955	12,070	2,070	1,961	666	1,067	1,181	163	3,161	307	977	82	435
1956	11,798	2,071	2,006	632	990	1,204	158	2,937	322	958	85	435
1957	11,554	2,046	2,001	589	915	1,208	150	2,848	339	932	88	438
1958	11,452	2,031	2,014	548	847	1,214	146	2,847	339	921	95	450

Source, by Column: (1) Sum of cols. 2 to 12; (2 to 12) Same procedure as for Table B-84, but applied to expenditures in 1947–49 prices (see Tables B-72, B-73, and B-74).

TABLE B-86

VALUE OF FARMERS' HOLDINGS OF MAIN TYPES OF CONSUMER DURABLE GOODS, CURRENT PRICES

(millions of dollars)

End of Year	Total (1)	Furniture (2)	Household Appliances (3)	China, Glassware, Tableware, and Utensils (4)	Household Furnishings (5)	Radio, TV, and Musical Instruments (6)	Books and Maps (7)	Passenger Cars (8)	Passenger Car Accessories (9)	Jewelry and Watches (10)	Ophthalmic Products, and Orthopedic Appliances (11)	Miscellaneous (12)
1945	5,018	1,302	551	425	870	298	151	430	50	658	79	204
1946	6,564	1,608	775	553	1,177	442	193	522	89	826	91	288
1947	8,051	1,879	1,123	643	1,321	638	210	783	132	867	101	354
1948	9,607	2,089	1,411	741	1,467	695	240	1,295	175	957	109	428
1949	10,516	1,980	1,442	734	1,455	673	228	2,368	181	928	101	426
1950	12,081	2,247	1,693	778	1,757	806	217	2,833	225	977	98	450
1951	13,276	2,291	1,859	852	1,743	826	223	3,582	263	1,037	104	496
1952	13,242	2,264	1,912	843	1,641	875	234	3,568	274	1,040	104	487
1953	13,814	2,252	1,935	836	1,535	894	221	4,214	293	1,044	103	489
1954	13,559	2,207	1,877	786	1,478	879	211	4,310	297	954	94	466
1955	13,314	2,161	1,816	790	1,400	886	202	4,242	319	941	93	464
1956	13,279	2,222	1,803	793	1,355	916	198	4,141	353	921	99	478
1957	13,233	2,195	1,761	756	1,289	954	216	4,249	377	880	102	482
1958	13,239	2,167	1,750	703	1,166	948	212	4,464	378	843	111	497

SOURCE, BY COLUMN: (1) Sum of cols. 2 to 12; (2 to 12) Cumulated depreciated capital expenditures in 1947–49 prices (Table B-85) multiplied by appropriate price index from Table B-33 (year-end average).

TABLE B-87
LIVESTOCK INVENTORIES: NUMBER OF HEAD ON FARMS
(thousands)

End of Year	All Cattle (1)	Milk Cows, 2 Years and Older (2)	Other Cattle (3)	Hogs (4)	Horses (5)	Mules (6)	All Sheep (7)	Stock Sheep (8)	Sheep and Lambs on Feed (9)	Chickens (10)	Turkeys (11)
1945	82,235	26,521	55,714	61,306	8,081	3,027	42,362	35,525	6,837	523,227	7,862
1946	80,554	25,842	54,712	56,810	7,340	2,789	37,498	31,805	5,693	467,217	5,879
1947	77,171	24,615	52,556	54,590	6,704	2,575	34,337	29,486	4,851	449,644	3,959
1948	76,830	23,862	52,968	56,257	6,096	2,402	30,943	26,940	4,003	430,876	4,622
1949	77,963	23,853	54,110	58,937	5,548	2,233	29,826	26,182	3,644	456,549	5,124
1950	82,083	23,568	58,515	62,269	7,036		30,633	27,251	3,382	430,988	5,037
1951	88,072	23,060	65,012	62,117	6,150		31,982	27,944	4,038	426,555	5,725
1952	94,241	23,549	70,692	51,755	5,403		31,900	27,593	4,307	398,158	5,086
1953	95,679	23,896	71,783	45,114	4,791		31,356	27,079	4,277	396,776	4,956
1954	96,592	23,462	73,130	50,474	4,309		31,582	27,137	4,445	390,708	4,917
1955	96,804	23,213	73,591	55,173	3,928		31,273	27,012	4,261	382,846	4,923
1956	94,502	22,916	71,586	51,703	3,574		30,840	26,538	4,302	390,137	5,799
1957	93,350	22,233	71,117	50,980	3,354		31,337	27,327	4,010	370,884	5,542
1958	96,851	21,606	75,245	57,201	3,079		32,644	28,364	4,280	383,257	5,861

SOURCE, BY COLUMN

Livestock inventory data published by the Department of Agriculture for January 1 are used here for December 31 of previous year. Cols. 2 and 3 are subclasses of col. 1; cols. 8 and 9 are subclasses of col. 7.

(1 and 2) 1945–58: *Livestock and Poultry Inventory, January 1,* Agricultural Marketing Service, released Feb. 13, 1956, p. 9, *Balance Sheet of Agriculture,* e.g., 1959, p. 14.

(3) 1945–58: Col. 1 minus col. 2.

(4) 1945–58: Same source as for col. 1.

(5 and 6) 1945–49: *Livestock and Poultry on Farms and Ranches,*
(7 and 9) 1950–58: *January 1,* Agricultural Marketing Service, released Feb. 14, 1955, p. 9.

1945–49: Same source as for col. 1. *Livestock and Poultry on Farms and Ranches, January 1,* Bureau of Agricultural Economics, Statistical Bull. no. 106, Feb. 1952, p. 2.

(8, 10, and 11) 1950–58: *Livestock and Poultry Inventory, January 1,* released Feb. 13, 1956, p. 10; *Balance sheet of Agriculture,* 1959, p. 14.

1945–58: Same source as for col. 1.

TABLE B-88

LIVESTOCK INVENTORIES: PRICE PER HEAD ON FARMS

(dollars)

End of Year	All Cattle (1)	Milk Cows, 2 Years and Older (2)	Other Cattle (3)	Hogs (4)	Horses (5)	Mules (6)	All Sheep (7)	Stock Sheep (8)	Sheep and Lambs on Feed (9)	Chickens (10)	Turkeys (11)
1945	76.20	112.00	59.00	24.00	57.50	133.00	9.69	9.57	10.30	1.27	5.75
1946	97.50	145.00	75.00	36.00	59.30	141.00	12.60	12.20	14.70	1.44	6.54
1947	117.00	164.00	94.40	42.90	55.70	133.00	15.40	15.00	17.70	1.44	6.97
1948	135.00	193.00	108.90	38.30	52.50	116.00	17.20	17.00	18.30	1.66	8.80
1949	124.00	177.00	100.00	27.10	46.00	99.10	17.80	17.80	18.10	1.36	6.34
1950	160.00	219.00	137.10	33.30	54.60		26.40	26.50	25.70	1.46	6.48
1951	179.00	252.00	153.10	29.90	53.90		27.80	28.00	26.50	1.53	6.99
1952	128.00	203.00	102.90	26.10	53.00		15.80	15.70	16.30	1.41	6.15
1953	92.00	147.00	73.70	36.60	52.90		13.90	13.80	14.50	1.43	6.32
1954	88.20	134.00	73.40	30.60	56.20		14.90	14.90	15.10	1.05	5.33
1955	88.00	139.00	72.07	17.70	62.60		14.26	14.30	14.32	1.26	5.50
1956	91.60	147.00	73.91	24.70	71.60		14.98	14.90	15.22	1.17	5.05
1957	119.00	176.00	102.00	30.20	83.90		19.22	19.40	18.20	1.26	4.67
1958	153.00	220.00	134.00	31.90	101.00		20.05	20.30	18.95	1.26	4.65

SOURCE, BY COLUMN

(1 and 2) 1945–58: *Livestock and Poultry Inventory, January 1,* Agricultural Marketing Service, released Feb. 13, 1956, p. 9; *The Balance Sheet of Agriculture,* e.g. 1959, p. 4.

(3) 1945–58: Table B-89, col. 4, divided by Table B-87, col. 3 (rounded).

(4) 1945–58: Same source as for col. 1.

(5 and 6) 1945–49: *Livestock and Poultry on Farms and Ranches, January 1,* Agricultural Marketing Service, released Feb. 14, 1955, p. 9.

(7) 1945–49: *Agricultural Statistics,* 1954, p. 335.
1950–58: Table B-89, col. 8, divided by Table B-87, col. 7.

(8) 1945–58: Same source as col. 1.

(9) 1945–49: *Agricultural Statistics,* 1954, p. 335.
1950–58: Table B-89, col. 10, divided by Table B-87, col. 9.

(10 and 11) 1945–58: Same source as for col. 1.

TABLE B-89

LIVESTOCK INVENTORIES; VALUE ON FARMS, CURRENT PRICES

(millions of dollars)

End of Year (1)	Total (1)	All Cattle (2)	Milk Cows 2 Years and Older (3)	Other Cattle (4)	Hogs (5)	Horses (6)	Mules (7)	All Sheep (8)	Stock Sheep (9)	Sheep and Lambs on Feed (10)	Chickens (11)	Turkeys (12)
1945	9,717	6,263	2,977	3,286	1,468	464	403	411	340	70	663	45
1946	11,916	7,858	3,754	4,104	2,046	435	392	473	389	84	673	38
1947	13,257	8,999	4,038	4,961	2,340	374	342	527	442	86	648	28
1948	14,426	10,382	4,615	5,767	2,154	320	280	532	459	73	716	41
1949	12,892	9,630	4,219	5,411	1,600	255	221	532	466	66	623	32
1950	17,099	13,174	5,152	8,022	2,073	384		808	722	87	627	33
1951	19,527	15,752	5,801	9,951	1,860	332		890	783	107	653	40
1952	14,778	12,045	4,769	7,276	1,350	286		504	434	70	562	31
1953	11,745	8,804	3,511	5,293	1,649	253		437	375	62	569	31
1954	11,210	8,517	3,148	5,369	1,542	242		471	404	67	411	26
1955	10,702	8,524	3,220	5,304	978	246		446	385	61	481	27
1956	11,132	8,653	3,366	5,287	1,275	256		462	396	66	457	29
1957	14,070	11,154	3,909	7,245	1,538	282		602	529	73	468	26
1958	18,111	14,809	4,744	10,065	1,826	312		655	574	81	482	27

SOURCE, BY COLUMN

(1) 1945–49: *Agricultural Statistics*, 1954, p. 432.
1950–52: Sum of cols. 2, 5 to 8, 11, and 12.
1953–55: *Livestock and Poultry Inventory, January 1*, Agricultural Marketing Service, released Feb. 13, 1956, p. 2.
1956–58: *The Balance Sheet of Agriculture*, e.g. 1958, p. 11.

(2 and 3) 1945–58: Same source as for col. 1.
(4) 1945–58: Col. 2 minus col. 3.
(5) 1945–58: Same source as for col. 1.
(6 and 7) 1945–49: *Livestock and Poultry on Farms and Ranches, January 1*, Agricultural Marketing Service, released–Feb. 14, 1955, p. 9.

(8) 1950–58: Same source as for col. 1.
1945–50: *Agricultural Statistics*, 1954, p. 335.
1951–52: Sum of cols. 9 and 10.
1953–55: *Livestock and Poultry Inventory, January 1*, released Feb. 13, 1956, p. 2, and Feb. 14, 1957, p. 9.

(9) 1956–58: Same source as for col. 1.
1945–58: Same source as for col. 1.
(10) 1945–52: *Agricultural Statistics*, 1954, p. 335.
1953–58: Col. 8 minus col. 9.

(11 and 12) 1945–58: Same source as for col. 1.

TABLE B-90

LIVESTOCK INVENTORIES: VALUE ON FARMS, CONSTANT (1947–49) PRICES

(millions of dollars)

End of Year	Total (1)	All Cattle (2)	Milk Cows 2 Years and Older (3)	Other Cows (4)	Hogs (5)	Horses (6)	Mules (7)	All Sheep (8)	Stock Sheep (9)	Sheep and Lambs on Feed (10)	Chickens (11)	Turkeys (12)
1945	14,884	10,354	4,721	5,633	2,213	415	351	713	590	123	780	58
1946	14,253	10,131	4,600	5,531	2,051	377	324	631	528	103	696	43
1947	13,586	9,694	4,381	5,313	1,971	345	299	578	490	88	670	29
1948	13,420	9,602	4,247	5,355	2,031	313	279	519	447	72	642	34
1949	13,608	9,717	4,246	5,471	2,128	285	259	501	435	66	680	38
1950	14,041	10,111	4,195	5,916	2,248	490		513	452	61	642	37
1951	14,564	10,678	4,105	6,573	2,242	429		537	464	73	636	42
1952	14,750	11,339	4,192	7,147	1,868	377		536	458	78	593	37
1953	14,628	11,510	4,253	7,257	1,629	334		527	450	77	591	37
1954	14,839	11,569	4,176	7,393	1,822	300		530	450	80	582	36
1955	14,969	11,572	4,132	7,440	1,992	274		525	448	77	570	36
1956	14,573	11,316	4,079	7,237	1,886	248		519	441	78	581	43
1957	14,342	11,147	3,957	7,190	1,841	234		526	454	72	553	41
1958	14,895	11,453	3,846	7,607	2,065	215		548	471	77	571	43

SOURCE, BY COLUMN

(1) Sum of cols. 2, 5 to 8, 11, and 12.
(2) Sum of cols. 3 and 4.
(3 to 7) Table B-87, cols. 2 to 7, multiplied by the 1947–49 price from Table B-88 (for horses and mules combined, the 1947–49 price is $69.70).
(8) Sum of cols. 9 and 10.
(9 to 12) Table B-87, cols. 8 to 11, multiplied by the 1947–49 price from Table B-88.

TABLE B-91

Value of Farm Land and Buildings
(millions of dollars)

Year	Land and Buildings		Buildings (3)	Land (4)
	March 1 (1)	December 31 (2)		
1945	53,854	59,790	16,320	43,470
1946	60,980	67,138	19,329	47,809
1947	68,373	72,711	22,938	49,773
1948	73,581	76,068	24,143	51,925
1949	76,566	75,475	24,571	50,904
1950	75,256	85,231	26,836	58,395
1951	87,231	95,564	29,254	66,310
1952	97,235	97,235	30,341	66,894
1953	97,235	95,162	30,946	64,216
1954	94,747	98,101	31,689	66,412
1955	98,774	102,024	33,012	69,012
1956	102,675	108,334	34,368	73,966
1957	109,469	115,133	35,190	79,943
1958	116,268	123,613	36,031	87,582
1959	125,086	—	—	—

Source, by Column

(1)   1945–56:   Department of Agriculture estimates.
      1957–59:   From "Balance Sheet of Agriculture," *Federal Reserve Bulletin*, e.g., Aug.
                 1958, p. 894.
(2)   Straight-line interpolation of figures in col. 1 (83.3% of first differences).
(3)   Table B-63, col. 11, plus Table B-80, col. 7.
(4)   Col. 2 minus col. 3.

TABLE B-92

CROP INVENTORIES: QUANTITY ON FARMS

End of Year	Corn	Wheat	Oats (thousand bushels)	Barley	Rye	Buckwheat	Tobacco (million pounds)	Peanuts
	(1)	(2)	(3)	(4)	(5)	(6)	(7)	(8)
1945	1,846,882	342,175	970,272	125,966	6,476	593	583	207
1946	2,111,821	356,180	882,805	110,060	3,864	841	810	206
1947	1,486,209	417,732	723,218	117,107	7,058	737	459	224
1948	2,394,651	333,831	906,456	155,519	8,605	709	479	258
1949	1,821,854	240,495	784,655	104,999	4,566	454	499	103
1950	1,905,943	276,529	879,673	139,818	6,779	417	463	155
1951	1,846,656	273,079	845,476	124,046	6,472	257	441	162
1952	2,068,135	328,726	786,560	98,680	3,649	304	494	137
1953	1,913,544	268,383	773,516	108,490	6,662	286	444	26
1954	1,927,083	201,718	920,789	165,195	9,582	455	448	37
1955	2,016,108	238,140	981,205	189,510	14,048	234	348	54
1956	2,129,304	225,921	696,376	159,561	7,280	265	309	121

(continued)

TABLE B-92 (concluded)

End of Year	Hay (thousand tons) (9)	Cotton Lint (million pounds) (10)	Potatoes (11)	Soybeans (thousand bushels) (12)	Flaxseed (13)	Sorghum Grain (14)	Rice (thousand cwt.) (15)	Dry Edible Beans (16)	Cotton Seed (thousand tons) (17)
1945	73,424	1,124	87,300	43,620	8,634	34,576	4,905	2,306	314
1946	68,836	1,322	117,900	37,908	4,955	44,754	4,138	2,467	190
1947	68,172	1,226	104,100	51,761	10,940	28,530	5,541	5,549	188
1948	65,040	1,593	101,300	75,013	8,756	53,685	9,204	8,144	279
1949	66,298	1,379	126,000	61,959	12,217	60,446	6,815	5,398	251
1950	69,720	644	155,300	101,728	10,942	78,286	6,331	4,763	170
1951	73,088	1,803	89,700	104,167	11,650	52,474	9,242	5,357	386
1952	68,126	2,151	107,200	83,621	9,424	23,803	4,860	5,200	215
1953	69,603	1,499	125,500	82,000	16,240	36,281	10,208	5,954	248
1954	72,667	1,315	120,300	149,000	15,608	54,733	17,761	6,718	152
1955	73,940	1,252	128,000	116,000	16,530	68,058	10,009	6,171	152
1956	73,489	1,115	77,800	168,949	21,976	58,686	11,856	6,060	81

SOURCE, BY COLUMN

(1 and 2) 1945–56: Excluding amounts stored on farms under Commodity Credit Corporation loan. (Table B-96, col. 1, minus col. 3, and col. 2 minus col. 4, respectively.)

(3 and 4) 1945–49: *Farm Stocks of Grains, Oilseeds, and Hay, Revised Estimates 1944–51*, Bureau of Agricultural Economics, Apr. 1952, pp. 1 and 2.

1950, 1951: *Stocks of Feed Grains*, Bureau of Agricultural Economics, Jan. 1, 1953, issued Jan. 23, 1953.

1952, 1953: *Stocks of Grains in All Positions*, Agricultural Marketing Service, Jan. 1, 1955, issued Jan. 21, 1955.

1954, 1956: *Ibid.*, Jan. 1, 1956, issued Jan. 23, 1956, and later issues.

(5) 1945–49: Same source as for col. 3.

1950, 1951: *Stocks of Wheat and Rye*, Bureau of Agricultural Economics, Jan. 1, 1953, issued Jan. 23, 1953.

1952–56: Same source as for col. 3.

(6 to 11) 1945–56: Department of Agriculture estimates.

(12) 1945–49: *Agricultural Statistics*, 1952, p. 160.

1950–53: *Ibid.*, 1954, p. 127.

1954, 1956: Department of Agriculture estimates.

(13) 1945, 1946: Department of Agriculture estimates.

1947–49: *Agricultural Statistics*, 1952, p. 150.

1950–53: *Ibid.*, 1954, p. 116.

1954, 1956: Department of Agriculture estimates.

(14) 1945–56: Same source as for col. 3.

(15 to 17) 1945–56: Department of Agriculture estimates.

NOTE: Crop.inventory data published by Department of Agriculture for Jan. 1 are used here for Dec. 31 of previous year.

TABLE B-93

CROP INVENTORIES: PRICE PER UNIT ON FARMS

(dollars)

End of Year	Corn	Wheat	Oats (per bushel)	Barley	Rye	Buckwheat	Tobacco (per pound)	Peanuts	Hay (per ton)
	(1)	(2)	(3)	(4)	(5)	(6)	(7)	(8)	(9)
1945	1.09	1.54	0.703	1.08	1.43	1.240	0.438	0.0833	19.50
1946	1.22	1.93	0.808	1.36	2.18	1.450	0.435	0.0889	21.90
1947	2.37	2.79	1.180	2.00	2.45	2.010	0.469	0.1010	23.00
1948	1.23	2.05	0.765	1.13	1.47	1.100	0.457	0.1050	23.80
1949	1.13	1.93	0.699	1.09	1.26	0.902	0.454	0.1040	21.90
1950	1.45	2.02	0.849	1.19	1.38	1.070	0.472	0.1090	21.80
1951	1.68	2.22	0.949	1.38	1.73	1.430	0.512	0.1030	24.40
1952	1.50	2.12	0.842	1.41	1.73	1.390	0.496	0.1100	26.40
1953	1.41	2.01	0.767	1.15	1.20	0.851	0.492	0.1100	23.00
1954	1.39	2.12	0.767	1.09	1.14	1.040	0.500	0.1250	23.30
1955	1.15	1.95	0.626	0.92	0.94	1.250	0.572	0.1190	21.30
1956	1.22	2.07	0.744	1.03	1.20	1.220	0.610	0.1100	22.70

(continued)

TABLE B-93 (concluded)

End of Year	Cotton Lint (per pound) (10)	Potatoes (cwt.) (11)	Soybeans (per bushel) (12)	Flaxseed (13)	Sorghum Grain (14)	Rice (per 100 pounds) (15)	Dry Edible Beans (16)	Cotton Seed (per ton) (17)
1945	0.2279	1.250	2.09	2.89	2.11	3.96	6.53	51.40
1946	1.2997	1.120	2.75	6.92	1.97	5.13	12.70	91.50
1947	0.3404	1.620	3.69	6.66	3.61	6.42	12.10	94.80
1948	0.2963	1.440	2.36	5.75	2.19	5.36	7.77	68.80
1949	0.2646	1.220	2.09	3.53	1.79	4.37	6.52	43.30
1950	0.4005	0.734	2.70	3.59	1.88	5.26	7.69	102.00
1951	0.4015	1.820	2.83	4.24	2.51	4.90	8.11	71.50
1952	0.3171	1.850	2.75	3.75	2.84	6.25	8.45	68.50
1953	0.3073	0.698	2.81	3.66	2.21	5.34	8.31	53.00
1954	0.3267	1.050	2.57	3.04	2.22	4.64	8.34	59.60
1955	0.3119	0.807	2.11	2.84	1.72	4.62	6.80	45.00
1956	0.3099	1.48	2.27	3.05	2.14	4.57	6.81	59.90

SOURCE, BY COLUMN

(1 to 6, 8, 10 to 14, 16 and 17)

1945–54: *Crops and Markets*, Agricultural Marketing Service, 1955 ed., pp. 68, 69.

1955: *Agricultural Prices*, Agricultural Marketing Service, released Jan. 31, 1956, p. 4, and later issues.

1956: *Agricultural Prices*, Jan. 30, 1957, p. 4.

(7 and 9) 1945–55: Agricultural Marketing Service figures.

1956: *Agricultural Prices*, p. 4.

(15) 1945–55: *The Wheat Situation*, Agricultural Marketing Service, WS-147, released Feb. 28, 1956, p. 34.

1956: *Ibid.*, p. 4.

TABLE B-94

CROP INVENTORIES: VALUE ON FARMS, CURRENT PRICES

(millions of dollars)

End of Year	Adjusted Total (1)	Corn (2)	Wheat (3)	Oats (4)	Barley (5)	Rye (6)	Buckwheat (7)	Tobacco (8)	Peanuts (9)
1945	5,961	2,013.1	526.9	682.1	136.0	9.3	0.7	255.4	17.2
1946	7,182	2,576.4	687.4	713.3	149.7	8.4	1.2	352.4	18.3
1947	9,244	3,522.3	1,165.5	853.4	234.2	17.3	1.5	345.6	22.6
1948	7,771	2,945.4	684.4	693.4	175.7	12.6	0.8	218.9	27.1
1949	6,044	2,058.7	464.2	548.5	114.4	5.8	0.4	226.5	10.7
1950	7,267	2,763.6	558.6	746.8	166.4	9.4	0.4	218.5	16.9
1951	8,609	3,102.4	606.2	802.4	171.2	11.2	0.4	225.8	16.7
1952	8,366	3,102.2	696.9	662.3	139.1	6.3	0.4	245.0	15.1
1953	7,162	2,698.1	539.4	593.3	124.8	8.0	0.2	218.4	2.9
1954	7,540	2,678.6	427.6	706.2	180.1	10.9	0.5	224.0	4.6
1955	6,681	2,318.5	464.4	614.2	174.3	13.2	0.3	199.1	6.4
1956	7,102	2,597.8	467.7	518.1	164.3	8.7	0.3	188.5	13.3

(continued)

TABLE B-94 (concluded)

End of Year	Hay (10)	Cotton Lint (11)	Potatoes (12)	Soybeans (13)	Flaxseed (14)	Sorghum Grain (15)	Rice (16)	Dry Edible Beans (17)	Cotton Seed (18)
1945	1,431.8	256.2	109.1	91.2	25.0	72.9	19.4	15.1	16.1
1946	1,507.5	396.2	132.1	104.2	34.3	88.2	21.2	31.3	17.4
1947	1,567.9	417.3	168.6	191.0	72.9	103.0	35.5	67.0	17.8
1948	1,547.9	472.0	145.9	177.0	50.3	117.6	49.3	63.3	19.2
1949	1,451.9	364.9	153.7	129.5	43.1	108.2	29.8	35.2	10.9
1950	1,519.9	257.9	114.0	274.7	39.3	147.2	33.3	36.6	17.3
1951	1,783.3	723.9	163.3	294.8	49.4	131.7	45.3	43.4	27.6
1952	1,798.5	682.1	198.3	229.9	35.3	67.6	30.4	43.9	14.7
1953	1,600.9	460.6	87.6	230.4	59.4	80.2	54.5	49.5	13.1
1954	1,693.1	429.6	126.3	382.9	47.4	121.5	82.4	56.0	9.1
1955	1,574.9	390.5	103.3	244.8	46.9	117.1	46.2	42.0	6.8
1956	1,668.2	345.5	115.1	383.5	67.0	125.6	54.2	41.3	4.9

SOURCE, BY COLUMN

(1) Sum of cols. 2 to 18 plus step-up of 5 per cent of that total, in order to adjust series for omission of corn silage and forage, and sorghums for silage and forage, for which

(2 to 18) long-time quantity and price series are not available. Table B-92, cols. 1 to 17, multiplied by appropriate price from Table B-93, cols. 1 to 17, respectively.

TABLE B-95

CROP INVENTORIES: VALUE ON FARMS, CONSTANT (1947–49) PRICES

(millions of dollars)

End of Year	Adjusted Total (1)	Corn (2)	Wheat (3)	Oats (4)	Barley (5)	Rye (6)	Buckwheat (7)	Tobacco (8)	Peanuts (9)
1945	7,863	2,918.1	773.3	854.8	177.6	11.2	0.8	268.2	21.4
1946	8,313	3,336.7	805.0	777.8	155.2	6.7	1.1	372.6	21.3
1947	7,119	2,348.2	944.1	637.2	165.1	12.2	1.0	211.1	23.1
1948	8,880	3,783.5	754.5	798.6	219.3	14.9	0.9	220.3	26.6
1949	7,465	2,878.5	543.5	691.3	148.1	7.9	0.6	229.5	10.6
1950	7,855	3,011.4	625.0	775.0	197.1	11.7	0.5	213.0	16.0
1951	8,011	2,917.7	617.2	744.9	174.9	11.2	0.3	202.9	16.7
1952	8,267	3,267.7	742.9	693.0	139.1	6.3	0.4	227.2	14.1
1953	7,803	3,023.4	606.5	681.5	152.9	11.5	0.4	204.2	2.7
1954	8,183	3,044.8	455.9	811.2	232.9	16.6	0.6	206.1	3.8
1955	8,391	3,185.5	538.2	864.4	267.2	24.3	0.3	160.1	5.6
1956	8,248	3,364.3	510.6	613.5	225.0	12.6	0.4	143.1	12.5

(continued)

319

TABLE B-95 (concluded)

End of Year	Hay (10)	Cotton Lint (11)	Potatoes (12)	Soybeans (13)	Flaxseed (14)	Sorghum Grain (15)	Rice (16)	Dry Edible Beans (17)	Cottonseed (18)
1945	1,681.4	337.6	124.6	118.2	45.8	87.5	26.4	20.3	21.7
1946	1,576.3	397.1	168.2	102.7	26.3	113.2	22.3	21.7	13.1
1947	1,561.1	368.3	148.5	140.3	58.1	72.2	29.8	46.2	13.0
1948	1,489.4	478.5	144.6	203.3	46.5	135.8	49.5	71.7	19.2
1949	1,518.2	414.2	179.8	167.9	64.9	152.9	36.7	47.5	17.3
1950	1,596.6	193.4	221.6	275.7	58.1	198.1	34.1	41.9	11.7
1951	1,673.7	541.6	128.0	282.3	61.9	132.8	49.7	47.1	26.6
1952	1,560.1	646.2	153.0	226.6	50.0	60.2	26.1	45.8	14.8
1953	1,593.9	450.3	179.1	222.2	86.2	91.8	54.9	52.4	17.1
1954	1,664.1	395.0	171.7	403.8	82.9	138.5	95.6	59.1	10.5
1955	1,693.2	376.1	182.6	314.4	87.8	172.2	53.8	54.3	10.5
1956	1,682.9	334.9	111.0	457.9	116.7	148.5	63.8	53.3	5.6

SOURCE, BY COLUMN

(1) Sum of cols. 2 to 18, raised by 5 per cent (see note to Table B-94, col. 1).

(2 to 18) Table B-92, cols. 1 to 17, multiplied by the 1947–49 price from Table B-93, cols. 1 to 17, respectively.

TABLE B-96

CORN AND WHEAT INVENTORIES

END OF YEAR	QUANTITY				ANNUAL AVERAGE PRICE	
	Stored on Farms		Stored on Farms Under Commodity Credit Corporation Loans			
	Corn	Wheat	Corn	Wheat	Corn	Wheat
	(thousand bushels)				(dollars per bushel)	
	(1)	(2)	(3)	(4)	(5)	(6)
1945	1,847,153	360,959	271	18,784	1.27	1.50
1946	2,112,113	366,003	292	9,823	1.56	1.91
1947	1,486,221	427,821	12	10,089	2.16	2.29
1948	2,479,619	387,450	84,968	53,619	1.30	1.99
1949	2,285,795	317,621	463,941	77,126	1.25	1.88
1950	2,106,698	335,748	200,755	59,219	1.53	2.00
1951	1,892,173	334,518	45,517	61,439	1.66	2.11
1952	2,154,757	401,110	86,622	72,384	1.53	2.09
1953	2,144,305	423,068	230,761	154,685	1.48	2.04
1954	2,093,235	321,321	166,152	119,603	1.51	2.12
1955	2,191,409	320,800	175,301	82,660	1.31	1.98
1956	2,330,920	292,804	201,616	66,883	1.32	1.98

SOURCE, BY COLUMN

(1)   Same source as for Table B-92, col. 3.
(2)   Same source as for Table B-92, col. 5.
(3 and 4)   Estimates of the Commodity Credit Corporation.
(5 and 6)   "Prices Received by Farmers," *Crops and Markets*, Agricultural Marketing Service, 1955 ed., p. 68. *United States 1908–55*, June 1956, pp. 3 and 6; *Crop Values*, (1956 preliminary), Dec. 1956, p. 3.

TABLE B-97
LIVESTOCK AND CROP INVENTORIES: VALUE ON FARMS
(millions of dollars)

End of Year	Current Prices			1947–49 Prices		
	Total (1)	Livestock (2)	Crops (3)	Total (4)	Livestock (5)	Crops (6)
1945	15,678	9,717	5,961	22,747	14,884	7,863
1946	19,097	11,916	7,181	22,566	14,253	8,313
1947	22,501	13,257	9,244	20,705	13,586	7,119
1948	22,197	14,426	7,771	22,300	13,420	8,880
1949	18,936	12,892	6,044	21,073	13,608	7,465
1950	24,366	17,099	7,267	21,896	14,041	7,855
1951	28,136	19,527	8,609	22,575	14,564	8,011
1952	23,144	14,778	8,366	23,017	14,750	8,267
1953	18,907	11,745	7,162	22,431	14,628	7,803
1954	18,750	11,210	7,540	23,022	14,839	8,183
1955	17,383	10,702	6,681	23,359	14,969	8,390
1956	18,234	11,132	7,102	22,821	14,573	8,248
1957	20,570	14,070	6,500	23,292	14,342	8,950
1958	26,155	18,111	8,044	25,545	14,895	10,650

SOURCE, BY COLUMN

(1) Sum of cols. 2 and 3.
(2) From Table B-89, col. 1.
(3) 1945–56 from Table B-94, col. 1; 1957 and 1958 estimated by applying 1955–56 ratios of adjusted totals to *Balance Sheet of Agriculture* figures, e.g., 1958, p. 14.
(4) Sum of cols. 5 and 6.
(5) From Table B-90, col. 1.
(6) 1945–56 Table B-95, col. 1; 1957 and 1958 derived by applying 1956 ratio in 1947–49 prices to 1940 prices as shown in *Balance Sheet of Agriculture*, e.g., 1958, p. 27.

TABLE B-98
BUSINESS EXPENDITURES ON PLANT CONSTRUCTION
(millions of dollars)

Year	Total (1)	Industrial (2)	Commercial		Public Utilities (5)	Miscellaneous Nonresidential Buildings (6)	Other Private Buildings (7)
			Warehouse, Office, and Loft Buildings (3)	Stores, Restaurants, and Garages (4)			
1946	4,358	1,689	331	801	1,374	111	52
1947	5,040	1,702	237	619	2,338	75	69
1948	5,875	1,397	352	901	3,043	117	65
1949	5,536	972	321	706	3,323	136	78
1950	5,925	1,062	402	886	3,330	133	112
1951	7,565	2,117	544	827	3,729	284	64
1952	7,833	2,320	515	622	4,003	288	85
1953	8,838	2,229	739	1,052	4,416	282	120
1954	8,968	2,030	958	1,254	4,284	321	121
1955	10,499	2,399	1,311	1,907	4,543	178	161
1956	12,143	3,084	1,684	1,947	5,113	195	120
1957	13,149	3,557	1,893	1,671	5,624	206	199
1958	11,999	2,443	1,986	1,575	5,554	252	189

SOURCE, BY COLUMN

(1) Sum of cols. 2 to 7.
(2 to 7) Departments of Commerce and Labor, *Construction Volume and Costs*, 1915–1956, pp. 2–5; various issues of *Construction Review*, e.g., June 1956, p. 14,

EXPENDITURES BY NONFARM PRODUCERS ON NEW DURABLE GOODS
(millions of dollars)

Year	Total (1)	Furniture and Fixtures (2)	Cutlery and Hand Tools (3)	Fabricated Metal Products (4)	Engines and Turbines (5)	Construction (6)	Mining and Oilfields (7)	Metal-working (8)	Special Industry (9)	General Industry (10)
1946	9,269	500	353	317	52	323	301	779	837	863
1947	13,893	690	348	506	148	408	352	834	1,340	1,170
1948	15,389	641	370	492	214	564	497	803	1,414	1,287
1949	13,266	583	336	390	196	402	413	619	1,144	1,024
1950	14,919	635	348	392	234	445	504	973	1,278	1,032
1951	17,379	893	425	433	292	539	711	1,127	1,588	1,271
1952	17,537	886	417	379	321	678	788	1,200	1,496	1,514
1953	18,870	856	391	423	344	563	784	1,531	1,590	1,743
1954	17,846	1,021	331	458	406	440	599	1,576	1,411	1,785

(continued)

TABLE B-99 (concluded)

Year	Office and Store Machines (11)	Service Industry Household Machines (12)	Electric Machinery (13)	Trucks, Buses, Trailers (14)	Passenger Cars (15)	Aircraft (16)	Ships and Boats (17)	Railroad Equipment (18)	Instruments (19)	Miscellaneous Equipment (20)
1946	443	456	1,129	1,241	315	156	174	359	226	445
1947	588	873	2,061	1,953	665	145	236	631	335	610
1948	680	1,263	1,895	2,223	816	75	120	1,004	360	671
1949	622	877	1,631	1,713	1,192	103	102	1,030	328	561
1950	684	867	1,836	2,247	1,526	60	95	756	356	651
1951	804	789	2,017	2,838	1,296	86	153	1,072	359	686
1952	956	921	2,247	2,169	1,142	174	207	953	362	727
1953	1,195	1,047	2,302	1,994	1,534	147	258	869	503	796
1954	1,161	1,027	2,282	1,705	1,463	173	283	541	490	694

SOURCE, BY COLUMN

(1) 1946–54: Sum of Cols. 2 to 20; figures for 1955, 19,761; 1956, 24,348; 1957, 25,623; 1958, 19,838; *Survey of Current Business*, July 1959, pp. 6 and 7. Private investment in producer durable equipment less business use of passenger cars, and farmers' expenditures for new trucks, tractors, and farm machinery as shown

(2 to 14, 16 to 20) (15)

1946–54: in Tables B-64, B-65, and B-67, plus expenditures for passenger cars from col. 15.

1946–54: *U.S. Income and Output*, p. 192.

1946–54: Table B-27, col. 2; figures for 1955, 2,093; 1956, 1,737; 1957, 1,918; 1958, 1,548.

NOTE: Expenditures by nonfarm producers include expenditures on equipment by institutions.

TABLE B-100

BUSINESS EXPENDITURES ON NEW PLANT AND EQUIPMENT BY TYPE OF BUSINESS

(millions of dollars)

Year	Total[a] (1)	Manufacturing (2)	Mining (3)	Railroads (4)	Transportation Other than Railroads (5)	Public Utilities (6)	Communications (7)	Other[b] (8)
1945	8,692	3,983	383	548	574	505	321	2,378
1946	14,848	6,790	427	583	923	792	817	4,516
1947	20,612	8,703	691	889	1,298	1,539	1,399	6,093
1948	22,059	9,134	882	1,319	1,285	2,543	1,742	5,154
1949	19,285	7,149	792	1,352	887	3,125	1,320	4,660
1950	20,605	7,491	707	1,111	1,212	3,309	1,104	5,671
1951	25,644	10,852	929	1,474	1,490	3,664	1,319	5,916
1952	26,493	11,632	985	1,396	1,500	3,887	1,537	5,557
1953	28,322	11,908	986	1,311	1,565	4,552	1,690	6,310
1954	26,827	11,038	975	854	1,512	4,219	1,717	6,513
1955	28,701	11,439	957	923	1,602	4,309	1,983	7,488
1956	35,081	14,954	1,241	1,231	1,712	4,895	2,684	8,364
1957	36,962	15,959	1,243	1,396	1,771	6,195	3,032	7,366
1958	30,526	11,433	941	754	1,500	6,088	2,615	7,195

SOURCE: 1946–47: *Survey of Current Business*, August 1952, p. 20.
1948–55: *Ibid.*, June 1956, pp. 6, 7.
1956–58: *Ibid.*, July 1959, p. 30.

Covers all industries except agriculture, banks, insurance carriers, real estate, professionals, and nonprofit organizations. For the covered industries, series represents expenditures for new depreciable fixed assets; it excludes purchases of land and secondhand plant and equipment. Derivation of series described in Dec. 1951 and Aug. 1952 issues of *Survey of Current Business*.

[a] Corporate and noncorporate business, excluding agriculture.
[b] Includes trade, service, finance, and construction.

TABLE B-101
Net Investment in Industrial Structures
(millions of dollars)

Year	Expenditures Original Cost (1)	Expenditures 1947–49 Prices (2)	Depreciation Original Cost (3)	Depreciation 1947–49 Prices (4)	Depreciation Replacement Cost (5)	Net Investment Original Cost (6)	Net Investment 1947–49 Prices (7)	Net Investment Replacement Cost (8)
1946	1,689	2,152	426	1,002	787	1,263	1,150	902
1947	1,702	1,814	461	1,021	958	1,241	793	744
1948	1,397	1,342	492	1,033	1,075	905	309	322
1949	972	952	516	1,037	1,059	456	−85	—87
1950	1,062	1,008	535	1,036	1,092	527	−28	—30
1951	2,117	1,796	569	1,047	1,234	1,548	749	883
1952	2,320	1,919	618	1,069	1,292	1,702	850	1,028
1953	2,229	1,806	667	1,086	1,340	1,562	720	889
1954	2,030	1,690	714	1,102	1,324	1,316	588	706
1955	2,399	1,952	763	1,126	1,384	1,636	826	1,015
1956	3,084	2,304	826	1,106	1,481	2,258	1,198	1,603
1957	3,557	2,506	901	1,279	1,815	2,656	1,227	1,742
1958	2,443	1,721	966	1,372	1,948	1,477	349	495

SOURCE, BY COLUMN

(1) Table B-98, col. 2.
(2) Col. 1 divided by Table B-106, col. 1.
(3) Col. 1 depreciated assuming an average life of forty years. Expenditure figures for years before 1946 from *A Study of Saving* . . . , worksheets, and *Construction and Building Materials, Statistical Supplement,* Department of Commerce, May 1954, p. 6.
(4) Col. 2 depreciated assuming an average life of forty years. Expenditures in 1947–49 prices for years before 1946 obtained by deflating expenditures in original cost (see col. 3) by index of industrial construction cost (for period 1915–45, index from same source as the later years; for years before 1915, extrapolated by index given in *A Study of Saving* . . . , Vol. I, Table R-20, col. 3).
(5) Col. 4 multiplied by Table B-106, col. 1.
(6) Col. 1 minus col. 3.
(7) Col. 2 minus col. 4.
(8) Col. 1 minus col. 5.

TABLE B-102

NET INVESTMENT IN COMMERCIAL STRUCTURES
(millions of dollars)

Year	Expenditures		Depreciation			Net Investment		
	Original Cost (1)	1947–49 Prices (2)	Original Cost (3)	1947–49 Prices (4)	Replacement Cost (5)	Original Cost (6)	1947–49 Prices (7)	Replacement Cost (8)
1946	1,132	1,593	409	952	677	723	641	455
1947	856	926	429	962	889	427	−36	−33
1948	1,253	1,208	450	969	1,005	803	239	248
1949	1,027	990	475	979	1,015	552	11	12
1950	1,288	1,230	500	990	1,037	788	240	251
1951	1,371	1,231	529	1,004	1,118	842	227	253
1952	1,137	989	556	1,015	1,167	581	−26	−30
1953	1,791	1,498	587	1,026	1,227	1,204	472	564
1954	2,212	1,786	633	1,047	1,297	1,579	739	915
1955	3,218	2,531	697	1,085	1,381	2,521	1,446	1,837
1956	3,631	2,736	777	1,132	1,506	2,854	1,604	2,125
1957	3,564	2,573	861	1,177	1,632	2,703	1,396	1,932
1958	3,561	2,485	945	1,227	1,761	2,616	1,258	1,800

SOURCE, BY COLUMN

(1)   From Table B-98, cols. 3 and 4.
(2)   Components of col. 1 deflated by indexes given in Table B-106, cols. 2 and 3.
(3)   Col. 1 depreciated assuming an average life of forty years. Expenditures for period 1920–45 from *Construction and Building Materials, Statistical Supplement*, Department of Commerce, May 1954, p. 40. Expenditures for years before 1920 obtained: (1) by deducting from *A Study of Saving*. . . estimates of commercial construction (see Vol. I, Table R-10, col. 1) expenditures for nonhousekeeping units (derived according to procedure described in Table R-10); and (2) by multiplying that residual by 80 per cent, the ratio estimated on the basis of the post-1920 relationship.
(4)   Col. 2 depreciated assuming an average life of forty years. Expenditures in 1947–49 prices obtained by deflating expenditures in original cost (col. 3) by index derived for period 1920–45 from same source as for later years (see col. 2); for years before 1920, extrapolated by index given in *A Study of Saving* . . . , Vol. I, Table R-20, col. 3.
(5)   Col. 4 multiplied by indexes described in col. 2, Table B-102.
(6)   Col. 1 minus col. 3.
(7)   Col. 2 minus col. 4.
(8)   Col. 1 minus col. 5.

TABLE B-103

NET INVESTMENT IN MISCELLANEOUS NONRESIDENTIAL STRUCTURES
(millions of dollars)

Year	Expenditures Original Cost (1)	Expenditures 1947–49 Prices (2)	Depreciation Original Cost (3)	Depreciation 1947–49 Prices (4)	Depreciation Replacement Cost (5)	Net Investment Original Cost (6)	Net Investment 1947–49 Prices (7)	Net Investment Replacement Cost (8)
1946	111	162	26	64	44	85	98	67
1947	75	82	29	66	60	46	16	15
1948	117	112	31	67	70	86	45	47
1949	136	130	34	69	72	102	61	64
1950	133	125	37	71	76	96	54	57
1951	284	251	42	75	85	242	176	199
1952	288	245	49	80	94	239	165	194
1953	282	230	56	85	104	226	145	178
1954	321	255	63	90	113	258	165	208
1955	178	138	69	94	122	237	44	56
1956	195	144	73	97	131	290	47	64
1957	206	146	78	99	140	128	47	66
1958	252	174	84	102	148	168	72	104

SOURCE, BY COLUMN

(1) From Table B-98, col. 6.
(2) Col. 1 deflated by Table B-106, col. 3, the index used by the Department of Commerce in its deflation of this category (see *Construction and Building Materials, Statistical Supplement*, May 1954, p. 82).
(3) Col. 1 depreciated assuming an average life of forty years. Expenditures for period 1920–45 from *ibid.*, p. 40. Expenditures for years before 1920 obtained: (1) by deducting from *A Study of Saving*. . . estimates of commercial construction (see Vol. I, Table R-10, col. 1) expenditures for nonhousekeeping units (derived according to procedure described in Table R-10); and (2) by multiplying that residual by 4 per cent, the ratio estimated on basis of the post-1920 relationship.
(4) Col. 2 depreciated assuming an average life of forty years. Expenditures in 1947–49 prices obtained: by deflating expenditures in original cost (col. 3) by index for period 1915–45, derived from same source as for later years (see col. 2); for years before 1915 extrapolated by figures given in *A Study of Saving* . . . , Vol. I, Table R-20, Col. 3.
(5) Col. 4 multiplied by Table B-106, col. 3.
(6) Col. 1 minus col. 3.
(7) Col. 2 minus col. 4.
(8) Col. 1 minus col. 5.

TABLE B-104

NET INVESTMENT IN PUBLIC UTILITY CONSTRUCTION
(millions of dollars)

Year	Expenditures		Depreciation			Net Investment		
	Original Cost (1)	1947–49 Prices (2)	Original Cost (3)	1947–49 Prices (4)	Replacement Cost (5)	Original Cost (6)	1947–49 Prices (7)	Replacement Cost (8)
1946	1,426	1,797	831	1,819	1,444	595	−22	−18
1947	2,407	2,571	860	1,829	1,712	1,547	742	695
1948	3,108	3,030	905	1,848	1,896	2,203	1,182	1,212
1949	3,401	3,225	961	1,877	1,980	2,440	1,348	1,421
1950	3,442	3,102	1,018	1,902	2,111	2,424	1,200	1,331
1951	3,793	3,110	1,077	1,918	2,340	2,716	1,192	1,453
1952	4,088	3,263	1,141	1,933	2,422	2,947	1,330	1,666
1953	4,536	3,454	1,213	1,954	2,566	3,323	1,500	1,970
1954	4,405	3,256	1,291	1,984	2,684	3,114	1,272	1,721
1955	4,704	3,370	1,370	2,013	2,810	3,334	1,357	1,894
1956	5,233	3,462	1,455	2,036	3,078	3,778	1,426	2,155
1957	5,823	3,618	1,548	2,054	3,305	4,275	1,564	2,518
1958	5,743	3,457	1,647	2,075	3,447	4,096	1,382	2,296

SOURCE, BY COLUMN

(1) Table B-98, col. 5 plus col. 7.
(2) From *Construction Volume and Costs, 1915–1956*, Department of Commerce, p. 41; and *Construction Review*, various issues, e.g., Feb. 1957, p. 15.
(3) Col. 1 depreciated assuming an average life of fifty years. Expenditures for period 1915–45 from *Construction Volume . . . , loc. cit.* Expenditures for years before 1915 obtained from *A Study of Saving . . . ,* Vol. I, Table R-16, col. 1.
(4) Col. 2 depreciated assuming an average life of fifty years. Expenditures for period 1915–45 from *Construction Volume . . . , loc. cit.* Expenditures for years before 1915 obtained by deflating original cost figures (col. 3) by index derived by linking *A Study of Saving . . . ,* Vol. I, Table R-20, col. 4, 1915, to the index described in Table R-15, col. 4 of that study.
(5) Col. 4 multiplied by Table B-106, col. 4.
(6) Col. 1 minus col. 3.
(7) Col. 2 minus col. 4.
(8) Col. 1 minus col. 5.

TABLE B-105
NET INVESTMENT IN SOCIAL AND RECREATIONAL BUILDINGS
(amounts in millions of dollars)

| Year | Expenditures | | Depreciation | | | Net Investment | | | Construction Cost Index (1947–49 = 100.0) |
	Original Cost (1)	1947–49 Prices (2)	Original Cost (3)	1947–49 Prices (4)	Replacement Cost (5)	Original Cost (6)	1947–49 Prices (7)	Replacement Cost (8)	(9)
1946	125	182	76	202	138	49	−20	−13	68.5
1947	99	108	78	201	184	21	−93	−85	91.5
1948	224	215	81	201	210	143	14	14	104.3
1949	262	251	85	203	212	177	48	50	104.3
1950	247	232	90	205	218	157	27	29	106.4
1951	164	145	94	206	233	70	−61	−69	113.1
1952	125	106	97	204	240	28	−98	−115	117.7
1953	163	133	99	203	249	64	−70	−86	122.7
1954	228	181	103	203	255	125	−22	−27	125.7
1955	239	185	107	203	262	132	−18	−23	129.3
1956	274	203	112	204	276	165	−1	−2	135.1
1957	311	220	118	205	289	193	15	22	141.1
1958	424	292	125	207	300	299	85	124	145.1

Source, by Column

(1) From Table B-46, col. 1.

(2) Col. 1 deflated by col. 9.

(3) Col. 1 depreciated assuming an average life of forty-five years. Expenditures for period 1920–45 from *Construction and Building Materials, Statistical Supplement*, May 1954, p. 7. Expenditures for years before 1920 obtained: (1) by deducting from *A Study of Saving . . .*, Vol. I, Table R-1C, col. 1, expenditures for nonhousekeeping units derived according to procedure described in Table R-10; and (2) by multiplying that residual by 16 per cent, the ratio estimated on basis of the post-1920 relationships.

(4) Col. 2 depreciated assuming an average life of forty-five years. Expenditures in 1947–49 prices obtained by deflating expenditures in original cost (col. 3) by index for the period 1915–45, derived from same source as for later years (see col. 9); for years before 1915, index extrapolated by figures given in *A Study of Saving . . .*, Vol. I, Table R-20, col. 3.

(5) Col. 4 multiplied by col. 9.

(6) Col. 1 minus col. 3.

(7) Col. 2 minus col. 4.

(8) Col. 1 minus col. 5.

(9) American Appraisal Company index from *Construction and Building Materials, op. cit.*, p. 32, as revised and brought up-to-date by the Department of Commerce.

NOTE: The buildings consist of "assembly buildings, auditoriums, community houses, golf and country club houses, athletic and social clubs, lodges, theatres, music conservatories, radio broadcasting studios, gymnasiums, indoor stadiums, indoor arenas, indoor coliseums, indoor courts, natatoriums, locker buildings, Y.M.C.A., bath houses at beaches, bowling alleys, billiard rooms, dance halls, indoor rinks, exhibit buildings, and other miscellaneous social and recreational buildings." Hence they include construction by institutions as well as construction by business.

TABLE B-106
Cost Indexes of Business Plant Construction
(1947–49 = 100)

| YEAR | ANNUAL AVERAGES | | | | YEAR-END (DEC.–JAN.) AVERAGES | | | |
| | Industrial (1) | Commercial | | Public Utility (4) | Industrial (5) | Commercial (6) | Public Utility (7) | Other Nonresidential Building (8) |
		Warehouse Office, and Loft Buildings (2)	Stores, Restaurants, and Garages (3)					
1945	64.9	64.8	57.7	70.5	69.4	61.8	72.2	60.1
1946	78.5	78.0	68.5	79.4	86.4	82.4	87.0	80.0
1947	93.8	95.2	91.5	93.6	99.6	100.0	96.6	100.0
1948	104.1	102.2	104.3	102.6	105.2	105.2	105.8	106.7
1949	102.1	102.7	104.3	105.5	101.5	102.5	106.0	103.1
1950	105.4	101.3	106.4	111.0	111.9	108.3	119.1	110.7
1951	117.9	108.9	113.1	122.0	120.6	113.0	122.4	115.0
1952	120.9	111.8	117.7	125.3	122.0	117.6	127.0	120.8
1953	123.4	115.3	122.7	131.3	122.4	121.4	133.2	124.4
1954	120.1	121.5	125.7	135.3	119.8	125.8	136.3	127.2
1955	122.9	124.2	129.3	139.6	126.4	131.2	140.8	132.0
1956	133.9	130.0	135.1	151.2	131.6	136.2	147.2	137.9
1957	141.9	136.3	141.1	160.9	143.2	140.6	164.3	143.1
1958	142.0	141.9	145.1	166.1	143.7	145.1	169.4	147.4

Source, by Column

Cost indexes are those applied by the Department of Commerce to the various types of construction in its deflation of expenditures from current to constant prices. All construction cost indexes are given in *Construction Volume and Costs, 1915–1956*, pp. 54–58 for 1945–56; *Construction Review*, e.g., Feb. 1957, p. 31; *Survey of Current Business*, various issues; *Engineering News-Record*, various issues; the *Handy-Whitman Index of Public Utility Construction Costs*; and miscellaneous Bureau of Labor Statistics publications for 1957 and 1958. The cost indexes utilized are as follows:

(1) Turner Construction Company index for industrial building.

(2) George A. Fuller Company index for commercial building.

(3) American Appraisal Company index.

(4) Obtained by dividing the Department of Commerce estimates of public utility expenditures in current prices by expenditures in 1947–49 prices (see Table B-104, cols. 1 and 2).

(5 to 7) Same procedure as for col. 4 except monthly values of construction from: Department of Labor, *New Construction Expenditures, 1915–51*, pp. 15–19, 40–42; Department of Commerce, *Construction Volume and Costs*, 1915–56, pp. 18–21, 56–57; Departments of Commerce and Labor, *Construction Review*, e.g., June, 1956, pp. 14–20; and Department of Labor releases on construction expenditures.

(8) American Appraisal Company index from *Construction Volume and Costs*, 1915–1956, pp. 56, 57; *Construction Review*, e.g., Feb. 1957, p. 31; and *Survey of Current Business*, various issues.

TABLE B-107

NET INVESTMENT THROUGH CAPITAL EXPENDITURES FOR PETROLEUM AND
NATURAL GAS WELL DRILLING, BASED ON DEPARTMENT OF COMMERCE
EXPENDITURE ESTIMATES
(millions of dollars)

Year	Expenditures Original Cost (1)	Expenditures 1947–49 Prices (2)	Depreciation Original Cost (3)	Depreciation 1947–49 Prices (4)	Depreciation Replacement Cost (5)	Net Investment Original Cost (6)	Net Investment 1947–49 Prices (7)	Net Investment Replacement Cost (8)
1946	653	832	272	556	436	381	276	217
1947	773	824	285	556	522	488	268	251
1948	1,059	1,017	308	564	591	751	453	468
1949	1,054	1,032	337	575	587	717	457	467
1950	1,261	1,196	370	591	623	891	605	638
1951	1,491	1,265	417	619	730	1,074	646	761
1952	1,683	1,392	474	653	789	1,209	739	894
1953	1,864	1,511	538	692	854	1,326	819	1,010
1954	2.043	1,701	610	738	886	1,433	963	1,157
1955	2,321	1,889	688	792	973	1,633	1,097	1,348
1956	2,445	1,826	773	840	1,125	1,672	986	1,320
1957	2,345	1,653	854	878	1,246	1,491	775	1,099
1958	2,400	1,690	934	911	1,294	1,466	779	1,106

SOURCE, BY COLUMN

(1)   1946–1957: *U.S. Income and Output*, p. 190. 1958: Estimated.
(2)   Col. 1 deflated by Table B-106, col. 1.
(3)   Col. 1 depreciated assuming a twenty-year life for expenditures during period 1921–29, and twenty-five year life for expenditures during 1930–58. Expenditures estimated for years before 1946 from *A Study of Saving* . . . , Vol. I, R-14, col. 1.
(4)   Same method as for col. 3, but expenditure figures of col. 2 used. Expenditure estimates in 1947–49 prices for years before 1946 obtained by deflating expenditures in original cost (see col. 3) by index of industrial construction cost (see Table B-101, col. 4).
(5)   Col. 4 multiplied by Table B-106, col. 1.
(6)   Col. 1 minus col. 3.
(7)   Col. 2 minus col. 4.
(8)   Col. 1 minus col. 5.

TABLE B-108

NET INVESTMENT THROUGH CAPITAL EXPENDITURES FOR PETROLEUM AND
NATURAL GAS WELL DRILLING, BASED ON ADJUSTED DEPARTMENT
OF COMMERCE AND OTHER EXPENDITURE ESTIMATES
(millions of dollars)

	Expenditures		Depreciation			Net Investment		
Year	Original Cost (1)	1947–49 Prices (2)	Original Cost (3)	1947–49 Prices (4)	Replacement Cost (5)	Original Cost (6)	1947–49 Prices (7)	Replacement Cost (8)
1946	914	1,164	277	563	442	637	601	472
1947	1,076	1,147	301	576	540	775	571	536
1948	1,458	1,401	339	598	623	1,119	803	835
1949	1,434	1,405	383	624	637	1,051	781	797
1950	1,697	1,610	433	655	690	1,264	955	1,007
1951	1,985	1,684	498	700	825	1,487	984	1,160
1952	2,213	1,830	575	752	909	1,638	1,078	1,304
1953	2,423	1,964	662	808	997	1,761	1,156	1,426
1954	2,656	2,211	757	874	1,050	1,899	1,337	1,606
1955	3,017	2,455	861	945	1,161	2,156	1,510	1,856
1956	3,179	2,374	974	1,015	1,359	2,205	1,359	1,820
1957	3,049	2,149	1,085	1,074	1,524	1,964	1,075	1,525
1958	3,120	2,197	1,192	1,128	1,602	1,928	1,069	1,518

SOURCE, BY COLUMN

(1) Department of Commerce figures; 1946–57, *U.S. Income and Output*, p. 190; 1958; *Survey of Current Business*, July 1959, p. 29, multiplied by step-up ratio obtained by interpolating between the 1947 and 1953 ratio of the Commerce estimates to the figures of col. 1 (1946 ratio taken at 1.4; 1954–58 ratios carried as 1.3).

(2) Col. 1 deflated by Table B-106, col. 1.

(3) Col. 1 depreciated assuming a twenty-year life for expenditures during period 1921–29 and twenty-five-year life for expenditures during 1930–58. Expenditure estimates for years before 1946 from *A Study of Saving* . . . , Vol. I, Table R-14, col. 1.

(4) Same method as col. 3, but expenditure figures of col. 2 used. Expenditure estimates in 1947–49 prices for years before 1946 obtained by deflating expenditures in original cost (see col. 3) by index of industrial construction cost (see Table B-101, col. 4).

(5) Col. 4 multiplied by Table B-106, col. 1.

(6) Col. 1 minus col. 3.

(7) Col. 2 minus col. 4.

(8) Col. 1 minus col. 5.

TABLE B-109

NET INVESTMENT THROUGH EXPENDITURES FOR MINING DEVELOPMENT
(millions of dollars)

Year	Expenditures		Depreciation			Net Investment		
	Original Cost (1)	1947–49 Prices (2)	Original Cost (3)	1947–49 Prices (4)	Replacement Cost (5)	Original Cost (6)	1947–49 Prices (7)	Replacement Cost (8)
1946	122	155	74	174	137	48	−19	−15
1947	178	190	76	174	163	102	16	15
1948	208	200	80	175	182	128	25	26
1949	154	151	84	176	180	70	−25	−26
1950	182	173	87	176	186	95	−3	−4
1951	202	171	91	176	208	111	−5	−6
1952	184	152	95	176	213	89	−24	−29
1953	186	151	98	175	216	88	−24	−30
1954	155	129	101	174	209	54	−45	−54
1955	185	151	104	173	213	81	−22	−28
1956	200	149	108	171	229	92	−22	−29
1957	209	147	110	168	238	99	−21	−29
1958	207	146	113	165	234	94	−19	−27

SOURCE, BY COLUMN

(1) From Table B-110, col. 5.
(2) Col. 1 divided by Table B-106, col. 1.
(3) Col. 1 depreciated assuming an average life of forty years. Expenditure estimates for years before 1946 from *A Study of Saving* . . . , Vol. I, Table R-15, col. 1.
(4) Col. 2 depreciated assuming an average life of forty years. Expenditure estimates in 1947–49 prices for years before 1946 obtained by deflating expenditures in original cost (see col. 3) by index of industrial construction cost (see Table B-101, col. 4).
(5) Col. 4 multiplied by Table B-106, col. 1.
(6) Col. 1 minus col. 3.
(7) Col. 2 minus col. 4.
(8) Col. 1 minus col. 5.

TABLE B-110

EXPENDITURES ON MINING DEVELOPMENT
(millions of dollars)

Year	Value of Output			Total (4)	Development Expenditures (5)
	Metallic Minerals (1)	Bituminous Coal (2)	Anthracite Coal (3)		
OLD BASIS					
1946	1,825	1,836	413	4,074	122
1947	2,909	2,623	413	5,945	178
1948	3,510	2,941	467	6,918	208
NEW BASIS					
1946	729	1,830	413	2,972	122
1947	1,084	2,615	413	4,112	178
1948	1,219	2,983	467	4,669	208
1949	1,101	2,126	358	3,585	154
1950	1,351	2,489	392	4,232	182
1951	1,671	2,614	406	4,691	202
1952	1,617	2,276	380	4,273	184
1953	1,811	2,233	299	4,343	186
1954	1,518	1,769	248	3,535	155
1955	2,055	2,092	206	4,353	185
1956	2,358	2,412	237	5,007	200
1957	2,129	2,504	228	4,861	209
1958	2,000	2,600	220	4,820	207

SOURCE, BY COLUMN

(1 to 3) 1946–57: *Statistical Abstract*, various issues: e.g., 1952, pp. 687–689; 1955, pp. 735–737. The 1946 figure in col. 2 (new basis) derived by extrapolation by means of the rate of change in output and price.

1958: Estimated.

(4) 1946–58: Sum of cols. 1 to 3.

(5) 1946–48: Estimated at 3 per cent of total value of output on old basis (see *A Study of Saving* . . . , Vol. I, Table R-15).

1949–58: Estimated at 4.3 per cent of col. 4, on the basis of the average relationship of 1946–48 development expenditures to the value of output on new basis.

TABLE B-111

EXPENDITURES BY NONFARM PRODUCERS ON NEW DURABLE GOODS, CONSTANT (1947–49) PRICES

(millions of dollars)

							Machinery			
Year	Total (1)	Furniture and Fixtures (2)	Cutlery and Hand Tools (3)	Fabricated Metal Products (4)	Engines and Turbines (5)	Construction (6)	Mining and Oil Field (7)	Metal Working (8)	Special Industry (9)	General Industry (10)
1946	11,282	626	435	412	60	413	380	924	1,008	1,100
1947	14,665	727	379	534	155	451	386	889	1,338	1,281
1948	15,226	632	367	480	211	555	491	796	1,400	1,286
1949	12,664	562	312	380	190	372	385	588	1,080	944
1950	13,918	585	300	366	222	401	459	873	1,168	912
1951	14,787	730	340	365	245	436	586	906	1,298	993
1952	14,798	732	333	322	260	543	643	941	1,220	1,189
1953	15,674	697	294	348	265	442	618	1,170	1,269	1,333
1954	14,644	821	238	371	304	341	461	1,187	1,106	1,328

(continued)

TABLE B-111 (concluded)

Year	Office and Store Machines (11)	Service Industry Household Machines (12)	Electric Machinery (13)	Trucks, Buses, Trailers (14)	Passenger Cars (15)	Aircraft (16)	Ships and Boats (17)	Railroad Equipment (18)	Instruments (19)	Miscellaneous Equipment (10)
1946	480	579	1,382	1,499	378	191	203	402	261	549
1947	593	930	2,125	2,095	716	156	252	659	351	648
1948	677	1,254	1,876	2,198	804	75	118	997	352	657
1949	620	834	1,599	1,621	1,128	97	97	993	320	542
1950	671	814	1,744	2,154	1,439	54	88	719	342	607
1951	757	671	1,722	2,508	1,170	71	131	955	317	586
1952	914	781	1,966	1,875	978	140	170	831	323	637
1953	1,132	862	1,986	1,742	1,345	112	200	727	437	695
1954	1,108	843	1,913	1,509	1,307	127	214	449	415	602

SOURCE, BY COLUMN

(1) 1946–54: Sum of cols. 2 to 20. Expenditures for 1955, 15,778; 1956, 18,286; 1957, 18,097, 1958, 13,716. These figures represent current expenditures shown in Table B-99, deflated by 1947–49 conversion of price deflators for producer durable equipment shown in *Survey of Current Business,* July, 1959, p. 40, and *U.S. Income and Output,* p. 221.

(2 to 20) Table B-99, cols. 2 to 20, deflated by Table B-118, cols. 1 to 19, respectively; passenger car expenditures for 1955, 1,796; 1956, 1,450; 1957, 1,521; 1958, 1,190.

DEPRECIATION ON NONFARM PRODUCERS' HOLDINGS OF DURABLE GOODS, ORIGINAL COST
(millions of dollars)

Year	Total (1)	Furniture and Fixtures (2)	Cutlery and Hand Tools (3)	Industrial Machinery and Equipment (4)	Office and Store Machines (5)	Electric Machinery (6)	Trucks, Buses, Trailers (7)
1946	3,937	254	163	1,563	190	333	494
1947	4,540	261	209	1,722	236	381	674
1948	5,468	272	248	1,946	295	440	1,978
1949	6,468	283	288	2,149	352	492	1,313
1950	7,488	397	322	2,342	410	541	1,635
1951	8,616	323	348	2,600	485	598	1,986
1952	9,648	360	362	2,917	577	662	2,238
1953	10,525	398	371	3,275	686	730	2,300
1954	11,253	439	373	3,637	791	796	2,225

Year	Passenger Cars (8)	Aircraft (9)	Ships and Boats (10)	Railroad Equipment (11)	Instruments (12)	Miscellaneous Equipment (13)
1946	125	23	99	337	81	275
1947	150	49	103	325	103	327
1948	242	70	105	332	131	409
1949	404	88	104	350	159	486
1950	627	103	103	369	186	553
1951	861	101	102	384	216	612
1952	1,037	97	104	398	248	648
1953	1,178	107	109	413	286	672
1954	1,305	121	116	423	329	698

SOURCE, BY COLUMN

(1) 1946–54: Sum of cols. 2 to 13. Subsequent years: 1955, 12,297; 1956, 13,031; 1957, 13,804; 1958, 14,496. These figures were derived by extending depreciation on items in Table B-99, col. 2 to 20, and estimating depreciation on aggregate producers' durables expenditures for 1955–58, as shown in Table B-99, except for passenger car depreciation, which is for 1955, 1,434; 1956, 1,526; 1957, 1,596; and 1958, 1,681.

(2 to 13) Table B-99, cols. 2 to 20, depreciated on basis of following average length of life:

	Years
Furniture and fixtures	20
Cutlery and hand tools	5
Industrial machinery and equipment (sum of cols. 4 to 10, and 12)	20
Office and store machines	8
Electric machinery	30
Trucks, buses, trailers	6
Passenger cars	6
Aircraft	5
Ships and boats	30
Railroad equipment	28
Instruments	10
Miscellaneous equipment	5

These estimates are based on data in Department of Treasury, Bureau of Internal Revenue, *Bulletin F*. Expenditures for years before 1946, required for the calculation of depreciation, for the period 1929–45 from *National Income Supplement to Survey of Current Business*, 1954, Table 32. For years before 1929, figures from *A Study of Saving . . .*, Vol. I, Tables P-5, P-13 and P-14, and related work sheets.

TABLE B-113

DEPRECIATION ON NONFARM PRODUCERS' HOLDINGS OF DURABLE GOODS,
CONSTANT (1947–49) PRICES
(millions of dollars)

Year	Total (1)	Furniture and Fixtures (2)	Cutlery and Hand Tools (3)	Industrial Machinery and Equipment (4)	Office and Store Furniture (5)	Electric Machinery (6)	Trucks, Buses, Trailers (7)
1946	5,733	361	215	2,389	211	446	712
1947	6,221	367	253	2,530	257	495	853
1948	6,939	370	298	2,709	313	553	1,043
1949	7,785	372	325	2,850	367	602	1,358
1950	8,611	378	340	2,974	422	649	1,645
1951	8,917	394	339	2,612	492	698	1,927
1952	9,589	420	325	2,834	576	751	2,079
1953	10,130	447	313	3,090	676	807	2,056
1954	10,554	476	298	3,340	770	860	1,929

Year	Passenger Cars (8)	Aircraft (9)	Ships and Boats (10)	Railroad Equipment (11)	Instruments (12)	Miscellaneous Equipment (13)
1946	187	30	157	535	102	388
1947	188	58	158	514	124	424
1948	263	80	158	515	150	487
1949	418	97	156	524	175	541
1950	627	111	153	532	199	581
1951	842	103	151	530	225	604
1952	989	89	150	523	246	607
1953	1,091	91	151	520	278	610
1954	1,185	98	154	512	313	619

SOURCE, BY COLUMN

(1)   1946–54: Sum of cols. 2 to 13. Subsequent years: 1955, 11,831; 1956, 11,996; 1957, 12,095; 1958, 12,111—derived as in Table B-112, using aggregate producer durables expenditures given in Table B-111.

(2 to 13)   Same method as in Table B-112, but expenditure figures given in Table B-111 used. Expenditures in 1947–49 prices for years before 1946, obtained by deflating expenditures in original cost (see Table B-112) by implicit price deflators given in *Survey of Current Business*, Nov. 1953, p. 19. Before 1929, figures extrapolated by indexes given in *A Study of Saving* . . . , Vol. I, Table P-10. Passenger car depreciation figures for subsequent years are: 1955, 1,283; 1956, 1,339; 1957, 1,370; 1958, 1,416.

TABLE B-114

DEPRECIATION ON NONFARM PRODUCERS' HOLDINGS OF DURABLE GOODS, REPLACEMENT COST
(millions of dollars)

Year	Total (1)	Furniture and Fixtures (2)	Cutlery and Hand Tools (3)	Industrial Machinery and Equipment (4)	Office and Store Machines (5)	Electric Machinery (6)	Trucks, Buses, Trailers (7)
1946	4,727	288	174	1,922	195	364	590
1947	5,883	348	232	2,388	255	480	795
1948	7,016	376	300	2,733	314	559	1,056
1949	8,167	386	350	3,024	368	614	1,435
1950	9,242	410	395	3,265	430	683	1,717
1951	10,418	482	423	3,205	523	817	2,179
1952	11,305	509	407	3,506	602	858	2,406
1953	12,098	549	416	3,930	714	935	2,356
1954	12,718	592	415	4,329	807	1,026	2,184

Year	Passenger Cars (8)	Aircraft (9)	Ships and Boats (10)	Railroad Equipment (11)	Instruments (12)	Miscellaneous Equipment (13)
1946	155	24	134	478	88	315
1947	174	54	148	492	118	399
1948	267	80	161	519	153	498
1949	441	103	164	543	179	560
1950	665	123	165	559	207	623
1951	932	124	177	595	254	707
1952	1,154	111	183	600	276	693
1953	1,244	119	195	621	320	699
1954	1,326	134	204	617	370	714

SOURCE, BY COLUMN

(1) 1946–54: Sum of cols. 2 to 13. Subsequent years: 1955, 14,648; 1956, 15,716; 1957, 16,817; 1958, 17,253—obtained by multiplying depreciation figures for these years as shown in Table B-113 by indexes used in Table B-111, except for passenger cars.

(2 to 13) Table B-113, cols. 2 to 13, multiplied by respective price indexes from Table B-118. Index for col. 4 is a weighted average of Table B-118, cols. 3 to 9, and 11, the weights being estimates of expenditures given in Table B-99, cols. 4 to 10, and 12. For passenger cars figures are: 1955, 1,495; 1956, 1,606; 1957, 1,727; and 1958, 1,842.

TABLE B-115

NET INVESTMENT IN PRODUCER DURABLE GOODS, ORIGINAL COST
(millions of dollars)

Year	Total (1)	Furniture and Fixtures (2)	Cutlery and Hand Tools (3)	Industrial Machinery and Equipment (4)	Office and Store Machines (5)	Electric Machinery (6)	Trucks, Buses, Trailers (7)
1946	5,332	246	190	2,365	253	796	747
1947	9,353	429	139	3,909	352	1,680	1,279
1948	9,921	369	122	4,588	385	1,455	1,245
1949	6,798	300	48	2,916	270	1,139	400
1950	7,431	338	26	3,383	274	1,295	612
1951	8,763	570	77	4,150	319	1,419	1,852
1952	7,889	526	55	4,380	379	1,585	−169
1953	8,345	458	20	4,750	509	1,572	−306
1954	6,593	582	−42	4,065	370	1,486	−520

Year	Passenger Cars (8)	Aircraft (9)	Ships and Boats (10)	Railroad Equipment (11)	Instruments (12)	Miscellaneous Equipment (13)
1946	190	133	75	22	145	170
1947	515	96	133	306	232	283
1948	574	5	15	672	229	262
1949	788	15	−2	680	169	75
1950	899	−43	−8	387	170	98
1951	435	−15	51	688	143	74
1952	105	77	103	555	114	79
1953	356	40	149	456	217	124
1954	158	52	167	118	161	−4

SOURCE, BY COLUMN

(1)   1946–54: Sum of cols. 2 to 13. Subsequent years: 1955, 7,464; 1956, 11,316; 1957, 11,819; 1958, 5,342—derived from expenditures as shown in Table B-99, minus depreciation from Table B-112.

(2 to 13)   Table B-99, cols. 2 to 20, minus Table B-112, cols. 2 to 13, respectively. Table B-112, col. 4, covers Table B-99, cols. 4 to 10, and 12. Passenger car net investment for 1955, 659; 1956, 210; 1957, 322; 1958, −333.

TABLE B-116

NET INVESTMENT IN PRODUCER DURABLE GOODS, CONSTANT (1947–49) PRICES
(millions of dollars)

Year	Total (1)	Furniture and Fixtures (2)	Cutlery and Hand Tools (3)	Industrial Machinery and Equipment (4)	Office and Store Machines (5)	Electric Machinery (6)	Trucks, Buses, Trailers (7)
1946	5,549	265	220	2,487	269	936	787
1947	8,444	360	126	3,434	336	1,630	1,242
1948	8,287	262	69	3,764	364	1,323	1,155
1949	4,879	190	−13	1,923	253	997	263
1950	5,307	207	−40	2,241	249	1,095	509
1951	5,870	336	1	2,888	265	1,024	581
1952	5,209	312	8	3,065	338	1,215	−204
1953	5,544	250	−19	3,217	456	1,179	−314
1954	4,090	345	−60	2,601	338	1,053	−420

Year	Passenger Cars (8)	Aircraft (9)	Ships and Boats (10)	Railroad Equipment (11)	Instruments (12)	Miscellaneous Equipment (13)
1946	191	161	46	133	159	161
1947	528	98	94	145	227	224
1948	541	−5	−40	482	202	170
1949	710	0	−59	469	145	1
1950	812	−57	−65	187	143	26
1951	328	−32	−20	425	92	−18
1952	−11	51	20	308	77	30
1953	254	21	49	207	159	85
1954	122	29	60	−63	102	−17

SOURCE, BY COLUMN

(1) 1946–54: Sum of cols. 2 to 13. Subsequent years: 1955, 3,947; 1956, 6,290; 1957, 6,002; 1958, 1,605—representing expenditures shown in Table B-111, less depreciation from Table B-113.

(2 to 13) Table B-111, cols. 2 to 20, minus Table B-113, cols. 2 to 13, respectively. Table B-113, col. 4, covers Table B-111, cols. 4 to 10, and 12. Net investment in passenger cars for 1955 is 513; 1956, 111; 1957, 151; 1958, −226.

TABLE B-117

NET INVESTMENT IN PRODUCER DURABLE GOODS, REPLACEMENT COST
(millions of dollars)

Year	Total (1)	Furniture and Fixtures (2)	Cutlery and Hand Tools (3)	Industrial Machinery and Equipment (4)	Office and Store Machines (5)	Electric Machinery (6)	Trucks, Buses, Trailers (7)
1946	4,542	212	179	2,006	248	765	651
1947	8,010	342	116	3,243	333	1,581	1,158
1948	8,373	265	70	3,801	366	1,336	1,167
1949	5,099	197	−14	2,041	254	1,017	278
1950	5,677	225	−47	2,460	254	1,153	530
1951	6,961	411	2	3,545	281	1,200	659
1952	6,232	377	10	3,791	354	1,389	−237
1953	6,772	307	−25	4,095	481	1,367	−362
1954	5,128	429	−84	3,373	354	1,256	−479

Year	Passenger Cars (8)	Aircraft (9)	Ships and Boats (10)	Railroad Equipment (11)	Instruments (12)	Miscellaneous Equipment (13)
1946	160	132	40	−119	138	130
1947	491	91	88	139	217	211
1948	549	−5	−41	485	207	173
1949	751	0	−62	487	149	1
1950	861	−63	−70	197	149	28
1951	364	−38	−24	477	105	−21
1952	−12	63	24	353	86	34
1953	290	28	63	248	183	97
1954	137	39	79	−76	120	−20

SOURCE, BY COLUMN

(1) 1946–54: Sum of cols. 2 to 13. Subsequent years: 1955, 5,113; 1956, 8,632; 1957, 8,806; 1958, 2,585—derived from original cost expenditures shown in Table B-99, less replacement cost depreciation from Table B-114.

(2 to 13) Table B-99, cols. 2 to 20, minus Table B-114, cols. 2 to 13, respectively. Table B-114, col. 4, covers Table B-99, cols. 4 to 10, and 12. Net investment in passenger cars for 1955 is 602; 1956, 131; 1957, 191; 1958, 294.

TABLE B-118

PRICE DEFLATORS FOR PRODUCER DURABLE GOODS (1947-49 = 100)

| Year | Furniture and Fixtures (1) | Cutlery and Hand Tools (2) | Fabricated Metal Products (3) | Engines and Turbines (4) | Machinery | | | | |
					Construction (5)	Mining and Oilfield (6)	Metal-working (7)	Special Industry (8)	General Industry (9)
1946	79.9	81.1	77.4	84.0	78.5	80.2	84.2	83.2	78.7
1947	94.9	91.7	95.5	93.0	90.8	92.4	93.6	93.5	91.7
1948	101.5	100.8	101.0	102.0	101.7	100.8	100.8	100.7	100.6
1949	103.7	107.6	103.5	104.9	107.6	106.9	105.6	105.8	107.7
1950	108.5	116.1	109.1	109.3	110.7	111.9	112.0	109.4	111.8
1951	122.4	124.9	117.8	122.0	123.0	124.8	125.8	121.7	126.8
1952	121.1	125.2	116.3	122.0	124.2	125.0	128.5	121.7	125.9
1953	122.9	132.8	117.5	126.0	126.9	130.8	131.1	124.4	129.3
1954	124.4	139.1	118.6	129.1	128.5	134.6	133.2	127.6	133.2
1955	124.8	149.9	121.5	132.8	133.8	143.1	142.5	130.6	137.7
1956	132.7	161.7	132.3	151.8	144.1	155.3	156.5	141.1	152.0

(continued)

TABLE B-118 (concluded)

Year	Office and Store Machines (10)	Service–Industry Household Machines (11)	Electric Machinery (12)	Trucks, Buses, Trailers (13)	Passenger Cars (14)	Aircraft (15)	Ships and Boats (16)	Railroad Equipment (17)	Instruments (18)	Miscellaneous Equipment (19)
1946	91.2	78.8	81.7	82.8	83.2	81.6	85.6	89.4	86.6	81.8
1947	98.0	96.6	97.0	93.1	92.8	93.2	93.5	95.6	95.5	94.9
1948	100.8	101.6	101.0	101.0	101.5	100.4	101.6	101.1	102.1	102.5
1949	101.1	101.6	102.0	105.6	105.7	106.3	104.9	103.3	102.3	102.5
1950	102.6	101.9	105.3	104.4	106.0	110.8	108.1	103.9	104.7	106.2
1951	109.3	109.1	117.1	113.0	110.7	120.5	117.1	110.9	113.9	118.1
1952	109.6	109.0	114.3	115.9	116.7	124.4	121.9	111.9	113.2	116.1
1953	112.3	110.3	115.9	114.9	114.0	131.2	129.1	118.0	116.3	117.2
1954	114.2	111.0	119.3	113.8	111.9	136.4	132.5	118.7	118.9	118.1
1955	117.3	108.9	115.7	116.2	116.5	141.3	132.4	123.9	123.2	120.3
1956	122.4	110.9	122.4	125.2	119.8	150.7	145.5	133.4	128.4	126.7

SOURCE: *Survey of Current Business*, Nov. 1953, p. 19, as revised and brought up to date by the Department of Commerce.

TABLE B-119

Nonfarm Producer Durable Goods 1955–58

(millions of dollars)

Year	Expenditures Original Cost (1)	1947–49 Prices (2)	Depreciation Original Cost (3)	1947–49 Prices (4)	Replacement Cost (5)	Net Investment Original Cost (6)	1947–49 Prices (7)	Replacement Cost (8)	Accumulated Stock Original Cost (9)	1947–49 Prices (10)	Stock Replacement Cost (11)
A. EXCLUDING PASSENGER CARS											
1954									100,147	98,908	124,063
1955	17,668	13,982	10,863	10,548	13,153	6,805	3,434	4,515	106,952	102,342	130,793
1956	22,611	16,836	11,505	10,657	14,110	11,106	6,179	8,501	118,058	108,521	149,216
1957	23,705	16,576	12,208	10,725	15,090	11,497	5,851	8,615	129,555	114,372	163,666
1958	18,290	12,526	12,815	10,695	15,411	5,475	1,831	2,879	135,030	116,203	169,424
B. PASSENGER CARS											
1954									4,179	3,721	4,249
1955	2,093	1,796	1,434	1,283	1,495	659	513	598	4,838	4,234	5,005
1956	1,737	1,450	1,526	1,339	1,606	211	111	131	5,049	4,345	5,344
1957	1,918	1,521	1,596	1,370	1,727	322	151	191	5,371	4,496	5,754
1958	1,548	1,190	1,681	1,416	1,842	−133	−226	−294	5,238	4,270	5,789
C. TOTAL, INCLUDING PASSENGER CARS											
1954									104,326	102,629	128,312
1955	19,761	15,778	12,297	11,831	14,648	7,464	3,947	5,113	111,790	106,576	135,798
1956	24,348	18,286	13,031	11,996	15,716	11,317	6,290	8,632	123,107	112,866	154,560
1957	25,623	18,097	13,804	12,095	16,817	11,819	6,002	8,806	134,926	118,868	169,420
1958	19,838	13,716	14,496	12,111	17,253	5,342	1,605	2,585	140,268	120,473	175,213

SOURCE, BY COLUMN

A. *Excluding Passenger Cars*

(1) Expenditures represent total expenditures for producer durable equipment as shown in *Survey of Current Business*, July 1959, p. 7, less current expenditures for passenger cars used by business (Table B-99), and farm tractors, machinery, and new trucks (Tables B-65, B-64 and B-67).

(2) Expenditures in constant (1947–49) prices derived by deflating total expenditures for producer durable equipment (as shown in *Survey of Current Business*, July 1959, p. 7,) by implicit price deflator for producer durable equipment (*ibid.*, p. 40, and *U.S. Income and Output*, p. 225, converted to a 1947–49 base), and then deducting expenditures in 1947–49 prices for passenger cars used by business, and farm tractors, machinery, and new trucks.

(3) Depreciation computed by extending depreciation on stocks of producer durable components shown in Table B-112, except passenger cars, and adding depreciation calculated on total expenditures for producer durables for years 1955–58. The depreciation rate for total producer durables was estimated at 7.16% (approximately 14-year life), based on the relation of actual depreciation to gross stock for the period 1952–54.

(4) Depreciation computed as in col. 3, except that depreciation rate for total producer durables for 1955–58 was estimated on basis of 16½-year life (6.10%).

(5) Col. 4 multiplied by average yearly deflator in source for col. 11.

(6) Col. 1 minus col. 3.

(7) Col. 2 minus col. 4.

(8) Col. 1 minus col. 5.

(9) 1954 value of original stock, excluding passenger cars, from Table B-127, plus net investment from col. 6.

(10) 1954 value of constant stock, excluding passenger cars, in (1947–49) prices, from Table B-128 plus net investment from col. 7.

(11) Col. 10 multiplied by year-end index of price deflators for producer durable equipment, converted to 1947–49 prices from 1954 prices (as shown in *U.S. Income and Output*, p. 221, and *Survey of Current Business*, July 1959, p. 40).

Year-end deflators obtained by averaging fourth and first quarter deflators of producer durables, as converted to 1947–49 prices from *Survey of Current Business*, e.g. July 1959:

	Average	Year-End
1955	124.7	127.8
1956	132.4	137.5
1957	140.7	143.1
1958	144.1	145.8

B. *Passenger Cars*

(1 to 8) Sum of Tables B-50 and B-120.

(9 and 10) Same method as for (9) and (10) above.

(11) From Table B-129.

TABLE B-120

NET INVESTMENT BY CORPORATIONS THROUGH PURCHASE OF PASSENGER CARS
(millions of dollars)

Year	Expenditures		Depreciation			Net Investment		
	Original Cost (1)	1947–49 Prices (2)	Original Cost (3)	1947–49 Prices (4)	Replacement Cost (5)	Original Cost (6)	1947–49 Prices (7)	Replacement Cost (8)
1946	105	126	42	63	52	63	63	53
1947	222	239	50	63	58	172	176	164
1948	272	268	81	88	89	191	180	183
1949	397	376	135	140	148	262	236	249
1950	509	480	209	209	222	300	271	287
1951	432	390	287	281	311	145	109	121
1952	381	326	346	330	385	35	−4	−4
1953	511	448	393	364	415	118	84	96
1954	488	436	435	395	442	53	41	46
1955	698	599	478	428	499	220	171	199
1956	579	483	509	447	536	70	36	43
1957	639	507	532	457	576	107	50	63
1958	516	397	560	472	614	−44	−75	−98

SOURCE, BY COLUMN

(1) From Table B-27, col. 4.
(2) Col. 1 divided by Table B-118, col. 14.
(3) Col. 1 depreciated assuming an average life of six years.
   Expenditures for years before 1946 from *A Study of Saving* . . . ,
   Vol I, Table P-14, col. 1.
(4) Same method as for col. 3, but expenditure figures of col. 2 used.
   Expenditures in 1947–49 prices for years before 1946 obtained

by deflating expenditures in original cost (see col. 3) by index
derived by extrapolating Table B-118, col. 14, from 1946 by
A Study of Saving . . . , Vol. I, Table P-10, col. 12.
(5) Col. 4 multiplied by Table B-118, col. 14.
(6) Col. 1 minus col. 3.
(7) Col. 2 minus col. 4.
(8) Col. 1 minus col. 5.

TABLE B-121

VALUE OF BUSINESS STRUCTURES, ORIGINAL COST
(millions of dollars)

End of Year	Total (1)	Industrial (2)	Commercial (3)	Miscellaneous Nonresidential (4)	Public Utility (5)
1945	38,707	8,380	8,211	580	21,536
1946	41,373	9,643	8,934	665	22,131
1947	44,634	10,884	9,361	711	23,678
1948	48,631	11,789	10,164	797	25,881
1949	52,181	12,245	10,716	899	28,321
1950	56,016	12,772	11,504	995	30,745
1951	61,364	14,320	12,346	1,237	33,461
1952	66,833	16,022	12,927	1,476	36,408
1953	73,148	17,584	14,131	1,702	39,731
1954	79,415	18,900	15,710	1,960	42,845
1955	87,143	20,536	18,231	2,197	46,179
1956	96,323	22,794	21,085	2,487	49,957
1957	106,085	25,450	23,788	2,615	54,232
1958	114,442	26,927	26,404	2,783	58,328

SOURCE, BY COLUMN

(1) Sum of cols. 2 to 5.
(2 to 5) Derived by addition of cumulated net investment, original cost, to estimated value for 1945, obtained by cumulating expenditures, less depreciation for number of years preceding 1945 corresponding to the assumed length of life of asset involved (see Tables B-101 to B-104).

TABLE B-122

VALUE OF BUSINESS STRUCTURES, CONSTANT (1947–49) PRICES
(millions of dollars)

End of Year	Total (1)	Industrial (2)	Commercial (3)	Miscellaneous Nonresidential (4)	Public Utility (5)
1945	78,571	18,056	17,998	1,326	41,191
1946	80,438	19,206	18,639	1,424	41,169
1947	81,953	19,999	18,603	1,440	41,911
1948	83,728	20,308	18,842	1,485	43,093
1949	85,063	20,223	18,853	1,546	44,441
1950	86,529	20,195	19,093	1,600	45,641
1951	88,873	20,944	19,320	1,776	46,833
1952	91,192	21,794	19,294	1,941	48,163
1953	94,029	22,514	19,766	2,086	49,663
1954	96,843	23,102	20,505	2,251	50,935
1955	100,466	23,928	21,951	2,295	52,292
1956	104,111	24,496	23,555	2,342	53,718
1957	108,345	25,723	24,951	2,389	55,282
1958	111,406	26,072	26,209	2,461	56,664

SOURCE, BY COLUMN

(1) Sum of cols. 2 to 5.
(2 to 5) Same procedure as for Table B-121, cols. 2 to 5, but applied to expenditures in 1947–49 prices.

TABLE B-123

VALUE OF BUSINESS STRUCTURES, CURRENT PRICES
(millions of dollars)

End of Year	Total (1)	Industrial (2)	Commercial (3)	Miscellaneous Nonresidential (4)	Public Utility (5)
1945	54,191	12,531	11,123	797	29,740
1946	68,909	16,594	15,359	1,139	35,817
1947	80,448	19,919	18,603	1,440	40,486
1948	88,362	21,364	19,822	1,584	45,592
1949	88,551	20,526	19,324	1,594	47,107
1950	99,405	22,598	20,678	1,771	54,358
1951	106,456	25,258	21,832	2,042	57,324
1952	112,791	26,589	22,690	2,345	61,167
1953	120,299	27,557	23,996	2,595	66,151
1954	125,756	27,676	25,795	2,863	69,424
1955	135,701	30,245	28,800	3,029	73,627
1956	146,622	32,237	32,082	3,230	79,073
1957	166,163	36,835	35,081	3,419	90,828
1958	175,111	37,465	38,029	3,628	95,989

SOURCE, by column: (1) Sum of cols. 2 to 5. (2 to 5) Cumulated depreciated capital expenditures in 1947–49 prices, multiplied by appropriate price deflator from Table B-106 (year-end figures used).

TABLE B-124

VALUE OF BUSINESS LAND

(millions of dollars)

End of Year	1947–49 Prices					Current Prices				
	Total (1)	Industrial (2)	Commercial (3)	Miscellaneous Nonresidential (4)	Public Utility (5)	Total (6)	Industrial (7)	Commercial (8)	Miscellaneous Nonresidential (9)	Public Utility (10)
1945	22,204	3,178	12,005	884	6,137	14,687	2,205	7,419	532	4,431
1946	22,896	3,380	12,432	950	6,134	19,262	2,291	10,244	760	5,337
1947	22,588	3,520	12,408	960	5,700	22,380	3,506	12,408	960	5,506
1948	22,993	3,574	12,568	990	5,861	24,239	3,760	13,221	1,057	6,201
1949	23,209	3,559	12,575	1,031	6,044	23,972	3,613	12,889	1,063	6,407
1950	23,015	3,554	12,735	1,067	5,659	25,690	3,977	13,792	1,181	6,740
1951	23,564	3,686	12,886	1,185	5,807	27,477	4,445	14,562	1,362	7,108
1952	23,972	3,836	12,869	1,295	5,972	28,963	4,680	15,134	1,564	7,585
1953	24,050	3,962	13,184	1,391	5,913	29,929	4,850	16,005	1,731	7,343
1954	24,898	4,066	13,677	1,501	5,654	30,812	4,871	17,325	1,910	7,706
1955	26,187	4,211	14,641	1,531	5,804	34,726	5,323	19,210	2,020	8,173
1956	27,547	4,311	15,711	1,562	5,963	38,004	5,674	21,399	2,154	8,777
1957	28,898	4,527	16,642	1,593	6,136	42,244	6,483	23,399	2,280	10,082
1958	29,766	4,354	17,481	1,641	6,290	45,034	6,594	25,365	2,420	10,655

SOURCE, BY COLUMN

(1) Sum of cols. 2 to 5.

(2 and 7) Estimated at 15 per cent of the total value of industrial real estate.

(3, 4, 8, 9) Estimated at 40 per cent of the total value of commercial

(5 and 10) real estate (see Tables B-122 and B-123, cols. 3 and 4). Rough extrapolation. See *A Study of Saving* . . . , Vol. III, Table W-1, col. 22.

(6) Sum of cols. 7 to 10.

353

TABLE B-125

VALUE OF SOCIAL AND RECREATIONAL REAL ESTATE
(millions of dollars)

End of Year	Structures			Land		Structures and Land	
	Original Cost (1)	1947–49 Prices (2)	Current Prices (3)	1947–49 Prices (4)	Current Prices (5)	1947–49 Prices (6)	Current Prices (7)
1945	1,861	4,494	2,701	2,997	1,802	7,491	4,503
1946	1,910	4,474	3,579	2,984	2,387	7,458	5,966
1947	1,931	4,381	4,381	2,922	2,922	7,303	7,303
1948	2,074	4,395	4,689	2,931	3,128	7,326	7,817
1949	2,251	4,443	4,581	2,963	3,056	7,406	7,637
1950	2,408	4,470	4,948	2,981	3,300	7,451	8,248
1951	2,478	4,409	5,070	2,941	3,382	7,350	8,452
1952	2,506	4,311	5,208	2,875	3,474	7,186	8,682
1953	2,570	4,241	5,276	2,829	3,519	7,070	8,795
1954	2,695	4,219	5,367	2,814	3,580	7,033	8,947
1955	2,827	4,201	5,545	2,802	3,699	7,003	9,244
1956	2,992	4,200	5,792	2,801	3,863	7,001	9,655
1957	3,185	4,215	6,032	2,811	4,023	7,026	10,055
1958	3,484	4,300	6,338	2,868	4,227	7,168	10,565

SOURCE, BY COLUMN

(1) Derived by addition of cumulated net investment, original cost, to estimated value for 1945, obtained by cumulating expenditures less depreciation for forty-five years, the assumed length of life of social and recreational buildings.

(2) Same procedure as for col. 1, but applied to expenditures in 1947–49 prices (see Table B-105, cols. 2 and 4).

(3) Cumulated depreciated capital expenditures in 1947–49 prices, multiplied by price index (year-end figures used; derived from same source as Table B-105, col. 9).

(4 and 5) Same procedure as for Table B-124, cols. 3 and 9.

(6) Sum of cols. 2 and 4.

(7) Sum of cols. 3 and 7.

TABLE B-126

VALUE OF UNDERGROUND MINING CONSTRUCTION
(millions of dollars)

| END OF YEAR | PETROLEUM AND GAS WELL DRILLING | | | | | | MINING DEVELOPMENT | | |
| | Estimate A[a] | | | Estimate B[b] | | | | | |
	Original Cost (1)	1947–49 Prices (2)	Current Prices (3)	Original Cost (4)	1947–49 Prices (5)	Current Prices (6)	Original Cost (7)	1947–49 Prices (8)	Current Prices (9)
1945	3,974	7,872	5,463	3,974	7,872	5,463	1,613	3,399	2,359
1946	4,355	8,148	7,040	4,611	8,473	7,321	1,661	3,380	2,920
1947	4,843	8,416	8,382	5,386	9,044	9,008	1,763	3,396	3,382
1948	5,594	8,869	9,330	6,505	9,847	10,359	1,891	3,421	3,599
1949	6,311	9,326	9,466	7,556	10,628	10,787	1,961	3,396	3,447
1950	7,202	9,931	11,113	8,820	11,583	12,961	2,056	3,393	3,797
1951	8,281	10,577	12,756	10,307	12,567	15,156	2,167	3,388	4,086
1952	9,490	11,316	13,806	11,945	13,645	16,647	2,256	3,364	4,104
1953	10,816	12,135	14,853	13,706	14,801	18,116	2,344	3,340	4,088
1954	12,249	13,098	15,691	15,605	16,138	19,333	2,398	3,295	3,947
1955	13,882	14,195	17,942	17,761	17,648	22,307	2,479	3,273	4,137
1956	15,554	15,181	19,978	19,966	19,007	25,013	2,571	3,251	4,278
1957	17,045	15,956	22,849	21,930	20,082	28,757	2,670	3,230	4,625
1958	18,511	16,735	24,048	23,858	21,151	30,394	2,764	3,211	4,614

SOURCE, BY COLUMN

(1, 4, and 7) Derived by addition of cumulated net investment, original cost, to estimated value for 1945, obtained by cumulating expenditures less depreciation for number of years preceding 1945 corresponding to the assumed length of life of asset involved (see Tables B-107, B-108, and B-109).

(2, 5, and 8) Same procedure as for col. 1, but applied to expenditures in 1947–49 prices.

(3, 6, and 9) Cumulated depreciated capital expenditures in 1947–49 prices multiplied by price index (year-end figures used; see Tables B-107, B-108, and B-109).

[a] Based on Department of Commerce figures (see Table B-107).
[b] Based on Department of Commerce and other expenditure estimates (see Table B-108).

355

TABLE B-127

VALUE OF STOCK OF PRODUCER DURABLE GOODS, ORIGINAL COST
(millions of dollars)

End of Year	Total (1)	Furniture and Fixtures (2)	Cutlery and Hand Tools (3)	Industrial Machinery and Equipment (4)	Office and Store Machines (5)	Electric Machinery (6)	Trucks, Buses, Trailers (7)
1945	33,901	2,282	379	16,977	717	5,488	1,313
1946	39,233	2,528	569	19,342	970	6,284	2,060
1947	48,586	2,957	708	23,251	1,322	7,964	3,339
1948	58,506	3,326	830	27,839	1,707	9,419	4,583
1949	65,305	3,626	878	30,755	1,977	10,558	4,984
1950	72,736	3,964	904	34,138	2,251	11,853	5,196
1951	81,499	4,534	981	38,288	2,570	13,272	6,448
1952	89,388	5,060	1,036	42,668	2,949	14,857	6,379
1953	97,733	5,518	1,056	47,418	3,458	16,429	6,073
1954	104,326	6,100	1,014	51,483	3,828	17,915	5,553

End of Year	Passenger Cars (8)	Aircraft (9)	Ships and Boats (10)	Railroad Equipment (11)	Instruments (12)	Miscellaneous Equipment (13)
1945	159	16	1,590	3,915	413	652
1946	349	149	1,665	3,937	558	822
1947	864	245	1,798	4,243	790	1,105
1948	1,438	250	1,813	4,915	1,019	1,367
1949	2,226	265	1,811	5,595	1,188	1,442
1950	3,125	222	1,803	5,982	1,358	1,540
1951	3,560	207	1,854	6,670	1,501	1,614
1952	3,665	284	1,957	7,225	1,615	1,693
1953	4,021	324	2,106	7,681	1,832	1,867
1954	4,179	376	2,273	7,799	1,993	1,813

SOURCE, BY COLUMN

(1) 1945–54: Sum of cols. 2 to 13. Subsequent years: 1955, 111,790; 1956, 123,107; 1957, 134,926; 1958, 140,268—obtained by adding net investment from col. 1, Table B-115.

(2 to 13) Derived by addition of cumulated net investment, original cost, to estimated value for 1945, obtained by cumulating expenditures less depreciation for number of years preceding 1945 corresponding to the assumed length of life of asset (see Table B-112). Passenger car values for subsequent years: 1955, 4,838; 1956, 5,049; 1957, 5,371; 1958, 5,238.

TABLE B-128

VALUE OF STOCK OF PRODUCER DURABLE GOODS, CONSTANT (1947–49) PRICES
(millions of dollars)

End of Year	Total (1)	Furniture and Fixtures (2)	Cutlery and Hand Tools (3)	Industrial Machinery and Equipment (4)	Office and Store Machines (5)	Electric Machinery (6)	Buses, Trucks, Trailers (7)
1945	49,450	3,282	507	25,101	796	7,585	1,854
1946	54,999	3,547	727	27,588	1,065	8,521	2,641
1947	63,443	3,907	853	31,022	1,401	10,151	3,883
1948	71,730	4,169	922	34,786	1,765	11,474	5,038
1949	76,609	4,359	909	36,709	2,018	12,471	5,301
1950	81,916	4,566	869	38,950	2,267	13,566	5,810
1951	87,734	4,902	870	41,838	2,532	14,590	6,391
1952	93,245	5,214	878	44,903	2,870	15,805	6,487
1953	98,539	5,464	859	48,120	3,326	16,984	5,873
1954	102,629	5,809	799	50,721	3,664	18,037	5,453

End of Year	Passenger Cars (8)	Aircraft (9)	Ships and Boats (10)	Railroad Equipment (11)	Instruments (12)	Miscellaneous Equipment (13)
1945	246	23	2,529	6,087	517	923
1946	437	184	2,575	5,954	676	1,084
1947	965	282	2,669	6,099	903	1,308
1948	1,506	277	2,629	6,581	1,105	1,478
1949	2,216	277	2,570	7,050	1,250	1,479
1950	3,028	220	2,505	7,237	1,393	1,505
1951	3,356	188	2,485	7,662	1,485	1,487
1952	3,345	239	2,505	7,970	1,562	1,517
1953	3,599	260	2,554	8,177	1,721	1,602
1954	3,721	289	2,614	8,114	1,823	1,585

SOURCE, BY COLUMN

(1)   1946–54: Sum of cols. 2 to 13. Subsequent years: 1955, 106,576; 1956, 112,866; 1957, 118,868; and 1958, 120,473—obtained by adding net investment from Table B-116 to 1954 stock.

(2 to 13)   Same procedure as for Table B-127, cols. 2 to 13, but applied to expenditures in 1947–49 prices. Passenger cars stock for 1955–58, respectively: 4,234, 4,344, 4,495, and 4,269.

TABLE B-129

VALUE OF PRODUCER DURABLE GOODS, CURRENT PRICES

(millions of dollars)

End of Year	Total (1)	Furniture and Fixtures (2)	Cutlery and Hand Tools (3)	Industrial Machinery and Equipment (4)	Office and Store Machines (5)	Electric Machinery (6)	Trucks, Buses, Trailers (7)
1945	39,296	2,537	396	19,428	720	5,863	1,469
1946	48,732	3,100	628	24,112	1,020	7,619	2,323
1947	62,169	3,837	821	30,308	1,398	10,050	3,774
1948	73,806	4,277	961	36,004	1,772	11,647	5,206
1949	81,420	4,625	1,016	39,646	2,042	12,933	5,564
1950	92,776	5,274	1,047	45,260	2,360	15,087	6,320
1951	104,573	5,971	1,088	51,544	2,669	16,896	7,302
1952	111,860	6,361	1,133	55,904	3,016	18,193	7,106
1953	120,104	6,759	1,167	61,786	3,499	18,816	6,660
1954	128,312	7,331	1,150	66,292	3,891	21,177	6,182

End of Year	Passenger Cars (6)	Aircraft (9)	Ships and Boats (10)	Railroad Equipment (11)	Instruments (12)	Miscellaneous Equipment (13)
1945	189	18	2,438	5,095	430	713
1946	384	161	2,307	5,513	615	950
1947	938	273	2,605	5,989	892	1,284
1948	1,560	286	2,716	6,726	1,130	1,521
1949	2,347	301	2,737	7,360	1,290	1,559
1950	3,283	255	2,821	7,867	1,513	1,689
1951	3,816	230	2,970	8,696	1,672	1,719
1952	3,856	305	3,144	9,333	1,774	1,735
1953	4,067	348	3,341	9,812	2,007	1,842
1954	4,249	403	3,505	10,094	2,193	1,845

SOURCE, BY COLUMN

(1)   1946–54: Sum of cols. 2 to 13; 1955–58 values: 135,798; 154,560; 169,420; 175,213, respectively.

(2 to 13)   Accumulated constant stock of producer durables from Table B-128 multiplied by year-end index of producer durables equipment obtained by converting 1954 price indexes to 1947–49 base and averaging fourth quarter and first quarter of succeeding year (from *Survey of Current Business*, July 1959, p. 40, and earlier and later issues). Passenger car values for subsequent years: 1955, 5,005; 1956, 5,344; 1957, 5,754; 1958, 5,789.

TABLE B-130

NONFARM BUSINESS INVENTORIES, BOOK VALUES
(millions of dollars)

	Book Value (end of year)			Change in Book Value		
Year	Total (1)	Corporations (2)	Unincorporated Business (3)	Total (4)	Corporations (5)	Unincorporated Business (6)
1945	34,288	26,316	7,972	75	−463	538
1946	47,606	37,546	10,060	13,318	11,230	2,088
1947	56,274	44,685	11,589	8,668	7,139	1,529
1948	61,812	48,890	12,922	5,538	4,205	1,333
1949	57,284	45,313	11,971	−4,528	−3,577	−951
1950	69,343	55,101	14,242	12,059	9,788	2,271
1951	79,926	64,852	15,074	10,583	9,751	832
1952	80,890	66,102	14,788	964	1,250	−286
1953	83,123	67,911	15,212	2,233	1,809	424
1954	81,361	66,302	15,059	−1,762	−1,609	−153
1955	88,781	72,965	15,816	7,420	6,663	757
1956	97,051	80,542	16,509	8,270	7,577	693
1957	100,094	83,274	16,820	3,043	2,732	311
1958	95,648	78,843	16,805	−4,446	−4,431	−15

	Inventory Valuation Adjustment			Adjusted Change in Value of Inventories		
Year	Total (7)	Corporations (8)	Unincorporated Business (9)	Total (10)	Corporations (11)	Unincorporated Business (12)
1945	−670	−564	−106	−595	−1,027	432
1946	−6,968	−5,263	−1,705	6,350	5,967	383
1947	−7,370	−5,899	−1,471	1,298	1,240	58
1948	−2,562	−2,152	−410	2,976	2,053	923
1949	2,319	1,856	463	−2,209	−1,721	−488
1950	−6,059	−4,965	−1,094	6,000	4,823	1,177
1951	−1,523	−1,196	−327	9,060	8,555	505
1952	1,182	981	201	2,146	2,231	−85
1953	−1,165	−997	−168	1,068	812	256
1954	367	−318	−49	−2,129	−1,927	−202
1955	−1,934	−1,736	−198	5,486	4,927	559
1956	−3,195	−2,693	−502	5,075	4,884	191
1957	−1,829	−1,532	−297	1,214	1,200	14
1958	−451	−408	−43	−4,897	−4,839	−58

SOURCE, BY COLUMN

(1 to 3) 1945–49: Derived by cumulating backward cols. 4 to 6, respectively, from 1950 value.
1950: *National Income Supplement* to *Survey of Current Business*, 1954, p. 136.
1951–58: Derived by cumulating forward cols. 4 to 6, respectively, from 1950 value.
(4 to 12) 1945: *National Income Supplement* to *Survey of Current Business*, 1954, p. 211.
1946–55: *U.S. Income and Output*, p. 193.
1956–58: *Survey of Current Business*, July 1958, p. 30.

TABLE B-131

Nonfarm Business Inventories, Constant (1947–49) Prices
(millions of dollars)

Year	Value (end of year)			Change in Value		
	Total (1)	Corporations (2)	Unincorporated Business (3)	Total (4)	Corporations (5)	Unincorporated Business (6)
1945	47,822	36,703	11,119	—	—	—
1946	55,292	43,607	11,684	7,470	6,904	565
1947	56,785	45,091	11,694	1,493	1,484	10
1948	58,645	46,385	12,260	1,860	1,294	566
1949	57,227	45,268	11,959	−1,418	−1,117	−310
1950	61,969	49,241	12,727	4,742	3,973	768
1951	69,743	56,590	13,154	7,774	7,349	427
1952	71,647	58,549	13,098	1,904	1,959	−56
1953	72,533	59,259	13,274	886	710	176
1954	70,934	57,805	13,129	−1,599	−1,454	−145
1955	74,356	61,110	13,246	3,422	3,305	117
1956	78,141	64,849	13,292	3,785	3,739	46
1957	79,503	66,143	13,360	1,362	1,294	68
1958	75,432	62,179	13,253	−4,071	−3,964	−107

SOURCE, BY COLUMN: (1 to 3) Table B-130, cols. 1 to 3, divided by fourth quarter average of Bureau of Labor Statistics monthly index of wholesale prices for commodities other than farm products and foods (*Federal Reserve Bulletin*, various issues, e.g., March 1952, p. 311); (4 to 6) First differences of cols. 1 to 3, respectively.

TABLE B-132

Value of Private Nonfarm Forest Land
(amounts in billions of dollars)

End of Year	Total		Index of Stumpage Prices National Forests (1947–49 = 100) (3)	Corporate Holdings	
	Current Values (1)	1947–49 Prices (2)		Current Values (4)	1947–49 Prices (5)
1945	3.09	6.40	48	2.30	4.80
1946	3.80	6.44	59	2.85	4.85
1947	6.09	6.48	94	4.55	4.85
1948	7.57	6.52	116	5.70	4.90
1949	8.33	6.56	127	6.25	4.90
1950	11.87	6.60	180	8.90	4.95
1951	14.31	6.64	216	10.75	5.00
1952	13.29	6.68	199	9.95	5.00
1953	11.95	6.72	178	8.95	5.05
1954	12.61	6.76	187	9.45	5.05
1955	15.02	6.80	221	11.25	5.10
1956	14.69	6.84	215	11.00	5.15
1957	15.03	6.88	219	11.25	5.15
1958	13.73	6.92	199	10.30	5.20

SOURCE, BY COLUMN

(1) 1946: Estimate of U.S. Forest Service, *Studies in Income and Wealth*, Vol. 12, p. 233.

Other years: Obtained by applying to 1946 value the changes in stumpage prices of lumber in national forests as shown in col. 3, after adjusting for an estimated 0.6 per cent annual increase in timber stands, derived from Stoddard, *Journal of Forestry*, July 1958.

(2) 1946: Col. 1 divided by col. 3.
Other years: Obtained on assumption of a 0.6 per cent annual increase in timber stands.
(3) Derived by converting stumpage prices for Douglas fir, southern pine, and ponderosa pine to 1947–49 = 100 base; averaging successive years for year-end values (*Statistical Abstract*, 1959, p. 700, and earlier issues). 1957 and 1958 values extrapolated in ratio of U.S. Forest Service estimated stumpage prices.
(4 and 5) Estimated at three-fourths of cols. 1 and 2, respectively, on basis of data on distribution of ownership in *Timber Resource Review*, Department of Agriculture, Forest Service, Chapter IV.D, 1955, p. 20 (figures rounded to nearest $50 million). This estimate is based on assumption that almost all forest industry holdings and other (nonfarm) private holdings of over 500 acres represent corporate holdings, and the likelihood that the average value per acre of large holdings is above that of small holdings (cf. *ibid.*, Chapter IX, p. 102).

TABLE B-133

Value of Subsoil Assets
(billions of dollars)

	Current Prices				1947–49 Prices			
End of Year	Total (1)	Oil and Gas (2)	Coal (3)	Other Minerals (4)	Total (5)	Oil and Gas (6)	Coal (7)	Other Minerals (8)
1945	6.2	3.0	1.1	2.1	9.7	4.7	1.7	3.3
1946	7.1	3.4	1.3	2.4	10.0	4.9	1.7	3.4
1947	9.4	4.7	1.5	3.2	10.2	5.0	1.7	3.5
1948	12.8	6.8	1.6	4.4	10.9	5.5	1.7	3.7
1949	11.9	6.2	1.6	4.1	11.4	5.8	1.7	3.9
1950	12.5	6.6	1.6	4.3	11.7	6.0	1.7	4.0
1951	14.3	7.8	1.6	4.9	12.6	6.6	1.7	4.3
1952	14.7	8.1	1.6	5.0	12.8	6.7	1.7	4.4
1953	16.3	9.1	1.6	5.6	13.4	7.1	1.7	4.6
1954	16.9	9.5	1.6	5.8	13.6	7.2	1.7	4.7
1955	17.9	10.2	1.6	6.1	13.7	7.2	1.7	4.8
1956	19.0	10.9	1.6	6.5	14.0	7.4	1.7	4.9
1957	20.7	12.0	1.6	7.1	14.1	7.4	1.7	5.0
1958	19.9	11.5	1.6	6.8	14.2	7.5	1.7	5.0

SOURCE, BY COLUMN

(1) Sum of cols. 2 to 4.
(2) From Table B-134, col. 8.
(3) Derived by adjusting Bain's estimate (H. Foster Bain, et al., "Subsoil Wealth," *Studies in Income and Wealth*, Vol. 12, NBER p. 270) for changes in average price of coal mined (*Statistical Abstract*, various issues, e.g., 1955, p. 743).
(4) Estimated at 52 per cent of sum of cols. 2 and 3, the 1946 relation indicated by Bain's figures.
(5) Sum of cols. 6 to 8.
(6) Value for 1946 obtained by adjusting col. 2 for change in crude oil price (*Business Statistics*, various issues, e.g., 1955, p. 169) for increase between end of 1946 and 1947–49 average. Figures for other years obtained by multiplying 1946 values by index of proved reserves, derived from *Petroleum Facts and Figures*, 1959 ed., p. 63.
(7) Value for 1946 derived in same way as col. 6. Figures for other years assumed equal to 1946 since small discoveries may be regarded as offset by depletion.
(8) Estimated at 52 per cent of sum of cols. 6 and 7.

TABLE B-134
VALUE OF OIL AND GAS RESERVES

END OF YEAR	VALUE OF PRODUCTION			VALUE OF UNDERGROUND RESERVES					
				Undiscounted				Discounted Total	
	Crude Oil	Natural Gasoline ($ million)	Natural Gas	Crude Oil	Natural Gasoline	Natural Gas ($ billion)	Total	A	B
	(1)	(2)	(3)	(4)	(5)	(6)	(7)	(8)	(9)
1945	2,094	210	220	3.66	0.37	0.86	4.89	2.95	2.95
1946	2,443	210	235	4.28	0.37	0.92	5.57	3.35	3.35
1947	3,578	295	275	6.26	0.52	1.07	7.85	4.70	4.80
1948	5,245	459	333	9.18	0.80	1.30	11.28	6.75	7.00
1949	4,674	402	344	8.18	0.70	1.34	10.22	6.15	6.45
1950	4,963	420	409	8.69	0.73	1.60	11.02	6.60	7.05
1951	5,690	508	543	9.96	0.89	2.12	12.97	7.80	8.45
1952	5,785	533	624	10.12	0.93	2.43	13.48	8.10	8.90
1953	6,317	598	775	11.05	1.05	3.02	15.12	9.10	10.15
1954	6,427	581	882	11.25	1.02	3.44	15.71	9.45	10.70
1955	6,870	619	978	12.02	1.08	3.81	16.91	10.15	11.65
1956	7,263	697	1,084	12.71	1.22	4.24	18.17	10.90	12.70
1957	8,079	679	1,202	14.13	1.19	4.69	20.01	12.00	14.20
1958	7,379	690	1,278	12.91	1.21	4.98	19.10	11.45	13.75

SOURCE, BY COLUMN

(1 to 3) Statistical Abstract of the United States, various issues, e.g.; 1959, pp. 730/31.

(4 to 6) Cols. 1 and 2 multiplied by 1.75, and col. 3 multiplied by 3.90, following Bains' procedure (Studies in Income and Wealth, Vol. 12, pp. 265–266).

(7) Sum of cols. 4 to 6.

(8) Total A: Estimated at 60 per cent of col. 7 and rounded to nearest $50 million. This method implies that Bain's assumptions regarding royalty rates (12.5 per cent for oil and 10 per cent for gas), reserves (14 times production in 1946 for oil and 39 times for gas), and

discounting factor (8 per cent return on invested capital with sinking fund of 3 per cent) are applicable throughout the decade.

(9) Total B: Estimated to rise from 60 per cent of col. 7 by 1 percentage point a year beginning with 1947, to reflect probable decline in discounting factor. Figures rounded to nearest $50 million. The 1958 estimates are equivalent to a valuation per average barrel of proved reserves of $0.31 and $0.37, respectively, rather low figures (Petroleum Facts and Figures, 1959 ed., p. 63).

TABLE B-135

DISTRIBUTION OF OWNERSHIP OF SUBSOIL ASSETS
(billions of dollars)

End of Year	Current Prices		1947–49 Prices	
	Corporations (1)	Other (2)	Corporations (3)	Other (4)
1945	5.6	0.6	8.7	1.0
1946	6.4	0.7	9.0	1.0
1947	8.4	1.0	9.1	1.1
1948	11.5	1.3	9.8	1.1
1949	10.7	1.2	10.2	1.2
1950	11.2	1.3	10.5	1.2
1951	12.8	1.5	11.3	1.3
1952	13.2	1.5	11.5	1.3
1953	14.5	1.8	12.0	1.4
1954	15.1	1.8	12.2	1.4
1955	16.0	1.9	12.3	1.4
1956	17.0	2.0	12.5	1.5
1957	18.5	2.2	12.6	1.5
1958	17.8	2.1	12.7	1.5

SOURCE: Obtained by allocating 85 per cent of ownership of oil and gas wells and 95 per cent of that of coal and other minerals to corporations (Table B-133). This allocation is based primarily, in the case of oil and gas wells, on the proportion of total depletion allowances claimed by corporations, and for other minerals, on the share of corporations in the value of mining output (see *A Study of Saving* . . . , Vol. I, Table C-16, p. 929).

TABLE B-136

CAPITAL OUTLAY OF STATE GOVERNMENTS
(millions of dollars)

| | Total (1) | Construction | | | Equipment (5) | Purchases of Land and Existing Structures (6) |
		Total (2)	Highway (3)	Other (4)		
		FISCAL YEAR				
1946	368	292	232	60	42	33
1947	975	832	599	233	91	52
1948	1,456	1,268	904	364	117	71
1949	1,901	1,669	1,205	464	131	101
1950	2,237	1,966	1,314	652	141	131
1951	2,483	2,196	1,548	648	148	142
1952	2,658	2,323	1,696	627	158	178
1953	2,847	2,472	1,863	609	157	218
1954	3,347	2,831	2,204	627	173	342
1955	3,992	3,404	2,729	675	177	412
1956	4,564	3,872	3,107	765	203	489
1957	5,158	4,313	3,391	922	251	593
1958	5,924	5,000	3,874	1,126	271	653
1959	(5,796)	(4,900)	(3,828)	(1,072)	(268)	(628)
		CALENDAR YEAR				
1946	672	562	416	146	67	43
1947	1,216	1,050	752	298	104	62
1948	1,678	1,468	1,054	414	124	86
1949	2,069	1,817	1,259	558	136	116
1950	2,362	2,081	1,431	650	145	136
1951	2,572	2,359	1,622	637	153	160
1952	2,753	2,398	1,780	618	157	198
1953	3,097	2,652	2,034	618	165	280
1954	3,670	3,118	2,467	651	175	377
1955	4,278	3,638	2,918	720	190	450
1956	4,861	4,093	3,249	844	227	541
1957	5,541	4,657	3,633	1,024	261	623
1958	(5,859)	(4,950)	(3,851)	(1,099)	(269)	(641)

SOURCE, BY COLUMN

Fiscal Year
(1)   1946, 1948, 1950: *Revised Summary of State Government Finances, 1942–1950*, Bureau of the Census, p. 5.

1947, 1949: Since Census Bureau's revision of data was limited to even numbered years for period 1942–50, probable revised figures for 1947 and 1949 were estimated by increasing the unrevised figures as given in *Compendium of State Government Finances in 1950*, Census, p. 6, by ratio of the unrevised to revised figures in adjoining years.

1951–55: *Summary of State Government Finances in 1955*, p. 7.
1956–58: *Ibid., in 1958*, p. 7.

(2)   1946, 1948: *Revised Summary of State Government Finances, 1942–1950*, p. 5.
1947, 1949: Sum of cols. 3 and 4.
1950–55: *Summary of State Government Finances in 1955*, p. 7.
1956–58: *Ibid., in 1958*, p. 7.

(3) 1946–50: *Compendium of State Government Finances*, various issues, (e.g., 1946, p. 23; 1947–50, p. 26). The Census Bureau constructed only total figures and did not develop construction figures by function. If it had, the figures shown in this table for highway construction, 1946–50, would have been slightly changed.

1951: Estimated at 90 per cent of capital outlay on highways (*ibid.*, 1951, p. 27) on basis of the 1946–50 relation of construction expenditures to capital outlay on highways (*ibid.*, various issues, e.g., 1950, pp. 26 and 27).

1952: *Summary of Government Finances in 1952*, Bureau of the Census, p. 31.

1953: *Ibid., in 1953*, p. 27.

1954: *Ibid., in 1954*, p. 32.

1955–56: Estimated by applying to figures of capital outlays on highways (*Summary of State Government Finances in 1955*, p. 14) the 1954 ratio of highway construction to highway capital outlays (*ibid., in 1954*, p. 14; *ibid., in 1956*, p. 14).

1957–58: *Ibid., in 1957*, Table 2, p. 9. *Ibid., in 1958*, Table 2, p. 8.

(4) 1946, 1948: Col. 2 minus col. 3.

1947, 1949: Col. 1 minus sum of cols. 3, 5, and 6.

1950–58: Col. 2 minus col. 3.

(5) 1946, 1948: *Revised Summary of State Government Finances, 1942–1950*, p. 5.

1947, 1949: *Compendium of State Government Finances in 1947*, p. 26 and *ibid., in 1949*, p. 26.

1950–58: *Summary of State Government Finances*, various issues, e.g., p. 7.

(6) 1946, 1948: *Revised Summary of State Government Finances, 1942–1950*, p. 5.

1947, 1949: Obtained by straight-line interpolation between the 1946 and 1948, and the 1948 and 1950 figures, respectively.

1950–58: *Summary of State Government Finances*, various issues, e.g., *in 1955*, p. 7.

Calendar Year

Figures for 1946–57 obtained by averaging fiscal year totals. Fiscal years of state governments, with a few exceptions, are for the twelve months ended June 30 (see *Revised Summary of State Government Finances, 1942–1950*, Table 2).

Calendar year figures for 1958 and fiscal year for 1959 estimated on basis of Department of Commerce figures (see Tables B-156 and B-140).

NET INVESTMENT THROUGH OUTLAYS FOR CONSTRUCTION BY
STATE GOVERNMENTS
(millions of dollars)

	Expenditures		Depreciation			Net Investment		
	Original Cost (1)	1947–49 Prices (2)	Original Cost (3)	1947–49 Prices (4)	Replacement Cost (5)	Original Cost (6)	1947–49 Prices (7)	Replacement Cost (8)
			FISCAL YEAR					
1946	292	396	450	793	592	−158	−397	−300
1947	832	969	466	811	705	366	158	127
1948	1,268	1,277	497	843	836	771	434	432
1949	1,669	1,569	539	883	940	1,130	686	729
1950	1,966	2,013	590	933	900	1,376	1,080	1,066
1951	2,196	2,105	646	988	1,023	1,550	1,117	1,173
1952	2,323	2,088	706	1,042	1,155	1,617	1,046	1,168
1953	2,472	2,149	769	1,094	1,255	1,703	1,055	1,217
1954	2,831	2,554	838	1,153	1,275	1,993	1,401	1,556
1955	3,404	3,140	921	1,225	1,332	2,483	1,915	2,072
1956	3,872	3,427	1,021	1,310	1,483	2,851	2,117	2,389
1957	4,313	3,571	1,134	1,402	1,692	3,179	2,169	2,621
1958	5,000	4,078	1,261	1,499	1,831	3,739	2,579	3,169
1959	(4,900)	4,045	1,395	1,600	1,935	3,505	2,445	2,965
			CALENDAR YEAR					
1946	562	682	458	802	648	104	−120	−86
1947	1,050	1,123	482	827	770	568	296	280
1948	1,468	1,423	518	863	888	951	560	581
1949	1,817	1,791	564	908	920	1,253	883	897
1950	2,081	2,059	618	960	962	1,463	1,099	1,119
1951	2,259	2,096	676	1,015	1,089	1,583	1,081	1,170
1952	2,398	2,118	738	1,068	1,205	1,660	1,050	1,193
1953	2,652	2,352	804	1,124	1,265	1,848	1,228	1,387
1954	3,118	2,847	880	1,189	1,304	2,238	1,658	1,814
1955	3,638	3,284	971	1,268	1,408	2,667	2,016	2,231
1956	4,093	3,499	1,078	1,356	1,588	3,015	2,143	2,505
1957	4,657	3,825	1,198	1,450	1,762	3,459	2,374	2,895
1958	(4,950)	4,062	1,328	1,550	1,883	3,622	2,512	3,067

SOURCE, BY COLUMN

Fiscal Year

(1) From Table B-136, col. 2; 1959 rough estimate (see Table B-136).

(2) Obtained by dividing the components of col. 1 (Table B-136, cols. 3 and 4) as derived from Department of Commerce figures (see Tables B-156 and B-140).

(3) Components of col. 1 depreciated assuming an average life of thirty years for highway construction and fifty years for other construction. Expenditures for years before 1946 from *A Study of Saving* ... , Vol. I, Table G-15, cols. 2 and 3. Col. 3 divided between other capital outlay and equipment in the ratio of 80:20 on the basis of the 1952–54 relationship.

(4) Same procedure as for col. 3, except expenditure figures from col. 2. Expenditures in 1947–49 prices for years before 1946 obtained by deflating expenditures in original cost (see col. 3) by appropriate price indexes. Indexes for period 1915–45 from same sources as the later figures; for years before 1915 indexes extrapolated by public construction index given in *A Study of Saving* ... , Vol. I, Table R-20, col. 8.

(5) Components of col. 4 multiplied by appropriate price indexes from Table B-143.

(6) Col. 1 minus col. 3.

(7) Col. 2 minus col. 4.

(8) Col. 1 minus col. 5.

Calendar Year

Figures, all columns, obtained by averaging fiscal year figures for current and succeeding year.

TABLE B-138

Net Investment and Accumulated Stock of Federal Aid Highway Construction
(millions of dollars)

| Year | Expenditures | | Depreciation | | | Net Investment | | | Accumulated Value | | |
	Original Cost (1)	1947–49 Prices (2)	Original Cost (3)	1947–49 Prices (4)	Replacement Cost (5)	Original Cost (6)	1947–49 Prices (7)	Replacement Cost (8)	Original Cost (9)	1947–49 Prices (10)	Replacement Cost (11)
1945									4,359	4,879	3,786
1946	180	218	222	228	188	−42	−10	−8	4,318	4,869	4,363
1947	296	316	230	236	222	66	80	74	4,384	4,948	4,894
1948	385	367	241	247	260	144	120	125	4,528	5,068	5,484
1949	406	401	253	246	249	153	155	157	4,682	5,223	4,936
1950	397	415	263	256	245	134	159	152	4,815	5,382	5,560
1951	397	372	274	266	284	123	106	163	4,939	5,488	6,020
1952	494	438	286	276	312	208	162	182	5,147	5,650	6,491
1953	507	456	300	288	320	207	168	187	5,354	5,818	6,237
1954	587	559	315	301	316	272	258	271	5,625	6,076	6,416
1955	635	598	333	316	336	302	282	299	5,927	6,357	6,917
1956	763	653	353	334	378	387	320	385	6,315	6,677	7,812
1957	1,217	1,038	384	358	420	833	680	797	7,148	7,357	8,622
1958	2,020	1,741	435	401	465	1,585	1,340	1,555	8,735	8,697	10,149

Source, by Column

(1) Expenditure figures from *Construction Volume and Costs, 1915–1956*, p. 11, as revised and brought up-to-date by Census Bureau.

(2) Original cost expenditures divided by annual index of highway construction from Table B-143, col. 2.

(3) Expenditure figures in col. 1 depreciated assuming an average life of thirty years. Figures for years before 1946 from *Construction Volume and Costs, 1915–1956*, p. 11.

(4) Same procedure as for col. 3 using expenditures in 1947–49 prices from col. 2.

(5) Col. 4 multiplied by Table B-143, col. 2.

(6) Col. 1 minus col. 3.

(7) Col. 2 minus col. 4.

(8) Col. 1 minus col. 5.

(9) Cumulated depreciated original cost value added to 1945 stock.

(10) Same procedure as for col. 9 using 1947–49 prices.

(11) Col. 10 multiplied by Table B-143, col. 5.

TABLE B-139
NET INVESTMENT THROUGH OUTLAYS FOR EQUIPMENT BY
STATE GOVERNMENTS
(millions of dollars)

	Expenditures		Depreciation			Net Investment		
	Original Cost (1)	1947–49 Prices (2)	Original Cost (3)	1947–49 Prices (4)	Replacement Cost (5)	Original Cost (6)	1947–49 Prices (7)	Replacement Cost (8)
				FISCAL YEAR				
1946	42	54	26	41	32	16	13	10
1947	91	104	29	44	38	62	60	53
1948	117	120	35	49	48	82	71	69
1949	131	127	43	55	57	88	72	74
1950	141	132	53	63	67	88	69	74
1951	148	131	62	69	78	86	62	70
1952	158	134	71	75	88	87	59	70
1953	157	132	82	82	97	75	50	60
1954	173	145	94	90	108	79	55	65
1955	177	144	107	100	123	70	44	54
1956	203	158	121	111	143	82	47	60
1957	251	184	139	123	168	112	61	83
1958	271	190	159	136	194	112	54	77
1959	(268)	184	176	145	211	92	39	57
				CALENDAR YEAR				
1946	67	79	28	42	35	39	37	32
1947	104	112	32	47	43	72	65	61
1948	124	124	39	52	52	85	72	72
1949	136	129	48	59	62	88	70	74
1950	145	132	58	66	73	87	66	72
1951	153	133	67	72	83	86	61	70
1952	157	133	76	79	92	81	54	65
1953	165	138	88	86	102	77	52	63
1954	175	145	100	95	115	75	51	60
1955	190	151	114	105	133	76	46	57
1956	227	171	130	117	155	97	54	72
1957	261	187	149	129	181	112	58	80
1958	(269)	187	167	140	202	102	47	67

SOURCE, BY COLUMN

Fiscal Year
(1) From Table B-136, col. 6; 1959 rough estimate derived from 1958 calendar year figure.
(2) Col. 1 divided by implicit price deflator of producer durable goods, *U.S. Income and Output*, pp. 220–221, as brought up to date from *Survey of Current Business*, July 1959, p. 41; index averaged to apply to fiscal years.
(3) Col. 1 depreciated assuming an average life of twelve years. Expenditures for years before 1946 obtained according to procedure described in Table B-137.
(4) Same procedure as for col. 3, but applied to figures of col. 2.
(5) Col. 4 multiplied by price deflator (see col. 1).
(6) Col. 1 minus col. 3.
(7) Col. 2 minus col. 4.
(8) Col. 1 minus col. 5.

Calendar Year
Figures, all cols., obtained by averaging fiscal year figures for current and succeeding year.

TABLE B-140

CAPITAL OUTLAY OF LOCAL GOVERNMENTS
(millions of dollars)

| Year | Total (1) | Construction | | | Equipment (5) | Purchases of Land and Existing Structures (6) |
		Total (2)	Highway (3)	Other (4)		
1946	937	678	140	538	147	112
1947	1,600	1,245	240	1,005	222	133
1948	2,269	1,817	340	1,477	298	154
1949	3,370	2,841	505	2,336	310	219
1950	3,810	3,203	570	2,633	323	284
1951	4,035	3,374	605	2,769	374	287
1052	4,778	4,063	651	3,412	426	289
1953	5,058	4,291	743	3,548	455	312
1954	5,778	4,907	778	4,129	527	344
1955	6,713	5,644	918	4,726	557	512
1956	6,843	5,482	874	4,608	649	712
1957	7,481	6,086	993	5,093	781	615
1958	8,009	6,651	1,132	5,519	754	604

SOURCE, BY COLUMN

Fiscal year taken as ending December 31 on basis of information given in *Historical Statistics on State and Local Government Finances, 1902–1953*, Bureau of the Census, p. 9.

(1)   1946, 1948, 1950: *Ibid.*, p. 21.

1947, 1949: Since Bureau of Census' revised data are limited to even numbered years for the period 1942–50, figures for 1947 and 1949 were obtained by interpolating between the 1946 and 1948, and the 1948 and 1950 figures, respectively, on the basis of unrevised data for cities having more than 25,000 inhabitants given in *Summary of City Government Finances in 1950*, Bureau of the Census, p. 4.

1951: Estimated by applying, to the revised data of capital outlay of cities of over 250,000 inhabitants, the average of the ratios of capital outlay of cities of over 250,000 inhabitants to capital outlay of all local governments in 1950 and 1952. Data from Census Publications: *Compendium of City Government Finances in 1954*, p. 6; and *Historical Statistics on State and Local Government Finances, 1902–1953*, p. 21.

1952–54: *Summary of Governmental Finances in 1954*, Bureau of the Census, p. 31; 1956, *ibid.*, *in 1956*, p. 30.

1955–58: *Summary of Governmental Finances*, various issues, e.g., *in 1957*, p. 31; *in 1958*, p. 17.

(2)   1946, 1948, 1950: *Historical Statistics on State and Local Government Finances, 1902–1953*, p. 21.

1947, 1949, 1951: Sum of cols. 3 and 4.

1952–58: *Summary of Governmental Finances*, various issues, e.g., *in 1954*, p. 31; *in 1955*, p. 29, *in 1956*, p. 30; *in 1957*, p. 31.

(3)   1946–51: Estimated at 15 per cent of col. 1, since this is the approximate relationship prevailing for both the cities of over 250,000 inhabitants and local government data in years for which the amount is known.

1952–58: *Summary of Governmental Finances*, various issues, e.g., *in 1954*, p. 32.

(4)   1946, 1948, 1950: Col. 2 minus col. 3.

Other Years: *Summary of Governmental Finances*, various issues.

(5 and 6)   1946, 1948, 1950: *Historical Statistics on State and Local Government Finances, 1902–1953*, p. 21.

1947, 1949: Straight-line interpolation between adjoining year values.

1952–58: *Summary of Governmental Finances*, various issues, e.g., *in 1954*, p. 31.

TABLE B-141

NET INVESTMENT THROUGH OUTLAYS FOR CONSTRUCTION BY LOCAL GOVERNMENTS
(millions of dollars)

Year	Expenditures		Depreciation			Net Investment		
	Original Cost (1)	1947–49 Prices (2)	Original Cost (3)	1947–49 Prices (4)	Replacement Cost (5)	Original Cost (6)	1947–49 Prices (7)	Replacement Cost (8)
1946	678	954	792	1,750	1,283	−114	−796	−605
1947	1,245	1,354	802	1,744	1,609	443	−390	−364
1948	1,817	1,740	826	1,751	1,830	991	−11	−13
1949	2,841	2,739	865	1,773	1,832	1,976	966	1,009
1950	3,203	3,071	915	1,806	1,860	2,288	1,265	1,343
1951	3,374	3,015	967	1,837	2,041	2,407	1,178	1,333
1952	4,063	3,476	1,026	1,868	2,171	3,037	1,608	1,892
1953	4,291	3,560	1,098	1,908	2,277	3,193	1,652	2,014
1954	4,907	4,026	1,179	1,954	2,338	3,728	2,072	2,569
1955	5,644	4,520	1,273	2,006	2,462	4.371	2,514	3,182
1956	5,482	4,182	1,372	2,058	2,657	4,110	2,124	2,825
1957	6,086	4,446	1,474	2,105	2,842	4,612	2,341	3,247
1958	6,651	4,754	1,589	2,154	2,979	5,062	2,600	3,672

SOURCE, BY COLUMN

(1) From Table B-140, col. 2.
(2) Obtained by dividing the components of col. 1 (Table B-140, cols. 3 and 4) by appropriate price indexes from Table B-143.
(3) Components of col. 1 depreciated assuming an average life of thirty years for highway construction and fifty years for other construction. Expenditures for years before 1946 from *A Study of Saving* . . . , Vol. I, Table G-6, cols. 2 and 6.
(4) Same procedure as for col. 3, except expenditure figures from col. 2. Expenditures in 1947–49 prices for years before 1946 obtained by deflating expenditures in original cost (see col. 3) by appropriate price indexes (indexes for period 1915–45 from same source as the later figures; for years 1915, extrapolated by public construction index, given in *A Study of Saving* . . . , Vol. I, Table R-20, col. 8).
(5) Components of col. 4 multiplied by appropriate price indexes from Table B-143.
(6) Col. 1 minus col. 3.
(7) Col. 2 minus col. 4.
(8) Col. 1 minus col. 5.

TABLE B-142

NET INVESTMENT THROUGH OUTLAYS FOR EQUIPMENT BY LOCAL GOVERNMENTS
(millions of dollars)

	Expenditures		Depreciation			Net Investment		
Year	Original Cost (1)	1947–49 Prices (2)	Original Cost (3)	1947–49 Prices (4)	Replacement Cost (5)	Original Cost (6)	1947–49 Prices (7)	Replacement Cost (8)
1946	147	180	71	113	92	76	67	55
1947	222	238	82	123	115	140	115	107
1948	298	295	99	136	137	199	159	161
1949	310	293	118	149	158	192	144	152
1950	323	299	138	162	175	185	137	148
1951	374	319	159	175	205	215	144	169
1952	426	361	183	188	222	243	173	204
1953	455	382	210	204	243	245	178	212
1954	527	439	245	230	276	282	209	251
1955	557	447	287	261	325	270	186	232
1956	649	490	334	297	393	315	193	256
1957	781	555	391	337	474	390	218	307
1958	754	521	448	372	538	306	149	216

SOURCE, BY COLUMN

(1) From Table B-140, col. 5.
(2) Col. 1, divided by implicit price deflator of producer durable goods (*U.S. Income and Output*, pp. 220–221) as brought up-to-date from *Survey of Current Business*, July 1959, p. 41.
(3) Col. 1 depreciated assuming an average life of twelve years. Expenditures for years before 1946 obtained from *A Study of Saving . . .*, Vol. I, Table G-6, col. 5.
(4) Col. 2 depreciated assuming an average life of twelve years. Expenditures in 1947–49 prices for years before 1946 obtained by deflating expenditures in original cost (see col. 3) by implicit price deflator (see col. 1).
(5) Col. 1, multiplied by price deflator (see col. 1).
(6) Col. 1 minus col. 3.
(7) Col. 2 minus col. 4.
(8) Col. 1 minus col. 5

TABLE B-143

Cost Indexes for Government Construction
(1947–49 = 100.0)

	Annual Averages			Year-End Averages		
	Nonresidential Building (1)	Highways (2)	Conservation and Development (3)	Nonresidential Building (4)	Highways (5)	Conservation and Development (6)
	CALENDAR YEAR					
1945	57.7	75.7	69.8	60.1	77.6	72.2
1946	68.5	82.6	78.6	80.0	89.6	85.9
1947	91.5	93.8	91.9	100.0	98.9	98.2
1948	104.3	105.0	102.4	106.7	108.2	105.4
1949	104.3	101.3	105.6	103.1	94.5	106.8
1950	106.4	95.6	111.8	110.7	103.3	116.6
1951	113.1	106.7	118.3	115.0	109.7	119.3
1952	117.7	112.8	123.0	120.8	114.9	126.4
1953	122.7	111.3	129.7	124.4	107.2	132.8
1954	125.7	105.0	135.6	127.2	105.6	137.9
1955	129.3	106.1	141.0	132.0	108.8	144.3
1956	135.1	113.4	148.1	137.9	117.0	151.3
1957	141.5	117.2	155.0	143.0	117.2	158.2
1958	146.1	116.0	161.4	147.0	116.7	164.0
	FISCAL YEAR					
1945	56.4	76.6	—	57.3	75.8	—
1946	61.1	77.6	—	68.4	80.3	—
1947	80.0	88.4	—	92.0	93.8	—
1948	99.4	99.2	—	104.2	105.2	—
1949	105.7	106.6	—	103.9	100.8	—
1950	103.6	94.9	—	106.4	94.0	—
1951	110.4	102.0	—	113.4	106.8	—
1952	115.1	109.9	—	117.6	113.1	—
1953	120.4	113.4	—	122.6	110.4	—
1954	124.4	107.5	—	125.5	104.2	—
1955	127.2	104.6	—	129.2	105.3	—
1956	132.1	109.1	—	135.3	114.0	—
1957	138.1	117.0	—	141.7	118.0	—
1958	144.8	117.4	—	145.0	116.0	—
1959	147.3	115.4	—	150.5	113.0	—

SOURCE: Cost indexes used are for the most part those applied by the Department of Commerce to the various types of construction in its deflation of expenditures from current to constant prices. For nonresidential building, the American Appraisal Company index is used; for highways, the Bureau of Public Roads index; and for conservation and development, an unweighted average of the construction indexes of the Associated General Contractors and the *Engineering News Record*.

The calendar-year annual average figures are from *Construction Volume and Costs, 1915–1956*, Department of Commerce, pp. 54, 55.

The calendar year-end indexes for nonresidential building, and conservation and development, are averages of December of the current year and January of the following year, from *ibid.*, pp. 30, 31; *Statistical Supplement to Survey of Current Business*, various issues; and *Construction Review*, e.g., March 1957, p. 39. For highways, the figures are from *Construction Cost Indexes*, Bureau of Labor Statistics, and various releases of Bureau of Public Roads, e.g., *Price Trends for Federal-Aid Highway Construction*, and *Survey of Current Business*, various issues, e.g., May 1957, S-8.

The fiscal-year annual average figures were obtained by averaging the indexes for the appropriate months from the sources listed above.

The fiscal year-end figures were obtained by averaging June and July indexes for nonresidential building, and second- and third-quarter indexes for highways from the sources listed above.

TABLE B-144

NET INVESTMENT AND ACCUMULATED STOCK OF STATE AND LOCAL RESIDENTIAL DWELLINGS, NONWAR HOUSING
(millions of dollars)

Year	Expenditures Original Cost (1)	Expenditures 1947–49 Prices (2)	Depreciation Original Cost (3)	Depreciation 1947–49 Prices (4)	Depreciation Replacement Cost (5)	Net Investment Original Cost (6)	Net Investment 1947–49 Prices (7)	Net Investment Replacement Cost (8)	Accumulated Value Original Cost (9)	Accumulated Value 1947–49 Prices (10)	Accumulated Value Replacement Cost (11)
1945	—	—	—	—	—	—	—	—	645	1,191	873
1946	65	82	15	27	21	50	55	44	695	1,246	1,042
1947	80	89	16	29	26	64	60	54	759	1,306	1,281
1948	113	108	18	31	32	95	77	81	854	1,383	1,472
1949	326	321	23	35	37	303	286	289	1,157	1,669	1,746
1950	330	307	29	41	45	301	266	285	1,458	1,935	2,225
1951	585	503	38	49	58	547	454	537	2,005	2,389	2,862
1952	638	537	51	60	73	587	477	565	2,592	2,866	3,545
1953	535	442	62	70	88	473	372	447	3,065	3,238	4,106
1954	331	277	71	77	97	260	200	234	3,325	3,438	4,394
1955	264	211	77	82	107	187	129	157	3,512	3,567	4,767
1956	275	212	82	86	118	193	126	157	3,705	3,693	5,138
1957	351	266	89	91	128	262	175	223	3,967	3,869	5,506
1958	483	363	97	97	139	386	266	344	4,354	4,135	6,033

SOURCE, BY COLUMN

(1) 1946–54, *Construction Volume and Costs*, 1915–1956, p. 10.
1957–58, *Construction Review*, Jan. 1959, p. 20.
(2) Col. 1 deflated by 1947–49 conversion index obtained by dividing original cost by 1947–49 cost of total public housing expenditures, from source shown in col. 1.
(3) Col. 1 depreciated using 50-year life.
(4) Col. 2 depreciated using 50-year life.

(5) Col. 4 multiplied by Table B-9, col. 2.
(6) Col. 1 minus col. 3.
(7) Col. 2 minus col. 4.
(8) Col. 1 minus col. 5.
(9) 1945 stock, plus cumulated savings from col. 6.
(10) 1945 stock, plus cumulated savings from col. 7.
(11) Col. 10 multiplied by year-end index from Table B-9, col. 4.

TABLE B-145
Net Investment in Veterans Re-use Housing
(millions of dollars)

Year	Expenditures		Depreciation			Net Investment			Accumulated Value		
	Original Cost (1)	1947–49 Prices (2)	Original Cost (3)	1947–49 Prices (4)	Replacement Cost (5)	Original Cost (6)	1947–49 Prices (7)	Replacement Cost (8)	Original Cost (9)	1947–49 Prices (10)	Replacement Cost (11)
1946	301	381	8	10	8	293	371	293	293	371	310
1947	111	124	18	22	20	93	102	91	386	473	464
1948	10	10	21	26	27	−11	−16	−17	375	457	486
1949	—	—	21	26	27	−21	−26	−27	354	431	451
1950	—	—	21	26	28	−21	−26	−28	333	405	466
1951	—	—	21	26	31	−21	−26	−31	312	379	454
1952	—	—	21	26	32	−21	−26	−32	291	353	437
1953	—	—	21	26	33	−21	−26	−33	270	327	415
1954	—	—	21	26	33	−21	−26	−33	249	301	385
1955	—	—	21	26	34	−21	−26	−34	228	275	367
1956	—	—	21	26	36	−21	−26	−36	207	249	346
1957	—	—	21	26	37	−21	−26	−37	186	223	317
1958	—	—	21	26	37	−21	−26	−37	165	197	287

Source, by Column

(1) 1946, *Construction Volume and Costs* 1915–1956, p. 10; federal aid plus $240 million of direct federal funds; 1947–58, *ibid*, federal aid only.
(2) See note to Table B-144, col. 2.
(3) Col. 1 depreciated using twenty-year basis.
(4) Col. 2 depreciated using twenty-year basis.
(5) Col. 4 multiplied by Table B-9, col. 2.
(6) Col. 1 minus col. 3.
(7) Col. 2 minus col. 4.
(8) Col. 1 minus col. 5.
(9) Depreciated 1946 stock plus cumulated savings from col. 6.
(10) Depreciated 1946 stock plus cumulated savings from col. 7.
(11) Col. 10 multiplied by Table B-9, col. 4.

TABLE B-146

NET INVESTMENT IN VETERANS RE-USE HOUSING TRANSFERRED TO PRIVATE OWNERSHIP

(millions of dollars)

Year	Expenditures[a]		Depreciation			Net Investment			Accumulated Value		
	Original Cost (1)	1947–49 Prices (2)	Original Cost (3)	1947–49 Prices (4)	Replacement Cost (5)	Original Cost (6)	1947–49 Prices (7)	Replacement Cost (8)	Original Cost (9)	1947–49 Prices (10)	Replacement Cost (11)
1946	—	—	—	—	—	—	—	—	—	—	—
1947	48	61	1	2	2	47	59	46	47	59	58
1948	104	132	5	6	6	99	126	98	146	185	197
1949	76	85	10	12	13	66	73	63	212	258	270
1950	55	71	13	16	18	42	55	37	254	313	360
1951	8	10	14	18	21	-6	-8	-13	248	305	365
1952	7	9	15	18	22	-8	-9	-15	240	296	366
1953	16	20	16	19	24	0	1	-8	240	297	378
1954	8	11	16	20	25	-8	-9	-17	232	288	368
1955	9	3	17	21	27	-8	-18	-18	224	270	361
1956	—	—	18	22	29	-18	-22	-29	206	248	345
1957	—	—	20	25	36	-20	-25	-36	186	223	317
1958	—	—	21	26	37	-21	-26	-37	165	197	287

SOURCE: See source to Table B-145.

[a] These are transfers rather than original expenditures.

TABLE B-147

Net Investment in Veterans Re-Use Housing Retained Under State and Local Ownership

(millions of dollars)

Year	Expenditures[a]		Depreciation			Net Investment			Accumulated Value		
	Original Cost (1)	1947–49 Prices (2)	Original Cost (3)	1947–49 Prices (4)	Replacement Cost (5)	Original Cost (6)	1947–49 Prices (7)	Replacement Cost (8)	Original Cost (9)	1947–49 Prices (10)	Replacement Cost (11)
1946	301	381	8	10	8	293	371	293	293	371	310
1947	63	63	17	20	18	46	43	45	339	414	406
1948	−94	−122	16	20	21	−110	−142	−115	229	272	289
1949	−76	−85	11	14	14	−87	−99	−90	142	173	181
1950	−55	−71	8	10	10	−63	−81	−65	79	93	106
1951	−8	−10	7	8	10	−15	−18	−18	64	74	89
1952	−7	−9	6	8	9	−13	−17	−17	51	57	71
1953	−16	−20	5	7	8	−21	−27	−25	30	30	37
1954	−8	−11	5	6	7	−13	−17	−16	17	13	17
1955	−9	−3	4	5	7	−13	−8	−16	4	5	6
1956	0	0	3	4	1	−3	−4	−7	1	1	1
1957	0	0	1	1	1	−1	−1	−1	—	—	—
1958	0	0	—	—	—	—	—	—	—	—	—

Source: See source to Table B-145.

[a] These are transfers rather than original expenditures.

TABLE B-148

VALUE OF GOVERNMENT STRUCTURES, ORIGINAL COST

(millions of dollars)

| End of Year | Federal Government (civilian) | | | Government Corporations (4) | State Governments (5) | Local Governments (6) | State and Local Residential (7) |
	Total (1)	Residential (2)	Nonresidential (3)				
1945	42,512	935	5,964	4,006	13,266	17,696	645
1946	42,666	759	6,157	3,851	13,329	17,582	988
1947	43,975	630	6,550	3,709	13,963	18,025	1,098
1948	46,427	502	7,194	3,574	15,058	19,016	1,083
1949	50,837	455	8,140	3,486	16,465	20,992	1,299
1950	55,805	394	9,102	3,431	18,061	23,280	1,537
1951	61,228	346	9,945	3,413	19,768	25,687	2,069
1952	67,405	296	10,687	3,419	21,636	28,724	2,643
1953	73,772	278	11,319	3,472	23,691	31,917	3,095
1954	80,733	235	11,768	3,543	26,200	35,645	3,342
1955	88,629	202	12,252	3,473	29,170	40,016	3,516
1956	96,862	185	12,953	3,369	32,523	44,126	3,706
1957	106,846	331	13,671	3,274	36,865	48,738	3,967
1958	118,628	666	14,564	3,169	42,075	53,800	4,354

SOURCE, BY COLUMN

(1) Sum of cols. 2 to 7.

(2) Depreciated original cost value of all federal residential construction less transfers to private housing (see Tables B-164 and B-165).

(3) Depreciated original cost value of federal nonresidential buildings, highways, and conservation and development construction. Derived by addition of cumulated net investment to estimated value for 1945, obtained by cumulating expenditures less depreciation for number of years preceding 1945 corresponding to the assumed length of life of asset involved (see Table B-158).

(4) Depreciated fixed assets of government corporations and Reconstruction Finance Corporation plant. (See Table B-160 and *A Study of Saving* . . . , Vol. I, Table F-14, col. 12.)

(5) Depreciated original cost value of state highway, Federal Aid highway, and other construction derived according to procedure described for col. 3. (see also Tables B-137 and B-138).

(6) Depreciated original cost value of local highway and other construction (see col. 3 and Table B-141).

(7) Depreciated original cost value of state and local housing less transfers to private housing (see Table B-146).

TABLE B-149

VALUE OF GOVERNMENT STRUCTURES, CONSTANT (1947–49) PRICES

(millions of dollars)

| End of Year | Total (1) | Federal Government (*civilian*) | | Government Corporations (4) | State Governments (5) | Local Governments (6) | State and Local Residential (7) |
		Residential (2)	Nonresidential (3)				
1945	85,589	1,668	12,915	8,110	21,421	40,284	1,191
1946	84,585	1,370	13,028	7,791	21,291	39,488	1,617
1947	84,416	1,151	13,293	7,478	21,676	39,098	1,720
1948	84,943	944	13,742	7,168	22,347	39,087	1,655
1949	87,496	852	14,463	6,902	23,384	40,053	1,842
1950	90,555	746	15,156	6,667	24,641	41,318	2,027
1951	93,595	663	15,686	6,457	25,830	42,496	2,463
1952	97,005	575	16,099	6,262	27,042	44,104	2,923
1953	100,475	525	16,391	6,098	28,437	45,756	3,268
1954	104,652	547	16,527	5,945	30,354	47,828	3,451
1955	109,355	440	16,673	5,678	32,650	50,342	3,572
1956	113,986	345	16,968	5,388	35,125	52,466	3,694
1957	119,657	448	17,228	5,137	38,168	54,807	3,869
1958	126,770	693	17,581	4,934	42,020	57,407	4,135

SOURCE, BY COLUMN

(1) Sum of cols. 2 to 7.
(2) Depreciated constant cost value of all federal residential construction less transfers to private housing (see Tables B-164 and B-165).
(3 to 6) Same procedure as for Table B-148, but applied to expen-

ditures in 1947–49 prices, as shown in Tables B-137, B-138, B-141, B-158, and B-160.

(7) Depreciated constant cost value of state and local housing, less transfers to private housing (see Table B-144).

TABLE B-150

VALUE OF GOVERNMENT STRUCTURES, CURRENT PRICES
(millions of dollars)

End of Year	Total (1)	Federal Government (civilian) Residential (2)	Nonresidential (3)	Government Corporations (4)	State Governments (5)	Local Governments (6)	State and Local Residential (7)
1945	57,384	1,207	8,887	4,874	15,950	25,593	873
1946	70,356	1,146	10,987	6,233	18,330	32,308	1,352
1947	83,910	1,129	13,127	7,478	21,470	39,019	1,687
1948	90,074	993	14,551	7,648	23,332	41,789	1,761
1949	88,923	891	15,219	7,116	23,060	40,710	1,927
1950	98,117	841	17,341	7,380	25,510	45,314	2,331
1951	106,910	994	18,468	7,426	28,762	48,509	2,951
1952	116,800	743	20,034	7,565	31,967	52,875	3,616
1953	120,980	665	21,237	7,515	31,690	55,730	4,143
1954	127,795	571	22,416	7,562	33,531	59,304	4,411
1955	138,367	521	23,294	7,494	37,549	64,736	4,773
1956	151,319	480	24,866	7,414	42,658	70,762	5,139
1957	163,077	638	26,302	7,356	46,936	76,339	5,506
1958	175,237	1,011	27,744	7,253	51,323	81,873	6,033

SOURCE, BY COLUMN: (1) Sum of cols. 2 to 7; (2 to 7) Cumulated depreciated capital expenditures in 1947–49 prices (Table B-149) multiplied by appropriate price index from Table B-143, and Table B-91, year-end averages.

379

TABLE B-151

VALUE OF PUBLIC LAND, CURRENT PRICES
(billions of dollars)

End of Year	Total (1)	Federal				State and Local (6)
		Total (2)	Forest Land (3)	Other Civilian (4)	Military (5)	
1945	20.5	6.3	1.8	2.4	2.1	14.2
1946	25.9	7.0	2.2	2.7	2.1	18.9
1947	29.7	8.3	3.5	3.0	1.8	21.4
1948	30.4	8.9	4.3	3.0	1.6	21.5
1949	29.6	9.1	4.7	2.9	1.5	20.5
1950	35.5	11.5	6.7	3.3	1.5	24.0
1951	37.6	13.4	8.1	3.8	1.5	24.2
1952	36.6	12.9	7.4	3.9	1.6	23.7
1953	36.0	12.0	6.6	3.8	1.6ᵃ	24.0
1954	36.5	12.4	7.0	3.8	1.6	24.1
1955	38.4	13.6	8.2	3.8	1.6	24.8
1956	39.7	13.4	8.0	3.8	1.6	26.3
1957	41.0	13.6	8.2	3.8	1.6	27.4
1958	40.8	12.8	7.4	3.8	1.6	28.0

SOURCE, BY COLUMN

(1) Sum of cols. 2 and 6.

(2) Sum of cols. 3 to 5.

(3) 1946: Obtained by assigning 92 per cent of total for all government forest land (J. E. Reeve, *et al.*, "Government Component in National Wealth," *Studies in Income and Wealth*, Vol. 12, (NBER, 1950, p. 233) to federal and 8 per cent to state and local governments. Allocation is based on ratio of timber stands in 1953 (*Timber Resources Review*, U.S. Forest Service, 1955, p. 50).

1945, 1947–58: Value for 1946 multiplied by index of stumpage prices in national forests (Table B-132, col. 3).

(4) 1946: Reeve's total for government (*ibid.*, 466–467) less col. 2.

1945, 1947–58: Value for 1946 multiplied by index of grazing land prices in western states, since a large proportion of federally owned civilian nonforest land is of this character. (The index rises by 133 per cent from 1939 to 1946, while the estimate of col. 4 increases by 93 per cent.)

(5) 1946: Reeve's estimates.

1945, 1947–58: Rough estimates.

(6) 1946: Reeve's estimates.

1947–58: Value of state and local land in constant prices Table B-152, col. 6, multiplied by Dec.–Jan. average wholesale price index. *Federal Reserve Bulletin*, various issues, e.g., July 1959, p. 788.

ᵃ This figure compares with $1,171 million of cost of about 7.1 million acres of land held by Department of Defense at end of 1953 (*Inventory Report on Federal Real Property in the U.S. as of December 1953*, 84th Cong., 1st sess., S. Doc. 32, p. 15). In addition there were 11.8 million acres from public domain on which no value was put (*Real and Personal Property of the Department of Defense as of 31 December 1954*, pp. 23, 31, 40). Since this acreage may easily have a value of $10 to $20 per acre (the estimated average for federal civil land in 1946 was about $12, Reeve, *et al.*, *op. cit.*, pp. 466–467), and the 1953 value probably was well above cost, the estimate of $1.6 billion for 1953 appears to be of the right order of magnitude.

TABLE B-152

VALUE OF PUBLIC LAND, CONSTANT (1947–49) PRICES
(billions of dollars)

End of Year	Total (1)	Federal				State and Local (6)
		Total (2)	Forest Land (3)	Other Civilian (4)	Military (5)	
1945	29.5	9.1	2.6	3.5	3.0	20.44
1946	28.2	7.7	2.5	2.9	2.3	20.54
1947	28.7	8.0	3.4	2.9	1.7	20.66
1948	29.4	8.6	4.1	2.9	1.6	20.80
1949	30.3	9.3	4.8	3.0	1.5	21.00
1950	31.3	10.2	6.0	2.9	1.3	21.11
1951	33.2	11.9	7.2	3.4	1.3	21.32
1952	33.3	11.7	6.6	3.6	1.5	21.55
1953	32.6	10.9	6.0	3.4	1.5	21.74
1954	33.2	11.2	6.2	3.5	1.5	21.98
1955	34.4	12.1	7.3	3.4	1.4	22.26
1956	34.0	11.4	6.7	3.3	1.4	22.58
1957	34.5	11.4	6.9	3.2	1.3	23.10
1958	34.2	10.8	6.3	3.2	1.3	23.43

SOURCE, BY COLUMN

(1) Sum of cols. 2 and 6.
(2) Sum of cols. 3 to 5.
(3) Derived from col. 3, Table B-151, applying relationship of constant to current prices in Table B-132.
(4) Table B-151, col. 4, divided by year-end index of average wholesale prices (*Federal Reserve Bulletin*, various issues, e.g., July 1959, p. 788).
(5) Same method as for col. 4 applied to Table B-151, col. 5.
(6) 1946: Reeve's estimate in current prices, from Table B-151, col. 6, deflated by Dec.–Jan. average of index of wholesale prices for all commodities, from *Federal Reserve Bulletin*, various issues, e.g., Mar. 1952, p. 311.
1945, 1947–58: Cumulated by adding to 1946 figure acquisition of land determined as follows:
State land, assumed to equal 80 per cent of purchases of land and existing structures, from Table B-136, col. 6 (calendar year basis).
Local land, assumed to equal one-half of purchases of land and existing structures, from Table B-140, col. 6.
Current prices converted to constant 1947–49 prices by multiplying the average of Nov. and Mar. to obtain year-end index of average value of farm real estate, from *Current Developments in the Farm Real Estate Market*, various issues, e.g., Mar. 1956, p. 20.

TABLE B-153

VALUE OF GOVERNMENT EQUIPMENT, ORIGINAL COST
(millions of dollars)

End of Year	Total (1)	Federal Government (civilian) (2)	State Governments (3)	Local Governments (4)	Government Corporations and RFC Civilian Industries (5)
1945	2,928	504	142	373	1,909
1946	2,580	577	181	449	1,373
1947	2,340	646	253	589	852
1948	2,317	770	338	788	421
1949	2,373	772	426	980	195
1950	2,491	688	513	1,165	125
1951	2,751	666	599	1,380	106
1952	3,123	715	680	1,623	105
1953	3,474	740	757	1,868	109
1954	3,794	696	832	2,150	116
1955	4,055	617	908	2,420	110
1956	4,378	536	1,005	2,735	103
1957	4,806	468	1,117	3,125	96
1958	5,163	430	1,219	3,431	83

SOURCE, BY COLUMN: (1) Sum of cols. 2 to 5; (2 to 5) Derived by addition of cumulated net investment, original cost, to estimated value for 1945, obtained by cumulating expenditures less depreciation for twelve years preceding 1945, the assumed length of life of government equipment, except for RFC, which is six years. For expenditure figures see Tables B-139, B-142, B-159, B-161, and *A Study of Saving . . .*, Vol. I, Table F-14, col. 11.

TABLE B-154

VALUE OF GOVERNMENT EQUIPMENT, CONSTANT (1947–49) PRICES
(millions of dollars)

End of Year	Total (1)	Federal Government (civilian) (2)	State Governments (3)	Local Governments (4)	Government Corporations and RFC Civilian Industries (5)
1945	4,187	739	216	578	2,654
1946	3,606	805	253	645	1,903
1947	3,097	846	318	760	1,173
1948	2,815	932	390	919	574
1949	2,678	897	460	1,063	258
1950	2,667	784	526	1,200	157
1951	2,780	725	587	1,344	124
1952	3,002	730	641	1,517	114
1953	3,214	718	693	1,695	108
1954	3,406	653	743	1,904	106
1955	3,539	564	789	2,090	96
1956	3,690	478	843	2,283	86
1957	3,884	404	900	2,501	79
1958	4,018	354	947	2,650	67

SOURCE, BY COLUMN: (1) Sum of cols. 2 to 5; (2 to 5) Same procedure as for Table B-153, but applied to expenditures in 1947–49 prices.

TABLE B-155

VALUE OF GOVERNMENT EQUIPMENT, CURRENT PRICES
(millions of dollars)

End of Year	Total (1)	Federal Government (civilian) (2)	State Governments (3)	Local Governments (4)	Government Corporations and RFC Civilian Industries (5)
1945	3,262	575	172	450	2,065
1946	3,153	704	222	564	1,663
1947	3,006	821	308	738	1,139
1948	2,910	964	402	950	594
1949	2,867	959	496	1,136	276
1950	3,003	883	592	1,351	177
1951	3,264	853	684	1,581	146
1952	3,560	866	760	1,799	135
1953	3,864	868	834	2,027	131
1954	4,155	804	919	2,302	130
1955	4,558	725	1,020	2,690	123
1956	5,040	653	1,149	3,119	119
1957	5,538	577	1,279	3,569	113
1958	5,868	516	1,390	3,864	98

SOURCE, BY COLUMN: (1) Sum of cols. 2 to 5; (2 to 5) Cumulated depreciated capital expenditures in 1947–49 prices (Table B-154) multiplied by implicit price deflator of producer durable goods, from *U.S. Income and Output*, p. 225; *Survey of Current Business*, July 1959, p. 40.

TABLE B-156

INVENTORIES OF GOVERNMENT CORPORATIONS AND STATE AND LOCAL GOVERNMENTS
(millions of dollars)

End of Year	Government Corporations		State and Local Governments	
	1947–49 Prices (1)	Current Prices (2)	1947–49 Prices (3)	Current Prices (4)
1945	3,540	2,584	101	70
1946	1,490	1,385	100	92
1947	980	1,102	100	104
1948	1,950	1,920	102	105
1949	3,680	3,278	105	103
1950	2,430	2,672	110	125
1951	2,030	2,243	115	130
1952	2,720	2,706	121	133
1953	5,820	5,590	127	140
1954	7,490	6,833	134	147
1955	8,360	6,977	142	158
1956	7,710	6,869	150	175
1957	6,360	5,926	159	189
1958	8,760	7,891	169	202

SOURCE, BY COLUMN

(1) Col. 2 deflated by average of Dec. and Jan. wholesale price index of farm products, *Federal Reserve Bulletin*, March 1952, p. 311, and later issues.

(2) "Commodities, supplies, and materials," plus Commodity Credit Corporation loans (here regarded as physical assets) of government corporations and credit agencies from *Federal Reserve Bulletin*, various issues, e.g., Feb. 1956, p. 148.
1956: *Ibid.*, June 1957, pp. 678, 679 (excludes General Services Administration inventory for "certain other activities").
1957 and 1958: *Ibid.*, June 1958; June 1959.

(3) Col. 4 deflated by average of Dec. and Jan. wholesale price index of all commodities (*Federal Reserve Bulletin*, March 1952, p. 311 and later issues).

(4) 1946: Rough estimates based on Reeve's figure, *Studies in Income and Wealth*, Vol. 12, p. 466.

TABLE B-157

CIVILIAN CAPITAL OUTLAY OF FEDERAL GOVERNMENT
(millions of dollars)

		Construction			
Year	Total (1)	Nonresidential Building (2)	Highways (3)	Conservation and Development (4)	Equipment (5)
1946	318	53	26	239	152
1947	525	103	34	388	157
1948	786	122	39	625	222
1949	1,102	291	57	754	108
1950	1,136	286	46	804	24
1951	1,032	259	42	731	86
1952	946	208	50	688	162
1953	849	168	58	623	145
1954	678	145	55	478	76
1955	725	91	75	559	34
1956	954	145	85	724	26
1957	985	141	109	735	36
1958	1,176	213	115	848	60

SOURCE, BY COLUMN

(1) 1946–58: Sum of cols. 2 to 4.

(2 to 4) 1946–58: Estimates of direct federal construction by type from *New Construction Expenditures, 1915–51: Labor Requirements 1939–51*, Bureau of Labor Statistics, pp. 28, 29, supplemented by data from BLS worksheets, adjusted to exclude military and atomic energy expenditures (*ibid.*) and government corporation capital outlays (*ibid.*, primarily construction expenditures of Tennessee Valley Authority, federal public housing agencies and Reconstruction Finance Corporation). Conservation and development revised because of adjustment in TVA and CCC outlays. See Table B-160, col. 1.

(5) 1946–48: From *A Study of Saving* . . . , Vol. I, Table F-16, col. 9.
1949–58: *The Budget of the United States Government*, Bureau of the Budget, various issues, e.g., 1955, pp. 1123–1124; 1957, p. 1111.

NOTE: Outlay excludes expenditures for military and atomic energy capital assets, and expenditures by government corporations.

TABLE B-158

NET INVESTMENT THROUGH OUTLAYS FOR CIVILIAN CONSTRUCTION BY
FEDERAL GOVERNMENT
(millions of dollars)

	Expenditures		Depreciation			Net Investment		
Year	Original Cost (1)	1947–49 Prices (2)	Original Cost (3)	1947–49 Prices (4)	Replacement Cost (5)	Original Cost (6)	1947–49 Prices (7)	Replacement Cost (8)
1946	318	412	125	299	224	193	113	94
1947	525	571	132	306	282	393	265	243
1948	786	764	142	315	326	644	449	460
1949	1,102	1,049	156	328	342	946	721	759
1950	1,136	1,036	173	343	370	963	693	766
1951	1,032	886	189	356	411	843	530	621
1952	946	780	204	367	440	742	413	506
1953	849	669	217	377	473	632	292	376
1954	678	520	229	384	494	449	136	184
1955	725	537	241	391	519	484	146	206
1956	954	671	253	399	556	701	272	398
1957	985	667	267	407	593	718	260	392
1958	1,176	770	283	417	627	893	353	549

SOURCE, BY COLUMN

(1) From Table B-157, col. 1.
(2) Obtained by dividing the components of col. 1 (Table B-157, cols. 2 to 4) by appropriate price indexes from Table B-143.
(3) Components of col. 1 depreciated assuming an average life of fifty years for non-residential building, thirty years for highways (based on data given in *Highway Facts*, Automotive Safety Foundation, 1952, p. 43), and eighty years for conservation and development. Expenditures for years before 1946 obtained from *A Study of Saving* . . . worksheets (see Tables F-2, col. 3 and F-16, col. 2 in *A Study of Saving* . . . , Vol. I).
(4) Same procedure as for col. 3 except expenditure figures from col. 2 used. Expenditures in 1947–49 prices for years before 1946 obtained by deflating expenditures in original cost (see col. 3) by appropriate price indexes (indexes for period 1915 to 1945 from same sources as the later figures; for years 1915 extrapolated by public construction index given in *A Study of Saving* . . . , Vol. I, Table R-20, col. 8).
(5) Components of col. 4 multiplied by appropriate price indexes from Table B-143.
(6) Col. 1 minus col. 3.
(7) Col. 2 minus col. 4.
(8) Col. 1 minus col. 5.

TABLE B-159

NET INVESTMENT THROUGH OUTLAYS FOR CIVILIAN EQUIPMENT BY
FEDERAL GOVERNMENT

(millions of dollars)

Year	Expenditures		Depreciation			Net Investment		
	Original Cost (1)	1947–49 Prices (2)	Original Cost (3)	1947–49 Prices (4)	Replacement Cost (5)	Original Cost (6)	1947–49 Prices (7)	Replacement Cost (8)
1946	152	186	79	120	98	73	66	54
1947	157	168	88	127	118	69	41	39
1948	222	220	98	134	135	124	86	87
1949	108	102	106	137	145	2	−35	−37
1950	24	22	108	135	146	−84	−113	−122
1951	86	73	108	132	155	−22	−59	−69
1952	162	137	113	132	156	49	5	6
1953	145	121	120	133	158	25	−12	−13
1954	76	63	120	128	156	−44	−65	−80
1955	34	27	113	116	145	−79	−89	−111
1956	26	20	107	106	140	−81	−86	−114
1957	36	26	104	100	141	−68	−74	−105
1958	60	41	98	91	132	−38	−50	−72

SOURCE, BY COLUMN

(1)   From Table B-157, col. 5.

(2)   Col. 1 divided by implicit price deflator of producer durable goods, *U.S. Income and Output*, pp. 220–221, as brought up to date from *Survey of Current Business*, July 1959, p. 41.

(3)   Col. 1 depreciated assuming an average life of twelve years. Expenditures for years before 1946 from *A Study of Saving* . . . , Vol. I, Table F-16, col. 9.

(4)   Col. 2 depreciated assuming an average life of twelve years. Expenditures in 1947–49 prices for years before 1946 obtained by deflating expenditures in original cost (see col. 3) by implicit price deflator of producer durable goods (see col. 1).

(5 to 8) Same as for Table B-158.

TABLE B-160

Net Investment in Construction by Government Corporations and Credit Agencies

(millions of dollars)

Year	Expenditures		Depreciation			Net Investment		
	Original Cost (1)	1947–49 Prices (2)	Original Cost (3)	1947–49 Prices (4)	Replace-ment Cost (5)	Original Cost (6)	1947–49 Prices (7)	Replace-ment Cost (8)
1946	19	28	174	347	237	−155	−319	−218
1947	32	35	174	348	318	−142	−313	−286
1948	40	38	175	348	363	−135	−310	−323
1949	88	84	176	350	366	−88	−266	−278
1950	124	117	179	352	374	−55	−235	−250
1951	163	144	181	354	400	−18	−210	−237
1952	191	162	185	357	420	6	−195	−229
1953	242	197	189	361	443	53	−164	−201
1954	265	211	194	364	458	71	−153	−193
1955	128	99	198	366	473	−70	−267	−345
1956	92	68	196	358	484	−104	−290	−392
1957	75	53	170	304	430	−95	−251	−355
1958	20	14	125	217	317	−105	−203	−297

Source, by Column

(1) Expenditures for construction assumed to be equal to ninety per cent of annual change in fixed assets of TVA and Commodity Credit Corporation converted from fiscal calendar year basis from *Annual Reports of TVA*, various issues, and *Treasury Bulletin*, e.g., April 1958.

(2) Col. 1 deflated by Table B-143, col. 1.

(3) Government corporations construction (col. 1) depreciated assuming an average life of fifty years. (For expenditures for years before 1946 see *A Study of Saving . . .*, Vol. I, Table F-14, col. 12.) Includes depreciation on plant of Reconstruction Finance Corporation in civilian industries during the period 1940 to 1945. (Expenditure figures from *A Study of Saving . . .*, Vol. I, Table F-14, col. 12.) Depreciation calculated on basis of fifteen-year life for plant expenditures.

(4) Government corporations construction (col. 2) depreciated assuming an average life of fifty years, except Reconstruction Finance Corporation which is fifteen years. Expenditures in 1947–49 prices for years before 1946 obtained by deflating expenditures in original cost (see col. 3) by index derived from same source as Table B-143, col. 1.

(5) Col. 4 multiplied by Table B-143, col. 1.

(6) Col. 1 minus col. 3.

(7) Col. 2 minus col. 4.

(8) Col. 1 minus col. 5.

TABLE B-161

NET INVESTMENT IN EQUIPMENT BY GOVERNMENT CORPORATIONS
AND CREDIT AGENCIES
(millions of dollars)

	Expenditures		Depreciation			Net Investment		
Year	Original Cost (1)	1947–49 Prices (2)	Original Cost (3)	1947–49 Prices (4)	Replacement Cost (5)	Original Cost (6)	1947–49 Prices (7)	Replacement Cost (8)
1946	2	2	538	753	614	−536	−751	−612
1947	4	4	525	734	684	−521	−730	−680
1948	5	5	436	604	609	−431	−599	−604
1949	10	9	236	325	344	−226	−316	−334
1950	14	13	84	114	123	−70	−101	−109
1951	18	15	37	48	57	−19	−33	−39
1952	21	18	22	28	33	−1	−10	−12
1953	27	23	23	29	35	4	−6	−8
1954	30	25	23	27	32	7	−2	−2
1955	14	11	20	21	26	−6	−10	−12
1956	10	8	17	17	22	−7	−9	−12
1957	8	6	15	14	20	−7	−8	−12
1958	2	1	15	13	19	−13	−12	−17

SOURCE, BY COLUMN

(1) Same procedure as in Table B-160 with equipment expenditures assumed to be 10 per cent.

(2) Col. 1 deflated by implicit price deflator of producer durable goods from *U.S. Income and Output*, pp. 225, 229, and *Survey of Current Business*, July, 1959, p. 40, converted to a 1947–49 base (see Table B-40, col. 9).

(3) Expenditure figures in col. 1 depreciated assuming average life of twelve years. Includes depreciation on equipment investment of RFC during the period 1940 to 1945, for which average life was assumed to be six years.

(4) Same procedure as in col. 3, using figures in col. 2.

(5) Col. 4 multiplied by Table B-40, col. 9.

(6) Col. 1 minus col. 3.

(7) Col. 2 minus col. 4.

(8) Col. 1 minus col. 5.

TABLE B-162

Net Investment and Accumulated Stock of Federally Owned Nonwar Housing

(millions of dollars)

Year	Expenditures		Depreciation			Net Investment			Accumulated Value		
	Original Cost (1)	1947–49 Prices (2)	Original Cost (3)	1947–49 Prices (4)	Replace-ment Cost (5)	Original Cost (6)	1947–49 Prices (7)	Replace-ment Cost (8)	Original Cost (9)	1947–49 Prices (10)	Replace-ment Cost (11)
1945									201	443	325
1946	3	4	5	12	9	−2	−8	−6	199	435	364
1947	—	—	5	12	11	−5	−12	−11	194	423	415
1948	—	—	5	12	12	−5	−12	−12	189	411	437
1949	—	—	5	12	12	−5	−12	−12	184	399	417
1950	—	—	5	12	13	−5	−12	−13	179	387	445
1951	—	—	5	12	14	−5	−12	−14	174	375	449
1952	—	—	5	12	14	−5	−12	−14	169	363	449
1953	20	16	5	12	15	15	−4	−5	184	367	465
1954	3	2	6	12	15	−3	−10	−12	181	357	456
1955	1	1	6	12	16	−5	−11	−15	176	346	462
1956	15	11	6	12	17	−9	−1	−2	185	345	480
1957	154	116	8	13	19	146	103	135	331	448	638
1958	348	262	13	17	25	335	245	323	666	693	1,011

Source, by Column

(1) 1946–56: *Construction Volume and Costs, 1915–1956,* p. 10, Federal Direct less AEC.
1957–58: *Construction Review,* Jan. 1959, p. 20. See note to Table B-144, col. 2.
(3) Col. 1 depreciated using fifty-year life.
(4) Col. 2 depreciated using fifty-year life.
(5) Col. 4 multiplied by Table B-9, col. 2.

(6) Col. 1 minus col. 3.
(7) Col. 2 minus col. 4.
(8) Col. 1 minus col. 5.
(9) 1945: stock plus cumulated savings from col. 6.
(10) 1945: stock plus cumulated savings from col. 7.
(11) Col. 10 multiplied by year-end index from Table B-9, col. 4.

TABLE B-163

Net Investment in Federal War Housing, Twenty-Year Life

(millions of dollars)

Year	Expenditures^a		Depreciation			Net Investment			Accumulated Value		
	Original Cost (1)	1947–49 Prices (2)	Original Cost (3)	1947–49 Prices (4)	Replacement Cost (5)	Original Cost (6)	1947–49 Prices (7)	Replacement Cost (8)	Original Cost (9)	1947–49 Prices (10)	Replacement Cost (11)
1945	—	—	—	—	—	—	—	—	1,265	2,112	1,548
1946	—	—	74	123	96	−74	−123	−96	1,191	1,989	1,663
1947	—	—	74	123	113	−74	−123	−113	1,117	1,866	1,831
1948	—	—	74	123	128	−74	−123	−128	1,043	1,742	1,853
1949	—	—	74	123	129	−74	−123	−129	969	1,619	1,693
1950	—	—	74	123	135	−74	−123	−135	895	1,496	1,720
1951	—	—	74	123	145	−74	−123	−145	821	1,373	1,645
1952	—	—	74	123	150	−74	−123	−150	747	1,249	1,545
1953	—	—	74	123	155	−74	−123	−155	673	1,126	1,428
1954	—	—	74	123	156	−74	−123	−156	599	1,003	1,282
1955	—	—	74	123	161	−74	−123	−161	525	879	1,174
1956	—	—	74	123	169	−74	−123	−169	451	756	1,052
1957	—	—	74	123	174	−74	−123	−174	377	633	901
1958	—	—	74	123	177	−74	−123	−177	303	509	743

Source, by Column

(3) Original cost expenditures depreciated using twenty-year life.
(4) Constant cost expenditures depreciated using twenty-year life.
(5) Col. 4 multiplied by Table B-9, col. 2.
(6) Col. 1 minus col. 3.
(7) Col. 2 minus col. 4.

(8) Col. 1 minus col. 5.
(9) 1945 stock plus cumulated savings from col. 6.
(10) 1945 stock plus cumulated savings from col. 7.
(11) Col. 10 multiplied by year-end index from Table B-9, col. 4.

^a Estimated expenditures for 1941–45: original cost, $1,472 million; constant (1947–49) prices, $2,466 million.

TABLE B-164
NET INVESTMENT AND ACCUMULATED VALUES OF FEDERAL WAR HOUSING TRANSFERRED TO PRIVATE OWNERSHIP
(millions of dollars)

Year	Expenditures[a]		Depreciation			Net Investment			Accumulated Value		
	Original Cost (1)	1947–49 Prices (2)	Original Cost (3)	1947–49 Prices (4)	Replacement Cost (5)	Original Cost (6)	1947–49 Prices (7)	Replacement Cost (8)	Original Cost (9)	1947–49 Prices (10)	Replacement Cost (11)
1945									531	887	666
1946	125	217	25	50	38	100	167	87	631	1,054	881
1947	81	143	31	59	54	50	84	27	681	1,138	1,117
1948	85	148	36	67	69	49	81	16	730	1,219	1,297
1949	7	18	39	71	74	−32	−53	−67	698	1,166	1,219
1950	22	44	40	73	80	−18	−29	−58	680	1,237	1,324
1951	11	23	42	75	89	−31	−52	−78	649	1,085	1,300
1952	13	28	42	76	93	−29	−48	−80	620	1,037	1,251
1953	2	8	43	77	97	−41	−69	−95	579	968	1,228
1954	10	23	44	78	99	−34	−55	−89	545	913	1,167
1955	0	0	46	78	102	−46	−78	−102	499	835	1,115
1956	0	0	48	79	108	−48	−79	−108	451	756	1,052
1957	0	0	74	123	174	−74	−123	−174	377	633	901
1958	0	0	74	123	177	−74	−123	−177	303	509	743

SOURCE: See notes to Table B-163.

[a] These are transfers rather than original expenditures.

TABLE B-165

NET INVESTMENT AND ACCUMULATED VALUES OF FEDERAL WAR HOUSING RETAINED UNDER FEDERAL OWNERSHIP

(millions of dollars)

	Expenditures[a]		Depreciation			Net Investment			Accumulated Value		
Year	Original Cost (1)	1947–49 Prices (2)	Original Cost (3)	1947–49 Prices (4)	Replacement Cost (5)	Original Cost (6)	1947–49 Prices (7)	Replacement Cost (8)	Original Cost (9)	1947–49 Prices (10)	Replacement Cost (11)
1945	−125	−217	49	73	58	−174	−290	−183	734	1,225	882
1946	−81	−143	43	64	58	−124	−207	−139	560	935	782
1947	−85	−148	38	56	58	−123	−205	−143	436	728	714
1948	−7	−18	35	52	54	−42	−70	−61	313	523	556
1949	−22	−44	34	50	55	−56	−94	−77	271	453	474
1950	−11	−23	32	48	57	−43	−71	−68	215	359	396
1951	−13	−28	32	47	57	−45	−76	−70	172	288	345
1952	−2	−8	31	46	58	−33	−70	−60	127	212	294
1953	−10	−23	30	45	57	−40	−68	−67	94	158	200
1954	0	0	28	45	59	−28	−46	−59	54	90	115
1955	0	0	26	44	60	−26	−44	−60	26	44	59
1956	0	0	0	0	0	—	—	—	—	—	—
1957	0	0	0	0	0	—	—	—	—	—	—
1958	0	0	0	0	0	—	—	—	—	—	—

SOURCE: See notes to Table B-163.

[a] These are transfers rather than original expenditures.

TABLE B-166

EXPENDITURES ON MILITARY DURABLES, CURRENT PRICES
(billions of dollars)

| Calendar Year | Major Procurement and Production | | | | Military Construction | |
	Aircraft[a] (1)	Naval Ships[b] (2)	Other' (3)	Total (4)	In U.S. (5)	Total (6)
1929	0.04	0.07	.008	0.19	0.02	0.02
1930	0.05	0.07	0.08	0.20	0.03	0.03
1931	0.05	0.07	0.08	0.20	0.04	0.04
1932	0.05	0.07	0.09	0.21	0.03	0.03
1933	0.05	0.07	0.08	0.20	0.04	0.04
1934	0.06	0.08	0.08	0.22	0.05	0.05
1935	0.08	0.10	0.13	0.31	0.04	0.04
1936	0.10	0.11	0.15	0.36	0.03	0.03
1937	0.10	0.15	0.15	0.40	0.04	0.04
1938	0.13	0.20	0.15	0.48	0.06	0.06
1939	0.16	0.25	0.18	.59	0.13	0.13
1940	0.50	0.50	0.50	1.50	0.39	0.39
1941	1.00	0.90	1.90	3.80	1.62	2.40
1942	5.10	4.30	8.10	17.50	5.02	6.00
1943	11.90	8.40	12.15	32.45	2.55	3.60
1944	14.80	9.50	11.60	35.90	0.84	1.10
1945	10.20	5.80	8.00	24.00	0.69	0.80
1946	1.50	0.50	0.30	2.30	0.19	0.70
1947	1.00	0.35	0.18	1.53	0.20	0.50
1948	1.00	0.30	0.18	1.48	0.16	0.28
1949	1.45	0.30	0.25	2.00	0.14	0.22
1950	1.80	0.30	0.70	2.80	0.18	0.32
1951	3.29	0.46	2.89	6.64	0.89	1.10
1952	6.18	0.92	8.03	15.13	1.39	1.93
1953	8.26	1.21	7.96	17.43	1.31	1.87
1954	8.17	1.02	5.00	14.19	1.03	1.52
1955	7.63	0.96	4.02	12.61	1.31	1.72
1956	8.04	0.95	4.86	13.85	1.36	1.76
1957	8.48	1.03	5.07	14.58	1.29	1.69
1958	8.21	1.34	5.25	14.80	1.40	1.80

SOURCE, BY COLUMN

(1) 1929–39: Result of rough allocation of col. 4.

1940–45: Total military expenditures as given in *Budget for 1947* (p. 786 and Appendix I), distributed among categories on basis of *Production* (War Production Board, Oct. 1, 1945), p. 29. Figures for 1940 and 1945 partly estimated.

1946–50: Obtained by splitting fiscal-year figures, as given in the Budget Messages, in accordance with the distribution of total military expenditures as shown in the *Federal Reserve Bulletin*, various issues. The figures for 1946 and the first half of 1947 are rough estimates.

1951–58: From *Status of Funds by Budget Category* (Office of Secretary of Defense, Controller, EISED), various issues. Obtained by aggregating monthly figures given in original source.

(2) 1929–58: Same sources and methods as for col. 1.
(3) 1929–58: Same sources and methods as for col. 1.

(4) 1929–31: Rough estimates based on total expenditures of War and Navy Departments.

1932–39: Derived from analysis of budget statements (unpublished War Production
Board memorandum of Oct. 24, 1942).

1940–58: Same sources and methods as for col. 1.

(5) 1929–53: *National Income,* 1954 ed., pp. 208, 209. Apparently does not include
industrial military facilities.

1954–58: *Survey of Current Business,* July 1959, p. 22.

(6) 1929–40: Assumed equal to col. 5.

1941–58: Same sources as for col. 1.

ᵃ Includes spare parts from 1940 on.

ᵇ Includes alterations from 1940 on.

TABLE B-167

EXPENDITURES ON MILITARY DURABLES, CONSTANT (1947–49) PRICES
(billions of dollars)

Calendar Year	Major Procurement and Production				Military Construction	
	Aircraftᵃ (1)	Naval Shipsᵇ (2)	Other (3)	Total (4)	In U.S. (5)	Total (6)
1929	0.06	0.10	0.11	0.27	0.04	0.04
1930	0.08	0.11	0.13	0.32	0.06	0.06
1931	0.09	0.12	0.14	0.35	0.09	0.09
1932	0.10	0.14	0.17	0.41	0.08	0.08
1933	0.09	0.13	0.15	0.37	0.09	0.09
1934	0.10	0.14	0.14	0.38	0.11	0.10
1935	0.14	0.17	0.22	0.53	0.09	0.09
1936	0.17	0.19	0.26	0.62	0.06	0.06
1937	0.15	0.22	0.22	0.59	0.09	0.09
1938	0.20	0.30	0.23	0.73	0.12	0.12
1939	0.25	0.38	0.28	0.91	0.26	0.26
1940	0.76	0.76	0.76	2.28	0.75	0.75
1941	1.46	1.31	2.77	5.54	2.95	4.36
1942	7.16	6.04	11.38	24.58	8.18	9.77
1943	16.76	11.83	17.11	45.70	3.94	5.56
1944	20.85	13.38	16.34	50.57	1.30	1.71
1945	14.25	8.10	11.17	33.52	1.03	1.20
1946	1.87	0.62	0.37	2.86	0.25	0.92
1947	1.08	0.38	0.20	1.66	0.21	0.54
1948	0.99	0.30	0.18	1.47	0.15	0.27
1949	1.36	0.28	0.24	1.88	0.14	0.21
1950	1.66	0.28	0.65	2.59	0.17	0.30
1951	2.77	0.39	2.43	5.59	0.77	0.95
1952	5.09	0.76	6.61	12.46	1.17	1.62
1953	6.72	0.98	6.47	14.17	1.08	1.54
1954	6.56	0.82	4.01	11.39	0.85	1.25
1955	5.94	0.75	3.13	9.82	1.05	1.38
1956	5.83	0.69	3.53	10.05	1.04	1.35
1957	5.80	0.70	3.47	9.97	0.94	1.24
1958	5.48	0.89	3.50	9.87	1.01	1.30

SOURCE, BY COLUMN: (1 to 3) Estimates of Table B-166 divided by Bureau of Labor
Statistics wholesale price index of machinery and motive products, linked in 1939 to
index of metals and metal products (Table B-181, col. 1). (4) Sum of cols. 1 to 3.
(5 and 6) Estimates of Table B-166, divided by Department of Commerce construction
cost index (Table B-181, col. 3).

ᵃ Includes spare parts from 1940 on.

ᵇ Includes alterations from 1940 on.

TABLE B-168

INVESTMENT IN MARITIME COMMISSION VESSELS

(dollars in billions)

End of Year	Size of Fleet[a] (1)	Undepreciated Value		Depreciated Value			Depreciation Allowances		
		Original Cost (2)	1947–49 Prices (3)	Original Cost (4)	1947–49 Prices (5)	Replacement Cost (6)	Original Cost (7)	1947–49 Prices (8)	Replacement Cost (9)
1945	40.0	5.00	7.00	3.95	5.50	4.00	0.65	0.91	0.65
1946	37.0	4.60	6.50	3.20	4.45	3.90	0.70	0.98	0.79
1947	27.6	3.45	4.85	2.05	2.90	2.80	0.60	0.84	0.78
1948	22.5	2.80	3.90	1.40	1.95	2.10	0.46	0.64	0.65
1949	22.1	2.75	3.85	1.10	1.55	1.65	0.40	0.56	0.60
1950	20.8	2.60	3.65	0.75	1.05	1.25	0.38	0.54	0.59
1951	20.8	2.60	3.65	0.50	0.70	0.85	0.38	0.52	0.62
1952	20.8	2.60	3.65	0.25	0.40	0.50	0.35	0.49	0.60
1953	21.0	2.65	3.70	0.10	0.14	0.17	0.25	0.35	0.43
1954	20.8	2.60	3.65	0.02	0.03	0.04	0.12	0.17	0.21
1955	20.6	2.60	3.65	—	—	—	0.03	0.04	0.05
1956	—	2.60	3.65	—	—	—	—	—	—

SOURCE, BY COLUMN

(1) From *Employment Report of U.S. Flag Merchant Seagoing Vessels . . .*, (Maritime Commission), various issues. Figures for ends of 1945 and 1946 obtained by adjusting reported data on fleet on September 30, 1946 for sales during 1946 from *Sale of Ships by the Maritime Commission* (Maritime Commission, Committee print, U.S. Senate, 82nd Cong., 1st sess., April 1951). From 1948 on, most of fleet was inactive.

(2) Col. 1 multiplied by $125 per D.W.T.[a] This was value obtained by dividing total expenditures on Maritime Commission vessels (J. E. Reeve et al., *Studies in Income and Wealth*, Vol. 12, New York, NBER, 1950, p. 505) by tonnage of ships constructed (*Statistical Abstract*, 1948, p. 558). Figures are too high after 1948 since sales were concentrated in vessels of above-average cost. (This also affects cols. 3 to 6.)

(3) Col. 1 multiplied by $175 per D.W.T., the value obtained by dividing original cost of $125 by Bureau of Labor Statistics' wholesale price index of machinery and

[a] Millions of dead weight tons.

motive products for 1942–45 (*Business Statistics*, various issues).

(4 and 5) Obtained by multiplying col. 1 by an average value per D.W.T., derived on assumption of original cost of $125 for col. 4 and $175 for col. 5; and straight-line depreciation of 10 percent per year. The expenditure figures for 1941 to 1945 underlying the calculation were derived by allocating total expenditures, in original cost ($7 billion), or 1947–49 prices ($9.8 billion), among individual years on basis of tonnage constructed and expenditures of Maritime Commission.

(6) Col. 5 multiplied by year-end value of BLS wholesale price index of machinery and motive products (Table B-181, col. 2).

(7 and 8) Obtained by straight-line depreciation and assumption of 10-year life.

(9) Col. 8 multiplied by annual average value of BLS wholesale price index of machinery and motive products (Table B-181, col. 1).

TABLE B-169

FEDERAL GOVERNMENT NET INVESTMENT IN MILITARY ASSETS, ORIGINAL COST
(millions of dollars)

	MILITARY ASSETS						World
		Structures		AEC			War II
	Movable	Continental U.S.		Fixed	Stockpiles		Merchant
YEAR	Assets	Inside	Outside	Assets	Strategic	AEC	Vessels
	(1)	(2)	(3)	(4)	(5)	(6)	(7)
1946	−9,280	−240	430	87	10	120	−750
1947	−7,800	−210	200	120	36	120	−1,150
1948	−6,040	−230	10	210	150	190	−650
1949	−4,420	−230	−30	198	456	260	−300
1950	−2,800	−180	30	225	455	290	−350
1951	900	530	100	660	745	400	−250
1952	7,550	960	410	977	1,106	520	−250
1953	6,950	820	390	983	841	610	−150
1954	1,760	480	300	799	996	750	−80
1955	−370	720	200	237	597	970	−20
1956	630	710	170	−53	450	1,210	0
1957	930	590	160	−46	597	1,460	0
1958	800	650	150	−68	481	1,710	0

SOURCE, BY COLUMN

(1 to 3) Obtained by depreciating expenditures for aircraft at 45 per cent per year, for
naval vessels at 15 per cent, for other equipment at 22.5 per cent, and for
structures at 7.5 per cent, using declining balance method and starting from
estimates for end of 1946 of $5.3 billion for structures, and $42.3 billion for
moveable assets (based on Reeve, *Studies in Income and Wealth*, Vol. 12, NBER,
p. 502; and *Real and Personal Property of the Department of Defense as of 31 December,
1954*, p. 71). Value of structures outside the U.S. put at $1,200 million as in
Table B-173, col. 3.
Expenditure figures used are shown in Table B-166, cols. 1 to 6.
(4) From Table B-176, col. 7.
(5) From Table B-180, col. 1, A and B.
(6) First differences of Table B-179, col. 8.
(7) First differences of Table B-168, col. 4.

TABLE B-170

FEDERAL GOVERNMENT NET INVESTMENT IN MILITARY ASSETS, CONSTANT (1947–49) PRICES
(millions of dollars)

	MILITARY ASSETS						World
		Structures		AEC			War II
	Movable	Continental U.S.		Fixed	Stockpiles		Merchant
YEAR	Assets	Inside	Outside	Assets	Strategic	AEC	Vessels
	(1)	(2)	(3)	(4)	(5)	(6)	(7)
1946	−15,280	−510	540	100	15	120	−1,050
1947	−12,750	−510	170	109	37	120	−1,550
1948	−9,940	−530	−50	178	142	190	−950
1949	−7,410	−500	−90	163	462	260	−400
1950	−5,290	−440	−30	180	436	290	−500
1951	−1,750	170	20	519	600	400	−350
1952	4,150	550	280	735	898	520	−300
1953	3,950	500	270	755	682	610	−260
1954	−20	240	190	605	707	750	−110
1955	−1,690	420	110	139	418	970	−30
1956	−1,210	370	80	−105	288	1,210	0
1957	−1,070	250	70	−108	434	1,460	0
1958	−910	300	50	−128	377	1,710	0

(1 to 3)   Same procedure as in Table B-169, except that expenditures are taken from
Table B-167. 1946 stock estimated in replacement cost at $8.1 billion for
structures and $58.4 billion for moveable assets (from same sources as noted
for Table B-169, cols. 1 to 3) is divided by Table B-181, cols. 2 and 4 to obtain
1947–49 prices. (Value of structures outside the U.S. at end of 1946 put at
$1.990 million as in Table B-174, col. 3.)

(4)   From Table B-176, col. 8.

(5)   From Table B-180, col. 3, A and B.

(6)   First differences of Table B-179, col. 8; 1947–49 values assumed equal to
original cost.

(7)   First differences of Table B-168, col. 5.

TABLE B-171

FEDERAL GOVERNMENT NET INVESTMENT IN MILITARY ASSETS, REPLACEMENT COST
(millions of dollars)

	MILITARY ASSETS						World War II
		Structures		AEC			
	Movable	Continental U.S.		Fixed	*Stockpiles*		Merchant
YEAR	Assets	Inside	Outside	Assets	Strategic	AEC	Vessels
	(1)	(2)	(3)	(4)	(5)	(6)	(7)
1946	−12,270	−390	−410	79	10	120	−845
1947	−11,800	−470	150	101	36	120	−1,435
1948	−10,040	−550	−60	183	150	190	−960
1949	−7,900	−500	−80	169	456	260	−425
1950	−5,760	−470	−30	193	455	290	−545
1951	−2,100	200	30	613	745	400	−415
1952	5,030	650	340	926	1,106	520	−365
1953	4,860	600	330	929	841	610	−320
1954	−30	290	230	745	996	750	−135
1955	−2,160	530	140	176	597	970	−40
1956	−1,660	520	100	−143	450	1,210	0
1957	−1,550	350	90	−162	597	1,460	0
1958	−1,350	420	70	−197	481	1,710	0

SOURCE, BY COLUMN

(1 to 3)   Same sources and procedures as Table B-169, except that depreciation
allowances were obtained by multiplying those used in Table B-170 by price
indexes of Table B-181, cols. 1 and 3.

(4)   From Table B-176, col. 9.

(5)   From Table B-180, cols. 1, A and B.

(6)   First differences of Table B-179, col. 8.

(7)   First differences in Table B-168, col. 5 multiplied by index of Table B-181,
col. 1.

TABLE B-172

STOCK OF AND INVESTMENT IN MILITARY ASSETS

(billions of dollars)

Year	Gross Stock (end of year)			Net Stock (end of year)			Net Investment		
	Original Cost (1)	1947–49 Prices (2)	Replacement Cost (3)	Original Cost (4)	1947–49 Prices (5)	Replacement Cost (6)	Original Cost (7)	1947–49 Prices (8)	Replacement Cost (9)
1945	143.26	208.05	150.18	63.28	100.28	72.71			
1946	145.29	210.24	185.28	53.62	84.21	74.51	−9.62	−16.07	−12.89
1947	140.58	202.42	196.64	44.97	69.84	68.16	−8.68	−14.37	−13.30
1948	128.81	183.83	196.52	38.61	58.88	63.26	−6.36	−10.96	−11.09
1949	115.83	163.57	172.49	34.54	51.37	54.30	−4.07	−7.52	−8.02
1950	108.94	152.05	177.40	32.21	46.01	54.41	−2.33	−5.35	−5.87
1951	148.43	155.05	186.30	35.30	45.62	54.81	3.09	−0.39	−0.53
1952	124.19	157.03	190.88	46.57	51.35	62.75	11.27	6.83	8.21
1953	130.48	153.33	189.46	57.01	57.86	71.28	10.44	6.51	7.85
1954	134.19	147.43	183.69	62.02	60.23	74.63	5.01	2.36	2.85
1955	140.33	146.85	192.72	64.35	60.56	79.25	2.33	0.34	0.21
1956	153.37	155.48	217.31	67.47	61.19	84.28	3.12	0.63	0.44
1957	159.25	157.44	231.85	71.16	62.23	86.58	3.69	1.04	0.79
1958	161.57	152.14	226.26	74.89	63.63	88.73	3.73	1.40	1.14

SOURCE, BY COLUMN

(1) From Table B-172A, sum of cols. 1 to 7.
(2) From Table B-172B, sum of cols. 1 to 7.
(3) From Table B-172C, sum of cols. 1 to 7.
(4) From Table B-173, sum of cols. 1 to 8.
(5) From Table B-174, sum of cols. 1 to 8.
(6) From Table B-175, sum of cols. 1 to 8.
(7) From Table B-169, sum of cols. 1 to 7.
(8) From Table B-170, sum of cols. 1 to 7.
(9) From Table B-171, sum of cols. 1 to 7.

TABLE B-172A

MAIN COMPONENTS OF GROSS STOCK OF MILITARY ASSETS, ORIGINAL COST
(millions of dollars)

END OF YEAR	Movable Assets (1)	MILITARY ASSETS *Structures* Continental U.S. Inside (2)	Outside (3)	*AEC* Structures (4)	Equipment (5)	Stockpiles (6)	Merchant Vessels (7)
1945	116,380	15,199	3,180	515	625	365	7,000
1946	117,460	15,368	3,690	577	703	495	7,000
1947	113,670	14,960	3,990	658	802	651	5,850
1948	103,030	13,565	4,110	795	945	991	5,370
1949	89,970	12,616	4,190	932	1,088	1,707	5,330
1950	81,970	12,635	4,330	1,075	1,265	2,452	5,210
1951	85,100	13,476	4,540	1,401	1,719	3,597	5,010
1952	90,980	14,841	5,080	1,871	2,389	5,223	3,810
1953	95,060	16,135	5,640	2,352	3,108	6,674	1,510
1954	95,950	17,156	6,130	2,674	3,856	8,420	—
1955	98,260	18,458	6,540	2,840	4,240	9,987	—
1956	107,620	19,807	6,940	2,966	4,392	11,647	—
1957	109,460	21,805	7,340	3,103	4,558	13,704	—
1958	107,510	22,470	7,740	3,235	4,719	15,895	—

SOURCE, BY COLUMN

(1) Expenditures in Table B-166, cols. 1, 2, and 3 cumulated on basis of five-, fifteen-, and ten-year lives, respectively.
(2) Expenditures in Table B-166, col. 5, cumulated on basis of thirty-year life.
(3) Same procedure as for col. 2, using expenditures in Table B-166, col. 6.
(4) Components of structures of AEC, fixed assets, in Table B-176, col. 2, cumulated on basis of fifty-year life for residential structures and forty-year for nonresidential structures.
(5) Equipment component of AEC fixed assets in Table B-176, col. 2, cumulated on basis of sixteen-year life.
(6) Table B-173, col. 6 plus col. 7.
(7) Cumulation of expenditures in Table B-168, col. 2 on basis of ten-year life.

TABLE B-172B

MAIN COMPONENTS OF GROSS STOCK OF MILITARY ASSETS, CONSTANT (1947–49) PRICES
(millions of dollars)

| END OF YEAR | MILITARY ASSETS | *Structures* Continental U.S. | | *AEC* | | Stockpiles | Merchant Vessels |
| | Movable Assets | Inside | Outside | Structures | Equipment | | |
	(1)	(2)	(3)	(4)	(5)	(6)	(7)
1945	164,210	26,667	5,200	826	876	390	9,880
1946	165,230	26,857	5,870	905	973	525	9,880
1947	159,370	25,569	6,200	992	1,080	682	8,530
1948	143,720	22,382	6,320	1,123	1,222	1,014	8,050
1949	124,330	20,486	6,390	1,257	1,356	1,736	8,010
1950	111,740	20,419	6,520	1,392	1,519	2,462	8,000
1951	112,500	21,099	6,700	1,669	1,901	3,462	7,720
1952	112,280	22,220	7,150	2,029	2,452	4,880	6,020
1953	108,050	23,272	7,610	2,414	3,037	6,172	2,770
1954	101,360	24,106	8,010	2,687	3,636	7,629	—
1955	97,590	25,141	8,340	2,822	3,936	9,017	—
1956	103,190	26,161	8,650	2,917	4,046	10,515	—
1957	101,830	27,079	8,950	3,014	4,160	12,409	—
1958	92,970	28,060	9,240	3,107	4,268	14,496	—

SOURCE: Same procedure as for Table B-172A, using expenditures in Table B-167 for cols. 1 to 3, and expenditures in constant (1947–49) prices from tables listed in sources for Table B-172A, except that Table B-174 is used for col. 7.

TABLE B-172C

MAIN COMPONENTS OF GROSS STOCK OF MILITARY ASSETS, CURRENT PRICES
(millions of dollars)

| END OF YEAR | MILITARY ASSETS | *Structures* Continental U.S. | | *AEC* | | Stockpiles | Merchant Vessels |
| | Movable Assets | Inside | Outside | Structures | Equipment | | |
	(1)	(2)	(3)	(4)	(5)	(6)	(7)
1945	119,052	18,507	3,609	576	635	640	7,163
1946	146,229	22,775	4,978	766	861	930	8,744
1947	153,633	25,467	6,175	989	1,041	1,110	8,223
1948	153,493	23,680	6,687	1,187	1,305	1,571	8,597
1949	131,790	20,834	6,499	1,277	1,437	2,159	8,491
1950	130,400	22,971	7,335	1,568	1,773	4,019	9,336
1951	135,901	24,728	7,852	1,956	2,296	4,240	9,326
1952	136,421	26,753	8,609	2,442	2,979	6,364	7,314
1953	134,414	28,322	9,261	2,942	3,778	7,294	3,446
1954	127,510	29,554	9,820	3,291	4,575	8,942	—
1955	129,990	31,879	10,575	3,577	5,243	11,470	—
1956	148,387	34,768	11,496	3,871	5,818	12,966	—
1957	152,134	37,098	12,262	4,118	6,215	13,806	—
1958	141,035	39,144	12,890	4,323	6,475	15,913	—

SOURCE: Gross stock values in constant (1947–49) prices from Table B-172B, multiplied by appropriate year-end deflator to obtain gross stock values in current prices; col. 6 taken directly from Table B-175, col. 6, plus col. 7.

TABLE B-173

MAIN COMPONENTS OF NET STOCK OF MILITARY ASSETS, ORIGINAL COST
(millions of dollars)

END OF YEAR	MILITARY ASSETS							
	Movable Assets	Structures Continental U.S.		AEC		Stockpiles		Merchant Vessels
		Inside	Outside	Structures	Equipment	Strategic	AEC	
	(1)	(2)	(3)	(4)	(5)	(6)	(7)	(8)
1945	51,580	5,540	770	498	572	45	320	3,950
1946	42,300	5,300	1,200	547	610	55	440	3,200
1947	34,500	5,090	1,400	613	664	91	560	2,050
1948	28,460	4,860	1,410	732	755	241	750	1,400
1949	24,040	4,630	1,380	848	837	697	1,010	1,100
1950	21,240	4,450	1,410	967	943	1,152	1,300	750
1951	22,140	4,980	1,510	1,263	1,307	1,897	1,700	500
1952	29,690	5,940	1,920	1,693	1,854	3,003	2,220	250
1953	36,640	6,760	2,310	2,122	2,408	3,844	2,830	100
1954	38,400	7,240	2,610	2,382	2,947	4,840	3,580	20
1955	38,030	7,960	2,810	2,480	3,086	5,437	4,550	—
1956	38,660	8,670	2,980	2,534	2,977	5,887	5,760	—
1957	39,590	9,260	3,140	2,598	2,872	6,484	7,220	—
1958	40,390	9,910	3,290	2,650	2,753	6,965	8,930	—

SOURCE, BY COLUMN

(1 to 3) Cumulation of net investment estimates of Table 169 starting with 1946 values given in footnotes for columns 1 to 3.

(4) Sum of Table B-177, col. 9, plus Table B-178, col. 9.

(5) From Table B-178A, col. 9.

(6) From Table B-180, col. 2, A and B. Figures include "additional stockpile" for 1952–55, on assumption that cost equals market value.

(7) From Table B-179, col. 8.

(8) From Table B-168, col. 4.

TABLE B-174

MAIN COMPONENTS OF NET STOCK OF MILITARY ASSETS, CONSTANT (1947–49) PRICES
(millions of dollars)

END OF YEAR	MILITARY ASSETS Movable Assets (1)	Structures Continental U.S. Inside (2)	Outside (3)	AEC Structures (4)	Equipment (5)	Stockpiles Strategic (6)	AEC (7)	Merchant Vessels (9)
1945	81,280	10,060	1,450	796	803	70	320	5,500
1946	66,000	9,550	1,990	854	845	85	440	4,450
1947	53,250	9,040	2,160	918	890	122	560	2,900
1948	43,310	8,510	2,110	1,023	963	264	750	1,950
1949	35,900	8,010	2,020	1,129	1,020	726	1,010	1,550
1950	30,610	7,570	1,990	1,232	1,097	1,162	1,300	1,050
1951	28,860	7,740	2,010	1,472	1,376	1,762	1,700	700
1952	33,010	7,190	2,290	1,787	1,796	2,660	2,220	400
1953	36,960	7,690	2,560	2,122	2,216	3,342	2,830	140
1954	36,940	7,930	2,750	2,327	2,616	4,049	3,580	30
1955	35,250	8,350	2,860	2,394	2,688	4,467	4,550	—
1956	34,040	8,720	2,940	2,418	2,559	4,755	5,760	—
1957	32,970	8,970	3,010	2,442	2,427	5,189	7,220	—
1958	32,060	9,270	3,060	2,459	2,282	5,566	8,930	—

SOURCE, BY COLUMN

(1 to 3) Cumulation of net investment estimates of Table B-170, starting with 1946 values which were obtained by dividing figures of Table B-169 by indexes of Table B-181.

(4) Sum of Table B-177, col. 10, and Table B-178, col. 10.

(5) From Table B-178A, col. 10.

(6) From Table B-180, cols. 4, and A and B. Figures include "additional stockpile" for 1952-55 using deflator of 1.25.

(7) From Table B-179, col. 8 (values in 1947–49 prices assumed equal to original cost).

(8) From Table B-168, col. 5.

TABLE B-175

MAIN COMPONENTS OF NET STOCK OF MILITARY ASSETS, CURRENT PRICES
(millions of dollars)

END OF YEAR	MILITARY ASSETS							
		Structures Continental U.S.		*AEC*		*Stockpiles*		Merchant
	Movable Assets	Inside	Outside	Structures	Equipment	Strategic	AEC	Vessels
	(1)	(2)	(3)	(4)	(5)	(6)	(7)	(8)
1945	58,940	6,980	1,010	556	582	320	320	4,000
1946	58,410	8,100	1,690	735	748	490	440	3,900
1947	51,330	9,000	2,150	915	858	550	560	2,800
1948	46,250	9,000	2,230	1,077	1,028	821	750	2,100
1949	38,060	8,150	2,050	1,145	1,081	1,149	1,010	1,650
1950	35,720	8,520	2,240	1,381	1,280	2,719	1,300	1,250
1951	34,860	9,070	2,360	1,769	1,662	2,540	1,700	850
1952	40,110	8,660	2,760	2,176	2,182	4,144	2,220	500
1953	45,980	9,360	3,120	2,595	2,757	4,464	2,830	170
1954	46,480	9,720	3,370	2,791	3,291	5,362	3,580	40
1955	46,950	10,590	3,630	3,026	3,580	6,920	4,550	—
1956	48,950	11,590	3,910	3,180	3,680	7,206	5,760	—
1957	49,260	12,290	4,120	3,477	3,626	6,586	7,220	—
1958	48,640	12,930	4,270	3,518	3,613	6,983	8,930	—

SOURCE, BY COLUMN

(1 to 3)   Obtained by multiplying value of Table 174 by appropriate indexes of Table 181.

(4)   Sum of Table B-177, col. 11, and Table B-178, col. 11.

(5)   From Table B-178A, col. 11.

(6)   From Table B-180, col. 6, A, and col. 5, B.

(7)   From Table B-179, col. 8 (current value assumed equal to original cost).

(8)   From Table B-168, col. 6.

TABLE B-176
ATOMIC ENERGY COMMISSION INVESTMENT IN FIXED ASSETS
(millions of dollars)

	Gross Expenditures			Depreciation Allowances			Net Expenditures			Accumulated Value		
	Fiscal Year (current prices)	Calendar Year		Original Cost	1947-49 Prices	Replacement Cost	Original Cost	1947-49 Prices	Replacement Cost	Original Cost	1947-49 Prices	Replacement Cost
		current prices	(1947-49 prices)									
Year	(1)	(2)	(3)	(4)	(5)	(6)	(7)	(8)	(9)	(10)	(11)	(12)
1943	—	250	377	5	8	6	245	369	244	245	369	244
1944	—	550	830	23	33	21	527	797	529	772	1,166	786
1945	—	340	495	42	62	43	298	433	297	1,070	1,599	1,138
1946	—	140	176	53	76	61	87	100	79	1,157	1,699	1,483
1947	—	180	194	60	85	79	120	109	101	1,277	1,808	1,773
1948	—	280	273	70	95	97	210	178	183	1,487	1,986	2,105
1949	—	280	268	82	105	111	198	163	169	1,685	2,149	2,226
1950	256	320	298	95	118	127	225	180	193	1,910	2,329	2,661
1951	459	780	659	120	140	167	660	519	613	2,570	2,848	3,431
1952	1,082	1,140	911	163	176	214	977	735	926	3,547	3,484	4,358
1953	1,126	1,200	975	217	220	271	983	755	929	4,530	4,338	5,352
1954	1,215	1,070	868	271	263	325	799	605	745	5,329	4,943	6,082
1955	843	550	434	313	295	374	237	139	176	5,566	5,082	6,606
1956	302	280	205	333	310	423	-53	-105	-143	5,513	4,977	6,860
1957	317	300	211	346	319	462	-46	-108	-162	5,467	4,869	7,103
1958	290	290	201	358	329	487	-68	-128	-197	5,399	4,741	7,131
1959	299	—	—	—	—	—	—	—	—	—	—	—

SOURCE, BY COLUMN

(1) *Radiation Safety and Major Activities in the Atomic Energy Program, July–December 1956,* Atomic Energy Commission, p. 373, and later bulletins.

(2) 1943–49: Estimated at about 75 per cent of total AEC disbursements in 1945 and 1944, as given in semiannual reports; 55 per cent in 1945; 45 per cent in 1946 and 1947; and 50 per cent in 1948 and 1949. These ratios are based on relationships in later years. The calendar-year estimates of total disbursements were obtained from the fiscal-year data given in AEC reports by application of interpolation formula:

$$y = \tfrac{1}{2}x_1 + \tfrac{1}{8}(x_0 - x_2)$$

y is expenditures in first half of fiscal year and $x_0, x_1,$ and x_2 are expenditures for preceding current year and following fiscal year, respectively.

Figures rounded to nearest $10 million. Very small expenditures attributable to 1942 ignored.

1950–58: Derived from col. 1 by interpolation formula for col. 2.

(3) Components of col. 2 deflated by appropriate index; residential housing by Table B-9, col. 1; other structures by Table B-106, col. 1; equipment by Table B-181, col. 1.

(4) Components of col. 2 depreciated on basis of fifty-year life for residential structures, forty-year life for other structures and seventeen-year life for equipment.

(5) Same method as col. 4, using components of expenditures in col. 3.

(6) Components of col. 5, multiplied by appropriate index.

(7) Col. 2 minus col. 4.

(8) Col. 3 minus col. 5.

(9) Col. 2 minus col. 6.

(10) Accumulated net investment from col. 7.

(11) Accumulated net investment from col. 8.

(12) Components of col. 11, multiplied by appropriate year-end index from tables listed in note to col. 3.

TABLE B-177

ATOMIC ENERGY COMMISSION INVESTMENT IN HOUSING

(millions of dollars)

Year	Gross Expenditures		Depreciation Allowances			Net Investment			Accumulated Value		
	Original Cost (1)	1947–49 Prices (2)	Original Cost (3)	1947–49 Prices (4)	Replacement Cost (5)	Original Cost (6)	1947–49 Prices (7)	Replacement Cost (8)	Original Cost (9)	1947–49 Prices (10)	Replacement Cost (11)
1943	39	65	0	1	1	39	64	38	39	64	40
1944	21	32	1	2	1	20	30	20	59	94	64
1945	9	13	1	2	1	8	11	8	67	105	76
1946	5	6	1	2	2	4	4	3	71	109	91
1947	9	10	2	2	2	7	8	7	78	117	117
1948	33	31	2	3	3	31	28	30	109	145	153
1949	33	32	3	3	3	30	29	30	139	174	176
1950	15	14	3	4	4	12	10	11	151	184	208
1951	10	9	3	4	5	7	5	5	158	189	222
1952	23	19	4	4	5	19	15	18	177	204	245
1953	1	1	4	5	6	−3	−4	−5	174	200	242
1954	2	2	4	5	6	−2	−3	−4	172	197	239
1955	1	1	4	5	6	−3	−4	−5	169	193	244
1956	2	2	4	5	6	−2	−3	−4	167	190	248
1957	1	1	4	5	7	−3	−4	−6	164	186	246
1958	1	1	4	5	7	−3	−4	−6	161	182	246

SOURCE, BY COLUMN

(1) Unpublished figures, Department of Labor, Construction Division.
(2) Col. 1 deflated by Table B-9, col. 1.
(3) Col. 1 depreciated assuming 2 per cent annual rate.
(4) Same method as for col. 3, using col. 2 expenditures.
(5) Col. 4 multiplied by Table B-9, col. 1.

(6) Col. 1 minus col. 3.
(7) Col. 2 minus col. 4.
(8) Col. 1 minus col. 5.
(9) Cumulated savings from col. 6.
(10) Cumulated savings from col. 7.
(11) Col. 10 multiplied by year-end index from Table B-9, col. 3.

TABLE B-178

ATOMIC ENERGY COMMISSION INVESTMENT IN OTHER STRUCTURES

(millions of dollars)

| | Gross Expenditures | | Depreciation Allowances | | | Net Investment | | | Accumulated Value | | |
Year	Original Cost (1)	1947–49 Prices (2)	Original Cost (3)	1947–49 Prices (4)	Replace-ment Cost (5)	Original Cost (6)	1947–49 Prices (7)	Replace-ment Cost (8)	Original Cost (9)	1947–49 Prices (10)	Replace-ment Cost (11)
1943	90	142	1	2	1	89	140	89	89	140	87
1944	215	357	5	8	4	210	349	211	299	489	306
1945	141	217	9	15	10	132	202	131	431	691	480
1946	57	73	12	19	15	45	54	42	476	745	644
1947	72	77	13	21	20	59	56	52	535	801	798
1948	104	100	16	23	24	88	77	80	623	878	924
1949	104	102	18	25	26	86	77	78	709	955	969
1950	128	121	21	28	30	107	93	98	816	1,048	1,173
1951	316	268	27	33	39	289	235	277	1,105	1,283	1,547
1952	447	341	36	41	50	411	300	397	1,516	1,583	1,931
1953	480	389	48	50	62	432	339	418	1,948	1,922	2,353
1954	320	266	58	58	70	262	208	250	2,210	2,130	2,552
1955	165	134	64	63	77	101	71	88	2,311	2,201	2,782
1956	124	93	68	66	88	56	27	36	2,367	2,228	2,932
1957	136	96	71	68	96	65	28	40	2,432	2,256	3,231
1958	131	92	74	71	101	57	21	30	2,489	2,277	3,272

SOURCE, BY COLUMN

(1) Expenditures in Table B-176, col. 2, minus housing and equipment.
(2) Col. 1 deflated by Table B-106, col. 1.
(3) Col. 1 depreciated assuming 2.5 per cent annual rate.
(4) Same method as for col. 3, using expenditures in col. 2.
(5) Col. 4 multiplied by Table B-106, col. 1.
(6) Col. 1 minus col. 3.
(7) Col. 2 minus col. 4.
(8) Col. 1 minus col. 5.
(9) Cumulated savings from col. 6.
(10) Cumulated savings from col. 7.
(11) Col. 10 multiplied by year-end index from Table B-106, col. 5.

TABLE B-178A

ATOMIC ENERGY COMMISSION INVESTMENT IN EQUIPMENT

(millions of dollars)

Year	Gross Expenditures		Depreciation Allowances			Net Investment			Accumulated Value		
	Original Cost (1)	1947–49 Prices (2)	Original Cost (3)	1947–49 Prices (4)	Replacement Cost (5)	Original Cost (6)	1947–49 Prices (7)	Replacement Cost (8)	Original Cost (9)	1947–49 Prices (10)	Replacement Cost (11)
1943	121	170	4	5	4	117	165	117	117	165	117
1944	314	441	17	23	16	297	418	298	414	583	416
1945	190	265	32	45	32	158	220	158	572	803	582
1946	78	97	40	55	44	38	42	34	610	845	748
1947	99	107	45	62	57	54	45	42	664	890	858
1948	143	142	52	69	70	91	73	73	755	963	1,028
1949	143	134	61	77	82	82	57	61	837	1,020	1,081
1950	177	163	71	86	93	106	77	84	943	1,097	1,280
1951	454	382	90	103	123	364	279	331	1,307	1,376	1,662
1952	670	551	123	131	159	547	420	551	1,854	1,796	2,182
1953	719	585	165	165	203	554	420	516	2,408	2,216	2,757
1954	748	600	209	200	249	539	400	499	2,947	2,616	3,291
1955	384	299	245	227	291	139	72	93	3,086	2,688	3,580
1956	52	110	261	239	329	−9	−29	−177	2,977	2,559	3,680
1957	166	114	271	246	359	−105	−132	−193	2,872	2,427	3,626
1958	161	108	280	253	379	−119	145	−218	2,753	2,282	3,462

SOURCE, BY COLUMN

(1) Expenditures in Table B-176, col. 2, minus A.E.C. housing from Table B-177, apportioned as follows: 1943–50: 57.6%; 1951, 59.0%; 1952–53, 60.0%; 1954–55, 70.0%; 1956–58, 55.0%.

(2) Col. 1 deflated by Table B-181, col. 1.

(3) Col. 1 depreciated assuming 6 per cent annual rate.

(4) Same method as col. 3, using expenditure figures of col. 2.

(5) Col. 4 multiplied by Table B-181, col. 1.

(6) Col. 1 minus col. 3.

(7) Col. 2 minus col. 4.

(8) Col. 1 minus col. 5.

(9) Cumulated savings from col. 6.

(10) Cumulated savings from col. 7.

(11) Col. 10 multiplied by year-end index from Table B-181, col. 2.

TABLE B-179

ATOMIC ENERGY COMMISSION INVENTORIES

(millions of dollars)

	Atomic Source Materials				Operating Expenditures		Estimated Total Inventory	
Year	Reported by AEC June 30 (1)	Annual Increase reported in Budget Fiscal Year (2)	Estimated Annual Increase Fiscal Year (3)	Cumulated Annual Increase June 30 (4)	Annual Fiscal Year (5)	Cumulated June 30 (6)	June 30 (7)	Dec. 31 (8)
1945	—	—	100	100	343	545	263	320
1946	—	—	90	190	201	746	384	440
1947	—	—	90	280	183	929	498	560
1948	—	—	150	430	239	1,168	611	750
1949	—	—	210	640	314	1,482	881	1,010
1950	—	186	—	826	414	1,869	1,130	1,300
1951	—	317	—	1,143	495	2,391	1,471	1,700
1952	—	421	—	1,564	684	3,075	1,934	2,220
1953	—	462	—	2,026	905	3,980	2,504	2,830
1954	1,000	514	—	2,540	1,039	5,019	3,151	3,580
1955	1,309	749	—	3,289	1,290	6,309	4,004	4,550
1956	1,574	998	—	4,287	1,608	7,917	5,096	5,760
1957	1,749	1,227	—	5,514	1,918	9,835	6,416	7,220
1958	2,000	1,546	—	7,060	2,299	12,134	8,030	8,930
1959	2,200	1,760	—	8,820	2,497	14,631	9,821	—

(Notes to Table B-179 on next page)

(Notes to Table B-179)

SOURCE, BY COLUMN

(1) 1954-57: Atomic Energy Commission, *19th Semiannual Report*, p. 190; *Major Activities*, July–Dec. 1956, p. 372. Figures include "Production inventories in process; source and special nuclear research material; stores; special reactor material; other special materials." In earlier annual reports, as well as from 1958 on, only the last three components–which in 1954 and 1955 accounted for less that 10 per cent of the total–were shown in the balance sheet. The figures still exclude "inventories of stockpile products," i.e., probably both source materials and refined products and possibly also weapons.

1958-59: Rough estimates based on changes in nonproduction inventories (financial reports of AEC) and earlier changes in production inventories.

(2) *Budget*, various issues: e.g., 1958, p. 1087; 1957, p. 1105; 1955, p. 1119; 1954, p. 1099; 1953, p. 1166; 1952, p. 970. It has been assumed that the budget item labelled "other physical assets" consist entirely of atomic source and nuclear materials. This is probably more nearly correct in the last few years than in the earlier period.

(3) Estimated as increasing by from 40 to 60 per cent of operating expenditures of AEC, as shown in col. 5. These ratios are based on the relations prevailing in later years.

(4) Cumulation of col. 3, assuming that additions to the stockpile in 1943 and 1944 were small enough to be disregarded.

(5) 1945-49: Total expenditures (AEC, *19th Semiannual Report*, p. 200) shifted to calendar year basis (cf. Table B-176, col. 2), less plant expenditures as shown in Table B-176, col. 2. This column includes depreciation, but excludes expenditures on research, administration, and community projects.

1950-59: From AEC semiannual reports.

(6) Cumulation of col. 5, assuming aggregate operation expenditures of about $200 million for the period before June 30, 1944.

(7) Average of nine-tenths of col. 4 and four-fifths of col. 6.

(8) Average of data for June 30 preceding and following (rounded to nearest $10 million).

TABLE B-180
FEDERAL GOVERNMENT INVESTMENT IN STRATEGIC STOCKPILE
(millions of dollars)

Year	Original Cost		1947–49 Prices		Market Value End of Year	
	Annual Expenditures (1)	Cumulated Expenditures (2)	Annual Expenditures (3)	Cumulated Expenditures (4)	Calculated (5)	Reported (6)
A. MAIN STRATEGIC STOCKPILE						
1945	45	45	70	70	40	320
1946	10	55	15	85	77	490
1947	36	91	37	122	119	550
1948	150	241	142	264	304	821
1949	456	697	462	726	665	1,149
1950	455	1,152	436	1,162	1,455	2,719
1951	745	1,897	600	1,762	2,190	2,540
1952	985	2,882	800	2,562	3,165	4,024
1953	720	3,602	585	3,147	3,940	4,226
1954	830	4,432	573	3,720	4,615	4,942
1955	500	4,932	350	4,070	6,350	6,300
1956	331	5,263	212	4,282	6,384	6,500
1953	308	5,571	224	4,506	5,844	5,700
1958	124	5,695	97	4,603	6,131	5,700
B. ADDITIONAL STOCKPILE						
1952	121	121	98	98	120	—
1953	121	242	97	195	238	—
1954	166	408	134	329	420	—
1955	97	505	68	397	620	—
1956	119	624	76	473	706	—
1957	289	913	210	683	886	—
1958	357	1,270	280	963	1,283	—

SOURCE, BY COLUMN

A. *Main Strategic Stockpile*
(1) 1945, 1946: Estimated on basis of expenditures before June 30, 1947, given in one aggregate figure in *Stockpile Report*, Jan.–June 1955, p. 15. This figure includes some stockpiles taken over without monetary consideration from war agencies.
    1947–52: From *Stockpile Report*, Aug. 15, 1953, p. 58. Figures are net, excluding revolving sales.
    1953–55: Year-end data from Office of Defense Mobilization (data for June 30 in *Stockpile Report*, July–Dec. 1955, p. 15).
    1956–58: Derived from col. 2.
(2) Cumulation of figures in col. 1, except figure for 1956 which is taken from *Stockpile Report*, July–Dec. 1956, p. 13.
(3) Col. 1 divided by Bureau of Labor Statistics index of wholesale prices of nonferrous metals.
(4) Cumulation of figures in col. 3.
(5) Col. 4 multiplied by year-end value of BLS index of wholesale prices of nonferrous metals.
(6) *Stockpile Report*, various issues. The figure for 1948 includes $424 million representing surplus property, apparently received from other federal agencies without monetary consideration and not included in cols. 1 through 5. All or part of these materials may be assumed to be included in later years. Figures for 1945–47 are rough estimates.

B. *Additional Stockpile*
(1) First differences of col. 2.
(2) Book value of stockpile obtained by averaging June 30 figures in *Budget* (e.g., 1958, p. 88).
(3) Col. 1 divided by BLS wholesale price index for nonferrous metals.
(4) Cumulation of col. 3.
(5) Col. 4 multiplied by year-end value of BLS wholesale price index for nonferrous metals.

TABLE B-181

DEFLATORS FOR MILITARY DURABLES
(1947–49 = 100)

	Equipment		Structures	
Year	Annual Average (1)	Year End (2)	Annual Average (3)	Year End (4)
1945	71.6	72.5	66.7	69.4
1946	80.3	88.5	76.5	84.8
1947	92.5	96.4	93.3	99.6
1948	100.9	106.8	104.0	105.8
1949	106.6	106.0	103.0	101.7
1950	108.6	116.7	106.5	112.5
1951	119.0	120.8	115.4	117.2
1952	121.5	121.5	119.1	120.4
1953	123.0	124.4	121.8	121.7
1954	124.6	125.8	121.6	122.6
1955	128.4	133.2	124.6	126.8
1956	137.8	143.8	130.7	132.9
1957	146.1	149.4	136.6	137.0
1958	149.8	151.7	138.5	139.5

SOURCE, BY COLUMN

(1) Bureau of Labor Statistics index of wholesale prices of "machinery and motive products" (*Business Statistics*, 1959, p. 34).

(2) 1945, 1946: Obtained by applying the Jan.–Dec. relation in the index of metal products prices to col. 1.
1947–58: *Survey of Current Business*, Mar. 1952, p. 23; and *Business Statistics*, various issues.

(3) Department of Commerce, composite construction cost index (*Business Statistics*, 1955, p. 38, and *Survey of Current Business*, July 1956, pp. 5–8); *Construction Review*, Feb. 1957, p. 31, and various issues.

(4) Average of Dec. and Jan. values of index in *Construction and Building Materials*, *Statistical Supplement*, Department of Commerce, May 1951, p. 44 and May 1952, p. 36; *Business Statistics*, 1955, p. 38; *Survey of Current Business*, July 1956, pp. 5–8, *Construction Review*, March 1957, p. 39, and various issues.

TABLE B-182

MONETARY GOLD AND SILVER

(millions of dollars)

End of Year	Gold			Silver			Total		
	Original Cost (1)	Current Prices (2)	1947–49 Prices (3)	Original Cost (4)	Current Prices (5)	1947–49 Prices (6)	Original Cost (7)	Current Prices (8)	1947–49 Prices (9)
1945	17,197	20,065	20,065	1,363	3,513	1,532	18,560	23,578	21,597
1946	17,661	20,529	20,529	1,342	3,514	1,532	19,003	24,043	22,061
1947	19,886	22,754	22,754	1,354	3,548	1,547	21,240	26,302	24,301
1948	21,376	24,244	24,244	1,371	3,597	1,568	22,747	27,841	25,812
1949	21,559	24,427	24,427	1,390	3,643	1,588	22,949	28,070	26,015
1950	19,838	22,706	22,706	1,430	3,697	1,612	21,268	26,403	24,318
1951	19,827	22,695	22,695	1,449	3,741	1,631	21,276	26,436	24,326
1952	20,319	23,187	23,187	1,464	3,794	1,654	21,783	26,981	24,841
1953	19,162	22,030	22,030	1,472	3,837	1,673	20,634	25,867	23,703
1954	18,845	21,713	21,713	1,490	3,887	1,695	20,335	25,600	23,408
1955	18,822	21,690	21,690	1,504	3,930	1,713	20,326	25,620	23,403
1956	19,081	21,949	21,949	1,566	4,064	1,772	20,647	26,013	23,721
1957	19,913	22,781	22,781	1,614	4,185	1,825	21,527	26,966	24,606
1958	17,666	20,534	20,534	1,709	4,363	1,902	19,375	24,897	22,436

SOURCE, BY COLUMN

(1) 1945–49: *A Study of Saving . . .*, Vol. III, p. 39. 1950–58: Col. 2 less devaluation profit of $2,868 million (*Banking and Monetary Statistics*, p. 538).

(2) 1945–49: *A Study of Saving . . .*, Vol. III, p. 39. 1950–58: *Federal Reserve Bulletin*, Feb. issues.

(3) 1945–58: Equal to col. 2.

(4) 1945–58: Col. 5 less accumulated seigniorage (*Treasury Bulletin*, April 1959, p. 59; and *A Study of Saving . . .*, Vol. 1, p. 997 for seigniorage before 1935).

(5) 1945–58: *Treasury Bulletin*, July 1951, p. 50, Mar. 1957, p. 54, and Apr. 1959, p. 57.

"Monetary stock", valued at $1.29 an ounce, includes silver bullion, standard silver dollars, and subsidiary silver coin.

(6) 1945–58: Col. 5 times ratio of bullion value of silver in 1947–49 (as given in *Statistical Abstract*, 1951, p. 385) to $1.29.

(7 to 9) 1945–58: Sum of cols. 1 and 4; 2 and 5; and 3 and 6, respectively.

TABLE B-183

DISTRIBUTION OF SILVER AND MINOR COIN, CURRENT PRICES
(millions of dollars)

End of Year	Total (1)	Held in Treasury (2)	Federal Reserve Banks (3)	Corporations (4)	Unincorporated Business (5)	Farmers (6)	Nonfarm Individuals (7)
				Outside of Treasury			
1945	3,830	2,590	21	94	128	158	839
1946	3,858	2,529	27	100	141	169	892
1947	3,902	2,530	29	103	148	175	917
1948	3,964	2,527	37	116	150	182	952
1949	4,019	2,561	40	121	157	187	953
1950	4,081	2,563	31	126	171	183	1,007
1951	4,138	2,538	17	136	188	201	1,058
1952	4,206	2,510	22	151	184	198	1,141
1953	4,267	2,492	42	153	192	192	1,196
1954	4,330	2,508	70	154	201	189	1,208
1955	4,386	2,496	47	162	212	199	1,271
1956	4,535	2,562	39	170	221	209	1,334
1957	4,683	2,442	57	193	252	238	1,503
1958	4,881	2,468	62	207	270	254	1,620

SOURCE, BY COLUMN

(1) Sum of Table B-182, col. 5, and minor coin outstanding from *Federal Reserve Bulletin*, Feb. issues.

(2) Total monetary silver less silver outside Treasury at $1.29 per ounce (*Treasury Bulletin*, July 1951, p. 50, and later issues, plus minor coin held in Treasury (*Federal Reserve Bulletin*).

(3) Standard silver dollars, subsidiary silver coin, and minor coin held by Federal Reserve banks (ibid.).

(4 to 7) Col. 1 minus sum of cols. 2 and 3, distributed among cols. 4 to 7, according to their currency holdings (*Federal Reserve Bulletin*, July 1955, p. 750 and Aug. 1955, p. 874). Estimates for 1955 through 1958 based on 1954 distribution of currency holdings, since no later figures were available.

TABLE B-184

DISTRIBUTION OF SILVER AND MINOR COIN, CONSTANT (1947–49) PRICES
(millions of dollars)

| End of Year | Total (1) | Held in Treasury (2) | Federal Reserve Banks (3) | Outside of Treasury | | | |
				Corporations (4)	Unincorporated Business (5)	Farmers (6)	Nonfarm Individuals (7)
1945	1,670	1,129	9	41	56	69	366
1946	1,682	1,103	12	44	61	74	389
1947	1,701	1,103	13	45	65	76	400
1948	1,728	1,102	16	51	65	79	415
1949	1,752	1,117	17	53	68	82	416
1950	1,779	1,117	14	55	75	80	439
1951	1,804	1,107	7	59	82	88	461
1952	1,834	1,094	10	66	80	86	497
1953	1,860	1,087	18	67	84	84	521
1954	1,888	1,093	31	67	88	82	527
1955	1,912	1,088	20	71	92	87	554
1956	1,977	1,117	17	74	96	91	582
1957	2,042	1,064	25	84	110	103	655
1958	2,128	1,077	27	90	118	111	706

SOURCE: Cols. 1 to 7 of Table B-183, multiplied by ratio of 43.6% as determined from Table B-182 col. 6, divided by col. 5.

TABLE B-185
United States Investments Abroad
(millions of dollars)

	1945	1946	1947	1948	1949	1950	1951	1952	1953	1954	1955	1956	1957	1958
1. Private investments, total	12,629	13,525	14,904	16,301	16,949	19,004	20,948	22,829	23,847	26,589	29,054	33,000	36,814	40,824
2. Long-term	11,677	12,263	13,446	14,727	15,637	17,488	19,295	21,090	22,259	24,365	26,668	30,082	33,632	37,336
3. Direct, held by:	6,723	7,227	8,366	9,625	10,700	11,788	13,089	14,819	16,329	17,626	19,313	22,177	25,238	27,075
4. Financial institutions	400	430	450	500	600	650	675	700	750	800	850	900	950	1,000
5. Other corporations	5,973	6,397	7,466	8,625	9,550	10,538	11,764	13,419	14,829	16,026	17,613	20,377	23,338	25,075
6. Individuals	350	400	450	500	550	600	650	700	750	800	850	900	950	1,000
7. Foreign dollar bonds	1,748	1,524	1,563	1,658	1,728	1,692	2,071	2,244	2,383	2,720	2,660	2,826	3,255	3,931
8. Other foreign securities, held (7 and 8) by:	2,241	2,572	2,482	2,425	2,073	2,641	2,674	2,431	2,048	2,406	2,821	3,022	2,693	3,690
9. Financial institutions	1,789	1,875	1,900	2,000	1,900	2,167	2,470	2,475	2,393	2,779	2,689	2,855	3,347	4,158
10. Individuals	2,200	2,221	2,145	2,083	1,901	2,166	2,275	2,200	2,038	2,347	2,792	2,993	2,601	3,463
11. Other, held by:	965	940	1,035	1,019	1,136	1,367	1,461	1,596	1,499	1,613	1,874	2,057	2,446	2,640
12. Financial corporations	170	145	225	199	296	512	591	701	574	658	924	1,084	1,428	1,570
13. Nonfinancial corporations	95	95	100	100	110	115	120	135	155	175	170	193	238	290
14. Individuals	700	700	710	720	730	740	750	760	770	780	780	780	780	780
15. Short-term	952	1,262	1,458	1,574	1,312	1,516	1,653	1,739	1,588	2,224	2,386	2,918	3,182	3,488
16. Deposits, held by:	320	365	308	313	293	487	332	320	371	502	447	417	424	498
17. Financial institutions	155	200	143	143	123	287	142	125	171	227	241	222	222	286
18. Nonfinancial institutions	65	65	65	70	70	100	90	95	100	125	106	95	102	112
19. Individuals	100	100	100	100	100	100	100	100	100	100	100	100	100	100
20. Other	632	897	1,150	1,261	1,019	1,029	1,321	1,419	1,217	1,722	1,939	2,501	2,758	2,990
21. U.S. government credits	2,144	5,168	12,132	13,143	13,716	13,840	14,007	14,424	15,720	15,620	15,893	16,476	17,478	18,331
22. Long-term	1,694	4,956	11,808	12,916	13,429	13,518	13,671	14,087	15,415	15,208	15,170	15,219	15,573	16,192
23. IMF and IBRD	—	323	3,385	3,385	3,385	3,385	3,385	3,385	3,385	3,385	3,385	3,385	3,385	3,385
24. British loan	—	600	3,450	3,750	3,750	3,750	3,705	3,660	3,614	3,567	3,519	3,470	3,470	3,419
25. Other	1,694	4,033	4,973	5,781	6,294	6,383	6,581	7,042	8,416	8,256	8,266	8,364	8,718	9,388
26. Short-term	450	212	324	227	287	322	336	337	305	412	723	1,257	1,845	2,139
27. Total	14,773	18,693	27,036	29,444	30,665	32,844	34,955	37,253	39,567	42,209	44,947	49,476	54,232	59,155

SOURCE, BY LINE

1, 2, 3, 7, 8, 11, 15, 16, 20, 21, 22, 26, 27.
Figures taken directly from international investment statistics as shown in *Survey of Current Business* (Balance of Payments Division, Department of Commerce), Aug. 1957 and Sept. 1958.

4. Investments in finance were put at $315 million for May 1953 in the Treasury Department's *Census of American Owned Assets in Foreign Countries* (T.F.R. 500), 1947; and at $425 million in *Foreign Investments of the U.S.* (1950 Census), Department of Commerce, 1953. These are largely owned by financial institutions in the United States. Financial institutions also have other interests in direct investments abroad, most prominently as holders of mortgages on ships (about $150 million in 1950), and holders of bonds of pipelines, etc. The ship mortgages were purchased mainly in 1948-50 and about half were liquidated in 1950-54.

5. Insurance company outflows, mainly reinvested earnings, were: 1946, $−26 million; 1947, $8 million; 1948, $7 million; 1949, $−42 million; 1950, $−9 million; 1951, $−42 million; 1952, $−24 million; 1953, $−20 million; 1954, $−39 million. (Annual data for banks unavailable.) Using these data as guides, the estimated total would be $400 million in 1945, increased to $650 million in 1950, and to $800 million in 1954.

6. Line 3 less sum of lines 4 and 6.
T.F.R. 500 gives $579 million for 1943, plus $162 million held through estates, making $741 million. About two-thirds was held by noncitizens who came to the United States after 1937. Holdings in Europe were $405 million, and of this some $250 million were either destroyed or had very little recoverable value after World War II. Properties reported by estates and trusts were concentrated in Panama ($36 million), Argentina ($60 million), and Spain ($31 million), so that, whatever their present status may be, they are probably not reflected to any extent in the currently published series. Taking these factors into account, about $350 million for individual holdings is used for 1945, based on the T.F.R. 500.
The Department of Commerce 1950 Census indicates individual holdings of about $600 million—$500 million in Canada and $100 million elsewhere. These are primarily holdings in foreign companies controlled in the United States and having stock traded on the markets. Starting with $350 million in 1945, and using $600 million in 1950, an increase of $50 million annually has been assumed, although the actual annual changes have probably been quite uneven.

9 and 10. According to the T.F.R. 500, 56 per cent of all foreign securities were held by individuals and estates, the remainder by corporations. In the period 1945-54, about $1 billion was added to holdings of dollar bonds, most of it purchases by financial institutions, so that at the end of the period the proportions were probably reversed. A fifty-fifty division in 1950 has been assumed with the proportions of financial institutions increasing over the whole period, except for 1954, when most of the increase was due to a rise in stock prices.

12, 13, and 14. At the end of 1945, (based on the T.F.R. 500) the total of $965 million included real property, insurance, estates claims of individuals totaling about $600 million, and other claims of about $100 million. This total was increased $10 million each year to account for market gains. Holdings by financial institutions include banks—amounting to $170 million in 1945 and $426 million in 1954—and insurance companies (mainly one large loan). Holdings of nonfinancial corporations were small, ranging from about $95 million in 1945 to about $175 million in 1954. Annual changes in holdings of financial and nonfinancial institutions are based largely on regular monthly or quarterly reports to the Treasury Department, included in *Treasury Bulletin*.

17, 18, and 19. Holdings of individuals are based on T.F.R. 500 and estimated at $100 million for each year. Holdings of nonfinancial corporations are based on quarterly Treasury reports (C-2) plus a small allowance for omissions. Holdings of financial institutions are based on monthly reports (B-2), plus a somewhat larger allowance for omissions.

23, 24, and 25. Largely as reported by the responsible agencies.

419

FOREIGN ASSETS IN THE UNITED STATES
(millions of dollars)

	1945	1946	1947	1948	1949	1950	1951
1. Long-term investments, private	7,322	6,985	6,820	6,756	7,122	7,744	8,450
2. Direct	2,470	2,503	2,603	2,787	2,941	3,138	3,330
3. Financial institutions	600	600	625	650	700	740	745
4. Nonfinancial institutions	1,870	1,903	1,978	2,137	2,241	2,398	2,585
5. Corporate stock	3,010	2,690	2,480	2,305	2,490	2,925	3,450
6. Financial institutions	100	100	100	100	100	110	120
7. Other corporations	2,910	2,590	2,380	2,205	2,390	2,815	3,330
8. Corporate, state, and municipal bonds	270	229	193	138	177	181	189
9. Corporate	170	129	93	38	77	81	89
10. State and municipal	100	100	100	100	100	100	100
11. Other	1,572	1,563	1,544	1,526	1,514	1,500	1,481
12. Estates and trusts	655	655	655	655	655	655	655
13. Other	917	908	889	871	859	845	826
14. Short-term investments, private	5,298	5,281	5,301	5,787	5,941	6,512	6,651
15. Deposits	4,966	4,894	4,903	5,298	5,461	5,831	5,783
16. With Federal Reserve Banks	862	508	392	642	767	895	526
17. Other	4,104	4,386	4,511	4,656	4,694	4,936	5,257
18. Other	322	387	398	489	480	681	868
19. With financial institutions	99	154	135	231	277	362	508
20. Other	223	233	263	258	203	319	360
21. Holdings of U.S. government securities	4,450	3,614	3,984	4,002	3,816	5,203	5,448
22. Long-term securities	609	380	461	470	528	1,470	810
23. Short-term securities	3,205	2,601	2,819	2,786	2,476	2,961	3,821
24. Currency	636	633	704	746	812	772	817
25. Total	17,070	15,880	16,105	16,545	16,879	19,459	20,549

(continued)

SOURCE, BY LINE

1, 2, 5, 8, 11, 14, 15, 18, 21, 22, 24, and 25. Figures are taken from international investment statistics (cf. Table B-185).

3. The total for June 1941, as published in the Treasury *Census of Foreign-Owned Assets in the U.S.* (T.F.R. 300), 1945, was $522 million. To these, $75 million have been added for insurance company reserves, and the figures have been adjusted annually on the basis of insurance company reinvested earnings and capital as included in the *Balance of Payments of the United States*.

4. Line 2 minus line 3.

6. A total of about $100 million was established for 1949 by a special Commerce Department study of withholding tax returns. This total was carried back to 1945 without change; increases after that date reflect primarily price rises.

7. Based on the 1949 special tabulation, carried back to 1945 and forward to 1954 on the basis of transactions as reported monthly to the Treasury (Form S1/3) and estimated price changes.

	1952	1953	1954	1955	1956	1957	1958
1. Long-term investments, private	8,929	9,172	11,025	12,587	13,354	12,834	15,219
2. Direct	3,519	3,776	3,981	4,255	4,547	4,782	4,940
3. Financial institutions	765	800	850	893	928	947	962
4. Nonfinancial institutions	2,754	2,976	3,131	3,362	3,619	3,835	3,978
5. Corporate stock	3,705	3,650	5,254	6,575	6,961	6,091	8,305
6. Financial institutions	130	140	150	160	170	150	200
7. Other corporations	3,575	3,510	5,104	6,415	6,791	5,941	8,105
8. Corporate, state, and municipal bonds	227	269	304	259	309	417	455
9. Corporate	127	169	204	159	209	317	355
10. State and municipal	100	100	100	100	100	100	100
11. Other	1,478	1,477	1,486	1,498	1,537	1,544	1,519
12. Estates and trusts	655	655	655	655	655	655	655
13. Other	823	822	831	843	882	889	864
14. Short-term investments, private	7,263	7,637	8,459	8,471	9,488	9,901	10,816
15. Deposits	6,230	6,530	7,437	7,416	8,056	8,072	9,184
16. With Federal Reserve Banks	550	423	490	402	332	356	262
17. Other	5,680	6,107	6,947	7,014	7,734	7,716	8,922
18. Other	1,033	1,107	1,022	1,055	1,432	1,829	1,632
19. With financial institutions	627	751	716	743	1,073	1,404	1,307
20. Other	406	356	306	312	359	425	325
21. Holdings of U.S. government securities	6,335	6,819	7,284	8,499	8,765	8,692	8,781
22. Long-term securities	113	1,019	1,059	1,636	1,501	1,449	1,480
23. Short-term securities	4,374	4,961	5,387	6,022	6,417	6,396	6,411
24. Currency	848	839	838	841	847	847	890
25. Total	22,527	23,628	26,768	29,557	31,607	31,427	34,816

9 and 10. State and municipal bonds are carried throughout at $100 million, based on the T.F.R. 300. Holdings of other bonds are based on a special tabulation of withholding tax returns, extrapolated as for line 6.

12 and 13. The breakdown between "estates and trusts" and other is derived from T.F.R. 300. The year-to-year changes are based on partial data regarding certain commercial liabilities reported to the Treasury Department. No estimates have been made of the changes in market values, or of new investments or liquidations.

2, 16, 17, 18, 19. Based essentially on data reported to the Treasury Department. Line 16 is taken from *Federal Reserve Bulletin*, various issues.

22 and 24. Long-term securities based on the T.F.R. 300 for 1941, with adjustments since then for known transactions. Short-term obligations are essentially as reported to the Treasury Department and published in the *Treasury Bulletin*, plus certain obligations of U.S. Government agencies to foreign governments. Figures for currency are published estimates of the Department of Commerce, e.g., *Survey of Current Business*, May 1954, and Aug. 1955.

TABLE B-187

SECTORING OF NET FOREIGN ASSETS, CURRENT PRICES
(millions of dollars)

Sector	End of year													
	1945	1946	1947	1948	1949	1950	1951	1952	1953	1954	1955	1956	1957	1958
U.S. Investments Abroad														
1. Financial institutions	2,514	2,650	2,718	2,842	2,919	3,616	3,878	4,001	3,888	4,514	4,704	5,061	5,947	7,014
2. Nonfinancial	6,765	7,454	8,781	10,056	10,749	11,782	13,295	15,068	16,301	18,048	19,828	23,166	26,436	28,467
3. Total corporate	9,279	10,104	11,499	12,898	13,668	15,398	17,173	19,069	20,189	22,562	24,532	28,227	32,383	35,481
4. Individuals	3,350	3,421	3,405	3,403	3,281	3,606	3,775	3,760	3,658	4,027	4,522	4,773	4,431	5,343
5. Government	2,144	5,168	12,132	13,143	13,716	13,840	14,007	14,424	15,720	15,620	15,893	16,476	17,418	18,331
6. Total	14,773	18,693	27,036	29,444	30,665	32,844	34,955	37,253	39,567	42,209	44,947	49,476	54,232	59,155
Foreign Assets in the U.S.														
7. Financial institutions	5,994	5,975	5,985	6,497	6,753	7,254	7,363	7,958	8,427	9,361	9,423	10,448	10,795	11,869
8. Nonfinancial	5,861	5,536	5,381	5,291	5,555	6,247	6,983	7,479	7,627	9,368	10,880	11,639	11,185	13,411
9. Financial and nonfinancial	11,855	11,511	11,366	11,788	12,308	13,501	14,346	15,437	16,054	18,729	20,303	22,087	21,980	25,280
10. Individuals	655	655	655	655	655	655	655	655	655	655	655	655	655	655
11. Government	4,550	3,714	4,084	4,102	3,916	5,303	5,548	6,435	6,919	7,384	8,599	8,865	8,772	8,881
12. Total	17,060	15,880	16,105	14,545	16,879	19,459	20,549	22,527	23,628	26,768	29,557	31,607	31,427	34,816
13. Net Foreign Assets	−2,287	2,813	10,931	12,899	13,786	13,385	14,406	14,726	15,939	15,441	15,390	17,869	22,805	24,339

SOURCE, BY LINE

1. Table 185, lines 4, 9, 12, and 17.
2. Table 185, lines 5, 13, 18, and 20.
3. Sum of lines 1 and 2.
4. Table 185, lines 6, 10, 14, and 19.
5. Table 185, line 21.
6. Sum of lines 3 to 5.
7. Table 186, lines 3, 6; 25 per cent of line 13; and lines 15 and 19.
8. Table 186, lines 4, 7, 9; 75 per cent of line 13; and line 20.
9. Sum of lines 7 and 8.
10. Table 186: line 12.
11. Table 186: lines 10 and 21.
12. Sum of lines 9 to 11.
13. Line 6 minus line 12.

TABLE B-188

CONVERSION INDEX FROM 1929 TO 1947–49 PRICES

	Index
1. Residential	205.85
2. Nonresidential	190.85
3. Institutional	200.20
4. Other nonresidential	190.19
5. Public	187.09
6. Producer durables	156.55
7. Consumer durables	130.77
8. Livestock	210.24
9. Other inventories	158.37
10. Crops	185.47
11. Nonfarm	154.74
12. Public	180.94
13. Monetary metals	174.69
14. Residential land	205.31
15. Nonresidential land	147.69
16. Public land	170.89
17. Net foreign assets	146.52
18. Agricultural land	150.41
19. Forests	170.98
20. Farm land	149.00

NOTE: Conversion index derived from *A Study of Saving* . . . , Vol. III, Tables W-1 and W-3. Aggregates for 1947–49 in current prices, divided by aggregates for 1947–49 in 1929 prices for each of the asset items listed.

TABLE B-189

NUMBER OF NEW PRIVATELY FINANCED NONFARM DWELLING
UNITS STARTED, 1946–58
(thousands)

Year	Total (1)	1-Family (2)	2-Family (3)	Total (4)	3-Family and Over	
					3- and 4-Family (5)	Multifamily (6)
1946	662.5	590.0	24.3	48.2	10.0	38.2
1947	845.6	740.2	33.9	71.5	14.0	57.5
1948	913.5	763.2	46.3	104.0	20.3	83.7
1949	988.8	792.4	34.7	161.7	31.5	130.2
1950	1,352.2	1,150.7	42.2	159.3	30.9	128.4
1951	1,020.1	892.2	40.1	87.8	17.0	70.8
1952	1,068.5	939.1	45.9	83.5	16.1	67.4
1953	1,068.3	932.9	41.5	93.9	18.1	75.8
1954	1,201.7	1,077.3	34.2	90.2	17.3	72.9
1955	1,309.5	1,190.0	32.8	86.7	16.3	70.4
1956	1,093.9	968.3	30.2	95.4	18.2	77.2
1957	992.8	831.6	31.7	129.5	24.7	104.8
1958	1,141.5	920.4	36.7	184.4	35.2	149.2

SOURCE, BY COLUMN

(1 to 4) 1946–53: *Housing Statistics*, Housing and Home Finance Agency, Jan. 1955, p. 4.

1954, 1955: Bureau of Labor Statistics estimates.

1956–58: *Construction Reports, Housing Starts*, Bureau of the Census, April 1960, pp. 2–3.

(5) 1946–47: From special tabulations supplied by Bureau of Labor Statistics.

1948–53: Estimated by applying to col. 4 the ratio of 3- and 4-family (col. 5) to 3-family and over (col. 4) which was obtained by straight-line interpolation between the 1947 and 1954 ratios of col. 5 to col. 4.

1954, 1955: Bureau of Labor Statistics estimates.

1956–58: Estimated as 19.1 per cent of col. 4, simple arithmetic average of three preceding years.

(6) 1946–58: Col. 4 minus col. 5.

TABLE B-190

AVERAGE VALUATION OF URBAN BUILDING AUTHORIZED,
BY TYPE OF BUILDING, 1946–56

	Average Valuation (dollars)			Ratio of Average Valuation of:	
			3-Family	3-Family and Over to Total	Multifamily to Total
Year	Total	1-Family	2-Family	and Over		(per cent)
	(1)	(2)	(3)	(4)	(5)	(6)
1946	4,916	5,110	4,236	3,804	77.38	78.93
1947	5,744	6,000	4,519	4,949	86.16	87.88
1948	6,631	6,994	4,999	5,681	85.67	87.38
1949	6,475	6,881	5,008	5,522	85.28	86.99
1950	7,288	7,769	5,373	5,608	76.95	78.49
1951	8,193	8,772	5,731	5,628	68.69	70.06
1952	8,253	8,856	5,708	5,591	67.74	69.09
1953	8,651	9,381	6,180	5,726	66.19	67.51
1954	—	—	—	—	—	67.01
1955	—	—	—	—	—	62.39
1956	—	—	—	—	—	59.10[a]

SOURCE, BY COLUMN

(1 to 4)   1946–53:   Derived from valuation and number figures given in *Construction*, Bureau of Labor Statistics, various issues.

(5)   1946–53:   Col. 4 divided by col. 1.

(6)   1946–53:   Col. 5 stepped up by 2 per cent on the basis of the 1954 relationship of the two ratios (a) the ratio of the average valuation of 3-family and over to total average valuation; (b) the ratio of the average valuation of multifamily to total average valuation.

1954, 1955:   Derived from Bureau of Labor Statistics figures for number and valuation of building permit activity by type of structure.

NOTE: The authorized building includes housekeeping units only.

  [a] 1956: Preliminary, based on first 11 months of 1956 from *Construction Review*, Feb. 1957, p. 24.

	Net Stock		Gross Stock[a]	
	Current	Constant	Current	Constant
		ABSOLUTE VALUES		
Aggregate National Wealth	1	2	1	2
By type of asset:				
All sectors	5	6	7	8
Nonfarm households	50	50	57	57
Nonprofit institutions	51	51	58	58
Unincorporated business	52	52	59	59
Agriculture	53	53	60	60
Corporations	54	54	61	61
State and local government	55	55	62	62
Federal government	56	56	63	63
By sector:				
Total tangible wealth	15	16	17	18
Total reproducible wealth	25	26	27	28
Residential structures	35	35	46	46
Nonresidential structures	36	36	47	47
Producer durables	37	37	48	48
Consumer durables	38	38	49	49
Inventories	39	39		
Residential land	40	40		
Nonresidential land	41	41		
Forest[a]	42	42		
Subsoil assets[a]	43	43		
Monetary metals	44	44		
Foreign assets	45	45		
		PERCENTAGE DISTRIBUTION		
Aggregate National Wealth, continued				
Tangible assets, by type	9	10	11	12
Tangible assets, by sector	19	20	21	22
Reproducible assets, by sector	29	30	31	32
		ANNUAL PERCENTAGE RATES OF CHANGE		
Aggregate national wealth	3	4	3	4
Tangible assets, by type		13		14
Tangible assets, by sector		23		24
Reproducible assets, by sector		33		34
		RATIO OF NET TO GROSS STOCK		
Reproducible assets, by type	64		64	
Reproducible assets, by sector	65		65	

[a] 1945-58 only.

INDEX TO APPENDIX B TABLES

	National Total	Nonfarm Household	Non-profit	Business			Farm	State and Local	Federal	Price Indexes
				Total	Unincor-porated	Corpo-rate				
Real estate and construction	13, 14		41, 42		54			137, 140, 141	157, 158, 160	4, 188
Land	11, 12, 17, 125, 151, 152 132		41, 42	124	59		62, 63, 91	136, 140, 151, 152	151, 152	188
Forests						132			151, 152	132, 188
Subsoil assets	133-135					135				
Structures			38, 41	98			62, 91	136, 140, 148-150		38
Residential	1, 11, 14						60, 80	144, 148-150	162, 148-150	4, 79, 188
1- to 4-family dwellings	1-5, 10, 12 189, 190									9
Multifamily dwellings	1, 6, 7, 10, 12, 189, 190			6, 7, 10	52					9
Nonhousekeeping	1, 8, 13				53, 54					9
War housing and re-use housing	145-146 163-165							147	145-147, 163-165	
Nonresidential				100					148-150, 157	106, 143, 188
Industrial, commercial, and miscellaneous				44, 98, 101-103, 121-123	44, 45, 47, 55-55B, 59					106
Mining	126			44, 109, 110	44, 45, 48, 56					
Petroleum and gas	126			44, 107, 108	44, 45, 48, 56					
Farm service							61, 80			79
Public utilities				44, 98, 100, 104, 121-123						106

(CONTINUED)

Index to Appendix B Tables (concluded)

	National Total	Nonfarm Household	Non-profit	Business				State and Local	Federal	Price Indexes
				Total	Unincorporated	Corporate	Farm			
Social and recreational buildings	46, 125		39, 42, 46	46, 105	46	46				105
Military and atomic energy									166, 167, 169-178, 181	
Highways								136, 138, 140	138, 157	143
Consumer durables		18-25, 31, 34-36					31, 71-78, 84-86			33
Passenger cars and accessories	26-28	18-30, 32, 34-37	46	26-28, 44, 51, 57, 111-119	27, 44, 50, 58	27, 120	26-29, 66, 82, 84-86			33, 79
Equipment	153-155		40, 43	44, 99, 100, 111-119, 127-129	44, 49, 58		65, 67-69, 81-83	136, 139, 140, 142, 153-155	153-155, 157, 159, 161	
Machinery				111-118, 127-129			64, 81			79
Military and atomic energy									166, 167, 178A, 181	
Maritime Commission vessels									168	
Inventories Livestock				130, 131	130, 131	130, 131	78-90, 97	156	156, 180	
Crops							92-97			
Military and atomic energy									179	
Monetary metals	183-184	183, 184			183, 184	183, 184	183, 184		182-184	188
Foreign assets and liabilities	185-187	187		187	187	187			187	188

RELATION OF THE DIRECTORS
TO THE WORK AND PUBLICATIONS
OF THE NATIONAL BUREAU OF ECONOMIC RESEARCH

1. The object of the National Bureau of Economic Research is to ascertain and to present to the public important economic facts and their interpretation in a scientific and impartial manner. The Board of Directors is charged with the responsibility of ensuring that the work of the National Bureau is carried on in strict conformity with this object.

2. To this end the Board of Directors shall appoint one or more Directors of Research.

3. The Director or Directors of Research shall submit to the members of the Board, or to its Executive Committee, for their formal adoption, all specific proposals concerning researches to be instituted.

4. No report shall be published until the Director or Directors of Research shall have submitted to the Board a summary drawing attention to the character of the data and their utilization in the report, the nature and treatment of the problems involved, the main conclusions, and such other information as in their opinion would serve to determine the suitability of the report for publication in accordance with the principles of the National Bureau.

5. A copy of any manuscript proposed for publication shall also be submitted to each member of the Board. For each manuscript to be so submitted a special committee shall be appointed by the President, or at his designation by the Executive Director, consisting of three Directors selected as nearly as may be one from each general division of the Board. The names of the special manuscript committee shall be stated to each Director when the summary and report described in paragraph (4) are sent to him. It shall be the duty of each member of the committee to read the manuscript. If each member of the special committee signifies his approval within thirty days, the manuscript may be published. If each member of the special committee has not signified his approval within thirty days of the transmittal of the report and manuscript, the Director of Research shall then notify each member of the Board, requesting approval or disapproval of publication, and thirty additional days shall be granted for this purpose. The manuscript shall then not be published unless at least a majority of the entire Board and a two-thirds majority of those members of the Board who shall have voted on the proposal within the time fixed for the receipt of votes on the publication proposed shall have approved.

6. No manuscript may be published, though approved by each member of the special committee, until forty-five days have elapsed from the transmittal of the summary and report. The interval is allowed for the receipt of any memorandum of dissent or reservation, together with a brief statement of his reasons, that any member may wish to express; and such memorandum of dissent or reservation shall be published with the manuscript if he so desires. Publication does not, however, imply that each member of the Board has read the manuscript, or that either members of the Board in general, or of the special committee, have passed upon its validity in every detail.

7. A copy of this resolution shall, unless otherwise determined by the Board, be printed in each copy of every National Bureau book.

(Resolution adopted October 25, 1926,
as revised February 6, 1933, and February 24, 1941)

NATIONAL BUREAU OF ECONOMIC RESEARCH PUBLICATIONS IN REPRINT

An Arno Press Series

Barger, Harold. **The Transportation Industries, 1889-1946:** A Study of Output, Employment, and Productivity. 1951

Barger, Harold and Hans H. Landsberg. **American Agriculture, 1899-1939:** A Study of Output, Employment, and Productivity. 1942

Barger, Harold and Sam H. Schurr. **The Mining Industries, 1899-1939:** A Study of Output, Employment, and Productivity. 1944

Burns, Arthur F. **The Frontiers of Economic Knowledge.** 1954

Committee of the President's Conference on Unemployment. **Business Cycles and Unemployment.** 1923

Conference of the Universities-National Bureau Committee for Economic Research. **Aspects of Labor Economics.** 1962

Conference of the Universities-National Bureau Committee for Economic Research. **Business Concentration and Price Policy.** 1955

Conference of the Universities-National Bureau Committee for Economic Research. **Capital Formation and Economic Growth.** 1955

Conference of the Universities-National Bureau Committee for Economic Research. **Policies to Combat Depression.** 1956

Conference of the Universities-National Bureau Committee for Economic Research. **The State of Monetary Economics.** [1963]

Conference of the Universities-National Bureau Committee for Economic Research and the Committee on Economic Growth of the Social Science Research Council. **The Rate and Direction of Inventive Activity:** Economic and Social Factors. 1962

Conference on Research in Income and Wealth. **Input-Output Analysis:** An Appraisal. 1955

Conference on Research in Income and Wealth. **Problems of Capital Formation:** Concepts, Measurement, and Controlling Factors. 1957

Conference on Research in Income and Wealth. **Trends in the American Economy in the Nineteenth Century.** 1960

Conference on Research in National Income and Wealth. **Studies in Income and Wealth.** 1937

Copeland, Morris A. **Trends in Government Financing.** 1961

Fabricant, Solomon. **Employment in Manufacturing, 1899-1939:** An Analysis of Its Relation to the Volume of Production. 1942

Fabricant, Solomon. **The Output of Manufacturing Industries, 1899-1937.** 1940

Goldsmith, Raymond W. **Financial Intermediaries in the American Economy Since 1900.** 1958

Goldsmith, Raymond W. **The National Wealth of the United States in the Postwar Period.** 1962

Kendrick, John W. **Productivity Trends in the United States.** 1961

Kuznets, Simon. **Capital in the American Economy:** Its Formation and Financing. 1961

Kuznets, Simon. **Commodity Flow and Capital Formation.** Vol. One. 1938

Kuznets, Simon. **National Income:** A Summary of Findings. 1946

Kuznets, Simon. **National Income and Capital Formation, 1919-1935:** A Preliminary Report. 1937

Kuznets, Simon. **National Product in Wartime.** 1945

Kuznets, Simon. **National Product Since 1869.** 1946

Kuznets, Simon. **Seasonal Variations in Industry and Trade.** 1933

Long, Clarence D. **Wages and Earnings in the United States, 1860-1890.** 1960

Mendershausen, Horst. **Changes in Income Distribution During the Great Depression.** 1946

Mills, Frederick C. **Economic Tendencies in the United States:** Aspects of Pre-War and Post-War Changes. 1932

Mills, Frederick C. **Price-Quantity Interactions in Business Cycles.** 1946

Mills, Frederick C. **The Behavior of Prices.** 1927

Mitchell, Wesley C. **Business Cycles:** The Problem and Its Setting. [1927]

Mitchell, Wesley C., et al. **Income in the United States:** Its Amount and Distribution 1909-1919. Volume One, Summary. [1921]

Mitchell, Wesley C., editor. **Income in the United States:** Its Amount and Distribution 1909-1919. Volume Two, Detailed Report. 1922

National Accounts Review Committee of the National Bureau of Economic Research. **The National Economic Accounts of the United States.** 1958

Rees, Albert. **Real Wages in Manufacturing, 1890-1914.** 1961

Stigler, George J. **Capital and Rates of Return in Manufacturing Industries.** 1963

Wealth Inventory Planning Study, The George Washington University. **Measuring the Nation's Wealth.** 1964

Williams, Pierce. **The Purchase of Medical Care Through Fixed Periodic Payment.** 1932

Wolman, Leo. **The Growth of American Trade Unions, 1880-1923.** 1924

Woolley, Herbert B. **Measuring Transactions Between World Areas.** 1966